The Speaker of the House

A Study of Leadership

Matthew N. Green

Yale UNIVERSITY PRESS

NEW HAVEN AND LONDON

Published with assistance from the foundation established in memory of James
Wesley Cooper of the Class of 1865, Yale College.

Set in Adobe Garamond type by The Composing Room of Michigan, Inc.,
Grand Rapids, Michigan.
Printed in the United States of America.

Library of Congress Cataloging-in-Publication Data

Green, Matthew N., 1970–
    The speaker of the House : a study of leadership / Matthew N. Green.
        p. cm.
    Includes bibliographical references and index.
    ISBN 978-0-300-15318-7 (pbk. : alk. paper)   1. United States. Congress.
House—Speakers.   2. United States. Congress. House—Leadership.   3. Political
leadership—United States.   I. Title.
    JK1411.G74 2010
    328.73′0762—dc22

                                                                    2009037085

A catalogue record for this book is available from the British Library.

This paper meets the requirements of ANSI/NISO Z39.48-1992 (Permanence of
Paper).

10 9 8 7 6 5 4 3 2 1

The Speaker of the House

Contents

Acknowledgments

My dad once said to me that the idea of the "self-made man" was a myth: no one can succeed without help from others. That has certainly been the case for the completion of this book, which was made possible with the assistance and guidance of many.

This includes a number of faculty, students, and staff at Yale University, where this book began as my dissertation. The chair of my dissertation committee, David Mayhew, was an incredible source of knowledge, direction, and encouragement; I could not have asked for a more dedicated and generous adviser as a graduate student. Stephen Skowronek and John Lapinski, who also served on my dissertation committee, devoted numerous hours to reading chapter drafts and offered useful criticisms and ideas. Other faculty and graduate students in the Political Science Department who took the time to review portions of the work and give comments include Alan Gerber, Donald Green, Gregory Huber, Ian Shapiro, Mayling Birney, Daniel Galvin, Matthew Glassman, Christopher Mann, and Colleen Shogan. The staff of the Yale University library, especially Julie Linden, lent their time and expertise to locating primary documents and research data.

Lots of people beyond the walls of Yale have given me invaluable help along the way. At the Brookings Institution, Sarah Binder provided insightful comments and feedback on the project; and my fellow Brookings research fellows Kathryn Pearson and Andrew Karch were remarkable comrades-in-arms. The staff of the Brookings Library patiently processed my interlibrary loan requests and reshelved the countless volumes of the *Congressional Record* that I copied. As I turned my dissertation into a book, I received many valuable suggestions and words of encouragement from my colleagues at the Catholic University of America, especially Sandra Hanson, Phillip Henderson, Alexander Russo, Stephen Schneck, John White, and James Youniss. Many thanks are owed to the anonymous reviewers for Yale University Press who provided critical suggestions that improved the manuscript immeasurably. Others who generously offered advice, data, constructive feedback, or support include Richard Bensel, Richard Beth, Deborah Jordan Brooks, Stephen Brooks, Robert Brookshire, Robert Christian, Jeffrey Crouch, Larry Evans, Laura Evans, Michael Heaney, Stephen Hess, Kenneth Kato, Sean Kelly, Jeffrey Lewis, Forrest Maltzman, Vincent Moscardelli, Ronald Peters, Keith Poole, Randall Ripley, Peter Schoettle, Barbara Sinclair, and Randall Strahan. I am also thankful to William Frucht and Keith Condon, my editors at Yale University Press, who were very supportive of the project and helped guide me through the publishing process.

Special gratitude goes to the people who were graciously willing to be interviewed for the project, including Speaker Jim Wright, Gary Hymel, and others who spoke with me on the condition of anonymity. My former colleagues on Capitol Hill, particularly Rochelle Dornatt and Debbie Merrill, were—and remain—indispensable sources of knowledge, contacts, and ideas for my research. Thanks are also due to the library staff and curators who helped me navigate the John McCormack Collection at Boston University; the O'Neill Papers at Boston College; the Rayburn Papers at the Center for American History, the University of Texas—Austin; and the Jim Wright Papers at Texas Christian University. Research assistance for this project came from a number of sources, including the Brookings Institution, the Dirksen Congressional Center, and a John Perry Miller Research Grant.

Finally, I am deeply thankful to my family for their love and support. From my parents, Simon and Kate, and my brother, Adam, I learned intellectual curiosity, a love of knowledge, and the courage to challenge myself. My wife Holly has been a foundation of strength and loving guidance, especially during the most trying periods of my research and my graduate school career. More than anything else, her confidence in my ability to succeed made the book possible. My daughter Olivia's energy and curiosity has been a joy and inspiration during the final stages of the project. I dedicate this book to them

Chapter 1 "An Office of Great Honor and Influence": The Speaker of the House of Representatives

As the moment of the vote approached, few were sure what would happen. It was June 2003, and the House of Representatives was considering one of the most important bills of the 108th Congress. The bill was a Republican measure to expand Medicare, the popular federal health care program for seniors, to include prescription drugs. If enacted, it would represent arguably the greatest enlargement of the American social welfare state since the creation of Medicare itself. But the legislation was contentious, invoking dissention within and across both parties. Democrats, who held a minority of seats in the House, claimed that the proposal did not provide sufficient benefit coverage. They opposed many of its elements, particularly the creation of a free market–style mechanism to induce competition with private insurance plans. Some legislators from both parties wanted the bill to allow importation of less expensive medications from other countries—primarily Canada—as a means of reducing drug costs and were against its requirement that such drugs first be certified for safety. Furthermore, a solid bloc of conservative Republicans hesitated at the expansion of Medicare benefits, especially at an estimated cost of $400 billion over ten years (an estimate that would later double). As a result, even with a 229 to 204 seat majority in the House, Republicans faced possible defeat. Days of extensive lobbying by party leaders and White House officials had converted many erstwhile GOP opponents, but the measure remained as many as twenty votes shy of passage (Adams 2003; Franzen 2003).

Nonetheless, party leaders gambled that the pressure of a floor vote would bring enough legislators their way. When the voting began on June 27, at around 2:00 in the morning, the Speaker of the House, Dennis Hastert of Illinois—who, along with other Republican Party leaders, had lobbied members of his caucus to support the measure—was on the floor, ready to lobby again. Hastert had already put months of work into the legislation, including negotiating details of the proposal with Senate Majority Leader Bill Frist (R-TN), House committee chairmen with jurisdiction over the bill, and Republican President George W. Bush, who had placed the measure high on his legislative agenda.

After the customary seventeen minutes for voting expired, the bill was losing, 210–214. But rather than accept defeat, Hastert ignored custom. Using his authority as Speaker, he kept the voting clock open and, with other Republican leaders, began searching the floor for more votes. A former high school wrestler and wrestling coach, Hastert was soon "towering over problem members" and asking for their support (Franzen 2003). He made progress, but after thirty minutes, he still needed at least two opponents to switch their votes for the measure to pass. C. L. "Butch" Otter, a Republican conservative from Idaho, eventually changed his vote to yes, and Hastert and other leaders focused their attention on Missouri Representative Jo Ann Emerson, one of the Republicans opposed to the bill's limits on importing cheaper medications. Hastert promised her that he would schedule a future vote to permit drug reimportation, and Emerson (tearful, by some accounts) went to the well of the chamber and voted yes. With the tally now at 216 to 215, Hastert immediately ended the vote (Adams 2003; Allen and Graham-Silverman 2003; Dewar and Goldstein 2003; Franzen 2003; Hastert 2004).

This was not the only occasion when Speaker Hastert used his authority so dramatically to steer legislative outcomes in a desired direction,[1] nor was he the first Speaker to do so. In 1941, for instance, Sam Rayburn (D-TX) used personal lobbying, swift closure of a floor vote, and other methods to successfully extend the Selective Service Act by a single vote. Some Speakers have gone so far as to exercise leadership on measures that were only weakly supported, or even opposed, by their own party in the House. In November 1993, Speaker Tom Foley (D-WA) worked with President Bill Clinton, albeit cautiously, to successfully ratify the North American Free Trade Agreement over the opposition of a majority of his own party.[2]

Why do Speakers sometimes act as assertive legislative leaders? What purpose motivates them to use their influence strategically to achieve legislative outcomes, even if those outcomes are resisted by many members of their own party? The answers to these questions, I argue, stem from the desire of every Speaker to satisfy key goals or objectives. The Speaker does not merely want to remain the favored leader of fellow partisans in the House; other objectives, derived from constitutional structure and the broader political environment, drive his or her behavior as much as do the preferences and electoral needs of the congressional majority party. The wish to satisfy these goals provides the basis for assertive, cross-partisan, and at times even independent legislative leadership on behalf of a variety of institutions or individuals. Thus while the majority party is the Speaker's most important constituency, the party's preferences may compete or join together with the preferences of other important players that matter to the Speaker, including the president, the legislature as a whole, constituents in the Speaker's congressional district, or even the Speaker himself or herself. Hastert's actions on the Medicare bill illustrate this phenomenon: not only did the measure's passage give credit-claiming opportunities to Hastert's party in Congress, but it was also an important priority for the president and an issue of considerable personal interest to the Speaker (Franzen 2003).

The Speaker of the House is an unusual office. Although it is one of the few specified in the U.S. Constitution (Article I, section 2), the Constitution says very little about its purpose, responsibilities, or proper role in national governance. The origins of the office go back at least as far as thirteenth century England, when the House of Commons was headed by a "Speaker." Over time, the role of the British Speaker shifted from representing the interests of the Crown within the legislature to serving more partisan interests in the seventeenth and eighteenth centuries and, finally, to presiding as a nonpartisan officer starting in the early nineteenth century. Legislative bodies in the American colonies also adopted the office of Speaker, but they did so at a time when the Speaker of the House of Commons was in its partisan phase of existence. As a consequence, by 1789 the most common experience of the Speakership in the former colonies was as a presiding officer with party-related duties (Fuller 1909, 1–17; Galloway 1976, 133; Peters 1997, 18–20). The Speaker of the U.S. House thus became a position with a hybrid of both partisan and nonpartisan responsibilities. By contrast, Speakers in other Anglo legislatures, like those in Australia, Canada, and New Zealand, have hewn more closely to the role of nonpartisan officer, though their selection from within the parliament presents the possibility of at least informal ties to their party or constituency.

There are several reasons why the Speaker of the House, and his or her reasons for exercising leadership, are worthy of detailed study. First, because the Speakership is the only leadership position in Congress whose existence and method of selection is mandated by the Constitution, the office possesses considerable prestige.[3] Second, the Speaker has a number of important internal duties and powers, such as establishing rule-making precedents, evaluating points of order related to floor procedure, referring legislation to committees, and influencing legislators' committee assignments. Perhaps the most important of these duties is the Speaker's ultimate responsibility for ensuring that the House enacts legislation —its fundamental task. Other House party officers may also help with that task, but they also usually have other day-to-day duties (setting the weekly calendar, for instance) that the Speaker does not. Only the Senate majority leader, a position that did not formally exist until the early twentieth century, is comparable in power.[4] In short, as House historian George Galloway described it, the Speakership "is an office of great honor and influence" (1955, 346).

Third, a study of how, when, and why the Speaker exercises leadership addresses a continuing debate over the proper conceptualization of congressional leadership. On one hand, as noted above, few political offices in American government possess greater authority than that of the Speaker. On the other hand, many scholars have identified significant constraints on the powers of leaders in Congress. They point out that these leaders, including the Speaker, face considerable risks when acting in ways that run contrary to the preferences of the party caucus that selects them. They also note that elements of the political environment—for instance, the decentralized nature of Congress, the weakness of congressional party structures, and the absence of centralized control over significant rewards and benefits—sharply limit what these leaders can accomplish. Thus even strong Speakers, like the infamous Joseph "Czar" Cannon from the early 1900s, are often described by scholars as "followers" or "agents" of their own party in the legislature, rarely able to exercise decisive organizational leadership except when the outcome is desired by their congressional party or by a majority of the House (Burns 1978, 345; Krehbiel and Wiseman 2001; Riker 1986, 129–30; Sinclair 1995, 1999).[5] This depiction of the Speaker as a constrained party agent is common in research studies that focus solely on the association between the House majority party and party leaders' behavior. These studies, however, understate the Speaker's independence from his or her party in Congress and fail to acknowledge the leadership goals that Speakers may achieve by acting both strategically and more autonomously. In this respect, I adopt the perspective of scholarly works that have identified how congressional leaders can be forceful and independent, such as Randall Strahan's analysis of selected House Speakers, Steven Smith's review of congressional leaders' direct and indirect sources of influence, and Charles Jones's discussion of Speaker Cannon and committee chairman Howard Smith (Jones 1968; Smith 2007; Strahan 2007).

Finally, understanding what drives the Speaker to exercise leadership has important applications beyond congressional politics. Speakers and party leaders in other national legislatures often have formal powers analogous to those of the U.S. Speaker and operate within similar institutions and political contexts—particularly those in presidential systems of government, as can be found in Latin America and elsewhere. More generally, political leaders (including the Speaker) can structure and limit the choices of others, undertake political and social reform, bring about procedural and policy changes within bureaucratic agencies, initiate significant institutional developments, or drive major political change more broadly (Burns 1978; Carpenter 2001; Miroff 2004; Riker 1986). Thus understanding not only what the U.S. Speaker does but also why he or she does it can provide useful insights into how and why leaders in other institutions and political contexts do what they do.

Speakers exercise leadership in a variety of ways. In examining why they seek to shape legislative outcomes, even when facing resistance from their own partisans, I focus on Speakers' *legislative leadership* in Congress, defined as the mobilization of resources to engage the interests of followers with respect to the legislative output of the House (Burns 1978, 18). Of all leadership behaviors in which Speakers may engage, legislative leadership is perhaps the most important to understand, since Speakers are judged on (if not presumably responsible for) legislative results and the ability to build substantive majorities in the House (Jones 1968). To explain their leadership on legislation, I build a series of original data sets to identify and analyze several kinds of legislative leadership as exercised by the nine Speakers who have served from 1941 through 2006 (listed in table 1.1). These Speakers differ in important ways—in their leadership style, degree of formal authority, and overall skill. More generally, however, they can be considered comparable insofar as they share several important features: the existence of the "modern" presidency, starting with Franklin Delano Roosevelt; general agreement on the Speaker's parliamentary versus partisan responsibilities; and a well-developed and firmly established set of leadership tools (Corwin 1940, 330–37; Peters 1997).

Table 1.1 Speakers of the House of Representatives, 1941–2006

Speaker	Party-State	Congresses	Dates
Rayburn, Sam	D-TX	77–79, 81–82, 84–87	1940–46, 1949–52, 1955–61
Martin, Joseph	R-MA	80, 83	1947–48, 1953–54
McCormack, John	D-MA	87–91	1962–70
Albert, Carl	D-OK	92–94	1971–76
O'Neill, Thomas P.	D-MA	95–99	1977–86
Wright, James	D-TX	100–101	1987–89
Foley, Thomas	D-WA	101–103	1989–94
Gingrich, Newt	R-GA	104–105	1995–98
Hastert, Dennis	R-IL	106–109	1999–2006

Speakers may exercise legislative leadership in several major spheres, including activity on the floor of the House, the content of the legislative agenda, the substance of particular legislation, and the behavior of committees. In a later chapter, I examine leadership in the latter three spheres (and in others as well), but the primary focus of this book is the first: Speakers' behavior during, or in proximity to, consideration of legislation on the House floor. This sort of behavior tends to involve at least one of five tactics: labeling a bill as "party policy" or a "party measure"; trading scarce benefits for votes; personally lobbying individual Representatives to vote in one direction; delivering floor statements that advocate a certain vote outcome; and extending or limiting the time available to vote on the floor.[6] The House floor is a particularly useful focal point for studying Speakers' legislative leadership. Since a bill must pass on the floor in some form to become law, the floor serves as the common arena for all legislative matters and the place where Speakers' strategic action can be best observed and evaluated. Speakers also have a measure of equality with all other legislators on the floor, in that each representative may vote, speak, or even introduce legislation. This allows one to compare the behavior of the Speaker with that of the majority party's rank and file and to compare different Speakers across time while holding most formal authority constant (though not all, because unlike his or her colleagues, the Speaker is also the House's official presiding officer). Focusing on the floor presents a test of whether Speakers can influence legislator vote choice, absent most of the other powers that give them an institutional advantage over other members of Congress.[7] By contrast, non-floor spheres of leadership activity are difficult to connect to legislative results or are largely un-observed and thus exceedingly challenging to verify.[8] In short, an examination of floor leadership can contribute to our understanding of the legislative process and the extent to which the Speaker affects political outcomes.

ACHIEVING LEADERSHIP GOALS

The idea that the Speaker exercises leadership on behalf of other individuals or entities besides the House majority party is not new. Speakers themselves have noted that the duties of the office encompass several, sometimes conflicting, ex-pectations (Albert 1976; O'Neill 1987, 327–28; Wright 1994). Some who study Congress have pointed to the president, the Senate, the Speaker's policy pref-erences, and his or her leadership style as other important influences (Evans and Oleszek 1999a; Palazzolo 1992; Peters 1997; Ripley 1969; Strahan 2007; Vega and Peters 1996).[9] Most relevant studies fail to provide theoretical justi-fications for the significance of these other factors or test their explanatory value for only a single Speaker or a limited number of leadership cases. Nonetheless, they do point the way toward a more complete and accurate explanation of why the modern Speaker of the House commits acts of legislative leadership.

Congressional leaders, as with legislators in general, are purposive actors: they have certain goals or objectives they wish to achieve while in Congress (Strahan 2007). In his book *Congressmen in Committees,* Richard Fenno iden-tified three basic legislator goals: reelection, passage of desired public policy, and internal influence in the legislature. Since Fenno's book, a number of other scholars have adopted this "multiple goals" approach in analyzing Congress, using these three goals as a starting point to explain committee selection, the internal organization and rules of the legislature, and leadership structure and authority (for example, Fenno 1973a; Schickler 2001; Sinclair 1995; Smith 2007).

Studies of congressional leaders, while acknowledging that leaders in Con-gress have goals, generally focus almost entirely on one goal—their reelection as leader—to explain their behavior. Emphasizing the partisan nomination process of the Speaker and other party leaders, these analyses assume that their actions are designed to satisfy the interests of the majority party, so that they can obtain and maintain their leadership positions (for example, Sinclair 1995, 65–66). This assumption provides a powerful and parsimonious explanation for leadership behavior, identifying the critically important relationship between leaders and the people who place them in their positions of authority. But such a narrow view of leadership goals is incomplete in at least two ways. First, it does not acknowledge that congressional leaders are also members of Congress and thus face an additional reelection goal: reelection to the legislature. This goal may lead them to exercise leadership on behalf of the policy preferences of their district or state constituencies. As the 1994 election defeat of Speaker Tom Foley aptly demonstrated, there is always a possibility that a Speaker can lose his or her House seat. Second, it neglects other important leadership goals that may lead to the exercise of legislative leadership on behalf of other individuals, institutions, or entities.

A theory of congressional leadership that incorporates these additional goals does not simply complicate the picture of what leaders in Congress do. It acknowledges that congressional leaders may face differing or even competing reasons to exercise (or not exercise) leadership in different political contexts. Their leadership may sometimes be overdetermined, satisfying more than one goal, while at other times leaders may choose to ignore some important entities—even the majority party in Congress—and act on behalf of other individuals or institutions in order to satisfy a certain goal. Perhaps more important, this sort of theory shifts the focus of congressional leaders from being implicitly passive to purposive and strategic. Congressional leaders do not merely respond to the desires and preferences of the majority party in Congress; they also possess particular objectives and, consequently, exercise legislative leadership to achieve those objectives.

In the discussion that follows, I outline this "multiple goals" leadership model, which I call the *theory of goal-driven leadership*.[10] As applied to the Speakership, the theory posits that the Speaker possesses an array of goals, with each specific goal associated with his or her position as either an official congressional leader or a member of Congress, and that the Speaker exercises legislative leadership to achieve one or more of these goals. This goal-centered view of leadership is similar to a related theory, Randall Strahan's "conditional agency" model (Strahan 2007). But the theory of goal-driven leadership identifies a different, and in some ways broader, set of Speaker objectives and applies them to all modern Speakers, not only transformative ones with a high personal tolerance for risk.[11] These general goals appear in table 1.2, along with the person, entity, or institution whose preferences or desires are most relevant to the achievement of each goal, and whether that goal is associated with the Speaker's position as leader or as a member of Congress. Note that some goals (namely, reelection and duty-fulfillment) have more than one element, and each element is associated with the preferences of a different individual or entity.

Table 1.2 Goals Motivating the Speaker's Legislative Leadership

Goal of Speaker	Relevant Person, Institution, or Entity	Associated Institutional Position of Speaker
Secure reelection	1. Party in Congress	Speaker
	2. District	Member of Congress
Enact policy	3. Speaker (personal policy preferences)	Member of Congress
Fulfill Speaker-related roles	4. Presidential party	Speaker
	5. Institutional presidency	Speaker
	6. Whole House	Speaker

The reelection goal. The Speaker of the House has two discrete sets of electoral constituencies, each with the power to deny the Speaker his or her position in Congress. The first is the Speaker's *party in Congress.* Several existing theories point to the congressional party as the fundamental influence on Speaker behavior. They include institutional context theory, which holds that the authority of congressional leaders, and their willingness to pursue assertive legislative leadership, is determined by the degree of ideological homogeneity within their party (Cooper and Brady 1981; Rohde 1991),[12] and procedural cartel theory, which views the Speaker as a party agent who helps resolve collection action problems, enforce intraparty policy agreements, and ensure that those agreements are enacted (Cox and McCubbins 1993, 2005). Another theoretical approach in this category applies the multiple goals framework to the demands of majority parties, positing that leaders provide assistance to the congressional party to achieve the three goals of party members (Sinclair 1995).

The importance of the majority party to the Speaker originates not only from the partisan nomination process but from the Constitution, which in its only reference to the office states, "the House of Representatives shall chuse their Speaker and other Officers" (Article I, section 2). With the creation of political parties, Speakers have usually been selected by a majority of the majority party: once the party chooses a nominee in its caucus, it nearly always votes unanimously for him or her in the subsequent House vote.[13] This electoral connection establishes a strong link between the Speaker and the objectives of the majority party. These partisan objectives can in turn be broken down into two components: maintaining the party's majority status and enacting its collective policy preferences (Cox and McCubbins 1993, 125–28; Sinclair 1995; Smith 2007).[14]

The majority party in Congress has electoral power over the Speaker, but the Speaker has a second important constituency: voters in his or her *congressional district*. The district matters because the norm in the House has been to choose Speakers from among other House members (though not technically a constitutional requirement). This means that Speakers, like their congressional colleagues, must run for reelection if they wish to stay in office, and thus they have an incentive to be responsive and attentive to their local constituencies. Even if House Speakers come from electorally safe districts, they may be concerned about the potential preferences of their constituents and will therefore act on behalf of those preferences, anticipating that they will become salient in a future election (Arnold 1990; Cox and McCubbins 1993; Mayhew 1974; O'Neill 1987, 327).

The policy goal. The Speaker has a second important objective. Because he or she is an elected representative, the goal of rank-and-file legislators to enact their *personal policy preferences* should—and, I argue, does—apply to the Speaker as well.[15] When the Speaker has strong preferences about a certain legislative outcome, he or she is likely to exercise leadership to achieve that outcome. While those preferences will usually coincide with those of the majority party, the Speaker's district, or both, they may not necessarily do so. They could instead derive from the Speaker's personal values, prior experiences, or deeply held beliefs (Galloway 1955, 347–48; Strahan 2002, 263).[16]

The role-fulfillment goal. The Speaker's leadership position is the basis for a third, more subtle, Speaker goal. When members of an organization choose a leader, that leader will naturally be concerned with the preferences and career concerns of the organization's members. But those members, as well as the leader himself and other individuals, will have additional expectations about the proper duties or responsibilities of the leader. These manifest themselves as another leadership goal: fulfilling key roles or duties related to serving as a leader. This way of thinking about the Speakership (and leadership generally) borrows from role theory, a paradigm from sociology and anthropology positing that a particular status position in society carries with it one or more duties or modes of conduct related to the behavior of others (Gerth and Mills 1964, 10; Linton 1936, 113–14; Mead 1934; Parsons 1951, 40). Indeed, several studies of Congress and legislative politics—including studies that do not draw from role theory —have also looked at legislator behavior as a function of particular duties or roles (for example, Davidson 1969; Mayhew 2000; Searing 1994; Sigel and Pindur 1973; Vega and Peters 1996; Wahlke et al. 1962).[17]

The fulfillment of leadership roles or duties is a goal for Speakers because of certain expectations that they achieve such a goal (Biddle 1979, ch. 5; Morris 1971, 397–98; Parsons 1951, 190–91). Even some advocates of "congressional party" theories of the Speaker acknowledge, at least implicitly, that expectations can drive leader behavior, though they usually identify the Speaker's party in Congress as the source of these expectations.[18] But expectations can come from a variety of places. For example, the codified rules or guidelines that define and describe the position of Speaker (that is, constitutional text and party rules) outline particular duties and responsibilities, and they may be taken seriously enough by Speakers to be followed, irrespective of the presence of formalized punishments (Biddle 1979, 116, 121–22; Searing 1994, 15; Wahlke et al. 1962, 11, 21). A second source of expectations is the views and beliefs of other actors (Biddle 1979, 117). These actors could include legislators as well as individuals outside of Congress, like the president or the public at large (Davidson 1969, 178; Wahlke et al. 1962, 171).[19] Their expectations could be enforced with electoral punishment, but social praise or similar rewards may alone encourage expectation-driven behavior, as may sanctions like ostracism, lack of trust, private rebuke, or open demonstrations of displeasure (Wahlke et al. 1962, 154, 168). A third source is internalized standards held by the individual Speaker (Biddle 1979, 117–18). Speakers may view their leadership position in a particular way and as a consequence have certain internal, often unexpressed, expectations of proper conduct when serving in that position. In a survey of legislators from the 88th Congress (1963–65), for example, Roger Davidson found that party leaders are not only partisan but also more nationally focused than other legislators (1969, 134–37, 151). Over time, any or all of these sources of expectations can become institutionalized (for example, Moe 1987) and will be followed by future Speakers as a matter of course.

Three specific elements of the role-fulfillment goal—deriving from such sources as constitutional text, the power and authority of the president, and the Speaker-selection process—are likely to encourage Speakers to exercise legislative leadership. The first is the duty to support the *presidential party.* Theories of congressional leadership that view the majority party as the causal variable of importance usually combine presidential and congressional party interests into a single, partisan motivation for behavior (for example, Sinclair 1995, 206–7). But while both are related—for example, shared party affiliation is likely to be highly correlated with common policy goals[20]—the Speaker does not serve at the pleasure of the president, and even with shared ideological beliefs, the policy preferences of the president and the congressional majority party are not always the same. The executive and legislative branches have different electoral bases, means of selection, and institutional sources of authority, which can contribute to ideological or policy divisions between the presidential and the congressional parties (Burns 1963, 196–203, 249–57; Pious 1979, 131–46; Truman 1959, 303). Thus while the president is often seen as the head of his party, presidential and congressional party imperatives may be distinct. For instance, a same-party president may propose legislation that is helpful to his own reelection but is not salient to his party in Congress, or a presidential candidate might see electoral gains from passage of a bill opposed by his legislative party.[21]

Despite these differences, the Speaker does have important reasons to support the presidential party, even when the policy or issue at hand is opposed by his or her congressional caucus. Constitutional text and other sources give the president considerable tools to influence the legislative process. There is also an expectation that part of the Speaker's responsibility as party leader in the House is to support, passively if not actively, the agenda of a same-party president or presidential candidate. This expectation comes from the so-called Washington community and also from the Speaker's party, since the party can benefit from having a president of the same party in the White House. As political scientist David Truman observed, Congress's "elective leaders are, and probably must be, both the President's leaders and the [congressional] party's leaders" (Ripley 1969, 5; Sinclair 1995, 206; Truman 1959, 291, quote p. 298).[22]

The Speaker's second role is to assist the *institutional presidency:* in other words, to aid the president not for partisan reasons but because of the president's electoral mandate, national stature, or traditional authority over defense and foreign policy.[23] Party-based theorists of congressional leadership tend to be skeptical of this duty: they note that because both the president and Speaker serve at the behest of separate constituencies, there is no immediate electoral inducement for the latter to assist the former, unless the president is popular and/or newly elected and, by granting him support, the Speaker can improve the reputation of the congressional majority party (Sinclair 1995, 273). In addition, Speakers often have much to gain from fighting a powerful president of the opposite party, whether it be to achieve a policy victory or to strengthen their party's reputation among core supporters.[24] But this perspective misses the effects of the Speaker's institutional position vis-à-vis the president, the powerful means of policy influence at the president's disposal, and a conditional norm of deference to the executive on certain issues.

For example, the constitutional powers and responsibilities of the president, including his veto authority and position as military commander in chief, serve as the basis for considerable influence over policy. Presidents, particularly when newly elected, often claim a national "mandate" for action as well, placing responsibility on the Speaker to accept, or at least respond to, his initiatives. Gary Hymel, a former aide to Speaker Tip O'Neill, recounted in an interview that O'Neill initially viewed President Ronald Reagan as an ideological foe, but that "the people elected him, so you've got to give him a chance" (interview with the author, May 2003).[25] In addition, the rise of the modern presidency, an expanded executive branch, and the use of modern media techniques in the late nineteenth and early twentieth centuries dramatically expanded the president's influence over Congress and constrained legislative leaders in what they could accomplish, giving congressional leaders an incentive to pursue outcomes that ensured cooperation from the president (Gould 2003; Hart 1995; James 2000, 21–22; Kernell 1997; Milkis 1993).[26] As one former legislator observed, not only does the president possess significant legislative powers, but "leaders of Congress have been reasonably deferential in the exercise of those powers," and the Speaker can acceptably defer to the president because of a sense of national unity (in his words, "we are all Americans") and because "when one looks at the Constitution, one can see that the president has his particular powers" he can exercise (interview with the author, January 2003). This extends in particular to foreign affairs and national defense issues, which became areas of major presidential influence (and congressional deference) with the growth of the domestic military establishment, the emergence of America as a state with imperial powers, and the endorsement of this influence by the Supreme Court in its 1936 *Curtiss-Wright* decision (Fisher 1995; Pious 1979, 184, 332, 354, 397; Sundquist 1981). If an expectation exists that the president has prerogatives in foreign policy, trade, or defense, the Speaker can feel beholden to uphold and support the president's position on these issues (for example, O'Neill 1987, 227).

In short, all Speakers must contend with the power of the president and may face situations in which deference is expected. Speaker John McCormack attributed considerable agenda-setting power to the president, whether Republican or Democrat, and famously remarked that he could never "say 'No' to a President" (*U.S. News and World Report,* 8 September 1969). Jim Wright noted that during his tenure in the House—in which, ironically, Wright would challenge a Republican president on a foreign policy issue (see chapter 4)—there was a "rather general perception . . . that we have only one president" and "that on matters of delicate national policy" there was a duty to "confront the world with an image of one nation, indivisible" (interview with the author, July 2003). In another example, one former aide to Speaker Newt Gingrich recounted in an interview his party's difficulties in defeating President Clinton during the 1995 government shutdown and the following year's White House–driven advertising campaign against congressional Republicans (interview with the author, June 2003). The expectation to exercise leadership on behalf of the institutional presidency appears most commonly when the president is from the opposite party of the congressional majority, but it is not exclusive to divided government: a Speaker may also support a same-party president for reasons related to the president's institutional authority.[27]

The Speaker's third duty is to serve the *whole House,* that is, the interests and concerns of all members of the House of Representatives regardless of political party. At first, the Speaker was primarily (though not entirely) a nonpartisan officer of the House, presiding over its deliberations and responsible for governing debate impartially (Peters 1997, ch. 1). Though this mode of behavior disappeared relatively quickly, the Speakership has never entirely lost its function as a House-wide office. This derives in part from the Constitution, which directs the entire House to select the Speaker rather than just the majority party. This function was reinforced early in congressional history when the Speaker was assigned important chamberwide functions, such as allocating committee assignments to all members of Congress and formally recognizing any member wishing to address the floor (Galloway 1955, 348–49; Peters 1997, 23, 26; Strahan, Gunning, and Vining 2006). The House-wide role of the Speaker has been interpreted to include a number of specific responsibilities, both internal (like protecting the rights of members of the House and ensuring the chamber's smooth operation) and external (defending the legislature's power, reputation, and authority).

Contemporary Speakers, even partisan ones, have acknowledged this role. In his survey of legislators, Roger Davidson found that party leaders, particularly Speaker Sam Rayburn, were more likely to be "ritualists," caring more about how Congress operates than about popular needs or wants (1969, 82, 93, 180). A later Speaker, Tip O'Neill, acknowledged in one floor speech, "When I am interviewed as Speaker, I have an official responsibility to be above the battle" (*Congressional Record,* 21 February 1978, 854; see also O'Neill 1987, 327).[28] Jim Wright observed after leaving Congress that "the Speaker has an obligation to uphold the public reputation of the House," and "it has been the goal of every Speaker to improve the public image of Congress" (Wright 1994, 241, 242). In a subsequent interview, Wright said that the Speaker as "a constitutional officer" has an obligation to defend the legislative branch, for "if he doesn't do it, who's going to?" (interview with the author, July 2003). Former Speaker Tom

Foley, in a television interview, acknowledged that the Speaker is both a party leader and "the Speaker of the whole House," and "when a great issue is at stake," Speakers must sometimes allow floor votes on bills opposed by their own party (Foley 2004). Former House minority leader Bob Michel noted that legislators have "mellowed" when becoming Speakers, because "they realized they're the Speaker of the whole House, not just one party" (quoted in Remini 2006, 394).

This role is not easily explained by partisan motivations for behavior. To be sure, one could argue that a fair and well-run legislature eases passage of party policy and may bolster the reputation of the majority party (Sinclair 1995, 69). In truth, however, the House majority party often writes chamber rules that disadvantage the minority, usually granting rights to the minority party only when they are demanded by a cross-party coalition (Binder 1997, Schickler 2000). In addition, the preferences and desires of the whole House and the congressional party may conflict. If the majority party wishes to enact legislation strongly opposed by the minority, for example, the Speaker may have an incentive to override or curtail the minority's parliamentary rights. As Speaker Jim Wright noted, "All Speakers face an occasional dilemma in their dual roles as activist and presiding judge. . . . How to reconcile the two—legislative effectiveness and fairness to the minority—is a challenge no Speaker escapes" (Wright 1994, 241).

CONSEQUENCES AND PREDICTIONS OF THE THEORY

Assuming that Speakers possess the electoral, policy, and duty-fulfillment goals outlined above, two associated problems emerge. First, if conflicts among particular entities or between different goals arise, how does the Speaker resolve them (Biddle 1979, 160; Davidson 1969, 74–76)? [29] Second, since the reelection goal includes a powerful constraint for noncompliance—removal from office—why would a Speaker follow any other goal if doing so conflicts with the needs or preferences of his or her electoral constituencies, especially those of the congressional majority party?

In general, Speakers can resolve conflicts among differing goals, or different aspects of the same goal (for example, aiding the presidential party versus the whole House, each a role-fulfillment goal), in several ways. If some individuals have strong preferences on a certain bill or measure, while others have weaker preferences on the same measure, the expectations of the former may trump those of the latter (Davidson 1969, 178–79; Merton 1968, 425–26;

Wahlke et al. 1962, 384). For example, the policy preferences of the majority party or voters in the Speaker's district may be uncertain, vague, or ill formed, creating an opportunity for the Speaker to achieve some other goal (Vega and Peters 1996). In addition, some individuals may have more influence or organize a more powerful coalition than others, allowing their interests and concerns to trump or cancel out competing ones (Merton 1968, 426–28). Speakers can take an active part in the process as well, using direct persuasion or the help of other actors like the president to convince skeptics of the need to follow one goal over another (for example, Maslin-Wicks 1998; Pious 1979, 197–98; Truman 1959, 294–97). Furthermore, if Speakers have the flexibility and desire to be a "role-determining" leader, they may even be able to ignore, interpret, or reshape particular duties or roles associated with their office (Gerth and Mills 1964, 420–25).

Besides these factors, the Speaker is also able to act on behalf of a range of goals because the relation between the Speaker and the majority party in Congress is more flexible than some party-based leadership theories posit or imply. If one assumes that individuals can be motivated by more than immediate self-interest, they may not always insist that leaders exercise leadership solely on behalf of their needs or preferences (Merton 1968, 436). Role-based studies of legislative politics suggest that this is the case among legislators. Davidson observed that "the folkways of legislatures are invariably tolerant," and constituencies are less insistent about things than political actors claim (Davidson 1969, 178). One set of surveys of state legislators revealed that elected representatives from partisan chambers see little conflict between the partisan and nonpartisan responsibilities of the chamber's presiding officer (Wahlke et al. 1962, ch. 8).[30]

Theoretically, this more flexible perspective of leadership can be understood by conceptualizing the Speaker as the political representative of the majority party in the House. Just as a member of Congress represents the citizens of her district, acting on their behalf in her legislative duties, Speakers can represent fellow legislators within Congress, acting on their behalf in certain activities that fall outside legislators' spheres of influence (such as media relations, high-level negotiations with other political actors, and coalition building). If Speakers are a representative of their party in the House, they are neither a delegate of the party, following its explicit directions or consulting with its members in advance, nor a trustee with considerable independence and leeway. Instead, like other representatives, they are a combination of the two, having many possible choices of action within the basic expectation of representing their "constituents" from the congressional party. This combination allows them to operate in an environment of diverse and often competing pressures for action, just as other elected representatives do (Pitkin 1967, 154, 166, 219–20). This is not to suggest that Speakers are undemocratic or unaccountable but rather that their followers grant them a degree of flexibility in exercising legislative leadership. Provided Speakers do not consistently and blatantly disregard the expressed preferences of the House majority party, they can act strategically to achieve their multiple goals.

In sum, the theory of goal-driven leadership paints a more complete picture of the goals and constraints driving congressional leadership behavior. Unlike institutional context theory, goal-driven leadership theory allows for varying motivations for the exercise of legislative leadership by individual Speakers in a given Congress. In contrast to party cartel theory and other multiple goal theories, it acknowledges that party leaders do not operate "in a vacuum" but exist in a "broader strategic context" (Evans and Oleszek 1999a, 3). Although it shares some important aspects of Randall Strahan's conditional agency theory, the theory of goal-driven leadership identifies a wider set of objectives that apply to Speakers in general, not solely to transformative-minded ones (Strahan 2007). Finally, unlike other studies that acknowledge the influence or importance of many factors, the theory explicitly connects the institutional foundations of the office of Speaker and a finite set of objectives that may be ever-present, so that even Speakers representing highly cohesive parties may still have the strategic incentive to achieve nonelectoral objectives.[31]

If the theory of goal-driven leadership is correct, at least four predictions follow. First, as already noted, Speakers may exercise legislative leadership on behalf of the preferences of others besides the majority party in Congress. To achieve each of their basic goals, Speakers will try to assist relevant individuals, groups, or institutions (as listed in table 1.2) when the issue or bill is salient to those individuals, groups, or institutions. This includes exercising leadership on behalf of the majority party in order to secure reelection as Speaker; representing his or her own district in order to ensure reelection to the House; pursuing issues that are personally salient in order to achieve his or her own preferred policy outcome; and helping the party's president, the institutional presidency, or the House as a whole in order to fulfill a leadership role. These predicted behaviors are each listed in the first column of table 1.3.

The conditions under which the Speaker is likely to pursue particular goals, or particular elements of a single goal, are not mutually exclusive. Therefore, a second prediction of the theory is that the Speaker may adopt a leadership strategy that satisfies the preferences or desires of more than one individual, institu-

Table 1.3 Predictions of Goal-Driven Leadership Theory

Goal and Associated Person, Institution, or Entity	Predicted Behavior	Example	When Likely to Occur	What Party-Based Theories Predict
Secure reelection				
1. Party in Congress				
a. majority status	Support majority coalition electoral objectives	Rayburn and civil rights legislation (ch. 3)	Issue is salient to majority party electoral goals	Same
b. policy	Support party platform	Gingrich and balanced budget amendment (ch. 4)	Issue is salient to majority party policy goals; majority party homogeneous	Same
2. District	Support constituency interests	Rayburn and natural gas regulation (ch. 3)	Issue is salient to district	May occur if not in conflict with majority party interests
Enact policy				
3. Speaker (personal policy preferences)	Pursue personally salient issues	Hastert and aid to Colombia (ch. 6)	Issue is of personal interest to Speaker	Does not occur

Fulfill leadership role

4. Presidential party	Support presidential party agenda	O'Neill and Carter energy bil (ch. 4)	Issue is salient to same-party incumbent president or candidate	Associated with majority party interests
5. Institutional presidency	Support executive-centered matters	Rayburn anc Formosa resolution (ch. 3)	Issue is salient to incumbent president and traditionally deferred to executive	Occurs if president(ial policy) is popular
6. Whole House				
a. internal	Impartiality, support House-wide interests	Wright and pay raise (ch. 4)	Issue is related to House internal procedure, process	Occurs if it helps achieve majority party interests
b. external	Protect institutional authority, reputation of House	McCormack and August recess (ch. 3)	Issue is related to House power, reputation	Occurs if it helps achieve majority party interests

tion, or entity, thus achieving one (or more) goals. This phenomenon is not simply of theoretical concern: such convergence may aid the process of persuading reluctant legislators, particularly if the president has a stake in the outcome, since the White House can provide potent leadership assistance to the Speaker.

Even though the third goal of the Speaker, role fulfillment, is institutionally grounded, its presence depends on factors that are less stable over time, like the expectations of other legislators, the public, or Speakers themselves. In addition, the failure to achieve the electoral goal generally has more severe consequences than the failure to enact personally desired policy or fulfill particular leadership duties or roles. A third prediction thus follows: leadership exercised to achieve reelection goals will occur the most often and the most consistently, followed by leadership exercised to achieve other goals. In particular, because the Speaker's leadership position is dependent on the votes of his or her party in Congress, the congressional party is expected to be the most common basis for legislative leadership. Evidence also suggests that the Speaker's role-fulfillment goal has shifted in importance across time, and although the theory makes no clear predictions about what has produced this shift, I discuss possible causes in the closing chapter.

Finally, while I test it only tangentially in this book, the theory suggests conditions when the Speaker is most likely to exercise legislative leadership (see the third column of table 1.3). Generally speaking, for any given bill or policy issue, two factors are likely to determine whether the Speaker is willing to use his or her leadership to shape legislative outcomes. The first is the degree of division in the majority party. This is important because, as noted above, the majority party is the electoral constituency that decides who is Speaker; thus the Speaker is unlikely to avoid serving his or her party or actively defy its policy interests if the party is more unified. The second factor is whether a particular bill or measure is salient to the actors or institutions related to the basic goals of the Speaker. Note that these predictions are not entirely new; others have argued that majority party divisions will increase the chances that the Speaker acts on behalf of nonparty interests, and a party whose members are discontented with the status quo may provide an opportunity for its leaders to seek major policy or institutional change (Strahan 2007; Vega and Peters 1996).

DETERMINING INFLUENCE ON FLOOR VOTES

Influence, like power, is very difficult to measure. Because the theory of goal-driven leadership is principally about why the Speaker acts, not whether his or her actions have a causal effect, I do not attempt to demonstrate conclusively that the Speaker caused all the legislative results documented in this book. I do, however, provide evidence when available (including interviews, statistical analyses, archival data, and legislator voting behavior) to show whether this type of causal relationship likely existed. I also indicate the intended legislative objective of the Speaker in selected case studies, which at least hints at whether the Speaker's leadership had its desired effect.[32] The counterfactual outcome is not necessarily a loss on the House floor; Speakers at times have exercised legislative leadership when the measure at hand was likely to pass or fail regardless, but this does not mean that their leadership did not matter. In fact, there are eight possible floor voting outcomes that a Speaker may seek, falling into two basic categories: winning on the floor and achieving some other result.[33]

Winning on the floor. The Speaker may exercise legislative leadership in order to win a vote on the House floor. In winning on the floor, however, the Speaker's choice of action depends on whether the "original" proposal—the bill, amendment, or other measure the Speaker wishes to see pass—is closer to the preferences of the majority party median legislator or the minority party median legislator. In the case of the former, the Speaker has one of four possible tactical objectives. First, the Speaker may seek to win over the floor median legislator. This is the most "conventional" case of legislative leadership: a proposal is supported by the party's median member but is opposed by the House's median member because the status quo is closer to that legislator's ideal preference point. This might occur, for instance, if the president is of the same party as the majority party and requests legislation desired by the majority party median member, but the status quo point is sufficiently close to the floor median that the legislation would lose on the House floor. The Speaker's aim in this strategic scenario is to persuade the pivotal floor member to vote contrary to her sincere preferences. Second, the Speaker may want to win over both the floor median legislator and the party median legislator. This case occurs when neither a majority on the floor nor a majority of the Speaker's own party prefers the legislative alternative to the status quo. This would occur, for example, if the president is of the same party as the majority and proposes legislation too extreme for even half of his or her congressional party to endorse, let alone a majority of the House. If the Speaker has some obligation or expectation to support such legislation, he or she will try to persuade his party's median member to vote for it, despite the fact that the status quo rests closer to that member's sincere preferences. Third, the Speaker may try to win a supermajority, that is, two-thirds of the voting members of the House. This scenario occurs in certain kinds of cases, such as overriding a presidential veto, passing a constitutional amendment, or enacting legislation under suspension of the rules. Finally, the Speaker may want to win both a supermajority and the party median legislator. Although theoretically possible, this scenario is unlikely to occur since it means that the Speaker desires a result so far to the extreme of the congressional majority party caucus, relative to the status quo, that it is opposed by a majority of the caucus as well as a nontrivial member of minority party members.

Two other tactical objectives related to winning on the floor involve the passage of proposals closer to the preferences of the minority party median legislator. In these cases, the Speaker wants to enact legislation that his or her own party opposes but the minority party endorses, a circumstance that applies most frequently to legislation proposed by a president of the opposite party that the Speaker wants to see pass. First, the Speaker may try to win over the floor median legislator. In this situation, the Speaker is trying to persuade the floor median (who is, by definition, a member of his or her own party) to vote for a proposal supported by the minority party. Second, the Speaker may try to win a supermajority. This is very uncommon since it means the Speaker desires an outcome endorsed by the minority party *and* in need of support from two-thirds of the House to pass. In the example of Rayburn and the natural gas bill (chapter 3), the Speaker could have followed this approach because both his party and President Harry Truman opposed the bill, but Rayburn chose not to —perhaps because the likelihood of success was so remote.

Alternative floor outcomes. Although winning a majority of votes on the floor might seem to be the only task of the Speaker, the appearance of a floor vote might provide additional political benefits for the majority party and/or achieve important goals of the Speaker. Two situations fit this category. First, the Speaker may seek to unify the majority party. In this case, floor success is likely, but the Speaker sees value in having as many legislators in the party caucus as possible voting in the same direction. This could be to enhance party reputation, bolster party harmony, or fend off procedural blockades from an institutionally powerful subset of the majority party. Second, the Speaker may wish to unify the House. In this situation, both the floor and the party median legislators support the Speaker's desired result, but the Speaker prefers that the House vote for it unanimously. The Speaker may pursue this result if, for example, Congress's reputation would be weakened by the sign of even minor dissent on a given issue or the Speaker wishes to send a public signal of strong bipartisanship.

Chapter 2 Speaking and

Voting on the House Floor

I have put serious effort and thought into these remarks that I am making today. . . . In this case, I hope we will act today to help the President to bring peace and stability in Lebanon, a country worthy of our attention, a country worthy of our assistance, a country worthy of our best efforts.
—Speaker Tip O'Neill (D-MA), *Congressional Record,* 28 September 1983, 26175–76

When Speaker O'Neill delivered these remarks on the House floor, he was speaking on behalf of a controversial resolution—to keep U.S. troops deployed in Lebanon—despite considerable opposition from many fellow Democrats. Yet the resolution passed, 270–161. Although a slim majority of his own party (134 of 264) voted against it, the Speaker's statements had been so effective, wrote one O'Neill biographer, that "it was one of those rare occasions, members of Congress said later, that a speech from the floor changed many votes" (Farrell 2001, 615).

This example illustrates a useful tool of legislative leadership at the Speaker's disposal: *floor advocacy,* or speaking on the House floor on behalf of a particular vote outcome.[1] Speakers at times have used floor advocacy to take strong positions on roll call votes. Three examples:

- Sam Rayburn (D-TX), on the rejection of a closed rule to consider trade legislation: "The House on this last vote has done a most unusual thing and under the circumstances a very dangerous thing . . . to proceed in this fashion, in my opinion, is a great mistake" (*Congressional Record,* 17 February 1955, 1678).
- Carl Albert (D-OK), on an amendment to an appropriations bill limiting certain spending on agriculture: "This is a cruel and inhumane amendment that will in my opinion start a depression in the United States and would destroy the livelihood of at least 100,000 farm families in America" (*Congressional Record,* 23 June 1971, 21637).
- Newt Gingrich (R-GA), on a major tax bill: "I urge every Member to look at this and ask yourself, in your constituents' lives, will not a little less money for Government and a little more money for . . . families be a good thing? And is not that what this Congress was elected to do?" (*Congressional Record,* 5 April 1995, H4314).

One may argue that floor advocacy is more symbolic position taking than an effort to alter legislative outcomes, or that it is used instead of other leadership tools because the majority party is divided or the Speaker has fewer available institutional powers (Cooper and Brady 1981; Mayhew 1974, 61). I contend, however, that regardless of the Speaker's formal authority, floor advocacy can be a potentially effective means of influencing floor outcomes—particularly when used with other leadership tactics—because the Speaker's stature, authority, and selective use of floor advocacy lend his or her floor statements a considerable degree of credibility and purpose. More important, evidence reveals that the Speaker can employ floor advocacy to achieve important goals, including (but not limited to) support from the House majority party.

In this chapter, I examine both floor advocacy and another floor-related activity Speakers may undertake, *floor voting.* I begin with floor advocacy, illustrating how the Speaker's use of floor statements has changed over time and how those changes demonstrate important shifts in Speakers' roles and duties. Next, I turn to a discussion of why floor advocacy can be an effective leadership tactic for contemporary Speakers. I then analyze instances of floor advocacy from Rayburn through Gingrich to explain why Speakers deliver speeches on the House floor. Since some of these analyses suffer from methodological limitations, I provide a more in-depth examination of select cases of floor advocacy, including their possible effect on final floor votes, in chapters 3 and 4. I then turn to nonpivotal floor voting, or voting in which the Speaker's vote does not itself decide the final result. Though such behavior, like public advocacy, has become more common for Speakers in recent years, evidence suggests that it is not consistently employed to affect legislative outcomes and that it reflects the leadership style and personal preferences of Speakers more than their position as House officer or party leader.

SHIFTING ROLES AND THE DEVELOPMENT OF SPEAKER FLOOR ADVOCACY

All Speakers have had the right to participate in floor debate. But although speaking on the floor might help the Speaker achieve particular goals, the decision to use floor advocacy may sacrifice one important objective for another (Peters 1997, 23). On one hand, as an officer of the entire House, the Speaker is expected to be above the fray of partisan disagreements and avoid advocating positions on issues divisive within the chamber. Indeed, the Speaker's traditional responsibility to preside over debate conflicts directly with participation in floor deliberation, since the latter requires him or her to literally leave the chair and thus abdicate, albeit temporarily, that responsibility.[2] On the other hand, using floor advocacy can accomplish both aspects of the Speaker's reelection goal: winning reelection to the House through the use of position taking and securing support from the party in Congress by openly lobbying legislators on party-preferred legislation. The Speaker may also achieve other goals by using floor advocacy, such as fulfilling the duty to help pass legislation preferred by the president or enacting personally desired public policy.

Early Speakers, particularly Jonathan Dayton (1795–99) and Henry Clay (who served three separate times, starting in 1811), experimented with the use of the floor to press for particular legislation, motions, or amendments (Strahan, Gunning, and Vining 2006). After Clay's final term as Speaker ended in 1825, subsequent Speakers rarely addressed the floor and usually did so only when they would not normally preside over debate (that is, when the House convened as the Committee of the Whole, where most amendments are debated). Speakers largely abstained from floor advocacy until the mid-twentieth century, when three developments distinguished the floor advocacy of Speaker Sam Rayburn and his successors from that of their predecessors. First, Speakers began delivering floor statements on a more consistent basis. The number

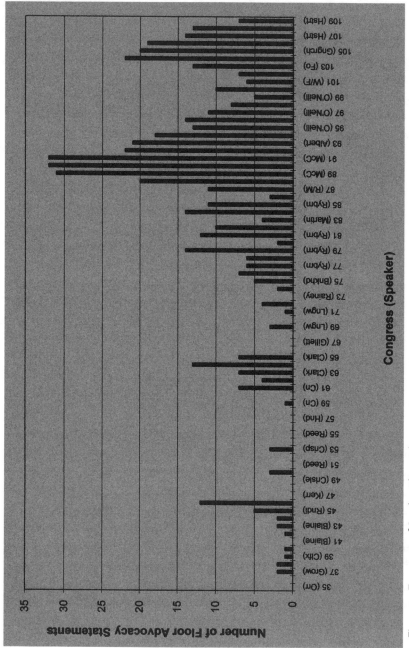

Figure 2.1 Frequency of Speaker Floor Advocacy, 1857–2006

of instances of Speaker floor advocacy from the 35th Congress (1857–59) through the 109th Congress (2005–6) is illustrated in figure 2.1. Each instance represents a speech, statement, or colloquy on the floor in which the Speaker advocated for or against a certain bill, amendment, motion, or other pending legislative vote. A few early Speakers, including Samuel Randall (D-PA, 1876–81), Joseph Cannon (R-IL, 1903–11), and Champ Clark (D-MO, 1911–19), used floor advocacy fairly often, but it was Rayburn who made it a regular practice that has continued to this day.[3] Although some contemporary Speakers have talked on the floor more than others—McCormack, in particular, stands out as especially loquacious—all Speakers since the 1930s share a general propensity to use floor advocacy, marking a decline in the expectation of the Speaker to avoid such activity.

In addition to the regular use of floor advocacy, a second development was the Speaker's expression of opinion on the floor more as a leader than as an individual legislator. Table 2.1 shows the number of floor statements delivered by selected Speakers from 1877 to 2006, the percentage of statements that included colloquial question-and-answer-type debate with members of Congress, and the percentage explicitly framed as being personal or without leadership intent.[4] Rayburn was the first contemporary Speaker to deliver floor speeches that were neither framed in explicitly personal terms nor delivered (except occasionally) as dialogue with other representatives. Both he and his successors have followed the norm of using floor advocacy primarily as a means of communicating general policy positions to their colleagues, not to debate others or convey personal opinions. Thus modern Speakers have seen floor statements as a way to advocate specific legislative outcomes, whether on behalf of the party in Congress, the president, or some other actor or institution.

Third, legislators since the 1940s have come to accept Speaker floor advocacy. Before then, Speakers sometimes faced criticism, notably from members of the minority party, for addressing the floor. In 1877, for example, Randall was cautioned against talking on the floor by Ohio Republican Charles Foster;[5] and in an 1893 speech, then-Congressman Thomas Reed (R-ME) questioned whether Speaker Crisp improperly made a floor speech. On other occasions, minority leaders explicitly allowed for or approved such statements,[6] or Speakers—anticipating disapproval—apologized to the House for talking on the floor. Speakers since Rayburn, by contrast, have virtually never been criticized for doing so.

Taken together, these developments suggest that the changing use of floor advocacy since the 1940s represents a basic decline in the importance of one

Table 2.1 Speaker Floor Statements: Summary Statistics

Speaker	Number of Statements	Mean per Congress	Percent Dialogue or Debate	Percent Framed as Personal
Randall (1876–80)	19	9.5[a]	47.3%	0.0%
Cannon (1903–11)	10	2.5	0.0%	50.0%
Clark (1911–19)	31	7.75	25.8%	3.2%
Bankhead (1936–40)	12	6	33.3%	0.0%
Rayburn (1940–46, 1949–52, 1955–61)	79	9.3[b,c]	5.1%	0.0%
McCormack (1962–70)	123	27.3[c]	14.6%	0.0%
Albert (1971–76)	61	20.3	4.9%	0.0%
O'Neill (1977–86)	51	10.2	3.9%	2.0%
Foley (1989–94)	24	6.4[d]	4.0%	2.5%
Gingrich (1995–98)	42	21.0	2.4%	0.0%
Hastert (1999–2006)	53	13.3	0.0%	0.0%

[a]Not counting the 44th Congress (during which Randall served only three months).
[b]Not counting the 76th Congress (during which Rayburn served only three months).
[c]Counting the 87th Congress as one-half. (Rayburn died midway through the 87th Congress, and McCormack became Speaker at the beginning of the second session.)
[d]Counting the 101st Congress as three-fourths. (Foley was sworn in June 1989.)

particular leadership duty: to represent the House as a whole. Not all Speakers since 1940 have followed this pattern exactly. McCormack's many appearances on the floor, often to enter into conversational dialogue or debate with other legislators (see figure 2.1), suggests that he may have viewed floor statements more as an outgrowth of his institutional position as an individual representative and thus separate from his duties and roles as Speaker. McCormack aside, however, Speakers since 1940 represented an important break from the past: no longer as worried about violating their role as a House-wide officer of the whole House, they regularly use floor advocacy as a congressional leader, pressing for desired legislative results.

THE SIGNIFICANCE OF FLOOR ADVOCACY

Floor advocacy by the Speaker is not always used to influence outcomes, but there are several reasons why it can serve as an effective tool of legislative leadership.[7] First, the stature and authority of the Speaker conveys additional gravitas to his public floor statements. The Speaker is not equal to any representative when he goes to the floor: his office is mandated by the Constitution, third in line to the presidency, and the top elected position of the majority party in the House. The practical and symbolic consequences of this give particular value to what he says publicly. For example, an aide to Speaker Tom Foley (D-WA) noted in an interview that a Speaker's speech can be influential because legislators assume that the Speaker possesses more information than they do and is more familiar with the arguments for and against a measure (interview with the author, March 2003).

Second, because Speakers address the floor more selectively than do other legislators, their statements have greater significance for lawmakers. In 1975, for example, then-Representative Tom Foley followed a floor speech by Speaker Carl Albert with a reminder to legislators that "it is a rare privilege that the House has to hear directly from the Speaker on a bill" (*Congressional Record,* 2 October 1975, 31440).[8] An opponent of Speaker O'Neill once remarked during floor deliberation that O'Neill's appearance "indicates the degree of importance placed by the majority on passing this legislation, because not often are we accorded this honor" (*Congressional Record,* 15 November 1979, 32749). Speaker Jim Wright (D-TX) stated in an interview that, as Speaker, "you have to pick and choose very carefully" when to address the floor because "if you went down there on every issue, it soon would wear out its appeal" (interview with the author, July 2003). A former aide to Speaker Foley remarked that Foley similarly felt "very strongly" that floor advocacy should be rarely used (interview with the author, August 2003). Greater demands on the Speaker's time, and a desire to minimize the risk of publicly losing a floor vote, probably also contribute to the paucity of Speaker floor statements.[9]

This selectivity is illustrated in figure 2.2, which compares the number of Speaker floor advocacy statements in every fifth Congress since 1907–8 (the 60th Congress) with the median number of speeches delivered by a random sample of legislators from the same Congress (as cited in the *Congressional Record* index). The figure shows that Speakers have almost always addressed the House less often than the average Representative (with McCormack being a notable exception). Using bootstrapping to estimate confidence intervals for the median number of legislator floor statements reveals that for all but the 65th and 85th Congresses, the differences in the frequency of floor statements between the Speaker and the random sample of other legislators are statistically significant at the $p < .05$ level.[10]

Third, a Speaker's rhetoric may itself be persuasive, at least on occasion. One should not exaggerate the influence of floor advocacy as a means of persuasion;

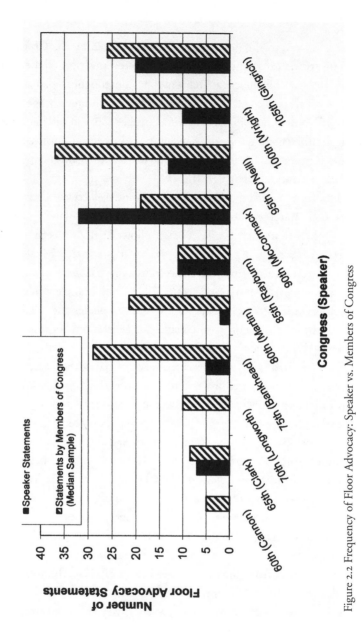

Figure 2.2 Frequency of Floor Advocacy: Speaker vs. Members of Congress

in an interview with the author, a former Democratic whip described Speaker floor statements as primarily "icing on the cake" compared with other means of influencing legislators' vote choice (interview with the author, December 2002). Nonetheless, as illustrated by the O'Neill speech on Lebanon discussed at the start of this chapter, floor advocacy can change minds. One past Foley staffer claimed that Foley was more likely to address the floor if "people felt that the vote was close or the people with us were a little shaky" (interview with the author, August 2003). Another Foley aide noted that persuasion was a legitimate reason for the Speaker to use floor advocacy, especially because, for difficult or controversial measures, some members of Congress will wait until the last minute to cast a vote (interview with the author, March 2003). An erstwhile House Democratic Party leader observed that although leaders have many means of influencing voting, "I don't want to underestimate the power of persuasion" (interview with the author, July 2003). And former Speaker Jim Wright opined in an interview that he may have used floor advocacy at least sometimes to win additional last-minute floor votes (interview with the author, July 2003).

A final reason why floor advocacy may be influential, as I discuss further below (and in subsequent chapters), is that Speakers have used it in conjunction with other kinds of leadership tactics, even when their party was divided on a particular issue. In fact, Speakers may find it necessary to talk on the floor irrespective of their ability to secure commitments in advance of a vote, particularly for contentious or divisive matters. Because the Speaker has always had some influence over the distribution of scarce benefits desired by fellow legislators, floor advocacy may even signal that obtaining such benefits in the future will be contingent upon supporting the Speaker's position. In a case from 1943, Rayburn indirectly acknowledged this function of legislative advocacy. Prefacing his floor remarks in support of a resolution to create a committee on aviation, he assured his colleagues that "I appear [on the floor] for nobody but myself and have no reason except reasons that I have within me. *This is not a leadership fight*" (*Congressional Record*, 2 March 1943, 1486, emphasis added). Even if Speakers do not, in their spoken words, explicitly connect a particular result with future benefits, they may commit other passive or active leadership activities in conjunction with floor statements that do draw such a connection.[11]

Vote margin data suggest that floor advocacy may be a useful and consequential means of influence. If Speakers use floor speeches to affect final vote totals, one should observe such activity when the passage of a measure is less certain. Although an expected vote outcome is difficult to measure, it can be

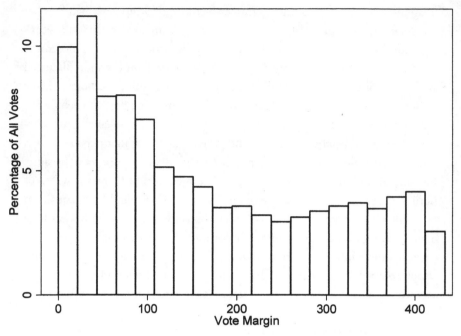

Figure 2.3 Vote Margins, All Roll Call Votes, 1971–2006
Sources: Rohde 2005 (for votes from 1971 to 2004), Keith Poole (http://voteview.com/) and author's estimates (for votes from 2005 to 2006).
Note: Data in this figure, and in figures 2.3, 2.4, 2.5, and 2.6, include only "majoritarian" votes, or those in which a simple majority is required for passage. Supermajority floor votes, as well as unrecorded votes (such as voice votes), are excluded.

approximated by looking at the final vote margin: if it is narrow, the probability that the result was uncertain and required leadership efforts is greater than if it is one-sided.[12] The distribution of vote margins for all roll call votes from 1971 (Carl Albert's first year as Speaker), when votes in the Committee on the Whole became recorded, through 2006 (the end of Dennis Hastert's Speakership) is shown in figure 2.3.[13] These data (which exclude supermajority votes, such as to override presidential vetoes) confirm both common wisdom and the findings of other scholars that such votes in the House tend to be relatively close, but with a significant proportion being one-sided (for example, Collie 1988, Groseclose and Snyder 1996). Contrast these numbers with those recorded in figure 2.4, which displays the distribution of margins for Speaker-advocated floor votes only (and also excludes supermajoritarian votes). Votes on which Speakers address the floor are far more likely to be close than lopsided. It should

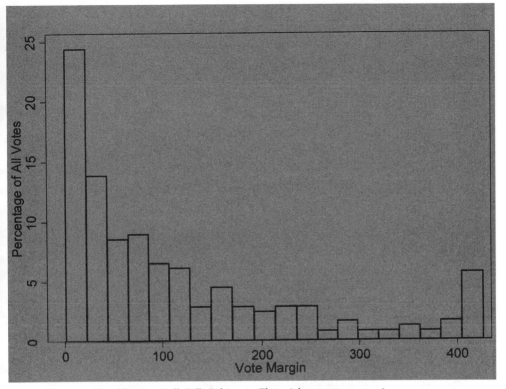

Figure 2.4 Vote Margins, Roll Calls Subject to Floor Advocacy, 1971–2006

be noted that before 1971, vote margins following floor advocacy were often not as narrow; however, this was likely because most of the votes were un- recorded and thus involved a different political dynamic.[14]

One may argue that despite these advantages of floor advocacy and its greater use for close than for lopsided votes, it is far less effective than other powers, like control of the agenda. Thus floor speeches signify meaningless position taking, serve as an outlet for a leader who otherwise suffers from major limita- tions in institutional power, or indicate the presence of internal party divisions that make it risky to rely on more assertive leadership methods (Cooper and Brady 1981). To be sure, the intent of floor advocacy may not always be to shape voting behavior: John McCormack, while verbose, was not known as an insti- tutionally powerful or legislatively active Speaker, and a number of his state- ments may have been delivered to express personal views without trying to in- fluence floor votes. But other Speakers with both more formal authority and a strong desire to shape legislative outcomes, such as Newt Gingrich, also made extensive use of floor advocacy. Furthermore, while Speakers may be more likely

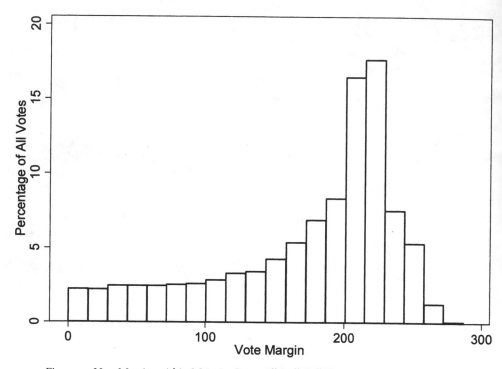

Figure 2.5 Vote Margins within Majority Party, All Roll Call Votes, 1971–2006

to talk on the floor when a vote is close, floor speeches do not happen only when the Speaker's party is clearly divided. The degree of unity in the House majority party on majoritarian (but not supermajoritarian) floor votes is shown in figures 2.5 and 2.6, which compare all such votes with those subject to the Speaker's floor advocacy. Both figures follow a similar distribution, with most of the Speaker's party voting one way in a plurality of roll call votes, regardless of whether the Speaker delivered a statement on the floor.

Furthermore, the testimony and behavior of other legislators suggest that Speaker floor statements can be consequential. House historian George Galloway observed that when the Speaker addresses the floor, "the House fills up, and everyone pays close attention" (Galloway 1976, 132). If a Speaker does so, remarked one leadership aide who served during O'Neill's tenure, "that's always a powerful signal" to legislators and others (interview with the author, June 2003). The same floor critic of Speaker O'Neill quoted earlier also remarked, "I can understand the need for the Speaker's speech, because this bill is [in] an awful lot of trouble" (*Congressional Record,* 15 November 1979, 32749). A one-time aide to Speaker Jim Wright observed that when Wright went to

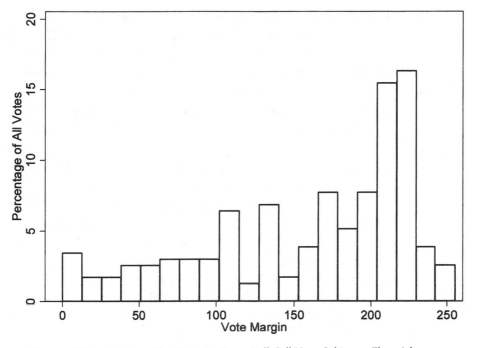

Figure 2.6 Vote Margins within Majority Party, Roll Call Votes Subject to Floor Advocacy, 1971–2006

the floor, "you knew it was [an] important" vote, and when the Speaker and Republican leader Bob Michel (IL) both closed debate, "it was high drama" (interview with the author, May 2003). A former congressional Democrat who served under several Speakers noted that whenever he would see the Speaker address the House, "you say [to yourself], 'this is something special, and I'd better pay attention'" (interview with the author, February 2003).

EXPLAINING WHY FLOOR ADVOCACY HAPPENS

Does the theory of goal-driven leadership explain why Speakers use floor advocacy? Answering this question poses some tricky methodological challenges. Ideally, one would measure each Speaker's expressed position on every legislative proposal subject to a floor vote and compare those positions with the prior preferences of other legislators, the president, the Speaker, and the Speaker's constituents. But measuring such prior preferences is difficult at best, and even if it were possible, doing so for all relevant votes since 1941 would be a daunting task. Instead, I use three techniques to estimate what incentives drove Speakers to talk on the House floor. First, I examine what kinds of legislative issues Speakers tend to discuss; second, I compare Speakers' actual stated positions on specific votes with approximate measures of the preferences of other actors and institutions, including the congressional party, the president, and Speakers and their congressional districts; and third, I examine those cases in which the Speaker's position was rejected by a majority of the House majority party.

Floor statements by issue. The content of a legislative proposal alone does not tell us the source or degree of support for that proposal. But some issues are more closely associated with certain institutions and actors and thus indirectly with the achievement of particular Speakers' goals. If Speakers address the floor disproportionately on behalf of issues connected with the White House, the Speaker's district, the House as a whole, or the Speaker personally, it suggests —even if those same issues are also supported by the majority party—that Speakers are using floor advocacy to satisfy an objective other than (if not in addition to) reselection as party leader.

I first coded all 418 Speaker floor statements from 1941 through 2000 into issue categories, using the nineteen-category coding scheme of the Policy Agendas Project (Baumgartner and Jones 2007). (Just the first two years of the Hastert speakership are included because, as of this writing, the Policy Agendas Project has coded only votes cast through 2000.) Each statement was coded based on the primary issue or topic of the measure, motion, or amendment subject to floor debate.[15] The results of this coding appear in table 2.2, which also notes whether an issue is associated with a Speaker goal other than reselection to their leadership position. Speaking on behalf of "executive-centered" issues, such as foreign affairs, defense, or trade, may stem from a desire to assist the institutional presidency,[16] whereas discussing government operations matters (which includes the internal operation of the House and congressional power and authority) may occur because the Speaker seeks to satisfy the preferences or concerns of the whole House. The goal of enacting preferred public policy is likely to explain advocacy on bills reflecting strong Speaker preferences, and the objective of reselection to the House may explain floor comments endorsing matters of great interest to the Speaker's district.[17] To be sure, a Speaker talking on these issues could be doing so to achieve other objectives as well, for example, if the particular legislation at hand was also of great concern to the House majority party. But if these issues are predominant, it at least sug-

Table 2.2 Speaker Floor Advocacy by Issue, 1941–2000

Issue Code	Frequency	Speakers for Whom Issue Is Strongly Salient (Personally or to District)
Macroeconomics	54	—
Civil rights, liberties	17	—
Health	10	Hastert
Agriculture	21	Rayburn, Albert, Foley
Labor, employment, immigration	20	—
Education	16	McCormack
Environment	3	—
Energy	13	Rayburn
Transportation	8	—
Law, crime, family issues	7	—
Social welfare	11	—
Housing, community development	10	—
Banking, finance, domestic commerce	5	—
Defense[a]	47	—
Space, science/tech, communications	5	—
Foreign trade[a]	16	—
International affairs[a]	55	McCormack, O'Neill, Wright
Government operations[b]	91	—
Public lands, water management	9	—
TOTAL (N)	418	

[a]Potential institutional presidency issue.
[b]Potential House-wide issue.

gests that Speakers might be using floor statements for more than advocacy of their party's policy or electoral objectives.

The data hint that goal-driven leadership may motivate Speaker floor advocacy. For example, Speakers often addressed the floor to discuss subject matters for which presidents have exercised considerable influence, including international affairs (which constituted 55 Speaker floor statements, or 13.2 percent of the total) and national defense (47 statements, or 11.2 percent). In addition, the largest proportion of Speaker statements (91, or 21.8 percent) were associated with government operations issues, which included (though were not limited to) the operations and functions of the legislative branch. McCormack's many floor statements might unfairly skew the results, but excluding them yields similar percentages: 12.3 percent on international affairs (36 statements),

10.9 percent on defense (32 statements), and 23.9 percent on government operations (70 statements).

This is suggestive, but it does not tell us whether certain issues show disproportionate attention from the Speaker compared to Congress's entire legislative agenda. I thus used the Policy Agendas Project data to compare the percentage of all House votes cast on each issue with the percentage of House votes cast on each issue that were also subject to Speaker advocacy.[18] Such a comparative analysis has some important limitations. Because floor advocacy is uncommon for Speakers, the variance for each set of floor statements per Congress is high and tests for statistical significance are less likely to infer causal relationships. Also, because votes in the Committee of the Whole were not recorded until 1971, many instances of Speaker floor advocacy before that year correspond to noncoded roll call votes. I therefore restricted the analysis to Speakers serving from 1971 to 2000 (Albert, O'Neill, Wright, Foley, Gingrich, and Hastert's first two years as Speaker).[19]

For each of the nineteen issue categories, the relative proportion of votes subject to Speaker Albert's floor advocacy, and whether its difference from the proportion of all votes cast on that issue is statistically significant, is listed in Table 2.3. As the table shows, Albert rarely addressed significantly greater or fewer roll call votes by issue than was represented by the full voting agenda. Nonetheless, the table indicates that issues both related and unrelated to Albert's congressional party may have motivated his use of floor advocacy. First, Albert avoided talking on defense policy–related votes over his full six-year term (1971–77). Such votes were usually associated with the Vietnam War, and (as I discuss in chapter 4) his abstention from discussing the war on the floor probably reflected concern for maintaining the unity of his congressional party, particularly given his personal views in favor of the conflict. Also, though the difference from the proportion of all votes is not statistically significant, Albert spoke a great deal on agriculture, an issue of much importance to his district. Of the combined three Congresses in which he served as Speaker, 10.5 percent of roll calls subject to Albert's floor advocacy were on the topic (versus just 2.8 percent of all floor votes). Similarly, perhaps to fulfill his role as House-wide officer, Albert addressed the floor quite often in the 93rd Congress (1973–75) on governmental operations issues (35.3 percent versus 22.6 percent overall), though this included matters both internal to the House (House procedure, construction of congressional facilities) and the investigation of presidential malfeasance (Watergate). Finally, the data show that Albert spoke disproportionately on civil rights–related votes,

Table 2.3 Roll Call Votes Subject to Speaker Albert's Floor Advocacy, Percent by Issue

Issue Code	Congress			
	92nd	93rd	94th	92nd–94th
Macroeconomics	9.1%	0.0%	16.7%	8.8%
Civil rights, liberties	31.8%*	0.0%	5.6%	14.0%*
Health	0.0%	5.9%	0.0%	1.8%
Agriculture	9.1%	5.9%	16.7%	10.5%
Labor, employment, immigration	4.5%	11.8%	5.6%	7.0%
Education	4.5%	0.0%	5.6%	3.5%
Environment	0.0%	0.0%	0.0%	0.0%
Energy	0.0%	11.8%	0.0%	3.5%
Transportation	4.5%	0.0%	11.1%	5.3%
Law, crime, family issues	0.0%	5.9%	0.0%	1.8%
Social welfare	9.1%	0.0%	0.0%	3.5%
Housing, community development	4.5%	5.9%	5.6%	5.3%
Banking, finance, domestic commerce	0.0%	0.0%	0.0%	0.0%
Defense	0.0%	5.9%	0.0%	1.8%*
Space, science/tech, communications	0.0%	0.0%	5.6%	1.8%
Foreign trade	4.5%	0.0%	0.0%	1.8%
International affairs	4.5%	11.8%	5.6%	7.0%
Government operations	13.6%	35.3%	11.1%	19.3%
Public lands, water management	0.0%	0.0%	11.1%	3.5%
TOTAL (*N*)	22	17	18	57

*Difference is significant at .05 level. Two-tailed t-test (using adjusted "t" scores for smaller *N*s).

both in the 92nd Congress and throughout his tenure. These were generally on matters salient to his party in Congress. They included an October 1971 speech on the Equal Rights Amendment to the Constitution, which addressed three roll calls on the topic: a vote to pass the amendment and two votes on proposed changes to the amendment. (If one excludes the latter two votes in the calculation of percentages, the difference is no longer statistically significant for all three Congresses but remains so for the 92nd Congress at the p < .10 level).[20]

Table 2.4 Roll Call Votes Subject to Speaker O'Neill's Floor Advocacy,
Percent by Issue

	Congress				
Issue Code	95th	96th	97th	98th	95th–99th
Macroeconomics	9.5%	7.7%	41.7%*	20.0%	20.0%*
Civil rights, liberties	0.0%	0.0%	8.3%	10.0%	3.3%
Health	0.0%	7.7%	0.0%	0.0%	1.7%
Agriculture	0.0%	0.0%	0.0%	0.0%	0.0%
Labor, employment, immigration	38.1%*	0.0%	8.3%	0.0%	15.0%*
Education	0.0%	15.4%	0.0%	0.0%	3.3%
Environment	0.0%	0.0%	0.0%	0.0%	0.0%
Energy	4.8%	7.7%	0.0%	0.0%	3.3%
Transportation	0.0%	0.0%	0.0%	0.0%	0.0%
Law, crime, family issues	0.0%	0.0%	0.0%	0.0%	0.0%
Social welfare	4.8%	0.0%	0.0%	20.0%	5.0%
Housing, community development	0.0%	0.0%	0.0%	0.0%	0.0%
Banking, finance, domestic commerce	9.5%	7.7%	0.0%	0.0%	5.0%
Defense	14.3%	0.0%	0.0%	20.0%	10.0%
Space, science/tech, communications	0.0%	0.0%	0.0%	0.0%	0.0%
Foreign trade	0.0%	0.0%	0.0%	0.0%	0.0%
International Affairs	0.0%	38.5%^	16.7%	20.0%	16.7%
Government operations	14.3%	15.4%	25.0%	10.0%	15.0%
Public lands, water management	4.8%	0.0%	0.0%	0.0%	1.7%*
TOTAL (N)	21	13	12	10	60

Note: 99th Congress not shown (no statistically significant differences).
*Difference is significant at .05 level; ^ significant at the 0.1 level. Two-tailed t-test.

Table 2.4 lists the results for Speaker O'Neill for all but the 99th Congress
(in which the Speaker made only four floor statements advocating a policy outcome that resulted in a roll call vote).[21] Macroeconomic issues attracted
O'Neill's disproportionate attention in both the 97th Congress and in the aggregate. This was due in part to the "must-pass" nature of bills in this category,
such as continuing appropriations needed to keep the federal government func-
tioning, but it also reflected the important partisan battles that emerged after

Table 2.5 Roll Call Votes Subject to Speakers Wright's and Foley's Floor
Advocacy, Percent by Issue

	Congress			
Issue Code	100th	102nd	103rd	102nd–103rd
Macroeconomics	8.3%	28.6%	35.3%*	33.3%*
Civil rights, liberties	0.0%	0.0%	0.0%	0.0%
Health	0.0%	0.0%	0.0%	0.0%
Agriculture	0.0%	0.0%	0.0%	0.0%
Labor, employment, immigration	0.0%	14.3%	0.0%	4.2%
Education	8.3%	0.0%	0.0%	0.0%
Environment	0.0%	0.0%	0.0%	0.0%
Energy	0.0%	0.0%	0.0%	0.0%
Transportation	0.0%	0.0%	0.0%	0.0%
Law, crime, family issues	0.0%	0.0%	5.9%	4.2%
Social welfare	0.0%	0.0%	0.0%	0.0%
Housing, community development	0.0%	0.0%	0.0%	0.0%
Banking, finance, domestic commerce	16.7%	0.0%	0.0%	0.0%
Defense	16.7%	14.3%	5.9%	8.3%
Space, science/tech, communications	0.0%	0.0%	0.0%	0.0%
Foreign trade	25.0%^	0.0%	11.8%	8.3%
International affairs	16.7%	0.0%	5.9%	4.2%
Government operations	8.3%^	42.9%	35.3%	37.5%
Public lands, water management	0.0%	0.0%	0.0%	0.0%
TOTAL (*N*)	12	7	17	24

*Difference is significant at .05 level; ^ significant at the 0.1 level. Two-tailed t-test.

the 1980 elections over federal spending and taxation policy. Besides budget
measures, O'Neill addressed international affairs votes disproportionately in
the 96th Congress, either to defend same-party presidential policy concerns
(such as the Panama Canal) or to support both his personal policy preferences
and his congressional party's policy objectives (for example, funding to
Nicaragua; see chapter 4). It should be noted, however, that one of his statements on Nicaraguan aid addressed two votes; the difference is no longer statistically significant if one of the votes is excluded from the analysis. Further-

more, the large proportion of labor, employment, and immigration votes were a series of amendments to a minimum wage bill, which O'Neill argued against in a single September 1977 floor speech; when excluding these amendments, the difference in percentages for the issue is no longer statistically significant. Nonetheless, O'Neill's floor statements suggest that he used floor advocacy not only to endorse his party's policy preferences but also to carry out his own policy objectives or those of an incumbent same-party president.

The patterns for Speakers Wright and Foley are shown in table 2.5, with the 101st Congress (1989–90) excluded (during which Wright spoke on the floor only twice before resigning from the Speakership, and Foley spoke on policy just four times). Despite Wright's few floor statements as Speaker in the 100th Congress (1987–88), he spoke significantly more often on foreign trade (with 25 percent of all votes subject to Wright's floor advocacy being cast on trade measures, versus just 2.4 percent of all floor votes) and less so on government operations (8.3 percent versus 24.5 percent). The former votes were on a major trade bill, an important measure for House Democrats for which Wright had exercised important committee-related leadership as well (see chapter 5). Foley spoke disproportionately on macroeconomic issues in the 103rd Congress and overall; these covered a variety of budget bills and probably reflected the importance of budget politics for House Democrats during the period.[22] Foley also addressed the House on a number of government operations bills in the 102nd and 103rd Congresses, primarily related to campaign finance reform or internal ethics investigations (the check-bouncing scandal in the 102nd Congress). This suggests that Speaker Foley was acting on behalf of House-wide concerns in these instances, though the differences from the entire roll call agenda are not statistically significant.

Finally, table 2.6 shows the percentage of roll call votes subject to Gingrich's floor statements broken down by issue.[23] In the 104th Congress, Gingrich spoke disproportionately on health care and government operations bills, but because many of these speeches addressed more than one vote (for example, against a motion to recommit and in favor of bill passage), his percentages in these categories are slightly inflated, and they are no longer statistically significant if only final passage votes are included. His attention to macroeconomic issues and government operations matters in the 105th Congress, however, are both statistically greater and more robust. The former points to the importance of budget and tax issues for House Republicans, and the latter involved disparate bills less associated with the Speaker's role as House-wide officer (such as funding for the District of Columbia). Thus for Gingrich especially, floor advocacy seems to have been a means of defending major party policy goals.

Table 2.6 Roll Call Votes Subject to Speaker Gingrich's Floor Advocacy, Percent by Issue

	Congress		
Issue Code	104th	105th	104th–105th
Macroeconomics	7.1%	28.0%*	17.0%^
Civil rights, liberties	0.0%	4.0%	1.9%
Health	14.3%^	4.0%	9.4%^
Agriculture	0.0%	0.0%	0.0%
Labor, employment, immigration	10.7%	0.0%	5.7%
Education	0.0%	12.0%	5.7%
Environment	7.1%	0.0%	3.8%
Energy	0.0%	0.0%	0.0%
Transportation	0.0%	0.0%	0.0%
Law, crime, family issues	7.1%	0.0%	3.8%
Social welfare	0.0%	8.0%	3.8%
Housing, community development	0.0%	0.0%	0.0%
Banking, finance, domestic commerce	0.0%	0.0%	0.0%
Defense	3.6%	8.0%	5.7%
Space, science/tech, communications	0.0%	0.0%	0.0%
Foreign trade	0.0%	0.0%	0.0%
International affairs	7.1%	20.0%	13.2%
Government operations	42.9%^	12.0%*	28.3%
Public lands, water management	0.0%	4.0%	1.9%*
TOTAL (*N*)	28	25	53

*Difference is significant at .05 level; ^ significant at the 0.1 level. Two-tailed t-test.

Comparison of preferences. Issues are, at best, an imperfect way to identify incentives for exercising leadership, particularly without knowing the actual position a Speaker takes on a bill or amendment. To address this problem, I also coded whether, in each floor speech, the Speaker expressed support for or opposition to the measure at hand. I also coded the incumbent president's party affiliation, whether the president had formally requested a particular vote outcome on that measure, and the likely preferences of the majority party.[24] Presidential requests were obtained from a data set compiled by Michael Malbin, which contains all written presidential legislative requests through 1988 and the floor votes associated with them (Swift et al. 2000).[25] Congressional party preferences were estimated with roll call votes: if a majority of the Speaker's party supported the result by more than a narrow margin (that is, 10 percent or more of the total votes cast as the margin between party supporters and opponents), the majority party was coded as being in favor of the endorsed outcome. Note that this measure is imprecise. For example, a roll call vote can reflect a variety of pressures, including the Speaker's own vote-building efforts. The congressional majority party's interests may also include things not easily measurable by a recorded vote, such as party reputation or other electoral concerns; and, as I discuss in subsequent chapters, a party that votes in favor of a measure may not necessarily have a strong preference for the particular result. Also, a party's preferences could not be estimated by voting behavior if a Speaker's statement was made on behalf of votes decided by division, teller, voice vote, or unanimous consent, which conceal the vote choice of individual legislators. As a result, 197 floor statements, or slightly less than half of the 400 delivered between 1941 and 1998, were included in the analysis.

Table 2.7 lists key observable conditions generally associated with each of the three goals of the Speaker, as well as two possible combinations of goals and three other hypothetical Speaker objectives. The first goal can manifest itself in a couple of ways. If the Speaker is responding to the wishes of his party in Congress by using floor advocacy, the congressional majority party should prefer the outcome endorsed by the Speaker, and the president (irrespective of party) should either oppose or be agnostic about it. If the Speaker is solely concerned about his reelection to Congress, then the issue at hand should not be endorsed by the president or the party in Congress but should be of special significance to the Speaker's congressional district. The second goal, to enact personally preferred policy, best explains floor advocacy if the Speaker asks for an outcome that neither the president nor the majority party in the House support or request, but which is related to the Speaker's personal policy objectives. The third goal, to fulfill leadership duties or roles, could be salient under several conditions. If the Speaker is acting to defend the presidential party, then a same-party president, but not the congressional majority party, should support the result, and the policy issue should be unrelated to the president's institutional authority (that is, not a defense, foreign affairs, or trade issue).[26] If the Speaker is acting out of deference to the institutional presidency, the particular legislative result should be requested only by the president (of either party) and be related to issues traditionally associated with the president's institutional authority, including defense and foreign affairs.[27] Finally, if the Speaker seeks to defend the House as a whole through floor advocacy, then neither the president nor the majority party in the House should support or request the particular outcome, and the issue should be a House-wide matter.

It may also be that the Speaker addresses the floor to satisfy aspects of both the reelection and role-fulfillment goals. For example, the concerns of the presidential party and the party in Congress could be jointly met by an act of floor advocacy, in which case the majority party and the same-party president should both support the final result. Or if the preferences of the congressional party and the institutional presidency are important, then the concerns of both should be related to the Speaker's floor statement.

There are three other combinations of the four conditions in table 2.7 that, if present, are not readily explained by the theory of goal salience. First, the Speaker may talk only on behalf of an opposite party president's policy objectives, but those objectives are unrelated to the institutional presidency; this is labeled "broad deference to opposite party president." Second, both the congressional party and an opposite-party president may support a legislative outcome unrelated to the institutional presidency; this is labeled "cooperative divided government." Finally, it may be that the Speaker alone advocates a result associated with neither personal policy concerns nor House-wide matters; this is labeled in table 2.7 as an "unknown/unclear" objective.[28]

The final column of table 2.7 contains the number and percentage of floor advocacy statements that fell within each category based on the method of measurement described above. In the majority of cases of floor advocacy, the Speaker was supported by a majority of his own party, and the president opposed or had no position on the outcome. Though not all of these may be cases of the reelection goal motivating (or solely motivating) floor advocacy,[29] it supports the chief contention of party-based leadership theories that the Speaker acts to help his party in the House. Many other cases of floor advocacy, however, cannot be explained by congressional party preferences alone. Another 13.7 percent of cases involved Speaker positions that were endorsed by both the House majority party and a same-party president on issues other than defense, foreign affairs, or trade, suggesting that the Speaker in these instances used floor statements to address the concerns of both the presidential party and the congressional party. Furthermore, although no cases involved the concerns of just the institutional presidency, ten were related to both the institutional presidency and the majority party in Congress. Finally, another ten instances were associated with the Speaker's district or with House matters, and

Table 2.7 Goals Motivating the Speaker's Floor Advocacy on Recorded Votes, 1941–1988

Goal and Associated Person, Institution, or Entity	Condition				Number of Floor Statements (%)
	Majority Party Supports Endorsed Outcome	President Requests Endorsed Outcome	Unified Government	Type of Issue	
Secure reelection					
Party in Congress	✓	No	—	Any	132 (67.0%)
District	No	No	—	Salient to Speaker's district	8 (4.1%)
Enact policy					
Speaker (personal policy preferences)	No	No	—	Salient to Speaker's personal policy preferences	0 (0%)
Fulfill leadership role					
Presidential party	No	✓	✓	Not defense/trade/foreign affairs	1 (0.5%)
Institutional presidency	No	✓	—	Defense/trade/foreign affairs	0 (0.0%)
Whole House	No	No	—	House-wide	2 (1.0%)

Both reelection and role-fulfillment goals

Party in Congress and presidential party	✓	✓	✓	Not defense/trade/foreign affairs	27 (13.7%)
Party in Congress and institutional presidency	✓	✓	—	Defense/trade/foreign affairs	10 (5.1%)
Other possible objectives					
Broad deference to opposite party president	No	✓	No	Not defense/trade/foreign affairs	2 (1.0%)
Cooperative divided government	✓	✓	No	Not defense/trade/foreign affairs	4 (2.0%)
Unknown/unclear	No	No	—	Not House-wide, nor salient to Speaker's personal policy preferences or to Speaker's district	11 (5.6%)

presidential party concerns (by themselves) explained one other case of floor advocacy: a July 1967 labor bill requested by President Lyndon Johnson but passed by only a slim voting majority of House Democrats.[30]

What about the remaining seventeen cases that appear to be unexplained by the theory of goal-driven leadership? A closer examination of these examples of floor advocacy reveals that the theory explains a majority of them. One instance of "broad deference to opposite party president" represented a rare moment when the Speaker supported the position of an opposite-party president against that of his own congressional party, and not on an institutional presidency issue. In August 1982, President Reagan reluctantly agreed to support a tax measure in the face of mounting budget deficits, and O'Neill spoke on its behalf despite the fact that many Democrats, looking to the impending midterm election, were wary of voting for any tax increase (and only a bare majority did so: 122, versus 118 against). O'Neill also supported the bill in the belief that, in exchange, Reagan would not veto a supplemental spending bill passed earlier by the House (Evans and Novak 1982). This case shows that Speakers may talk on behalf of opposite-party presidents on issues other than defense, foreign policy, and trade, though it may require some compromise and logrolling by the White House (which I discuss further in chapter 7). But the other case of such deference—a surtax bill from 1969—can be explained by the theory of goal-driven leadership. Although a Republican president, Richard Nixon, had initiated the tax package, in his floor statement McCormack remarked that it had been originally proposed by a Democratic president, Lyndon Johnson, and shepherded through the House by a Democratic committee chairman (*Congressional Record,* 30 June 1969, 17862). McCormack may also have been responding to a possible threat to an important constitutional function of the House as a whole. Failure to enact the surtax would have increased the chances that the Senate would pass the tax bill first, ignoring the House's prerogative to initiate all tax measures and thus weakening its independence.[31]

The four "cooperative divided government" votes suggest that agreement between a congressional majority party and opposite-party president is possible on some nonexecutive issues and can occasionally explain Speaker floor statements, a possibility I examine in more detail in chapter 7. In March 1969, the House approved an increase in the federal debt ceiling, endorsed (through not originally desired) by President Nixon, with support from a majority of both Democrats and Republicans (*Congressional Quarterly Almanac* 1969, 171–72).[32] In August 1973, Albert went to the floor to deliver a statement by President Nixon on behalf of a bill constructing an Alaska pipeline, which later passed 356–60. For the other two votes, in December 1985 and September 1986, Speaker O'Neill urged passage of a major tax reform bill that was endorsed by both President Reagan and Ways and Means Chairman Dan Rostenkowski (D-IL); in both speeches, O'Neill emphasized the bipartisan nature of the legislation (Birnbaum and Murray 1987, 165–74).

Finally, a careful analysis of the speeches in the "unknown/unclear" category reveals that most of them can be explained by one or more of the Speaker's three goals. Deference to the institutional presidency explains six of the eleven instances; in these cases, the opposite-party president took a position on a foreign affairs or national security matter, but because he did not do so in writing, they were excluded from the Malbin database (Swift et al. 2000).[33] These included a May 1971 vote to restore funding for a supersonic transport vehicle, a 1974 proposal to limit the number of troops deployed overseas, two attempts by Speaker Albert in 1974 to prevent the House from voting to ban foreign aid to Turkey, a September 1982 effort to end economic sanctions imposed by President Reagan against the Soviet Union, and the example that opened this chapter: the September 1983 resolution supporting U.S. Marines in Lebanon (*Congressional Quarterly Almanac* 1971, 146; *Congressional Quarterly Almanac* 1974, 54-H; *Congressional Record*, 29 September 1982, H7929).[34] A seventh case, from 1978, involved a House-wide expectation to protect legislators' prerogatives on spending: Speaker O'Neill was attempting to override President Carter's veto of a public works bill, which would have distributed funds for local projects in many congressional districts. An eighth case, Jim Wright's support for increasing the borrowing authority of the Federal Savings and Loan Insurance Corporation to bail out savings and loan institutions, was associated, at least partly, with the preferences of Wright's district. Wright had originally opposed such an increase, but he reversed himself in order to stem damaging media criticism of his position and after getting assurances that regulators would be restrained from arbitrarily closing failing savings and loan banks—a number of which were located in Texas. House Democrats remained worried by the possibility of premature bank closings, however, and they soundly rejected the increase (Barry 1989, 216–17, 239–40; Yang 1987).[35]

The final three floor statements in this category indicate that Speakers may, on occasion, deliver floor statements out of deference to specific legislators or congressional committees. In August 1969, a major tax reform bill drafted by the Ways and Means Committee was threatened with failure when the rule for floor debate was nearly rejected. In April 1977, Speaker O'Neill stood behind that year's congressional budget resolution, supported by the House Budget Committee, despite the fact that it had been amended on the floor in such a way so as to alienate both Republicans and Democrats. The third case involved an amendment by Congressman Claude Pepper (D-FL) to a Social Security reform bill to substitute an increase in the program's retirement age with a hike in payroll taxes. O'Neill and party liberals opposed raising the retirement age, and O'Neill may have supported Pepper's amendment as a favor to Pepper, a longtime Social Security advocate and the chairman of the Rules Committee. But many Democrats also feared the electoral consequences of voting for a tax increase, and half of the party voted against the amendment (Light 1985).[36] I discuss this particular exception to the theory in chapter 7.

In short, although the desire to assist the majority party is a powerful motivator for the Speaker's use of the floor, the concerns of other individuals, institutions, or entities—sometimes with the endorsement of the party in Congress, sometimes not—matter as well. Although about two-thirds of the 197 cases of floor advocacy examined here can be plausibly explained as a sole consequence of the Speaker's desire to remain Speaker by helping his party, conceptualizing the Speaker as a leader with other goals allows one to explain far more—nearly 97 percent—of his floor statements. Thus despite the limitations of this aggregate analysis, the results provide further support for the theory of goal-driven leadership.

The Speaker versus his party. To give a clearer picture of the dynamics that compel Speakers to advocate for legislation opposed by their own congressional party, I examined all cases of floor advocacy in which the House majority party voted against the Speaker's expressed preferences (see table 2.8).[37] Such events seldom occur, but they have happened at least once to all of the Democratic Speakers who served between 1941 and 2006 (though not to the three Republican Speakers: Joseph Martin, Newt Gingrich, and Dennis Hastert). Many of these votes have been on matters of important national policy: ten of the cases are categorized as "key votes," or recorded votes that, according to the journal *Congressional Quarterly* (*CQ*), are controversial, significant for Congress or the presidency, or concern major national policy. Some of the subsequent floor votes were quite close, and others ended in a wider margin but were nonetheless bitterly fought. In at least three cases (documented in subsequent chapters), floor advocacy was just one of the tools used by the Speaker to influence the outcome, despite the division within his party.[38] Though the Speaker usually won these votes, in all cases he clearly acted without the policy agreement of his own party.[39]

Although it is possible that in these cases the Speaker was using floor advocacy on behalf of his congressional party's electoral interests (such as their collective reputation), a close study reveals that the Speaker was likely using such advocacy to satisfy other leadership goals. Two cases can be explained by a combination of objectives: a 1969 Nixon bill to extend the federal surtax, discussed earlier, and Speaker Foley's support for the North American Free Trade Agreement, which would have helped his district, implemented the president's prerogatives on trade matters, and achieved a major policy objective of the Clinton White House (see chapter 4). In another six cases, the Speaker went against his party's preferences on behalf of the institutional presidency, defending an opposite-party president on a defense, foreign affairs, or trade-related matter. In eight other cases, the Speaker used floor advocacy on behalf of a district or regional concern. The energy-related votes involving Sam Rayburn, the first two of which are discussed in more detail in chapter 3, were on measures to exempt small producers of natural gas from the threat of federal price regulation, an issue of considerable importance to Rayburn's state. Carl Albert's outspokenness on the four agriculture votes can be explained by the salience of that issue to his Oklahoma district and to his local livestock industry in particular. The eighth case, mentioned earlier, involved Speaker Wright's decision to support a banking bill amendment after calculating the impact of doing so on his electoral reputation and on local financial institutions. Finally, Albert twice addressed the floor to fulfill his role to defend matters salient to the House as a whole: once on a proposal to extend the west front of the Capitol, a contentious construction project criticized by many legislators for its high cost and dubious necessity, and once on an amendment to eliminate funding for Eisenhower College, including a library containing the collection of former Speaker Sam Rayburn.

The remaining three cases cannot be readily explained by the theory of goal-driven leadership. One involved deference to an opposite-party president on an issue unrelated to the institutional presidency: Speaker Foley's support for an October 1990 budget resolution, which had resulted from bipartisan negotiations with President George H. W. Bush (*Congressional Quarterly Almanac* 1990, 136–37).[40] The 1983 O'Neill speech on Social Security, discussed above, stemmed from the Speaker deferring to a key committee chairman. Finally, O'Neill's support for a 1977 House budget resolution, also discussed previously, reflected Speaker deference to the output of congressional committees. I discuss these possible counterexamples to the theory further in chapter 7.

Table 2.8 Cases When the Speaker's Public Position Was Rejected by the Majority Party

Speaker	Issue	Cases (Date)	Speaker Position (Majority Party Vote)	Floor Vote	Primary Goal (Relevant Individual/Entity/Institution)	CQ Key Vote?
Rayburn	Energy	Natural gas deregulation (8/49)	Pro (93–97)	183–131	Reelection (district)	Yes
Rayburn	Energy	Natural gas deregulation (3/50)	Pro (97–115)	176–174	Reelection (district)	Yes
Rayburn	Energy	Natural gas deregulation (7/55)	Pro (86–136)	209–203	Reelection (district)	Yes
McCormack	Tax	Surtax bill (6/69)	Pro (56–179)	210–205	Several	Yes
Albert	Transportation	SST funding (5/71)	Pro (106–129)	201–195	Role fulfillment (institutional presidency)	No
Albert	House-wide	Extension of west front (6/72)	Pro (106–111)	181–198[a]	Role fulfillment (whole House)	No
Albert	Agriculture	Economic Policy Act, Gonzalez amendment (8/72)	Pro (91–102)	177–158	Reelection (district)	No
Albert	Agriculture	Food bill, Findley amendment (7/73)	Con (120–104)	246–163[a]	Reelection (district)	No
Albert	Defense	Troop deployment, O'Neill amendment (5/74)	Con (128–96)	163–240	Role fulfillment (institutional presidency)	No
Albert	Federal government	Eisenhower library, Wylie amendment (9/74)	Con (99–86)	166–169	Role fulfillment (whole House)	No

Speaker	Issue area	Bill	Committee position	Floor vote	Explanation	
Albert	Foreign affairs	Foreign aid bill, Rosenthal amendment (9/74)	Con (180–38)	307–90[a]	Role fulfillment (institutional presidency)	Yes
Albert	Foreign affairs	Relations with Turkey (10/74)	Pro (65–142)	171–187[a]	Role fulfillment (institutional presidency)	No
Albert	Agriculture	Beef bill (10/75)	Pro (135–139)	229–189	Reelection (district)	No
Albert	Agriculture	Beef bill, conference report (5/76)	Pro (118–127)	200–170	Reelection (district)	No
O'Neill	Budget	Budget resolution (4/77)	Pro (82–135)	84–320[a]	Other (committee deference)	No
O'Neill	Foreign affairs	Russian sanctions (5/82)	Pro (82–146)	206–203	Role fulfillment (institutional presidency)	Yes
O'Neill	Social Security	Social Security tax amendment (3/83)	Pro (131–131)	132–296[a]	Other (chairman deference)	No
O'Neill	Defense	Troops in Lebanon (9/83)	Pro (130–134)	270–161	Role fulfillment (institutional presidency)	Yes
Wright	Banking	FSLIC, St. Germain amendment (5/87)	Pro (81–150)	153–258[a]	Reelection (district)	Yes
Foley	Budget	Budget resolution (10/90)	Pro (108–149)	179–254[a]	Other (broad deference to opposite party president)	Yes
Foley	Trade	NAFTA (11/93)	Pro (102–156)	234–200	Several	Yes

[a]Speaker's position was also rejected on the floor.

In short, Speakers have used their ability to deliver floor speeches as a means of satisfying a range of goals. Speakers discuss legislative items that reflect electoral, presidential, personal, and chamber-related concerns; speak on matters salient to their party, the White House, and/or the House as a whole; and, when they defy the policy preferences of their party, they do so to achieve goal-related outcomes.

NONPIVOTAL FLOOR VOTING:
ANOTHER LEADERSHIP TOOL?

Just as Speakers have the power to address the floor on behalf of legislative results, yet only occasionally do so, they can also (but traditionally seldom do) cast recorded votes on the House floor. And just as using floor advocacy can forfeit one Speaker goal for another, the same may occur when a Speaker votes on the floor. As a House-wide officer, Speakers should in principle avoid the position taking that follows from floor voting, particularly since they preside over all floor votes (at least in theory).[41] But Speakers are also representatives and thus may want to bring about certain outcomes by casting a vote. Tension between these two objectives has led to several changes in the rules governing Speaker floor voting. When the first Congress convened in 1789, the House determined that the Speaker would participate in balloted votes but would otherwise be prohibited from voting except when pivotal—that is, to break or make a tie.[42] Speaker Henry Clay ignored this prohibition and starting in 1817 cast votes in a nonpivotal fashion; in 1850, the House lifted the earlier restriction on voting, albeit with some debate over its possible effect on the Speaker's impartiality. Thirty years later, House rules were changed to require, rather than permit, the Speaker to vote when making or breaking a tie or establishing quorum, a requirement that remains in the chamber's rules today. Irrespective of these varying rules changes, a strong norm against nonpivotal Speaker floor voting existed for most of the history of the House, as well as the custom that Speakers cast their vote last, to avoid influencing other legislators (Follett 1896, 149–53, 158; Hinds 1907, 5964; U.S. Congress 2005, rule 1, clause 7).

Figure 2.7 shows the percentage of recorded roll call votes on which Speakers since 1881 have cast a ballot when it was nonpivotal in making a quorum or deciding the final result of the vote. Such floor voting by Speakers has tended to swing rather dramatically in frequency over time. Individual Speakers, such as Joseph Cannon and Henry Rainey (D-IL, 1933–34), frequently voted, but the practice rarely continued with their successors. The first modern Speaker to cast many nonpivotal floor votes was Carl Albert, and although Speaker vot-

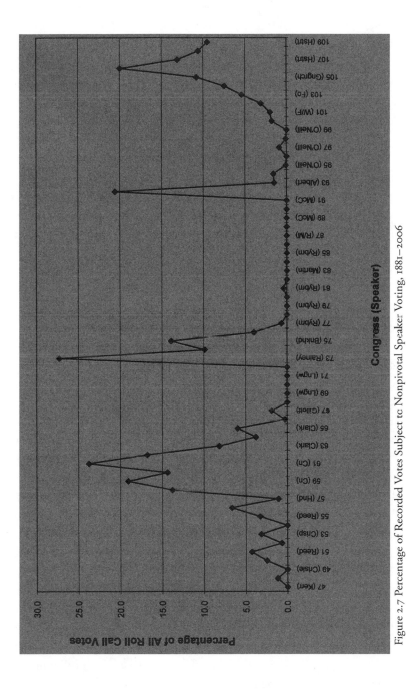

Figure 2.7 Percentage of Recorded Votes Subject to Nonpivotal Speaker Voting, 1881–2006

ing quickly dropped in frequency after his departure, it never completely disappeared. It is now more common for Speakers to cast nonpivotal votes, suggesting that, as with floor advocacy, it measures a considerable decline in the House-wide role of the Speakership.[43]

Is floor voting, like floor advocacy, a useful means of exercising leadership or shaping legislative outcomes? Speakers may vote because they have strong personal preferences on a certain bill and wish to express them, because the matter at hand is important to their constituents, or just to show loyalty to their party on an issue that is highly salient to the majority caucus. Floor voting is also risky. If a Speaker votes against a winning side, it suggests that he or she suffers from a lack of majority support within Congress. On the other hand, Speaker voting can signal to fellow majority party members the importance of a measure, as well as suggest possible connections between vote choice and future leadership benefits. It may also send a message that the Speaker is willing to risk his or her own reelection by casting an unpopular vote, an act of self-sacrifice that may convince other partisans to face the same electoral hazard.

A closer examination of the conditions under which modern Speakers have cast nonpivotal votes suggests that it has been used less often to alter legislative results than to express personal preferences; and when it has been committed, it is usually on issues highly salient to the Speaker's party, though the reasons have varied across votes and from one Speaker to another. Carl Albert was the first modern Speaker to revive the practice of floor voting, and he cast a stunning 170 roll call votes in his six years of service as Speaker—including 21 percent of all recorded votes in the 92nd Congress alone (1971–72)—setting a record that, in percentage terms, has yet to be broken. But, like McCormack's use of floor advocacy, Albert stands as an outlier, and it seems unlikely that he was attempting to influence outcomes on such a large number of votes. One study of Albert's voting behavior found that when he voted against his own party, it was primarily on foreign policy, an issue on which the Speaker had strong inclinations to support the president over his own caucus (Peters 1997, 173; see also chapter 4). Most likely, Albert's voting was an experimental and short-lived innovation associated with the introduction of recorded voting in the Committee of the Whole in 1971.[44] Albert soon abandoned his experiment, as can be seen in figure 2.8, which shows the percentage of roll call votes on which Albert cast a vote divided into three-month intervals.[45]

No Speaker has yet voted at such a high rate as did Albert (though Hastert came close in the 106th Congress), but his successors have not shied away from nonpivotal floor voting, though the evidence suggests they have usually done so

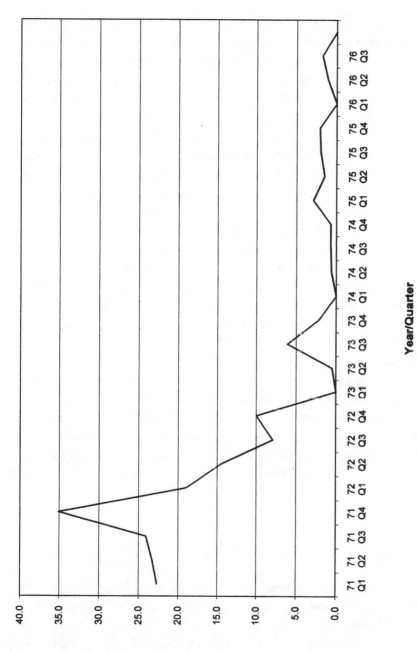

Year/Quarter

Figure 2.8 Percentage of Roll Calls on Which Speaker Albert Voted, 1971–1976

for reasons unrelated to a desire to influence events. Tip O'Neill cast twenty-two recorded floor votes; in nine of them, either the vote was decided by three votes or fewer (suggesting O'Neill might have tried to use his vote to bring others with him), O'Neill is known to have voted early, or evidence suggests he was unsure of the outcome (see table B.1 in appendix B). But most of his remaining votes were either pivotal (a situation in which Speaker voting is acceptable, if not mandatory), on matters salient to O'Neill personally (for example, limiting funds for the Nicaraguan Contras), a means of demonstrating solidarity with his party, or some combination of these conditions. Wright voted seventeen times, but none of his votes appear to have been cast to change final vote totals, suggesting he used the tactic to express his position as an individual legislator, demonstrate unity with his party, or both.[46] Foley voted even more often: 108 times between 1987 and 1994.[47] Available evidence on these votes, however, reveals that Foley rarely voted on close votes and often did so early or when he was unsure of the outcome of the vote. Interestingly, Foley did occasionally vote on issues related to House-wide matters, such as internal ethics investigations or reform, suggesting he was acting in these cases as a leader concerned with matters of the House as a whole, if not with partisan ones.

In short, Speakers are increasingly willing to vote on the floor, undertaking an activity that was once seen as unacceptably threatening to their position as an officer of the whole House. But just as frequent use of floor advocacy makes it a less effective leadership tool, the popularity of Speaker voting also undercuts its influence: as one former House leader observed in an interview, a Speaker who votes too much "dilutes the importance of it" as a significant activity (interview with the author, December 2002). Used mostly on votes that are neither close nor unclear in their final result, Speaker voting should not be seen in the same light as floor advocacy.

SUMMARY

Floor advocacy has become an increasingly utilized element in the Speaker's battery of strategic leadership tools. Legislative advocacy by the Speaker during floor deliberation can be simple position taking (as may be the case with certain Speakers, such as John McCormack), but it can also be a useful leadership tactic: it can persuade legislators through force of argument, signal that scarce goods will be provided contingent on supporting the Speaker's position, and carry additional weight due to the rarity and gravity of the act itself. The evidence presented here indicates that the contemporary Speaker's use of the floor to deliver speeches reflects the multiple goals that drive his or her exercise of legislative leadership. Floor advocacy most commonly reflects the policy preferences of the Speaker's congressional caucus, but it is also related to the Speaker's goals of election to the House, enactment of desired public policy, and fulfillment of leadership duties to the president or the House as a whole. Furthermore, its change in usage over time is a useful measure of how the duty to serve as a House-wide officer has declined in salience since World War II. The growth in floor voting suggests a similar development, though it appears to be motivated by reasons other than to influence floor outcomes.

Chapter 3 Sam Rayburn
and John McCormack

The standard wisdom about two Democratic Speakers, Sam Rayburn of Texas and John McCormack of Massachusetts—who together served almost continuously from 1941 to 1970—is that their leadership was limited in important ways. Historical narratives often relate that neither Speaker possessed or made frequent use of such powers as committee appointments, the selection of committee chairmen, or agenda control. Together with the presence of a sizable southern conservative wing of the Democratic Party, whose members chaired many significant committees and were willing to align with Republicans on key issues, this lack of formal authority constricted both Speakers' ability to elicit political change or influence legislative outcomes.[1]

It would be incorrect, however, to conclude that these Speakers were weak, inactive, or without influence over the legislative process. To be sure, the twin problems of party division and limited institutional authority meant that both men had to work hard at times to build successful winning coalitions (Cooper and Brady 1981). Indeed, one of the persistent political dynamics evident in the cases discussed in this chapter is the ongoing challenge to the Speaker's leadership from the "conservative coalition" of Republicans and rightward-leaning Democrats. Nonetheless, a careful analysis of both Speakers' tenures reveals that Rayburn and McCormack were quite willing and able to shape policy outcomes, although it might have required going to the House floor to do it.[2]

The theory of goal-driven leadership posits that Speakers may exercise leadership not only to ensure reelection to their position as Speaker—by satisfying the interests of the majority party in Congress—but to achieve other objectives, such as satisfying district needs, achieving personal policy interests, carrying out presidential initiatives, and/or addressing House-wide matters. In this chapter, I test this and other predictions of the theory using key acts of legislative leadership committed on or near the House floor by Speakers Rayburn and McCormack. Evidence shows that the theory provides a more complete explanation of these cases than do party-based models of congressional leadership.

To find "key" leadership acts by Speakers, I conducted a "sweep" of major histories of Congress and congressional leadership, identifying and recording any instance when the Speaker allegedly acted to influence a specific legislative outcome. The twenty-three cases of legislative leadership derived from these sweeps that involved Speakers McCormack and Rayburn exercising leadership during or in temporal proximity to legislative activity on the House floor are listed in tables 3.1 and 3.2 (see appendix A for a description of the sweep methodology).[3] I discuss thirteen of these cases in detail, including the goal or goals that the Speaker most likely sought to accomplish in each case.[4] These goals (and the individuals, institutions, or entities associated with satisfying those goals) were identified using historical and journalistic accounts, archival data, and other material and were coded as follows:

- the *reelection (to the Speakership) goal,* if evidence indicates that the specific legislative outcome (1) was expected to help the reelection chances of the Speaker's congressional party, (2) would have satisfied a clearly identified, well-developed, and widely held policy goal or preference of the party, or (3) otherwise matched the strongly held policy goals of an influential and sizeable majority of the Speaker's party;[5]
- the *reelection (to the House) goal,* if the issue at hand was described (or was indicated by poll data, if available) as being highly salient to a large number or pivotal set of voters in the Speaker's district, was of great economic impor-

Table 3.1 Rayburn as Legislative Leader

Case	Date of Floor Vote(s)	Speaker's Primary Floor-Related Activity	Source(s)	Key Vote(s) All Members	Key Vote(s), Maj. Party	Motivating Speaker Goal(s) and Relevant Individual/Entity	
						Primary	Secondary
Draft extension	August 1941	Lobbying, vote clock management	Various (10)[a]	203–202	181–65	Role fulfillment • Pres. party • Inst. presidency	—
Neutrality Act revision[b]	November 1941	Floor advocacy	Gould and Young (1998)	212–194	188–53	Reelection • Party in Congress Role fulfillment • Pres. party • Inst. presidency	—
Emergency Price Control Act[b]	June 1944	Floor advocacy	Galloway (1976), Bolling (1968)	64–153, 170–44	n/a	Reelection • Party in Congress	Role fulfillment • Pres. party
21-day rule enactment	January 1949	Lobbying (in caucus)	Various (6)[c]	275–142	225–31	Reelection • Party in Congress Role fulfillment • Pres. party	—
Taft-Hartley repeal[b]	May 1949	Lobbying, floor advocacy	Bolling (1968)	212–209	193–62	Reelection • Party in Congress Role fulfillment • Pres. party	—
Natural Gas Act[b]	August 1949, March 1950	Lobbying, floor advocacy, clock management	MacNeil (1963), Truman (1959)	183–131, 176–174	93–97, 97–116	Reelection • District	—
21-day rule repeal[b]	January 1950	Floor advocacy	Truman (1959)	183–236	85–171	Reelection • Party in Congress	—

Issue	Date	Tactics	Sources	Votes	Votes	Speaker's goals	Outcome
Point Four Program[b]	March 1950	Floor advocacy	Truman (1959)	141–189, 150–220	n/a; 31–190	Role Fulfillment • Pres. party	—
Formosa resolution[b]	January 1955	Lobbying, floor advocacy	Josephy (1979), Mooney (1964)	410–3	225–1	Role fulfillment • Pres. party • Inst. presidency	—
Reciprocal Trade Act[b]	February 1955	Floor advocacy, lobbying	Bolling (1964), Dexter (1977), Gould and Young (1998), Mooney (1964)	191–193, 193–192	82–134, 128–88	Role fulfillment • Inst. presidency	Policy enactment • Speaker
Restoring foreign aid[b]	June 1956	Floor advocacy	MacNeil (1963)	192–112	n/a	Role fulfillment • Inst. presidency	—
Civil rights	July 1956, June and August 1957	Lobbying, other	Bolling (1964, 1968), Remini (2006)	279–126, 286–126, 279–97	111–102, 118–107, 129–82	Reelection • Party in Congress	Policy enactment • Speaker
Labor reform	August 1959	Lobbying, other	Bolling (1964), Peters (1997)	215–200, 229–201	n/a; 95–183	Reelection • Party in Congress	Role fulfillment • Pres. party
Rules Committee expansion[a]	January 1961	Lobbying, floor advocacy	Several (19)[d]	217–212	195–64	Reelection • Party in Congress • Role fulfillment • Pres. party	Role fulfillment • Pres. party

[a] Barone (1990), Bolling (1968), Fenno (1973b), Galloway (1976), Gould and Young (1998), Josephy (1979), MacNeil (1963), Mooney (1964), Remini (2006), and Riddick (1949).

[b] Rayburn spoke on House floor on behalf of the measure.

[c] Bolling (1968), *Congressional Quarterly*, Fenno (1973b), Josephy (1979), Peters (1997), and Truman (1959).

[d] Barone (1990), Bolling (1964, 1968), *Congressional Quarterly*, Fenno (1973b), Galloway (1976), Gould and Young (1998), Grantham (1976, 1987), Jones (1970), Josephy (1979), MacNeil (1963), Mooney (1964), Peters (1997), Remini (2006), Ripley (1967), Sinclair (1995, 2004), and Thurber (2004).

tance to the district or region, or was otherwise seen by the Speaker as potentially having a great impact on his or her reelection to the House;

- the *policy enactment goal,* if evidence indicates that the matter was of great personal interest to the Speaker;[6]

- the *role-fulfillment goal of assisting the presidential party,* if evidence shows that
the matter was initiated or given high priority by a same-party White House,
and/or was considered by the Speaker's party to be of great importance to
their candidate for the White House (and perhaps viewed as affecting the result of the next presidential election);

- the *role-fulfillment goal of assisting the institutional presidency,* if evidence indicates that the matter was initiated or given high priority by the incumbent
president (of either party) and was on defense, foreign affairs, trade, or another issue closely associated with the unique power and authority of the
White House; and/or

- the *role-fulfillment goal of aiding the whole House,* if the case involved the internal function of the House or its external reputation or authority, and affected legislators regardless of their party affiliation.

A goal is considered the primary explanation of Speaker behavior if the pre-
ponderance of evidence indicates it was of greatest importance to the Speaker,
and a secondary explanation if evidence suggests the goal may have mattered
to the Speaker but was unlikely to have been the pivotal reason for exercising
legislative leadership.

I also present evidence, when available, of the degree to which the Speaker's
leadership affected the final legislative result. As one might expect, such evidence is often scarce or absent as Rayburn and McCormack rarely identified or
kept records of the legislators they had lobbied or sought to persuade.[7] But the
dynamics of floor votes—such as close outcomes, vote switching by legislators,
or members of Congress voting contrary to expectation—often implied such influence. Using the taxonomy of strategic floor scenarios outlined in chapter 1,
ten Rayburn cases and seven McCormack cases out of the twenty-three captured in the sweeps involved an attempt to win over the floor median legislator
with the votes of a majority of the majority party; one concerned winning on
the floor without the support of the majority of the majority party; one was associated with unifying the majority party; two were attempts to unite the House
as a whole; and the remaining two more involved ambiguous floor objectives.

Tables 3.1 and 3.2 show that although the Speaker's party in the House motivated legislative leadership in a majority of the sweep-captured cases (fifteen of

twenty-three), it often did so in conjunction with the needs or preferences of other institutions or political actors. As a primary factor, the concerns of just the congressional party explain five of the Rayburn and McCormack cases. The most common pattern is leadership that was driven by both the party in Congress and the presidential party, appearing in a plurality of cases (seven). Other goals sometimes mattered as well. Aiding the congressional party, the presidential party, and the institutional presidency appears in another three instances. In several cases, the Speaker's party in the House is not the primary entity of importance. The Speaker focused on the institutional presidency three times, the institutional presidency together with the presidential party twice, his own congressional district once, the concerns of the whole House once, and enacting policy goals while aiding the institutional presidency once.

I begin by looking at cases in which the Speaker acted not out of concern for the majority party in the House but to accomplish the goals associated with his position as individual representative (reelection to the House or passage of preferred policy) or to fulfill his role as an officer of the whole House. I follow with a discussion of some of the instances that are best explained as the fulfillment of two other leadership roles: aiding the presidential party and assisting the institutional presidency. Next, I examine a subset of the cases in which Rayburn and McCormack were acting on behalf of both their party in Congress and the presidential party. I conclude with an analysis of several cases in which the Speaker most clearly acted as an agent of his congressional majority party's policy preferences, showing that, even in this situation, other goals can be of some importance.

SERVING ONE'S DISTRICT, ENACTING ONE'S
POLICY PREFERENCES, OR AIDING THE HOUSE

In two cases from the data set, Rayburn and McCormack exercised significant legislative leadership because doing so would contribute to their reelection to Congress, enact personally preferred policy, or fulfill House-wide leadership duties. Neither the interests nor objectives of the Speaker's party in Congress dictated the particular final result in either case. In one instance, in fact, the Speaker's preferred outcome was opposed by a majority of his caucus in the House. Although only two instances fell into this category, they involved significant issues (national energy policy and congressional representation), and evidence in both points to the Speaker as being critical in influencing the final legislative outcome.

Table 3.2 McCormack as Legislative Leader

Case	Date of Key Floor Vote(s)	Speaker's Primary Floor-Related Activity	Source(s)	Key Vote(s), All Members	Key Vote(s), Maj. Party	Motivating Speaker Goal(s) and Relevant Individual/Entity	
						Primary	Secondary
House expansion	March 1962	Other	Peabody (1977)	n/a	n/a	Role fulfillment • House-wide	—
Tax bill	March 1962	Lobbying	Ripley (1964)	219–196	218–34	Reelection • Party in Congress Role fulfillment • Pres. party	—
Trade bill[a]	June 1962	Lobbying, floor advocacy	Ripley (1964)	171–253	44–210	Reelection • Party in Congress Role fulfillment • Pres. party • Inst. presidency	—
Farm bill[a]	September 1962	Lobbying, floor advocacy, other	MacNeil (1963)	202–197	200–37	Reelection • Party in Congress Role fulfillment • Pres. party	—

Measure	Date	Actions	Sources	Vote 1	Vote 2	Goals	Additional
Rules Committee expansion[a]	January 1963	Lobbying, trading benefits, floor advocacy	Bolling (1964), Galloway (1976), Ripley (1967)	235–196	207–48	Reelection • Party in Congress Role fulfillment • Pres. party	—
Debt limit increases[a]	May, August, and November 1963	Lobbying, floor advocacy	Ripley (1964, 1967)	213–204, 221–175, 187–179	212–32, 219–17, 187–32	Reelection • Party in Congress Role fulfillment • Pres. party • Inst. presidency	—
Modified 21-day rule[a]	January 1965	Floor advocacy	Bolling (1968), Fenno (1973b), Galloway (1976)	224–202	208–79	Reelection • Party in Congress	Role fulfillment • Pres. party
Vietnam War measures[a]	1965–69	Floor advocacy, other	Josephy (1979)	various	various	Policy enactment • Speaker Role fulfillment • Inst. presidency	Role fulfillment • Pres. party
Voting Rights Act extension[a]	June 1970	Lobbying, floor advocacy	Sinclair (1995)	224–183	165–66	Reelection • Party in Congress	—

[a]McCormack spoke on House floor on behalf of the measure.

Rayburn and the Natural Gas Act, 1949–50

One legislative initiative important to the voters in Speaker Rayburn's district yet contrary to the policy preferences of his own party and, ultimately, the Democratic president was a proposal to amend the 1938 Natural Gas Act to exclude independent natural gas producers from federal regulation. The act, as interpreted by a 1947 Supreme Court decision, allowed the Federal Power Commission (FPC) to regulate intrastate sales of natural gas. Fuel producers feared such regulation was likely because both the use of natural gas and exports of natural gas from the southern United States to the north had grown since the mid-1940s.

A majority of House Democrats worried that prohibiting such regulation could lead to rising prices for consumers—a particular concern among Democrats representing colder climates—and give the gas industry an unfair economic advantage. Rayburn, however, strongly supported exempting producers from the act. His motivation for doing so was primarily regional: "As Rayburn saw it," according to one biography, "Texas interests were at stake."[8] Although his district did not produce natural gas at the time, it was close to major gas fields and to pipelines used for shipping the fuel elsewhere, primarily to the northeastern United States, and Rayburn had strong electoral reasons to stand behind Texas energy interests (Hardeman and Bacon 1987, 349; Sanders 1981, 29, 58–64). Independent gas producers, concerned that FPC regulation was on the horizon, urged Rayburn and other congressional allies to approve an exemption. Rayburn was thus willing to push for the natural gas exemption in spite of the sentiments of his caucus (Hardeman and Bacon 1987, 351, 393; *New York Times*, 6 August 1949).[9]

Not only did an exemption of independent producers from FPC regulation go against the preferences of Rayburn's congressional party, but it was not sought by the Truman White House. To be sure, President Truman's initial unwillingness to oppose the exemption measure, and possible consultations on the issue between his administration and the Speaker, may have given Rayburn hope that the president would sign an exemption into law. But the measure was not on Truman's legislative agenda, the president did little to actively push it through Congress, and its passage placed Truman in a tight spot between bill supporters in Congress and the influential party liberals who opposed it. Nor would the exemption enhance or protect the institutional authority of the president; arguably, by limiting the jurisdiction of a commission whose members were appointed by the White House (with Senate approval), it would do the reverse. Thus Rayburn's decision to help enact the gas regulation exemption cannot be explained as an effort to aid the presidential party or the institutional presidency (Clark 1950; Trott 1950; Waggoner 1950).

On at least two occasions, Rayburn did not shy from using his authority as Speaker to pass the measure. First, in August 1949, Rayburn employed (in the words of political scientist David Truman) "one of his rare appeals from the floor" in support of the House version of exemption legislation. In a short speech, he emphasized his many years of experience dealing with the issue in the House of Representatives, and argued that the legislation would merely ensure that Congress, not "a commission by regulation," would continue to have authority over natural gas sales.[10] The speech was presumably one of several tactics Rayburn used (others being more hidden) in which he "threw his support to [the bill] and helped put it over," as one news story put it. The bill passed, 183–131, though it was narrowly rejected by Democrats by a 93–97 margin (*Congressional Record*, 4 August 1949, 10779; *New York Times*, 6 August 1949; Truman 1959, 25).

The second occasion occurred after the Senate passed its version of a natural gas exemption the following March. When some legislators refused to let the Senate bill come to the House floor by unanimous consent, the Speaker called for a special meeting of the Rules Committee—which has the power to set the rules for considering legislation on the floor—to quickly clear the measure for floor debate over the objections of at least one progressive Democrat on the committee. The next day, Rayburn delivered a speech on the House floor arguing against granting the FPC such regulatory power and claiming that the exemption would "not raise the price of natural gas to any consumer in the United States one red penny." When representatives recorded their votes, however, the initial results revealed that the measure would fail. Rayburn recruited several bill proponents to ask the presiding officer how their votes had been recorded. This delayed an announcement of the final count; Rayburn then asked Republican Charles Halleck of Indiana to lobby his partisan colleagues. Three members of Congress switched their votes, and the measure passed by 176–174.[11] Interestingly, Democrats had voted against the bill by an even larger margin than before (97 to 116). Legislators from leading gas-producing states, including Kansas, Louisiana, and Oklahoma, as well as Texas, voted nearly unanimously for the bill, and delegates from states with the greatest consumption of natural gas cast votes against it (Carper 1962, 37; *Congressional Record*, 31 March 1950, 4566; Lapham 1988, 268–69; MacNeil 1963, 359; Sanders 1981, 91–92; *Washington Post*, 31 March 1950).

Truman subsequently vetoed the measure, killing the exemption. Nonetheless, Rayburn's efforts had clearly helped bring the legislation to the president's desk, despite the sentiments of his own party in the House.

McCormack and House Expansion, 1962

After the 1960 census, several states were threatened with a loss of congressional seats due to reapportionment. Though the House had not added members since 1913, the recent admission of Hawaii and Alaska as states had temporarily expanded the size of the House by two, and a number of legislators hoped this might lead to a permanent creation of new seats in the chamber before the 1962 elections. Several bills were introduced in 1961 to increase House membership by as many as thirty-four representatives, but Speaker Rayburn was against such moves, and the Judiciary Committee rejected two expansion bills that year. But when McCormack became Speaker following Rayburn's death in late 1961, he proved more supportive of House expansion and even openly endorsed a modest addition of three or four seats (*Congressional Quarterly Almanac* 1962, 394–95).

The expansion proposal ultimately agreed upon would have increased the House by three additional seats and would have accomplished several objectives of importance to legislators of both parties. One of the three seats would likely have gone to Pennsylvania, where Republican Ivor Fenton was otherwise in danger of being redistricted out of his seat. Of benefit to Democrats (including, perhaps, McCormack himself)[12] was a potentially new seat for Massachusetts, which would have alleviated an intrastate conflict stemming from the state's post-census loss of two congressional districts. Furthermore, because the proposal would have only added a few new members to the House, it would have posed less of a threat to the chamber's efficiency, which had been Rayburn's stated reason for opposing any expansion (*Congressional Quarterly Almanac* 1962, 395). Since the creation of new congressional seats was beneficial not so much to the majority party in the House as to legislators generally, McCormack's endorsement of the plan is best understood as driven by a duty to serve the entire House.

Although it is not known what specific actions McCormack took on behalf of the proposal, his support was cited as key to bringing it to the House floor. The chairman of the Judiciary Committee, a former opponent of expansion, explained his newfound endorsement as a result of "the solid leadership support behind it" (*Congressional Quarterly Almanac* 1962, 395). Democratic leaders also conducted an advance whip count on the expansion proposal, in which party "whips" polled fellow Democrats to determine their likely vote (Evans 2007). As it happened, however, McCormack would also be partly culpable for the bill's failure. Republicans, led by Minority Leader Charles Halleck (R-IN), worried that the Democratic Pennsylvania legislature would not draw a new seat for Congressman Fenton, forcing him to run as an at-large representative elected by the entire state. Halleck convinced the bill's sponsor, Francis Walter (D-PA), to offer a floor amendment requiring that any state given an extra seat would have to draw new congressional districts and not simply create a single at-large district. Misinformed that his amendment was endorsed by the leaders of both parties, a majority of congressmen voted for it, and it passed by both voice vote and a 128–54 standing vote (also known as a "division" vote, in which legislators stand and are counted without being identified individually). But McCormack, who did not want to impose redistricting requirements on states and feared that such requirements might not pass legal muster, publicly withdrew his support for the amended bill. The Speaker was joined by Pennsylvania legislators, who worried that if their state failed to redraw its districts, the amendment would force the entire delegation to run as at-large representatives. The bill was quickly recommitted by voice vote and subsequently died in committee (*Congressional Quarterly Almanac* 1962, 395–96; *Newsweek,* 19 March 1962; Peabody 1977, 384).

McCormack's critics were quick to point to the bill's death as a sign that the Speaker was less able than his predecessor, Sam Rayburn. Various press accounts called McCormack's move "an ignominious retreat," a "debacle," and a "bitter" defeat that "showed that . . . [he] was unable to keep control of the House of Representatives" (*Business Week,* 17 March 1962; *Newsweek,* 19 March 1962). While McCormack had exercised considerable influence in this particular case, the proposal's collapse—and McCormack's failure to anticipate either the Walter amendment or its consequences—had probably been avoidable; it marked an inauspicious start to his first year as Speaker of the House.

FULFILLING PRESIDENT-ORIENTED ROLES OR DUTIES

Neither Rayburn nor McCormack depended on presidents to sustain their formal leadership positions in the House. Nonetheless, both Speakers at times exercised significant legislative leadership on matters that were initiated or strongly endorsed by the White House and which their party in the House opposed, was ambivalent about, and/or did not perceive as having significant electoral benefits. Such leadership occurred out of deference to the president as an independent constitutional officer, as an important party leader, or both.

In this section, I examine five of the six cases concerning Rayburn or Mc-Cormack that can be explained by one or both of these two role-related goals. Some important general characteristics of all six cases should be noted. First, they all were associated with legislative matters related to defense or foreign affairs. Since such issues have traditionally fallen under the purview of the president, particularly since World War II, this should not come as a great surprise.[13] Second, in two of the cases the Speaker's personal policy objectives coincided with the preferences of an opposite-party president. Although it is unlikely that the Speaker's policy objectives were the primary motivation to exercise legislative leadership, it illustrates how more than one goal of the Speaker may jointly point to a particular course of action. Having strong private interests in the desired legislative outcome may have allowed the Speaker to make a personal appeal for legislators' support, a potentially quite effective tactic. Third, in all of the recorded votes associated with these instances of leadership, a majority of the majority party voted in favor of the president's policy. This does not mean, however, that the Speaker was acting as an agent of the congressional party or that his leadership was unnecessary. In fact, the Speaker in these cases often acted forcefully, sometimes before the particular measure came to a final floor vote, against both potential and actual opposition within his party in the House; and in at least one case, the Speaker's objective was to achieve unanimity, not merely floor passage.

Rayburn and Draft Extension, 1941

The House's extension of the military draft in August 1941 involved one of the most impressive and consequential examples of leadership undertaken by a contemporary Speaker. Not only was the extension's passage in the House in doubt until the final moment, but the proposal proved remarkably prescient when Japan launched its surprise attack on Pearl Harbor just three months later. For many years afterward, both Speaker Rayburn and his majority leader at the time, John McCormack, made frequent references to the vote in floor speeches and private interviews.[14]

In 1940, worried by the expanding war in Europe, both the House and Senate agreed to enact a one-year military draft. But a temporary draft seemed less and less sufficient as the international situation deteriorated further: Germany launched an invasion of the Soviet Union in June 1941, and many were alarmed by Japan's territorial ambitions in China and the Pacific. Rayburn, serving his first term as Speaker, soon faced pressure from the White House to renew the draft. By mid-1941, President Roosevelt had asked Congress to extend military conscription, and both the army chief of staff and the secretary of war had met with the Speaker to enlist his aid.[15] Meanwhile, even though a majority of Democrats had supported the draft in 1940, the prospect of continued conscription and a possible military campaign gave many House Democrats pause. Northern liberals especially were sympathetic to the isolationist cause, and a number of them had already cast votes earlier that year against Roosevelt's Lend-Lease program to provide military supplies to Great Britain. Their concerns reflected those of many Americans, and McCormack himself later speculated that at that time "probably 75 percent of the American people were opposed" to U.S. involvement overseas.[16] Furthermore, the party's own campaign platform opposed draft extension, and Democrats of all stripes feared electoral retaliation from constituents with children who had already been drafted but were expected to return home in a matter of months (Dorough 1962, 313; Hardeman and Bacon 1987, 259, 261; Keegan 1989, 245–48; McCormack Papers, McSweeny interview, box 195, tape 6; Sanders 2001; Steinberg 1975, 169–70).

Given these political dynamics, Rayburn's decision to push an extension of the draft through the House can be best explained as fulfilling two leadership-related duties: to assist a same-party president for partisan reasons, since a defeat in Congress would hurt Roosevelt's image and reputation; and to aid the nation's commander-in-chief, regardless of his party affiliation. By contrast, neither the congressional party's policy objectives nor its short-term electoral fate would be clearly secured by pursuing draft extension. Furthermore, while some biographers have emphasized Rayburn's personal backing of the draft extension, the Speaker had not initially supported it, suggesting that Rayburn was not driven by a desire to enact personally desired policy (see, for example, Sanders 2001).

Rayburn's efforts to pass the military draft bill occurred in three stages. The first involved deciding how long to extend the draft.[17] Roosevelt insisted on an open-ended extension, but a whip count in the House indicated that only a one-year extension had a chance of getting a majority vote on the floor. Nonetheless, Rayburn decided that a bill the Senate had passed earlier that year, which renewed the draft for eighteen months, could possibly garner a majority, though getting that majority would not be easy. The second stage of the Speaker's campaign was to lobby individual members to vote for an extension. With the help of other party leaders, Rayburn relied on both personal persuasion and promises of future benefits to win over legislators. Providence also stepped in at this stage when, on August 10, Representative Albert Rutherford (R-PA) passed away. Rayburn, still lacking a majority, had an excuse to hold the House in a one-day recess, during which time he worked hard to recruit more supporters (Hardeman and Bacon 1987, 262–64; Steinberg 1975, 170).

The final stage of Rayburn's leadership took place on the floor itself. The bill still did not have the votes of a majority of representatives, and on August 12, as floor debate on the measure proceeded, the Speaker and other party leaders lobbied members of both parties. In the short time remaining, Rayburn had managed to persuade four additional Democrats to vote for the extension (Hardeman and Bacon 1987, 265–66; Steinberg 1975, 170–71). When all time for debate expired, as then–Majority Leader McCormack later recalled, he and Rayburn "did not know if we had the votes" but "knew the vote was going to be close." A motion to recommit the bill and strike all after the enacting clause (thus killing the measure) failed, 190–215. All that remained was the vote on final passage of the draft extension, but Rayburn had very little room to maneuver: he possessed no more than two "pocket" votes that could be called upon if last-minute switches were needed to pass the bill.[18] When the initial voting was completed, Rayburn, who was presiding over the House, saw that the bill would narrowly lose, and he quickly called over several Democratic draft opponents to the Speaker's dais to make a last-minute plea for their votes. Meanwhile, would-be draft opponents, seeking either to buy time or switch their votes from yes to no, were asking Rayburn to officially recognize them on the floor. When one legislator asked how his vote had been recorded, Rayburn replied that he had voted for the bill, whereupon—to the Speaker's chagrin—the congressman then switched his vote from yes to no. The vote count, which had been 204–201 for the bill, was now a precarious 203–202. Lest any of the other representatives seeking to be recognized planned to vote against the bill, Rayburn immediately declared the vote to be final (*Congressional Record,* 12 August 1941, 7075; Hardeman and Bacon 1987, 267–68; McCormack Papers, McSweeny interview, box 195, tape 6; Steinberg 1975, 171).

Given the closeness of the vote and Rayburn's many efforts to enact the bill, it seems reasonable to surmise that Rayburn's legislative leadership had been critical to the measure's passage. Although the switch of just one Democrat would have been sufficient to change the result, Rayburn lobbied scores of Democrats in the days before the vote. Rayburn did lose twelve party members to the opposition[19] after the recommittal vote, gaining only two southerners, Robert Sikes (FL) and John Rankin (MS). But the broader extent of Rayburn's lobbying is revealed by examining whether legislators subject to such efforts voted contrary to their own preferences. A useful method of approximating such preferences is the NOMINATE classification model (Poole and Rosenthal 1997), which estimates legislators' ideal preference points for a given Congress based on their roll call voting behavior.[20] The model can identify preferences for many dimensions, but two—generally interpreted as an ideological "left-right" dimension and a cross-cutting dimension (such as race or region)—usually explain most of the variation in voting behavior. A hypothetical "cut point line" dividing yes and no votes is then determined for each roll call, and legislators who are mistakenly classified for a roll call vote are considered "error" terms associated with that vote. Of course, such mistaken estimates are not direct proof of leader influence; they could be within the margin of error associated with the model or caused by other idiosyncratic factors. When combined with evidence of lobbying efforts by the Speaker, however, they strongly suggest that the Speaker affected others' voting behavior.[21]

Figure 3.1 shows the estimated ideal preference points in two dimensions for all members of the House in the 77th Congress (1941–42) and the estimated yes-no cut line for the vote on final passage of the draft extension bill. (The preference points are W-NOMINATE coordinates; W-NOMINATE is a version of the NOMINATE procedure that generates estimates applicable to single congresses.) The points are arrayed horizontally according to each legislator's relative conservatism or liberalism (those placed further to the left are more liberal, those further to the right are more conservative), and arrayed vertically based on each legislator's preferences on a second, cross-party division (southern Democrats are toward the top of the circle, northerners further down). Solid circles represent legislators who voted for the draft extension bill, and solid squares represent legislators who voted against it; thus, circles to the right of the line (in the "predicted as voting no" region) and squares to the left of the line (in the "predicted as voting yes" region) are legislators who voted contrary to prediction, based on their estimated ideal preferences. The figure shows that ten Democrats voted for the bill contrary to their own approximated preferences. Many of those Democrats are quite close to the cut line, suggesting that their falsely predicted vote choice may be due to errors in the statistical model rather than to actual leadership pressure. One should recall, however, that the switch of one Democrat would have reversed the outcome. Furthermore, a similar analysis shows that four of the ten unexpected Democratic bill supporters were also falsely predicted to vote for the previous motion to recommit (and thus kill) the bill: John Dingell (MI), William Fitzgerald (CT), Augustine Kelley (PA), and John Lesinski (MI).[22] If even one of these Democrats voted

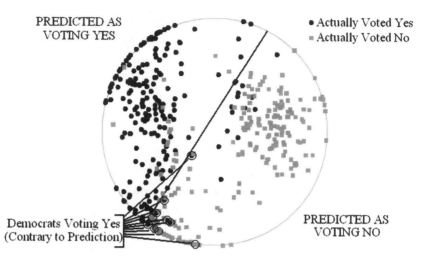

PREDICTED AS
VOTING YES

• Actually Voted Yes
▪ Actually Voted No

Democrats Voting Yes
(Contrary to Prediction)

PREDICTED AS
VOTING NO

Figure 3.1 W-NOMINATE Estimates of Legislator Vote Choice, 1941 Draft Extension
Bill, Final Passage

as they did because of Rayburn's influence, it meant the Speaker had made the
difference in determining the bill's fate.

Rayburn and the Point Four Program, 1950

In his 1949 inaugural address, President Truman proposed a major new program designed to broadly distribute U.S. aid to underdeveloped countries.
Known as "Point Four" for appearing in the fourth section of the address, his
proposal would later include $45 million in funding for international organi-
zations to provide technical assistance overseas and the granting of authority to
the Export-Import Bank to give financial guarantees for economic development programs. Point Four represented a major new direction for American
foreign relations, establishing as a national policy the granting of development
aid to needy nations (Butterfield 2004, 2–5).

If Speaker Rayburn were to exercise leadership to guide the plan through
Congress, it would most clearly be to defend both Truman's policy preferences
and his presidential authority in setting foreign policy. Point Four had originated in the executive branch (specifically, from a public affairs staffer in the
State Department), and Truman chose to include it in his inaugural address despite the doubts of higher-level officials in the department (Butterfield 2004;
Gosnell 1980, 441). After Truman's surprise announcement of the initiative, he
and other officials pressed aggressively for it, with State Department officials
making several public speeches and appearing at congressional committee hear-

ings on its behalf (*Congressional Quarterly Almanac* 1949, 393–95; McCullough 1992, 730). By contrast, House Democrats were decidedly ambivalent about the new foreign aid program. Many more Democrats than Republicans were consistent internationalists (Kesselman 1961), but Point Four would have given few benefits to their districts, and it was not closely associated with the party's platform or ideological bent. Furthermore, as two foreign policy scholars noted a few years later, because there had been "little if any consultation with Congressional figures prior to the Truman inaugural address and little improvement in this respect until late in 1949, the support of even the Democratic members of the legislative branch was scarcely hearty" (Cheever and Haviland 1952, 117).

Point Four was incorporated into a larger foreign aid authorization bill that came to the House floor in March 1950. House Republicans were the most vocal opponents of Point Four as well as other elements of the authorization bill, but at least some budget-minded (primarily southern) Democrats could be expected to vote against the program as well. In a bad omen for the program, champions of the bill failed to block two major amendments to the bill even before Point Four came up for deliberation. The first amendment, which withheld Marshall Plan aid to England until that country agreed to end the partition of Ireland, passed in a 99–66 teller vote over the opposition of the president and the chairman of the Foreign Affairs Committee.[23] (In a teller vote, legislators walk past two representatives each serving as a vote counter, or "teller"; the vote choice of individuals is not recorded.) The second, offered by Texas Democrat Omar Burleson, required that $1 billion of European aid be spent to purchase U.S. agricultural goods; it passed the House by teller, 119–107, even though Truman opposed such an explicit dedication of funds (Belair 1950; *Congressional Quarterly Almanac* 1950, 211).

When the Point Four provisions came up for debate, Wisconsin Republican Lawrence Smith offered an amendment to strike Title III of the bill, effectively killing the entire Point Four program. In response, after a number of smaller amendments to alter Title III were considered, Speaker Rayburn went to the floor to speak on behalf of Point Four. As the *New York Times* somewhat dramatically described the event, the Speaker was the first during the bill's debate to "receive the undivided attention of the members [of the House]. . . . An unfamiliar quiet gripped the House as Mr. Rayburn spoke, and it prevailed until he had yielded the floor." In the end, the Smith amendment failed in a 141–189 teller vote. The Republicans offered a motion to recommit the bill, which would have also eliminated the Point Four plan, but it failed in a 150–

220 roll call vote (Belair 1950; *Congressional Quarterly Almanac* 1950, 211–12; *Congressional Record*, 31 March 1950, 4518, 4550).[24]

Given the fact that neither the teller nor the recorded vote was particularly close, and that Rayburn's legislative leadership appears to have manifested itself primarily in his floor speech, the evidence that Rayburn's leadership was pivotal to the final result in this case is not as persuasive.[25] What was perhaps most significant was Rayburn's willingness to speak on the floor to defend Point Four, given his party's ambivalence about the plan and the Speaker's relative reluctance to use the floor in this manner (see chapter 2).

Rayburn and the Formosa Resolution, 1955

In late 1954, China began a series of aggressive military actions against nationalist-held territory off its coast, including attacks against the islands of Quemoy, Ichiang, and Matsu, and threatened to send an invasion force to Taiwan. Although President Dwight Eisenhower opted not to respond immediately with military force, he determined that an open statement of American preparedness might be sufficient to deter an immediate invasion of the islands, and in early 1955 he formally asked Congress to pass a resolution that would grant him the power to deploy American troops in their defense (Fisher 1995, 105; Steinberg 1975, 292–93; White 1955a).

Many Democrats opposed or were wary of such a resolution, for several reasons: it would allocate considerable authority to the president; it could involve the United States in a war with China; and any negative consequences could hurt the Democrats' reputation for having voted for it. Speaker Rayburn, however, believed that Congress (and, by extension, the Speaker) was expected to grant the president, as commander in chief, whatever authority he deemed was necessary to defend U.S. interests overseas. Rayburn took this view even though he himself was not particularly in favor of such a resolution, judging it unnecessary in light of what he perceived to be the president's existing powers. Thus this case was not an attempt by Rayburn to enact personally desired public policy, nor to implement his congressional party's interests, but rather to fulfill the Speaker's duty to assist the president on defense matters (Dorough 1962, 478; Josephy 1979, 356; Mooney 1964, 173; White 1955a; White 1955b).

The Speaker almost certainly had no need to worry about whether there were enough votes in the House to approve Eisenhower's request. But Rayburn was still concerned by the possible behavior of his own party, which had become increasingly critical of Eisenhower's foreign policy the previous year

(Reichard 1978, 57–59). Specifically, Rayburn feared that any open dissent on the House floor by Democrats, particularly via floor amendments, could undermine the image of bipartisan deference to the executive on foreign policy making, encourage some Democrats to vote against the resolution, and convey the impression that Democrats opposed using military force against communism.[26] Rayburn thus sought to sharply limit consideration of the measure on the floor and wanted to obtain a unanimous vote, or a vote as close to unanimous as possible, on the resolution.

In a private meeting with key House Democrats, Rayburn denied a request to hold extended debate on the floor, which might have given opponents a chance to critique Eisenhower's foreign policy and encourage further Democratic opposition. Rayburn instead argued for party unity, saying that "the country comes first" (Dorough 1962, 477–78). Rayburn also urged all Democrats to be present for the vote and took "personal responsibility" for what was a rather restrictive floor rule governing its consideration, denying any opportunity to offer amendments (Abel 1955; White 1955b). Finally, when the House debated the measure, Rayburn delivered a rare floor speech on its behalf. In his brief remarks, he made clear his view of the proper role of the president in foreign affairs, a role that he believed made the resolution unnecessary. "I do not think," he said, "that anyone who has ever studied our Constitution or the makeup of our Government denies that the President of the United States, as Commander in Chief of the Armed Forces, has this power" (*Congressional Record* 25 January 1955, 672).

Though the resolution passed easily, the Speaker's efforts may have been key to repressing all potential dissent. Only three congressmen voted against the resolution (one of them a Democrat), and the president had obtained the authority he wanted without any open display of division within either political party.

Rayburn and the Reciprocal Trade Act, 1955

Later that same year, Speaker Rayburn again helped with the passage of a presidential initiative, contrary to the preferences of many congressional Democrats. The Reciprocal Trade Act, which established conditions for trade between the United States and other countries, would expire in 1955. Prior extensions in 1953 and 1954 had been for one year only, but President Eisenhower now sought a longer, three-year extension. Eisenhower's request for a renewal involved both institutional and policy considerations: it would give him the authority to negotiate trade agreements, which he could then use to lower import tariffs.

Congressional Democrats (including Speaker Rayburn and the chairman of the House Ways and Means Committee, Tennessean Jere Cooper) were generally more sympathetic than Republicans toward liberalizing trade. Unfortunately for Eisenhower, however, many Democrats were increasingly unhappy with the president's foreign policy, at least in the areas of defense and foreign aid (as noted above), and their support for Eisenhower's request could not be automatically assumed (Reichard 1978). More specifically, sympathy toward protectionism was gaining ground among House Democrats. Some key Democratic regions, such as Appalachia and the state of Rhode Island, were suffering from high unemployment, and there were claims that increased imports from overseas were to blame. In addition, textile companies in the largely Democratic South initiated a tremendous lobbying effort to convince their representatives that they should be granted protections against competing imports. Even Speaker Rayburn, an opponent of protectionist tariffs from the very start of his congressional career, faced some resistance from key industries in his native state of Texas, including southern oil producers concerned about increased fuel imports under earlier trade agreements and organizations representing livestock farms. This, together with the same Republican resistance to the act that Eisenhower had grappled with in the previous, GOP-controlled Congress, made it much less certain that a renewal would pass on the House floor. It also meant that if Rayburn were to endorse Eisenhower's proposal, it would be as much to achieve a personal policy goal and to fulfill his leadership role to protect the White House's prerogatives on international and trade matters (a deference widely acknowledged, at least in principle, by many congressional Democrats in the early 1950s) as it would be to satisfy the policy preferences of House Democrats (Bauer, Pool, and Dexter 1963, 59–62; Dexter 1977, 21–23; Drury 1955a; Reichard 1978, 53; Steinberg 1975, 40; *Washington Post*, 17 January 1954).

This was the path that Rayburn chose to follow. He endorsed the renewal early on, and to send a signal of the bill's importance and the need for its swift passage, he gave the legislation the lowest possible number (H.R. 1). Protectionist-minded legislators in Ways and Means, meanwhile, tried to amend the bill to protect key industries, including oil. When those amendments failed, opponents turned their focus to amending or killing the renewal bill on the House floor. In a sign of both the bill's significance and that it could easily lose, the White House's legislative liaison office tried to gauge the preferences of House members from both parties, though with mixed success. Rayburn lobbied fellow Democrats in advance of the floor vote, and a whip count was also taken before the vote. Rayburn's leadership, however, proved even more critical on the floor, where the difference between supporters and opponents was so slim that it took no fewer than three roll call votes just to consider the bill for debate (Bauer, Pool, and Dexter 1963, 59–60; Conley and Yon 2007; Evans 2007; *New York Times*, 10 February 1955).

As was custom for trade legislation, the rule for considering the extension bill limited what amendments could be offered. Bill opponents hoped to defeat this "closed" rule, which would then permit them to offer more amendments and register their opposition less directly than would voting against renewal itself. On February 17, after debate on the rule was finished, the House defeated (178–207) a motion to proceed to a vote on the rule, with only a slim majority of Democrats (116 of 217) having voted to pass the motion. Though this did not kill the rule or the bill, it did surrender control of the floor to the bill's opponents, and Ohioan Clarence Brown (R) immediately offered an amendment to the rule that would allow for unlimited amendments. In response, Rayburn took to the floor and delivered an unusually lengthy speech defending Trade Act renewal; the purpose was both to persuade legislators and to buy time for bill supporters to lobby their colleagues. Rayburn succeeded on both fronts. As fellow Democrat Richard Bolling later described it, during Rayburn's speech "a few of his lieutenants [had time] to carry the message to some of Rayburn's friends and debtors that this was one issue 'the Speaker really wants you on.'" As for the rhetoric itself, one newspaper recounted (in somewhat colorful language) that it was a "spine-tingling speech that few will forget" and "may prove to have been the most electrifying single address in the 84th Congress" (Bolling 1964, 69; Strout 1955).

The Brown amendment was subsequently defeated by a narrow 191–193 vote. At first, the pro-Brown side had been ahead by seven votes, but nine legislators switched from accepting to rejecting the amendment. The House then considered again whether to proceed to a vote on the (unamended) rule, which it agreed to do by voice vote. The original rule now came up for a vote, and the margin proved extremely close: with one congressman switching his vote from no to yes (Robert Jones, D-AL) and another legislator voting in favor at the last minute (Chet Holifield, D-CA), the rule passed 193–192, the closest recorded vote in the House since the final passage of the draft extension bill fourteen years earlier (Bauer, Pool, and Dexter 1963, 64; Strout 1955).[27]

Although Eisenhower aides later lobbied legislators on passage of the bill (Bauer, Pool, and Dexter 1963, 64), it was Rayburn's efforts on the rule-related votes that had saved the measure from amendment or defeat. Looking at how

Table 3.3 Analysis of the 1955 Reciprocal Trade Act Floor Votes

Specific Roll Call Vote (Feb. 17, 1955)			
Previous Question	Brown Amendment to Rule	Rule	Democrats Voting in This Direction
No	No[a]	Yes[a]	Boykin (AL), Chelf (KY), Doyle (CA), Miller (CA), Richards (SC), Rivers (SC), and Sullivan (MO)
No	No[a]	No	Aspinall (CO), Bell (TX), Green (OR), Huddleston (AL), Metcalf (MT), Pfost (ID), Quigley (PA), Rogers (CO), Rogers (TX), Roosevelt (CA), Sisk (CA), and Tumulty (NJ)
No	Yes	Yes[a]	Abbitt (VA), Burleson (TX), Carnahan (MO), Fernandez (NM), Mack (IL), Thompson (LA), Watts (KY), Whitten (MS), and Willis (LA)

[a]Voting with House Democratic Party leadership

Democrats voted across the three recorded votes—to proceed to a vote on the rule, to approve the Brown amendment, and to enact the original rule—suggests where Rayburn and others applied the greatest pressure to win on the floor (see table 3.3). Seven Democrats originally voted against ending debate but then decided to go with party leaders on the next two recorded votes, rejecting Brown and voting for the original rule. An additional twenty-one Democrats voted against ending debate but were subsequently willing to either vote against Brown or for the original rule, though not both. Together with a few Republican switchers, this gave Rayburn the bare margin he needed to win the last two floor votes.[28] Unfortunately, the W-NOMINATE scaling procedure cannot be used in this case to identify whether these legislators voted against their preferences, because many members of Congress voted along nonideological lines: the estimated cut line fails to predict more than one hundred legislators on each of the three votes.

The bill remained controversial, and on the following morning, prior to the vote on the bill, the Speaker held a private breakfast meeting with twenty newly elected Democrats, urging them to back the measure by giving his signature advice that "those who go along, get along" (Dorough 1962, 477; quote from Dexter 1977, 26). The motion to recommit the bill failed by 199 to 206, and the bill ultimately passed, 295–110. Interestingly (and perhaps unsurprisingly), representatives from higher-unemployment districts were more likely to reject the bill, and those with large numbers of manufacturing jobs in their districts were more likely to cast votes in favor of free trade (Conley and Yon 2007).

McCormack and Vietnam
War Measures, 1965–69

This case of legislative leadership is more diffuse than others in this chapter. Congressional historian Alvin Josephy argues that McCormack exercised leadership several times from the mid- to late-1960s to limit significant opposition to the Vietnam War on the House floor. Working with the chairman of the Armed Services Committee, L. Mendel Rivers (SC), he "held the Democrats in line" and scheduled "an avalanche of loyal votes" to keep legislators on record in favor of the war (1979, 361).[29] Few Democrats initially expressed opposition to the conflict, or even public doubts about its direction or progress, but McCormack wanted to ensure that there was no open dissent. McCormack's active and enthusiastic championing of the war continued even as Republicans won control of the White House and as sentiment against the conflict gradually grew within his party in the House. This strongly suggests that the Speaker was acting neither on behalf of the policy objectives of his party in Congress nor to fulfill a responsibility toward the presidential party.

It could be argued that, initially, McCormack was seeking to accomplish the latter goal by defending the war, since Democrat Lyndon Johnson had great stakes riding on the outcome of the conflict during his presidency. But McCormack's enthusiasm did not wane with the election of Richard Nixon in 1968: in fact, McCormack continued to champion the president's conduct of the war, although he was markedly more circumspect with his endorsements in public (see, for example, Davidson, Hammond, and Smock 1998, 320). Furthermore, even under Johnson's presidency, the Speaker's support was often couched in terms related to the presidency as an institution, not to party politics. For instance, just before the passage of a supplemental military funding bill in May 1965, he argued that "the action of the House today is a clear indication to the entire world that our people are united behind the President of the United States, and not whether a Democrat or Republican presently occupies the White House, but our President" (*Congressional Record*, 5 May 1965, 9525). McCormack may have used such rhetoric to win votes from Republicans, but it nonetheless implies that the Speaker's actions were motivated by a duty to defend the prerogatives and powers of the institutional presidency on military matters.

McCormack may have been working to achieve another goal as well: passage of personally desired policy. His strong anticommunist views dated at least as far back as the 73rd Congress (1933–35), when he had chaired a special committee to investigate possible subversion activities by communist (as well as fascist) organizations. He also repeatedly touched on both his political and religious objections to communism in floor speeches and interviews throughout his career and saw the war in Vietnam largely in these terms (for example, McCormack Papers, McSweeny interview, box 195, tape 6). In one notable example from October 1967, McCormack seemed to reveal his strong personal views on the war in a speech delivered on the House floor. Public antiwar demonstrations and protests had been growing in size and frequency that year, and in mid-October the *New York Times* reported that North Vietnam's defense minister was encouraged by such activity, describing it as a "valuable mark of sympathy." In response, McCormack made a floor appearance during the morning hour of debate, proclaiming, "I would never exercise my right of dissent . . . if I thought that anything I said might directly or indirectly be adverse to the national interest of my country." With a copy of the day's *Times* in hand, and "pounding it on a table for emphasis," he closed with the remark that if he were making such criticism, "my conscience would be such that it would disturb me the rest of my life" (*Congressional Record*, 11 October 1967, 28611; Finney 1967; Schickler 2001, 172; Smith 1967; Swift et al. 2000).[30]

During the latter half of the McCormack Speakership, the House considered a number of bills related to the Vietnam War. Most passed with virtually no opposition, including:

- in May 1965, a bill to provide $700 million in supplemental funding for Vietnam, which McCormack endorsed in a floor speech (and which passed by 408 to 7);
- in February 1966, a $415 million supplemental foreign aid bill that included $275 for Vietnam (which passed, 350–27);
- in March 1966, a $4.8 billion military authorization bill, which McCormack also endorsed (passing 393–4);
- in March 1967, a $12 billion supplemental appropriations bill for the war (passing 385–11);
- in July 1968, a supplemental appropriations bill that included $6 billion in funding for Vietnam (which passed by voice vote).

It seems unlikely that the efforts of Speaker McCormack made much difference in the easy passage of these measures; nor is it known what McCormack may have done on their behalf, apart from sometimes speaking on the House floor. But the bills' appearance on the House floor may have nudged potential war opponents into declaring favorable positions on U.S. military policy early and often, while framing the war in terms of financial assistance rather than military strategy or the direction of the conflict. They also passed at a time of heightening opposition to the Vietnam War in Congress. In the Senate, this opposition was led most notably by Arkansas Senator J. William Fulbright, Democratic chairman of the Foreign Relations Committee; in the House, it emerged as early as 1965 when twenty-eight congressional Democrats openly petitioned the Foreign Affairs Committee to conduct hearings on the war (Josephy 1979, 361). By having these measures win by such wide margins, McCormack not only ensured their passage but also sent an important countersignal of party and congressional unity to the electorate and the White House.[31]

The result of at least one floor vote, however, can be attributed in part to McCormack's leadership. Despite the Speaker's efforts, throughout 1968 and early 1969 an expanding number of House Democrats and some liberal Republicans expressed reservations about the war, began fomenting legislative strategy, and introduced resolutions calling for the immediate withdrawal of U.S. troops. In late 1969, Congressman (and later Speaker) Jim Wright (D-TX) stepped in with a legislative initiative he hoped would signal bipartisan defense of the recently elected president, Richard Nixon, and perhaps move the peace talks forward as well, thus also achieving war opponents' goals. On November 4, Wright introduced a resolution that expressed the House's support for the president "in his efforts to negotiate a just peace in Vietnam" and for democratic elections in South Vietnam. As Wright later described it, "I felt that he [Nixon] was embattled" at the time and needed the help of Congress "because he was the president, and I didn't want the president to be embarrassed in the eyes of the world" (Finney 1969d; Wright 1996, 156–57; Jim Wright interview, July 2003).

From the perspective of McCormack and House leaders, the measure achieved more than just nonbinding support for the president (who had also endorsed the resolution). Because the resolution framed the war in terms of achieving a "just peace" and "free elections," it would be difficult for war opponents to vote against it. It also followed a contentious session the previous month, during which a scheduled series of late-night speeches by congressional war critics was abruptly ended by a 112–110 procedural vote, conducted by teller. Angry liberal Democrats had responded by killing a Republican resolution on Vietnam the following day, and they threatened to sponsor future debates on the floor (Finney 1969a; 1969b; 1969c; *New York Times,* 1 November 1969). The resolution would thus counter the perception of Democratic division on Vietnam and contain congressional opposition to the conflict.

The resolution drew backing from fifty Democrats and an equal number of Republicans, and the Speaker publicly endorsed it in early November. Sure enough, the measure put war critics on the defensive. Given a choice between endorsing the president and opposing a peaceful resolution of the conflict, many of them felt compelled to express their ideological preferences off the floor: eighty Democrats signed a letter stating that even if they did vote for the measure, they did not endorse the president's Vietnam policy. The resolution passed the House Foreign Affairs Committee after a meeting that was closed to the public, and liberals failed to win a floor vote to allow amendments, losing 132–225. Indicating its importance to the Speaker and Democratic leaders, a whip count was conducted before the measure went to the floor (Evans 2007). When it did, McCormack engaged in a short debate with California Democrat John Tunney. Tunney complained that the resolution could be interpreted as endorsing an indefinite deployment of U.S. troops in Vietnam, but McCormack replied simply that the goal of the United States should be to prevent "an imposed Communist coalition government" in South Vietnam. Despite the reservations of Tunney and others, the resolution passed by 334 to 55, with many war opponents feeling compelled to vote for the measure (Finney 1969c; 1969d; 1969e; *Congressional Record,* 1 December 1969, 36103).

HELPING THE PARTY IN CONGRESS
AND THE PRESIDENTIAL PARTY

Eight cases captured in the literature sweeps provide evidence for the claim that Speakers exercise leadership to aid the congressional party that nominated them to their leadership position. But these cases also reveal that Speakers can, at the same time, also seek to support the presidential party. A congressional party–oriented theory of leadership may therefore miss the importance of the presidential party in explaining Speakers' legislative activity. This is particularly so when the Speaker's actions threaten the objectives of a significant proportion of the majority party in Congress.

In this section I discuss four of the ten cases that are best explained by a combination of these two Speaker goals. The four present the strongest evidence among the ten of Speaker influence and demonstrate how both Rayburn and McCormack could exercise leadership to help fellow House Democrats and their presidential party.

Rayburn and the 21-Day Rule, 1949–50
(two cases)

Since the mid-1930s, the ability of the House Democratic Party to implement more liberal policy objectives had been hindered by the existence of a "conservative coalition" of loosely organized Republicans and southern conservative Democrats sharing similar ideological predispositions. In particular, the coalition's control of the Rules Committee, which sets the rules for considering legislation on the floor of the House, gave it the ability to block or modify liberal bills or to subject them to unfriendly floor amendments. After more than a decade of the conservative coalition's de facto control of the committee, however, liberal Democrats saw an opportunity to limit that influence: the 1948 elections brought the Democrats a party majority of 263 seats, taking control of the House from Republicans.

Shortly after the 1948 elections, several Democrats began considering ways to more permanently restrict the power of the conservative coalition. In private correspondence with Rayburn, the chairman-elect of the Rules Committee, A. J. Sabath (IL), proposed adding an additional Democrat to the committee, giving liberals a one-vote edge "so that we would have nine of thirteen that will go along and won't make yours [*sic*] and my life miserable" (Sam Rayburn Papers, letter from A. J. Sabath, 11 November 1948, box 3R341). But a more organized group of liberal members of the caucus, including Andrew Biemiller (WI), Herman Eberharter (PA), and Chet Holifield (CA), were developing a possible change to House rules to achieve the same objective. Speaker Rayburn, perhaps in response to their initiative, sent a letter to Eberharter in mid-November, asking to speak with him on the matter. Eberharter replied that, unlike Sabath, he believed "the problem is not so much the composition of the Committee, as the function it has exercised in reviewing and vetoing the substance of bills reported by the other committees" (Rayburn Papers, letter to Herman Eberharter, 15 November 1948, and letter from Herman Eberharter, 23 November 1948, box 3R341). With Rayburn's input, Eberharter and his allies eventually drafted a rule that would allow a committee chairman to forcibly discharge a bill—provided it had been approved by his committee and a request to consider it on the floor had stalled in the Rules Committee for at least twenty-one days—by mandating that the Speaker recognize the chairman on the floor for that purpose (Bolling 1968, 179; Schickler 2001, 173–75).

A party-based view of leadership in Congress might explain the attempt to enact such a rule as deriving from the Speaker's fundamental responsibility to ensure floor passage of caucus-preferred policy (Cox and McCubbins 1993; 2004). In this case, however, although the ideological concerns of House Democrats were important to Rayburn, just as important was his goal of helping the same-party president carry through his legislative program. Truman had been newly reelected, and Rayburn and other Democrats were doubtless aware that the Rules Committee could slow down or even stop the president's agenda (Truman 1959, 18). The chairman of the Democratic Caucus, Francis Walter of Pennsylvania, argued that the rule "means Mr. Truman's program can now go through the House," and newspaper coverage of the rule emphasized that its ultimate approval would be an indicator of Truman's influence in the House (Albright 1949a; Whitney 1949). By contrast, other goals of the Speaker were much less salient: the rule was not directly connected to the power or authority of the institutional presidency, it was unrelated to the interests of Rayburn's district, and at least one historical account suggests that Rayburn was much less enthusiastic about the rule than were liberal activists in his party (Goodwin 1970, 212–13; Lapham 1988). Nor was this case the same as the adoption of a 21-day rule four years later (see table 3.2), which was much less important for the presidential party: that rule was adopted under a same-party president with masterful legislative skills, large Democratic majorities in the House and Senate, and a Rules Committee with more sympathetic party members.

Rayburn's leadership on the 21-day rule was most evident in his negotiations with Eberharter on the nature of the rule, in securing its passage in the party caucus and on the floor, and in fighting against its repeal the following year. When the rule was proposed in the Democratic Caucus in January 1949, the party held a rare "binding" vote;[32] "guided" by Rayburn, who publicly endorsed it, the rule passed 176–48 (Albright 1949a; Bolling 1968, 179; Truman 1959, 18, 197). It is not known what lobbying efforts Rayburn undertook to secure its passage on the floor, but his endorsement was probably an important factor in the 275–143 vote to move the previous question and end debate on the measure. Rayburn then rushed it to passage as quickly as possible. After a short debate, he ignored one southerner's request for additional debate time and immediately called for a vote; and when it passed by a voice vote, Rayburn ruled that an insufficient number of legislators had risen to require a second, recorded vote (Albright 1949b).[33]

In 1950, conservative Democrats attempted to overturn the 21-day rule on the floor, hoping to recruit southerners by connecting the vote to the possible consideration of a bill creating a federal antidiscrimination commission. When a resolution repealing the rule was introduced, Rayburn, together with Majority Leader McCormack, decided to schedule floor consideration of the resolution in a way that would maximize votes for the 21-day rule. In a floor speech, the Speaker cited the rule's importance in enacting the president's agenda and that of his own congressional party, asking rhetorically, "Who won the election in 1948, anyhow?" (*Congressional Record,* 20 January 1950, 708). The resolution lost, 183–236, and the 21-day rule remained in place. Compared with the 1949 vote, northern Democrats had remained largely unified; however, while fifteen more Republicans voted for the rule than had the year before, more than fifty additional southern Democrats voted against the rule, indicating that raising the issue of civil rights had had some effect (Lapham 1988, 243; Schickler 2001, 177, 287).

An analysis of both the 1949 and 1950 votes on the 21-day rule shows the importance of both a reelection goal and support for the presidential party in explaining the Speaker's leadership. Eric Schickler, combining congressional and presidential party objectives into a single partisan motivation for behavior, finds that party ideology (as measured by NOMINATE data and party affiliation) has a strong and statistically significant effect in predicting the likelihood of voting for the rule on the floor in both 1949 and 1950 (2001, 174–78). But treating the two concerns separately reveals how they may have independently shaped legislator behavior and, by extension, the Speaker's leadership. Table 3.4 shows the results of the logit statistical models used by Schickler to predict the 1949 and 1950 votes compared with results reached by adding two dummy variables equal to 1 if a legislator's state gave a majority of its votes in the 1948 election to either Truman or Strom Thurmond, the southern Dixiecrat candidate who ran in opposition to Truman's civil rights platform.[34] The revised analysis of the 1949 vote reveals that although cross-party divisions (as captured by the W-NOMINATE second-dimension scale) fail to show significant predictive power, the success of Thurmond in a given congressman's state had a strongly negative effect on the likelihood of voting for the 21-day rule. These legislators had less incentive to stand behind Truman's policy agenda and may have feared that civil rights legislation would more easily reach the floor with the new rule. As further evidence of presidential party influencing support for the rule in 1949, a W-NOMINATE spatial map of voting behavior (not shown) reveals that of the eleven Democrats falsely predicted to vote for the rules change, all came from southern or border states, and seven represented pro-Thurmond states (Alabama, Louisiana, Mississippi, and South

Table 3.4 Logit Analysis of House Votes on 21-Day Rule, 1949–50

Variable	Model 1 (1949 Vote, Schickler Model)	Model 2 (1949 Vote, Adding Pres. Dummy)	Model 3 (1950 Vote, Schickler Model)	Model 4 (1950 Vote, Adding Pres. Dummy)
W-NOMINATE, 1st dimension	−8.928***	−9.503***	−9.279**	−10.569**
	(1.636)	(1.769)	(1.712)	(1.870)
W-NOMINATE, 2nd dimension	−1.529^	−1.228	−4.452***	−3.869***
	(0.805)	(0.873)	(0.830)	(0.853)
Democrat	−0.386	−0.170	−2.236	−2.861*
	(1.359)	(1.436)	(1.379)	(1.426)
Truman won state	—	−0.274	—	−0.303
		(0.454)		(0.459)
Thurmond won state	—	−2.230**	—	−3.729**
		(0.762)		(1.340)
Constant	2.124**	2.529**	2.259**	3.018**
	(0.760)	(0.879)	(0.762)	(0.879)
N	416	416	423	423
Pseudo-R^2	.585	.606	.511	.670

Note: Coefficients in models 1 and 3 differ slightly in size, though not in sign, from Schickler (2001) due to the use of a slightly different measure of legislator preference points (W-NOMINATE) to measure legislator ideology.

^ $p < 0.1$, * $p < 0.05$, ** $p < 0.01$, *** $p < .001$ (two-tailed test)

Carolina). The cross-party divisions were more salient in the 1950 vote, probably because rule opponents, as noted above, sought to connect the rule explicitly to the potential passage of a civil rights bill.

The rule did not have the effect its supporters had hoped for. It was used only eight times during the 81st Congress, and although the threat of its use may have compelled the Rules Committee to release additional bills, it was not employed for any significant Democratic legislation. In the end, the rule did not survive the 1950 elections. Democrats lost nearly thirty seats in the House that year, the conservative coalition regained its majority status on the floor, and the 21-day rule was quickly revoked at the start of the next Congress (Galloway 1976, 186; Schickler 2001, 177–78).

Rayburn and Taft-Hartley Repeal, 1949

When Democrats regained control of the House and Senate in the 1948 elections, and Truman narrowly won reelection to the White House, the party set its sights on repealing the Taft-Hartley Act, a stringent antilabor measure passed in the previous Republican Congress. Taft-Hartley had become law in response to accusations of improper union activity and a growing number of labor strikes. It contained provisions that organized labor considered particularly onerous, including a ban on union-only (or "closed") shops, a requirement that union officers affirm that they were not communists, and a greater ability for the government to halt potential labor strikes (Stark 1949; Taft 1964, 579–84).

For Rayburn and a majority of House Democrats, weakening Taft-Hartley achieved important policy and electoral objectives of the congressional party. The Democratic Party's 1948 platform called explicitly for ending Taft-Hartley, which was also a top priority for organized labor, an important Democratic constituency. But an explanation of leader behavior looking only at the congressional party ignores Rayburn's desire to help his presidential party by revisiting Taft-Hartley. Truman had vetoed the original Taft-Hartley bill; after the 1948 election, he made Taft-Hartley repeal a part of his "Fair Deal" legislative agenda; his staff would later work with congressional party leaders in crafting a compromise prolabor bill that could pass the House; and he even went so far as to threaten Democratic labor opponents in Congress with a loss of patronage (Johnson and Porter 1973, 433; *New York Times,* 29 April 1949; Pomper 1959, 164–65; Steinberg 1975, 251). In pressing for repeal of Taft-Hartley, the Speaker thus could satisfy the goal of achieving the same-party president's policy objectives as well as champion the interests of the majority of his party in Congress.

Rayburn and other Democratic leaders had to find a way to revoke as much of Taft-Hartley as possible over the likely opposition of the conservative coalition of Republicans and their Democratic allies. Thus their initial bill did not repeal Taft-Hartley outright. Known by the name of its original sponsor, Michigan Democrat John Lesinski, the measure was introduced in early 1949 and later approved by the House Education and Labor Committee. It would effectively replace Taft-Hartley with the prolabor Wagner Act of 1935 but retain some limits on unions, such as a prohibition on some secondary boycotts and strikes.

Meanwhile, Republicans and southern Democrats crafted a substitute amendment, sponsored by conservative southerner John Wood (D-GA), which made only cosmetic changes to the Taft-Hartley Act. Rayburn responded by employing a legislative tactic to head off Wood's substitute amendment. Fearing that it might draw enough votes from moderate Democrats to pass on the floor, Rayburn and labor supporters endorsed a second substitute amendment, to be offered by Representative Hugo Sims (D-SC) in the event that Wood's amendment were to pass. The Sims bill put some limits on labor unions but was less stringent than Taft-Hartley; its provisions had been drafted in negotiations between unions, House Democratic leaders, and the Truman White House. Many labor leaders were unhappy with the union limits in the Sims amendment, but some at least recognized that if the Sims amendment passed, it would make the Wood proposal more labor-friendly, perhaps forcing the conservative coalition to reject it entirely (Loftus 1949; Pomper 1959, 147–48, 163–67; Taft 1964, 587; Truman 1959, 20–21).

Because the Lesinski bill and the Wood and Sims amendments would be considered under an open floor rule, Taft-Hartley defenders had a key strategic advantage: the ability to freely modify the Wood substitute amendment to gain more votes, if necessary.[35] The Wood amendment to the bill was offered first, but when pro-Wood legislators perceived that their measure was too antilabor to pass, conservatives successfully amended the measure several times to build support among moderate Representatives. In a rare move, Rayburn cast a vote himself (against the Wood language),[36] but it nonetheless passed the House on May 3 by a 210–196 teller vote. An attempt to defeat it in a second, roll call vote also failed: Wood passed, 217–203, with Rayburn failing to prevent sixty-nine southern Democrats from voting for the antilabor amendment. The original Lesinski bill had now been altered by the Wood amendment to effectively keep the Taft-Hartley law as it was (Pomper 1959, 162–63, 168; Truman 1959, 21; Stavisky 1949).

Rayburn's second line of defense, the Sims amendment, also failed to garner a majority. Although the Speaker spoke on its behalf and against Wood, arguing that the Sims substitute represented "the proper approach to passing legislation the vast majority of the people will feel is fair" (*Congressional Record,* 3 May 1949, 5512), the Sims amendment failed by a vote of 183–211, with "several conspicuous labor supporters" among those voting no (Truman 1959, 21).

With only one day left to consider the newly amended Lesinski bill, two votes remained: a motion to recommit the bill (now consisting of the labor-unfriendly Wood provisions) to committee, and final passage of the bill. Rayburn and other leaders promptly undertook what one historian described as a "herculean" lobbying campaign, making every effort to convince at least eight Democratic supporters of Wood to switch their position and vote for the motion to recommit.[37] Passage of the motion would keep the amended bill from a final floor vote and give Democrats a chance to weaken Taft-Hartley at some future point. The focus on getting Wood endorsers to vote for the motion to recommit also made sense, because doing so would be a less obvious reversal (and had less serious consequences) than voting to kill the bill completely. Rayburn's efforts paid off: on May 4, by a slim vote of 212–209, the labor bill was recommitted to the Education and Labor Committee. A photo in the next day's *New York Times* showed Lesinski and two other gleeful congressmen each holding up three fingers, representing the size of their victory (Loftus 1949; Pomper 1959, 168; Taft 1964, 587; Truman 1959, 21).

Ten Democrats, all but one from the South, had gone from supporting the Wood amendment the previous day to voting for recommittal (Pomper 1959, 168–69). Although the press made much of these apparent "reversals" (for example, Loftus 1949), the recommittal vote was not technically the same as voting for Wood, so their behavior alone does not tell us whether these ten legislators voted as they did because of personal preferences or due to outside pressure. A W-NOMINATE estimation of legislator preferences can better identify voting behavior that cannot be explained by ideology. Specifically, I use it to test the "true" preferences of two types of Democrats: those who voted for the Wood amendment but then voted for recommittal (and were thus possibly subject to leadership lobbying between votes), and those who voted against Wood and for recommittal (thus possibly subject to leadership lobbying before either vote was cast).

Of the ten from the first category, four voted for recommittal contrary to their estimated preferences; all four had voted for Wood as predicted by those same preferences (see table 3.5). These four most clearly "reversed" themselves and are the likeliest candidates for having responded to pressure from Rayburn and/or other party leaders. (Three others voted for recommittal as expected, but their votes for Wood were contrary to prediction; they may have voted for Wood under pressure from conservatives but subsequently followed their ideological beliefs to support the motion.) Of Democrats in the second category, six cast a pair of votes in the leadership-preferred direction (that is, against Wood and for recommittal), but their votes were not correctly predicted by W-NOMINATE. It is therefore quite possible that at least four House Democrats, and perhaps six others, were influenced in their vote choice by Rayburn's leadership.

This case represented both a failure and a success for the Speaker. Rayburn had been unable to significantly amend or repeal the Taft-Hartley Act, but he had prevented passage of additional antilabor legislation, denied conservatives a major victory on the floor, and left open a second opportunity for labor-friendly legislation in the 81st Congress—though union supporters were unable

Table 3.5 Analysis of the 1949 Taft-Hartley Repeal Votes

Category of Legislator	Member (Democrat)	W-NOMINATE predicts vote for Wood?	W-NOMINATE predicts vote for recommit?
Voted for Wood, then for motion to recommit	*Norrell (AR)*	Yes	No
	Herlong (FL)	Yes	No
	Tackett (AR)	Yes	No
	Harris (AR)	Yes	No
	Fallon (MD)	No	Yes
	Evins (TN)	No	Yes
	Hays (AR)	No	Yes
	Bolton (MD)	Yes	Yes
	Peterson (FL)	Yes	Yes
	Hardy (VA)	Yes	Yes
Voted against Wood, then for motion to recommit, both votes unpredicted[a]	*Burleson (TX)*	No	No
	Thompson (TX)	No	No
	Bennett (FL)	No	No
	Jones (NC)	No	No
	Sikes (FL)	No	No
	Smathers (FL)	No	No

Note: Italicized names indicate those legislators more likely to have voted for the motion to recommit due to factors beyond ideological preferences (for example, influence by party leaders).

[a] In addition, at least three Democrats voted against the Wood amendment and for the motion to recommit, but only their first vote was unpredicted (Asa Allen, LA; John Lyle, TX; and Wilbur Mills, AR). These are likely to be "true" errors in the model since it is unlikely that Rayburn would have failed to persuade these Democrats to vote to recommit after they had already rejected the Wood amendment, though they could have been successfully lobbied by Wood supporters to do so.

to craft an acceptable bill that could pass on the House floor, and no such legislation became law in that Congress.

Rayburn and Rules Committee Expansion, 1961

The initial expansion of the House Rules Committee in 1961 is perhaps the most famous case involving Rayburn's leadership. It represented arguably the boldest challenge to the chamber's conservative coalition and served as a capstone to the career of the Speaker, who died later that year. John McCormack later described it in an interview as "one of the most dramatic legislative fights that I've ever participated in" (McCormack Papers, McSweeny interview, box 196, tape 11).

Much has been written about the campaign to add three legislators to the Rules Committee and why it happened at the beginning of the 87th Congress.[38] Both Democratic liberals and newly elected President John F. Kennedy were the crucial actors that pressed for a change to the committee. Support from within the congressional party can be traced to the midterm elections of 1958, when Democrats gained nearly fifty seats in the House, many of which were won by young left-leaning candidates. As a result, the party saw an opportunity to limit the independence of the conservative-dominated Rules Committee, and in early 1959, a group of more than one hundred progressive Democrats sent two of their members to discuss some possible changes to the committee with Rayburn. The Speaker balked at endorsing a new 21-day rule, which he felt gave committee chairmen too much authority (see discussion of earlier 21-day rule above) and resisted making any change to the personnel of the Rules Committee. Instead, Rayburn agreed to make every effort to keep the committee from being unduly obstructionist, with help from his friend and colleague Joe Martin, the Republican minority leader. But Rayburn was unable to fulfill his promise when Charles Halleck, a more conservative Republican from Indiana, was elected minority leader and subsequently placed two like-minded Republicans on the committee. Halleck's move strengthened the conservative coalition's control over Rules, which proceeded to kill or modify several pieces of liberal legislation, renewing the complaints of liberal Democrats (Bolling 1964, 207; Cummings and Peabody 1969, 256–59; Kofmehl 1964, 263; Reston 1959).

Ideological pressures from within his caucus may have led Rayburn to reform the Rules Committee after 1960, but a focus on congressional party policy concerns fails to explain why the Speaker did not seek to impose institutional changes in 1959, when such concerns were also salient. However, by taking into account a second goal of the Speaker—to assist a same-party president—one can explain both the timing of, and the motivation for, Rayburn's leadership. In January 1961, with a Democrat in the White House for the first time in eight years, Rayburn did not want to see the president's partisan agenda curtailed by conservative congressmen. President Kennedy himself was keenly concerned about the power of the conservative coalition and expressed as much to Rayburn during a preinaugural meeting with the Speaker and other top congressional leaders; in an early private conference with select leaders and representatives, Rayburn also framed the matter as hindering Kennedy's legislative agenda. In addition, the president's initial lack of involvement in pressing for changes to the committee was due primarily to the Speaker, who first insisted that outside lobbying would backfire and potentially threaten the independence of the House. When Rayburn later changed his mind, Kennedy and his aides made both public statements and phone calls to legislators to urge support for changing the balance of power on the committee. Indeed, Kennedy's use of direct phone calls to even "obscure" representatives on behalf of committee expansion left those legislators "flabbergasted" (Berman 1964, 84; Bolling 1964, 209–10; Hardeman and Bacon 1987, 450–59; Remini 2006, 384; Steinberg 1975, 335). [39]

Rayburn first had to choose from among several possible methods for weakening the conservative coalition's control over Rules. One plan, to remove the conservative Mississippi Democrat William Colmer from the committee, would be relatively easy to accomplish—it required only a vote in the party caucus, not a change to House rules—but could easily instigate an open revolt by southern Democrats. Rayburn decided instead to threaten such a purge to gain southerners' backing for a less drastic approach: changing the House rules to add two additional Democrats and one new Republican to the committee. This rule change would apply only to the current Congress and would have to be renewed two years later, making it more palatable to skeptics. After negotiations between Rayburn, southerners, and Rules Chairman Howard Smith, the Speaker's gambit worked: the caucus endorsed the expansion in mid-January, albeit with much personal lobbying by the Speaker, and Smith agreed to have his committee report a resolution expanding Rules by three (Bolling 1964, 211–12, 215–16; Cummings and Peabody 1969, 261; Hardeman and Bacon 1987, 452–56; Remini 2006, 385; Steinberg 1975, 335–36).

But the rule change would still have to pass on the floor of the House, the other principal platform of the conservative coalition. Several factors would make the battle difficult for Rayburn: Democrats had lost twenty House seats in the 1960 election, most southerners were likely to oppose the committee expansion, and the House Republicans' leadership was working hard to keep its partisans united. Rayburn and his Democratic allies began an intensive lobbying campaign, using "every possible persuasive technique" to win on the floor (Bolling 1964, 217). The party conducted a whip count to determine likely supporters and opponents; the Speaker met with freshmen Democrats, who had not yet been given committee assignments and were thus more susceptible to leadership influence; and Rayburn lobbied his own Texas delegation, persuaded one Democrat to cancel a trip planned for the day of the vote, and called upon outside organizations and elected officials to lobby legislators (Bolling 1964, 217–18; Evans 2007; Hardeman and Bacon 1987, 456–59). Majority Leader John McCormack, recalling the lobbying campaign years later, noted that both the presidential and congressional parties were salient: "Speaker Rayburn and I would talk to, to try and persuade them [doubtful supporters] and convince them to vote for this change . . . in the interest of good government and in the interest of the program of the Democratic Party, and the program submitted to the Congress by President Kennedy" (McCormack Papers, McSweeny interview, box 196, tape 11).

Rayburn delayed the vote for several days, gaining precious time to lobby legislators. On the day of the vote, party leaders counted on at least two or three "pocket" ballots, or legislators willing to switch their votes if needed, and Rayburn personally may have had more. Nonetheless, as McCormack later recounted, "Rayburn and I felt we had the votes, but we weren't sure." Finally, Rayburn delivered a floor speech endorsing the measure right before the vote took place. The result was a 217–212 victory for Rayburn (Bolling 1964, 219; Cummings and Peabody 1969, 273n43; Hardeman and Bacon 1987, 459–60, 462–63; quote McCormack Papers, McSweeny interview, box 196, tape 11).

The outcome was likely due to a combination of factors. District and ideological concerns may have played a part: according to one study, the twenty-two Republicans who voted for the committee expansion were either relatively liberal or represented urban or pro-Kennedy districts, whereas many of the thirty-six Democratic supporters from the South were more left-leaning and had fewer African Americans in their districts than their fellow southern brethren. More important, Rayburn influenced the vote choice of a number of legislators. Two observers subsequently noted that "a sense of personal loyalty to the Speaker" seemed to drive the votes of several southern Democrats, such as Georgian John Pilcher (who admitted as much), and Rayburn probably took advantage of "state delegation solidarity" to bring over some fellow Texans (Cummings and Peabody 1969, 266n36, 270–72, 273–77).[40] Though Rayburn kept hidden the identity of the legislators he lobbied, a W-NOMINATE analysis (not shown) indicates that, of the fourteen Democrats falsely predicted to oppose the bill, four were from Texas (J. T. Rutherford, Olin Teague, W. R. Poage, and Robert Casey) and a fifth was Congressman Pilcher.[41]

The result was a clear victory for Kennedy and the party's liberal and mainstream members. Although the newly expanded Rules Committee did not always perform as hoped in the 87th Congress, occasionally blocking the administration's more objectionable bills, it nonetheless was much more compliant to the Speaker's wishes than the previous Congress's committee had been (Morris 1962b; Peabody 1963). When Rayburn's successor, John McCormack, succeeded in making the expansion permanent two years later, he did so on behalf of a similar array of interests (see table 3.2).

McCormack and the Farm Bill, 1962

Beginning in the 1950s, American farmers faced a growing problem of sinking farm prices and profits, caused in part by overproduction of such agricultural commodities as grains and cotton. Federal farm policy was limited in what it could do to help. Because the federal government established price supports by purchasing surplus goods, it incurred rising storage costs when production expanded. The few production controls it did impose were limited to certain crops and were widely seen as both ineffective and outdated (Cochrane and Ryan 1976, 76–79; *Congressional Quarterly Almanac* 1962, 94; Hadwiger and Talbot 1965, 8–12).

In response, in January 1962 President Kennedy proposed what one account termed "the most stringent permanent production and marketing controls in history" (*Congressional Quarterly Almanac* 1962, 94). Kennedy's plan would limit production of key surplus commodities, particularly wheat, feed grains, and dairy goods, using new mandatory programs to curtail agricultural supply. His plan would also reduce the amount of cropland by converting it to other uses, such as park or timber land. The ultimate objective was to reduce supply without significantly increasing costs to consumers or the federal government (Cochrane and Ryan 1976, 42; *Congressional Quarterly Almanac* 1962, 94, 96).

The proposal was of considerable importance to the president. During his election campaign two years before, Kennedy had promised to address the farm crisis by reducing supply, and he claimed an electoral mandate for such policy when he received large numbers of votes from farmers in the 1960 election. Kennedy had formally requested legislation to implement agricultural reform in March of 1961, but with only minimal success: the bill that passed Congress temporarily extended some existing agricultural programs and included voluntary (but not mandatory) reductions of acreage dedicated to wheat cultivation. In short, as one press account put it, the 1962 proposal was "clearly was among the 'most wanted' measures on President Kennedy's legislative program." The high priority Kennedy placed on agriculture reform meant that Speaker McCormack would satisfy an important goal of aiding the same-party president by standing behind the measure (Cochrane and Ryan 1976, 41; Hadwiger and Talbot 1965, 25–27; Morris 1962a).

But passing Kennedy's reform bill would help House Democrats, too. Many of them had criticized the Eisenhower administration's plan to resolve the overproduction problem by ending farm price supports and using free market mechanisms. By campaigning, often successfully, on a platform attacking this approach, House Democrats may have felt the need to endorse a positive alternative to the Eisenhower policy. A number of congressional Democrats also came from agricultural states where farmers' incomes had been affected by overproduction (Cochrane and Ryan 1976, 78; Hadwiger and Talbot 1965, 13). By contrast, other goals of the Speaker were not salient in this particular case. The proposal was unrelated to the institutional presidency or the House as a whole, and it seems unlikely that McCormack, coming from a northeastern urban district, had a personal or constituent-driven motive for championing the bill.

Unfortunately for McCormack, both ideological and regional considerations made enactment of the bill very problematic. Many House Republicans and some southern Democrats, who opposed expanding the power of the federal government, were likely to reject the measure's imposition of major federal controls over agriculture. Some legislators from agricultural districts were wary of its mandatory limits on farmers' production and unhappy that it would phase out existing monetary payments to farmers. Furthermore, Republicans from urban and suburban districts, concerned about increasing food prices, worried that production limits would hinder full competition and thereby keep commodity prices high. Thus while a majority of Democrats initially were in favor of the bill, enough House members opposed individual portions of the measure to put its passage on the floor in doubt (Cochrane and Ryan 1976, 42; *Congressional Quarterly Almanac* 1962, 106, 114).

This opposition initially caused serious problems for Kennedy and McCormack. The bill first passed the Senate, but after a series of delays, it was approved in a tumultuous meeting of the House Agriculture Committee by a mere one-vote margin.[42] Although the Kennedy administration had initially predicted a legislative victory in the House, Agriculture Secretary Orville Freeman soon voiced concern that the bill's fate on the floor, just as in committee, might be determined by an extremely narrow vote. Meanwhile, the possibility of winning congressional seats in the 1962 midterm elections encouraged House Republicans to oppose the bill, seeing its defeat as an opportunity to embarrass the president. Bolstered by unanimous opposition to the farm bill from the Republican Policy Committee, Minority Leader Charles Halleck urged his colleagues to reject the measure. Unable to garner pledges of support from a majority of the House, Democratic party leaders postponed the vote for several days while White House officials and others continued to lobby legislators and McCormack urged supporters, such as Frank Boykin (D-AL), to be present for the vote (Blair 1962a; *Congressional Quarterly Almanac* 1962, 113; Hadwiger and Talbot 1965, 144–69, 194–95, 197; Hansen 1991, 150; McCormack Papers, telegram to Boykin, 19 June 1962, box 108 folder 1; Morris 1962a; *New York Times,* 13 June 1962).

Despite the Speaker's efforts, lobbying by the White House, and the possession of four pocket votes by Majority Leader Carl Albert (D-OK), a motion to recommit the bill passed by 215 to 205. McCormack and fellow party leaders had been stymied by near-unanimous Republican opposition and absences among pro-bill Democrats. Most notably, forty-eight Democrats voted against the bill. Many had done so either in retaliation for being denied the chance to speak or offer amendments on the floor, or because of a haphazard, confusing, and last-minute attempt by bill supporters to gain votes through floor amendments (Hadwiger and Talbot 1965, 203–9; Hansen 1991, 150; Mac-Neil 1963, 361).

Farm bill supporters quickly dropped the measure's most controversial element, mandatory production controls for feed grains, and succeeded in passing the bill in July 1962. But new problems arose after members of the House and Senate met in conference committee to work out differences between their respective measures. The completed conference report omitted the original production controls, but it did include other, potentially controversial programs, such as a reduction of acreage allotments for wheat production. House Republicans and the American Farm Bureau complained about the bill's newly restrictive production and marketing limits. By September 20, the scheduled day to vote on the conference report, party leaders believed the bill was doomed because of the nearness of the election and the departure of some House Democrats to their districts to campaign (Blair 1962b; *Congressional Quarterly Almanac* 1962, 94, 123; MacNeil 1963, 361).

McCormack and his fellow party leaders, however, managed to pull out a last-minute victory. When voting began on the House floor, they assumed that the conference report would fail, but the running vote tally soon suggested there was momentum building toward passage. Albert and Congressman Hale Boggs quickly lobbied likely Democratic opponents, while McCormack, presiding over the House, "beckoned a couple of Representatives to come to the Speaker's chair, where he asked them, desperately, to support the President's bill" (MacNeil 1963, 362). Stalling, Democratic members started asking how their votes were recorded, and McCormack overruled a Republican point of order against their requests. Finally, what had been an eight-vote deficit was turned into five-vote victory, and the conference report passed by a narrow 202–197. As reporter Neil MacNeil later put it, party leaders "had at the last moment plucked victory out of seemingly certain defeat with a few half-spoken words and great tactical skill" (Duscha 1962; MacNeil 1963, 361–63).

Although it is not known who specifically was lobbied by McCormack or other party leaders on the day of the vote, three Democrats—Hugh Carey (NY), Donald Magnuson (WA), and J. T. Rutherford (TX)—are noted in the *Congressional Record* as having switched their votes from opposing to favoring the bill, with one Republican (Chester Merrow of New Hampshire) flipping the opposite way. McCormack and his colleagues may have helped persuade at least some of the twenty Democrats who opposed the original bill but voted for the conference report, countering the eleven Democrats who had switched their votes in the other direction (*Congressional Quarterly Almanac* 1962, 123; *Congressional Record*, 20 September 1962, 20129–30).

HELPING THE PARTY IN CONGRESS

In five of the cases captured in the literature sweeps, either Rayburn or Mc-Cormack acted principally to defend his congressional party's policy interests and/or bolster its majority status. In these cases, a particular legislative outcome was believed to contribute to the reelection chances of the Speaker's party in the House, was a clearly identified and developed policy objective of a substantial majority of the party, or was both. Thus they represent the strongest evidence for party-oriented theories of leadership in Congress, though they sometimes were associated with major disagreements within the Democratic Caucus.

While congressional party preferences were paramount to the Speaker in these specific instances, other Speaker goals sometimes mattered as well, albeit secondarily (see tables 3.1 and 3.2). In some cases, evidence suggests that the Speaker also considered how his leadership could aid the presidential party, even if presidential party considerations were secondary to, or overshadowed by, the concerns of the Speaker's party in the House. On occasion, the Speaker may also have sought to enact policy he personally desired. Even these examples, then, suggest a more nuanced portrayal of Speaker leadership than party-based theories offer. The two cases I focus on below both involve Rayburn, and provide strong evidence of Speaker influence and also suggest the importance of other leadership goals in driving the Speaker.

Rayburn and Civil Rights, 1956–57

One of Rayburn's most concealed uses of legislative leadership involved civil rights for African Americans, an issue that cut across Democratic Party lines more deeply than perhaps any other. The repression of southern blacks, particularly the denial of their right to vote, reflected the strong preferences of most southern House Democrats and their voting constituents and represented a critical pillar of the southern white political regime. Northern Democratic liberals, by contrast, were more sympathetic to the civil rights cause, and for decades they had tried to enact legislation against lynching and race-based voting restrictions, usually with the help of some congressional Republicans.[43] But southern Democrats possessed important structural and procedural advantages in Congress that allowed them to block such measures, including chairmanships of key committees, positions of leadership within their party, and the Senate filibuster (see, for example, Bolling 1964, 174–75).

Two events in the mid-1950s helped shift the political equation in the liberals' favor. In 1954, the Supreme Court in *Brown v. Board of Education* nullified the "separate-but-equal" doctrine and mandated school desegregation. This pushed civil rights further up the national agenda and pressed the federal government to intercede on blacks' behalf against defiant southern whites. The ruling also encouraged civil rights lobbying groups and key Democratic constituencies, such as organized labor and the National Association for the Advancement of Colored People (NAACP), to petition Congress on behalf of civil rights legislation. The second event was the 1955 lynching of Chicago youth Emmett Till in Mississippi. Widespread coverage of the murder, and the subsequent show trial, in northern black publications and in the national press further raised awareness of southern racial discrimination and violence (Bolling 1964, 175–76; Caro 2002, 702–9; Whitfield 1988, 145–47).

According to Missouri Democrat Richard Bolling, a well-respected member of Congress and supporter of civil rights at the time, the campaign to enact a voting rights bill for African Americans began in late 1955. After a private meeting with NAACP representatives and other favorable legislators, Bolling consulted with Rayburn and proposed that the House pursue civil rights legislation. This placed the Speaker in a political dilemma. On the one hand, such legislation would badly split House Democrats and, even if it were to pass, would face almost certain defeat in the Senate. On the other hand, a majority of Democrats in the House (as well as some Republicans) were in favor of federal civil rights protections to at least some degree, and failure to act could risk the congressional party's national reputation and push northern blacks, an important and growing constituency, away from the Democratic Party. This latter concern may have been somewhat hypothetical in 1955, but it became more tangible when the 1956 elections showed greater-than-expected numbers of northern blacks voting for Eisenhower and Republican candidates for public office (Bolling 1964, 175–77; Caro 2002, 841–43).[44] On balance, the future of the party as the majority in the House seemed contingent upon positive action of some sort.

Although the congressional party was probably first and foremost in Rayburn's mind, two other considerations played a secondary role. The first was achieving the goals of the presidential party. The Eisenhower administration espoused expanded rights for African Americans (and formally introduced civil rights bills in 1956 and 1957), but the president's support for the issue was often limited and equivocal. For Democrats, however, lack of progress on civil rights legislation could harm the party's chances for retaking the White House if the matter became an election-year issue. Inaction on, or public opposition to, civil rights threatened to openly divide the Democratic Party, a result that could be a serious blow to their presidential prospects. By contrast, a successful bill—particularly one with at least some southern Democrats on record in favor—would counter the perception that the party could not provide national leadership on the issue. Second, the Speaker himself may have had personal reasons for endorsing civil rights legislation. Though a longtime segregationist, Rayburn was becoming more sympathetic to the idea of granting voting rights for blacks. An electoral incentive to remain in Congress, however, was not salient in this case: in fact, Rayburn's district was solidly conservative on racial issues and against granting civil rights protections to African Americans (Ambrose 1984, 406, 413; Bolling 1964, 177–78; Caro 2002, 781–82; Champagne 1984, 12; Hardeman and Bacon 1987, 420–21). In short, by supporting civil rights legislation, Rayburn would help secure his Speakership by ensuring his party remained in the majority, but he could also, to a lesser extent, achieve two other goals: passage of personally desired policy and fulfillment of his responsibility to help the presidential party.

Ultimately, Rayburn opted to stand behind Bolling's efforts to enact a voting rights bill, but do so covertly. His decision to avoid taking a public position on the bill but to lend quiet support for it when needed reflected in part his desire not to alienate southern conservatives in his party, and in part his awareness of the segregationist sentiments of his constituents (Peters 1997, 134).

Rayburn's basic legislative strategy (as recommended by Bolling) was to delay meaningful consideration of a civil rights bill until late 1956, denying Senate Democrats enough time to mount an embarrassing filibuster before adjournment, and to make a stronger effort to enact legislation the following year.[45] Although he kept his influence largely concealed from the public eye and delegated legislative leadership to others, Rayburn "gave it his all-out support" in both 1956 and again in 1957 (Bolling 1968, 193). When the first bill came to the floor in 1956,[46] House southerners, who had developed an organized strategy against the measure, tried several procedural tactics to weaken or kill it. At one point, they attempted to pass an anti–civil rights amendment by surrendering all of their allotted time for debate, hoping to force an early vote before the amendment's opponents could get to the floor. Rayburn encountered Bolling just outside the House chamber and immediately alerted him to the gambit (Bolling 1964, 179–81; 1968, 193–94; Caro 2002, 791–92; Remini 2006, 372–73). Although the bill did ultimately pass in July of that year, 279–126, the Senate adjourned as expected, avoiding the possibility of a filibuster.

When a civil rights bill was reintroduced in 1957 and came to the floor in June, the Speaker lobbied key uncertain or resistant legislators, including southerners, to vote for it. In addition, after conservative southerner Howard Smith offered a procedural objection that could have derailed the bill, Rayburn used his authority to interpret House rules to dismiss the objection (Bolling 1964, 184; Hardeman and Bacon 1987, 421–22). The measure passed, 286–126, although Rayburn had failed to recruit many southern representatives: as with the 1956 bill, virtually all northern and southern Democrats were on opposite sides of the vote. When the final conference version of the bill was scheduled for an August floor vote, Rayburn lobbied his delegation, keeping a personal "work list" of Texas Democrats' positions on the bill. Aided by changes to the bill that weakened certain civil rights provisions, Rayburn's efforts this time were more successful: although all twenty-one Texans had voted against the original House legislation, six of the eight delegation members whose intentions were undetermined told Rayburn that they would support the conference report,[47] and Texas representatives voted 12–7 in favor of it (Rayburn Papers, file 3R451). In "unexpected . . . one-sidedness" (Caro 2002, 997), the report itself passed on the floor by a vote of 279–97, with twenty-two southern Democrats voting for it.

Notwithstanding the large margins by which both bills passed, the Speaker's lobbying, procedural rulings, and strategic assistance at key moments played an important role in the final vote. Interestingly, a two-dimensional W-NOMI-

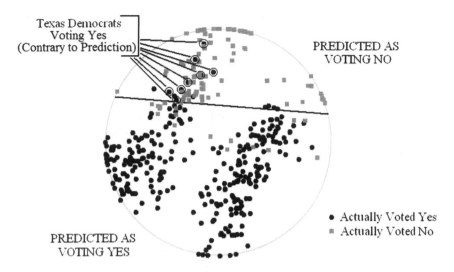

Figure 3.2 W-NOMINATE Estimates of Legislator Vote Choice, 1957 Civil Rights Bill, Conference Report

NATE estimation of likely legislator vote choice, shown in figure 3.2, reveals that eight of the eleven House members voting for the bill contrary to prediction were from Rayburn's home state, including four of the formerly uncommitted Texans lobbied by Rayburn.[48] In addition to the eight Texans, two Oklahoma representatives voted for the bill contrary to prediction (Toby Morris and Thomas Steed), as did a legislator from Missouri (William Hull).

Rayburn and Labor Reform, 1959

A decade after the passage of the Taft-Hartley Act, which imposed a number of legal restrictions on labor union organization and activity (see above), House Democrats faced renewed pressure to curtail organized labor. Though major work stoppages and media reports of union corruption had become more frequent in the mid- to late-1950s, the catalyst for action occurred in the 85th Congress (1957–58), when a special Senate select committee, chaired by Arkansas Democrat John McClellan, began a series of public hearings on the subject of union mismanagement. The televised hearings, and the committee's 1958 report, highlighted illegal activity within several union organizations and "materially changed the climate for labor legislation." President Eisenhower also urged Congress to enact legislation addressing union corruption.[49] Passage of legislation to stem labor corruption thus appeared highly probable (Bolling 1964, 156–57; Patterson 1966, 1; Peters 1997, 134–35; quote from Bolling 1964, 157).

Unlike in 1947, when sympathetic Republican majorities in Congress made passage of the Taft-Hartley Act possible, Democrats controlled both chambers in the 85th Congress; and those Democrats could, in theory, prevent any labor reform bill from being considered. But while northern liberals in the House were generally allied closely with labor unions, southern conservatives not only were much less sympathetic to unions but could form a majority with Republicans to pass more strict labor reform in the House (Peters 1997, 135). Yet even pro-union Democrats felt pressure to pass such legislation. This pressure derived from two sources: the Senate, where reform legislation was certain to be introduced, and the public, which Gallup opinion polls revealed was both familiar with the Senate investigation and decreasingly supportive of labor unions.[50]

The Senate moved quickly, approving a union reform bill in June 1958. Rayburn delayed the bill's referral to the House Education and Labor Committee, however, in order to ensure the committee successfully approved another worker-related bill already under consideration. Although the AFL-CIO had helped write the Senate reform bill and had endorsed its passage, the delay gave bill opponents (both conservative groups and other unions) the chance to mobilize against the measure, and it lost on the House floor, 190–198 (Bolling 1964, 157–58; Patterson 1966, 3).[51]

Advocates of organized labor took heart when the 1958 elections brought almost fifty new Democrats to the House, many of them left-leaning, resulting in a swollen 283-seat Democratic majority. But there were still dangers if Rayburn failed to act on behalf of union reform. With both the public and the media expressing concern about corruption,[52] even party liberals and union leaders acknowledged that legislation was necessary and/or that inaction could hurt congressional Democrats in the elections of 1960. In addition to the electoral worries of Rayburn's congressional party, the fate of the presidential party may have been a secondary consideration for the Speaker, even though neither party had yet chosen their presidential nominee. Since Democrats were more closely associated with unions than Republicans, there was some fear that failure to act on labor legislation could hurt Democratic candidates for the White House as well as for other offices (Bolling 1964, 159; Patterson 1966, 4, 18).

The Speaker faced a serious problem, however, when the Senate passed a new reform bill in April 1959: unlike the previous year's measure, this bill was much more stringent, with criminal penalties for unions that failed to protect the "rights" of workers and additional limits on picketing and the ability of workers to refuse handling goods from another "struck plant." Labor opposed it, but the mood of the House seemed to point toward passage of a bill at least as restrictive as the Senate measure, if not more so (Bolling 1964, 161–62; Patterson 1966, 13–15, 20; *Congressional Quarterly Almanac* 1959, 166).

Rayburn calculated that the Senate's approach, though repellant to labor, was better than trying to enact a more pro-union bill, which could lose—or worse, attract even more stringent amendments on the House floor. When the House Education and Labor Committee narrowly approved its version of the Senate bill in July, later sponsored by Representative Carl Elliott (D-AL), Rayburn endorsed it. But the Elliott measure represented "a mix of compromises" that failed to satisfy either liberals or conservatives and was passed "purely for the sake of getting the bill to the floor" (Bolling 1964, 162, 167; *Congressional Quarterly Almanac* 1959, 166; Patterson 1966, 20, quote p. 20).

As a result, two alternative union reform bills were introduced. The AFL-CIO stood behind a more labor-friendly proposal, sponsored by former union leader John Shelley (D-CA), which had fewer restrictions and limits on unions. On the other side of the idelogical spectrum, Republicans and conservative Democrats supported a bill sponsored by two Education and Labor Committee members, Phil Landrum (D-GA) and Robert Griffin (R-MI). Their legislation, supported by President Eisenhower, contained even more restrictions on union activities than the Elliott plan (Bolling 1964, 167; *Congressional Quarterly Almanac* 1959, 166; Patterson 1966, 20–21).

With three measures to choose from—the union-friendly Shelley bill, the Speaker-endorsed compromise Elliott bill, and the management-friendly Landrum-Griffin bill—legislators were lobbied from all sides, some quite intensively. Both business and labor organizations undertook major lobbying campaigns. The former used letter-writing campaigns and radio, television, and newspaper advertising on behalf of Landrum-Griffin; the latter sent lobbyists to meet with persuadable legislators and even threatened to oppose the reelection of Democrats who voted for Landrum-Griffin. Rayburn, meanwhile, put an unusual amount of effort into passing the Elliot measure. He gave "support and encouragement" to a core set of House members, known as the "Speaker's group," who worked to defeat the conservative Landrum-Griffin measure and pass the Elliott bill instead. When Eisenhower made a last-minute address on TV and radio in early August extolling the virtues of the Landrum-Griffin plan, Rayburn followed with a radio appearance of his own, opposing Landrum-Griffin and advocating the Elliott compromise bill (Bolling 1964, 168–69, 172; *Congressional Quarterly Almanac* 1959, 167; Patterson 1966, 23–25, 27, quotes p. 24).[53]

When the Elliott proposal came to the House floor in August, the first scheduled vote was on the prolabor Shelley bill, which was offered as a substitute amendment. Opposed by both House conservatives and Elliott bill proponents, the Shelley measure was soundly rejected in a 132–245 teller vote. With labor unions' favored bill out of the way, the next vote would be on the legislation they disliked the most, the Landrum-Griffin measure, also to be offered as a substitute amendment. The conservative coalition of Republicans and southern Democrats commanded a powerful bloc of floor votes, and to garner more support for Landrum-Griffin, they proposed and passed two amendments to their measure. The first, reducing criminal penalties for a union that inhibited the rights of its members, was added to make the bill less onerous for labor. The second limited the authority of the secretary of labor to protect workers against union violations of their rights; this was added to assuage the fears of southern Democrats that Landrum-Griffin gave the federal government potential powers to enforce civil rights laws. These changes, and Elliott's own absence due to poor health, overcame Rayburn's leadership against the measure. The Landrum-Griffin proposal passed the House, first by a 215–200 teller vote, following considerable "confusion" on the House floor, and again by a roll call vote, 229–201. Only ten of the 229 supporters in the second vote were from outside the House's conservative coalition (Bolling 1964, 170–71; Patterson 1966, 27–28, quote p. 28).[54]

As a result of these votes, the original language of the Elliott bill had now been replaced by the Landrum-Griffin measure. Though their proposal had been gutted, Elliott bill supporters could still stop the Landrum-Griffin proposal either by passing a motion to recommit the bill to committee (which would allow the bill to be rewritten later or to simply die in committee) or by voting to kill the bill outright on the House floor. However, not many Democrats were willing to delay or defeat labor reform. The motion to recommit the bill failed, 149–279, with a majority of Democrats and all but a handful of Republicans voting against the motion; and on final passage, the bill passed, 303 to 125 (Patterson 1966, 28–29).

President Eisenhower and the conservative coalition had won a decisive victory. Rayburn had not succeeded in stopping conservatives from passing a union bill to their liking, though his lobbying and other acts of leadership may have convinced a number of legislators to vote against Landrum-Griffin, making at least some of the floor votes closer than they might otherwise have been. A modified version of the Landrum-Griffin bill, with minor concessions to organized labor, later passed both the House and Senate and was signed into law by the president that same year (Patterson 1966, 32–33).

CONCLUSION

The cases of legislative leadership discussed in this chapter provide evidence for the four predictions of the theory of goal-driven leadership. First, both Speakers Rayburn and McCormack exercised legislative leadership on behalf of a variety of goals, not merely the objective of securing their leadership position in the House. In at least one instance, the Speaker acted out of concern for a second electoral objective, to win reelection to the House, by espousing the preferences of his local constituency (Rayburn and the Natural Gas Act extension). In other cases, Rayburn or McCormack sought to enact a personally desired policy initiative or to fulfill certain duties associated with the Speakership —such as support for the presidential party, defense of the institutional presidency, or support for the whole House—even if doing so did not satisfy the interests of the majority party in the House or the Speaker's own congressional district. Furthermore, the Speakers' leadership on or near the House floor was often consequential, even in a period when the majority party in the House was fairly divided.

Second, the cases illustrate that two or more goals (or multiple aspects of a single goal) can jointly explain the particular direction of the Speaker's leadership. The most common such combination for Rayburn and McCormack was the goals of reelection to leadership and fulfilling the role of aiding the presidential party: that is, both the Speaker's party in Congress and his party's president (or future presidential candidate) wanted or would clearly benefit from enacting a certain policy. But the goal to remain Speaker also sometimes joined with other leadership objectives, such as to pass preferred policy, as occurred with civil rights, the Reciprocal Trade Act, and the war in Vietnam. In short, evidence shows that Rayburn and McCormack were nested within a broader set of goals that at times combined to give them a strong incentive to exercise leadership. Theories of leadership that focus on the Speaker's desire to stay in office, and by extension on solely the House majority party, fail to fully capture this interlocking set of leadership objectives.

The cases provide some support for the theory's third prediction: that the goal of remaining Speaker is the most frequent explanation of the Speaker's legislative leadership. In the twenty-three cases discussed in this chapter, the most common goal-related explanation for such leadership was a desire to remain Speaker by defending the interests or preferences of the House caucus (which occurred in fifteen cases). The desire to support the presidential party, however, also appeared frequently as an explanation (twelve cases), usually in conjunction with the leadership reelection goal. Rayburn and McCormack, then, appear to have been more willing to exercise significant legislative leadership to address this second goal than the theory would suggest. This may be a result of how these earlier Speakers balanced and prioritized their objectives, a point I return to in chapter 7.

Finally, though the case study analysis does not allow for a full test of the conditions under which Speaker leadership will most likely occur, it does suggest what those conditions are, at least for leadership on or near the House floor. One factor suggested by the theory, issue salience, does seem to matter. For example, in all but one case, the Speaker acted to achieve the goal of aiding the institutional presidency when the matter at hand involved national defense or foreign affairs and the president strongly desired a particular legislative result. But the second hypothesized factor, party division, did not seem to hinder the Speaker's use of leadership to satisfy party-wide concerns. Both Rayburn and McCormack often had significant numbers of Democrats vote against them on major bills, such as occurred with labor reform, civil rights, and expansion of the House Rules Committee. In some instances, the Speaker seems to have stepped forward nonetheless because leadership on the particular issue was seen as necessary to aid the party's collective electoral status (as with civil rights and labor reform). In other cases, however, this contrary finding appears to stem from my definition of the "needs," "preferences," or "concerns" of the congressional party. These terms mean more than just the degree of unity exhibited by the majority party on a particular bill or measure: they also include issues for which the party is not homogeneous but nonetheless has a sizable majority strongly in favor of the particular outcome. Under these conditions, the Speaker was willing to tolerate party defections in order to retain or cement support from the (liberal) majority of the majority party by helping implement its policy objectives.

Chapter 4 Speaker Leadership in the Reform and Post-Reform House

The modern history of the House is often divided into *pre-reform,* *reform,* and *post-reform* periods (for example, Rohde 1991). During the pre-reform period, which lasted until the 1970s, seniority was largely sacrosanct, younger legislators had little power, and party leaders relied on informal means of influence to achieve desired goals.[1] Party discipline was also less rigid, with conservative Democrats and moderate Republicans often crossing party lines when voting.

Politics in the House underwent a gradual but significant shift in the reform era of the 1970s. Young, activist, liberal, and more independent Democrats grew in number, and they proved willing to challenge internal House procedures and power structures. Together with reform-minded Republicans and more junior legislators from both parties, these Democrats pressed for significant institutional changes that redistributed authority over agenda setting, committee assignments, and policy making. New powers were given to more members of Congress, as well as to subcommittees, the party caucus, and party leaders—particularly the Speaker. In 1975, for example, Carl Albert

Table 4.1 Reform and Post-Reform Speakers as Legislative Leaders

Speaker	Case	Date of Key Floor Vote(s)	Speaker's Primary Floor-Related Activity	Source(s)	Key Vote(s), All Members	Key Vote(s), Maj. Party	Motivating Speaker Goal(s) and Relevant Individual/Entity Primary	Secondary
Albert	Vietnam withdrawal[a]	1971–72	Lobbying (in caucus), floor advocacy	Josephy (1979), Maney (1998), Peters (1997)	Several	Several	Role fulfillment • Inst. presidency	Policy enactment • Speaker
Albert	Public works bill	April and June 1971	Lobbying	Peters (1997)	Several	Several	Reelection • Party in Congress	—
Albert	Job creation bill	May and June 1971	Lobbying	Peters (1997)	Several	Several	Reelection • Party in Congress	—
Albert	Minimum wage bill	1972–73	Lobbying	Peters (1997)	Several	Several	Reelection • Party in Congress	—
O'Neill	Energy legislation[a]	August 1977, October 1978	Lobbying, vote labeling, floor advocacy	Kaufman (1993), Peters (1997), Sinclair (1998)	199–227, 207–206	72–210, 199–79	Reelection • Party in Congress; Role fulfillment • Pres. party	—
O'Neill	Debt limit increase	February and March 1979	Lobbying, trading benefits, clock management	Sinclair (1995)	Several	Several	Reelection • Party in Congress; Role fulfillment • Pres. party • Inst. presidency	—
O'Neill	Gramm-Latta I budget resolution[a]	May 1981	Lobbying, vote labeling, floor advocacy	Barone (1990), Peters (1997), Remini (2006)	253–176	63–176	Reelection • Party in Congress	—

Speaker	Issue	Date	Activities	Sources	Vote(s)	Vote(s)	Goals	
O'Neill	Supplemental appropriations veto override[a]	September 1982	Lobbying, vote labeling, floor advocacy	Peters (1997)	301–117	220–13	Reelection • Party in Congress	—
O'Neill	Contra funding[a]	1983–86	Lobbying, floor advocacy	Peters (1997)	Several	Several	Reelection • Party in Congress	Policy enactment • Speaker
Wright	Budget reconciliation[a]	October 1987	Lobbying, vote labeling, floor advocacy, clock management	Several (5)[b]	206–205	205–41	Reelection • Party in Congress	—
Wright	Contra funding[a]	February, March 1988	Lobbying, floor advocacy	Connelly and Pitney (1994)	211–219 208–216	47–207 202–46	Reelection • Party in Congress	Policy enactment • Speaker
Wright	Congressional pay raise	February 1989	Lobbying, other	Peters (1997)	88–238	82–107	Role fulfillment • House-wide	—
Foley	Congressional pay raise	November 1989	Lobbying	Peters (1997), Sinclair (1995)	252–174	168–85	Role fulfillment • House-wide	—
Foley	Flag burning constitutional amendment[a]	June 1990	Lobbying, floor advocacy, other	Sinclair (1995)	254–177 (failed)	95–160	Reelection • Party in Congress	Policy enactment • Speaker
Foley	Spending rescission	April 1993	Lobbying, clock management	Connelly and Pitney (1994), Sinclair (1995)	212–208	210–42	Reelection • Party in Congress Role fulfillment • Pres. party	—
Foley	Budget reconciliation[a]	May, August 1993	Lobbying, floor advocacy	Patashnik (2004), Peters (1997)	219–213 218–216	218–38 217–41	Reelection • Party in Congress Role fulfillment • Pres. party	—

(continued)

Table 4.1 (continued)

Speaker	Case	Date of Key Floor Vote(s)	Speaker's Primary Floor-Related Activity	Source(s)	Key Vote(s), All Members	Key Vote(s), Maj. Party	Motivating Speaker Goal(s) and Relevant Individual/Entity	
							Primary	Secondary
Foley	North American Free Trade Agreement[a]	November 1993	Floor advocacy	Sinclair (1995)	234–200	102–156	Role fulfillment • Pres. party • Inst. presidency Reelection • District	—
Gingrich	Balanced Budget Amendment	January 1995	Lobbying	Killian (1998)	300–132	228–2	Reelection • Party in Congress	—
Gingrich	Income tax reduction[a]	April 1995	Lobbying, floor advocacy	Killian (1998), Sinclair (1999b), Strahan and Palazzolo (2004)	246–188	219–11	Reelection • Party in Congress	—
Gingrich	Endangered species funding[a]	July 1995	Floor advocacy	Killian (1998)	132–289	93–133	Policy enactment • Speaker	—
Gingrich	Labor-HHS appropriations	August 1995	Lobbying	Killian (1998)	219–208	213–18	Reelection • Party in Congress	—
Gingrich	Medicare reform[a]	October 1995	Lobbying, floor advocacy	Killian (1998), Sinclair (1999a)	231–201	227–6	Reelection • Party in Congress	—

Speaker	Issue	Date	Activity	Source	Vote	Vote	Goals	
Gingrich	Balanced budget initiative/government shutdown	January 1996	Lobbying	Aldrich and Rohde (2001), Killian (1998), Rae and Campbell (1999), Remini (2006)	401–17	214–15	Reelection • Party in Congress	—
Gingrich	Everglades protection[a]	February 1996	Floor advocacy, other	Killian (1998)	299–124	155–79	Reelection • Party in Congress	—
Gingrich	Welfare reform	July 1996	Lobbying	Killian (1998)	168–258	9–221	Reelection • Party in Congress Role fulfillment • Pres. party	—
Gingrich	Campaign finance reform[a]	July 1996	Floor advocacy	Killian (1998)	162–259	162–68	Reelection • Party in Congress	—
Gingrich	Committee funding	March 1997	Lobbying	Killian (1990)	210–213	210–11	Reelection • Party in Congress	—

[a]The Speaker addressed the House floor on behalf of the measure.

[b]Connelly and Pitney (1994), Peters (1997), Remini (2006), and Sinclair (1995, 1998).

(D-OK) became the first Speaker in sixty-five years to possess appointment power for all of his party's seats on the Rules Committee, and three incumbent committee chairmen were ousted by a secret vote in the Democratic Party Caucus (Polsby 2004; Rohde 1991; Schickler 2001).

Most significant for the Speaker were those institutional changes that granted party leaders additional legislative control and authority. These changes gave Democratic Speakers in the reform and post-reform eras, including Albert, Tip O'Neill (D-MA), Jim Wright (D-TX), and Tom Foley (D-WA), a greater ability to shape legislative outcomes prior to floor activity. Following the election of a Republican majority to the House of Representatives in 1994, more powers were given to Speaker Newt Gingrich (R-GA), including expanded authority over the referral of legislation to committees, more extensive powers to appoint Republicans to committees, and greater control over the administration of the House (Evans and Oleszek 1997). Yet all of these Speakers, Gingrich included, sometimes faced difficult circumstances that compelled them to exercise legislative leadership on or near the House floor, just as their predecessors had.

In this chapter, I examine specific instances of legislative leadership involving the first five Speakers serving in the reform and post-reform eras. Using the same method of literature sweeps employed in chapter 3, I identified twenty-seven cases of leadership, listed in table 4.1;[2] as in chapter 3, I discuss a subset (just over half, or sixteen) of these cases. As in the previous chapter, and drawing on similar evidence, I discuss whether an instance of legislative leadership is best explained by the Speaker's electoral, policy, and/or role-fulfillment goals. I also introduce evidence, when available, that the Speaker's leadership was effective in achieving the desired result, that is, to win a majority or supermajority of the House or the majority party, or to unify the House or the majority party. In most (but not all) cases, the Speaker's objective was to win over the floor median member on a bill supported by his party.[3]

Besides having more extensive institutional powers, there were two other major differences between these Speakers and those discussed in chapter 3. The first was in the frequency of divided government. Presidents and Speakers came from opposite parties for ten of the thirty years from 1941 to 1970 but for twenty-two of the twenty-eight years that followed. The increased frequency of divided government often challenged the Speaker's ability to accomplish his congressional party's objectives in the face of a presidential veto. But it also affected one of the Speaker's basic goals—fulfillment of leadership roles—in two ways. First, Speakers became less willing to defer to opposite party presidents on defense and foreign policy issues. The catalyst for this change was the Vietnam War. As had prior Speakers, Carl Albert was at first willing to support the president's war policy, even if the chief executive was from the opposite party (in his case, Richard Nixon). But war opponents came to dominate the House Democratic Caucus in the early 1970s, and eventually Albert turned against the conflict. Speakers since Albert have generally been less willing to go against their congressional party on such issues. For example, O'Neill and Wright fought against President Ronald Reagan's attempt to fund a guerilla army in Nicaragua, and Wright even went so far as to initiate foreign policy making directly within his leadership office (Roberts 1988).[4]

Second, divided government (along with other factors, including changes in voter behavior and preferences and, more broadly, the loss of the Democratic South) helped to unify and galvanize both parties in Congress. The majority party in the House, first Democrats and later Republicans, sought ways to oppose incumbent opposite-party presidents and regain same-party control of the White House (Nivola and Brady 2006; Peters 1997; Polsby 2004). Supported by activists within their parties, Speakers in turn began asserting themselves more forcefully against presidents of the opposing party and deferring to them less readily. This development also undermined the Speaker's role as an officer of the entire House: by more aggressively resisting opposite-party presidents, Speakers often alienated the House minority party, making it harder for both parties to unite on issues of importance to all legislators.

The nature of the goals motivating Speakers in the sweep-captured cases from 1971 through 1998 illustrates these two developments. Unlike the cases discussed in chapter 3, those involving Speakers Albert through Gingrich can be much more readily explained as a function of the preferences and goals of the House majority party. Seventeen of the twenty-seven instances involved leadership motivated primarily by the congressional party. Four others involved both the congressional and presidential parties, and two cases exemplified the Speaker acting on behalf of the House as a whole. Four additional explanations each appeared once: aiding the institutional presidency; enacting Speaker-desired policy; jointly helping the Speaker's party, the presidential party, and the institutional presidency; and aiding the institutional and partisan presidency while also pursuing an individual policy goal.

This decline in the exercise of legislative leadership on behalf of institutions and entities besides the House majority party suggests how certain Speaker goals may be diminished under extended periods of divided government. Nonetheless, leadership roles and duties have not vanished entirely, and Speakers who choose not to fulfill these duties and instead act as partisan agents can face serious peril. For example, Wright's attempt to forge Central American foreign policy independently of the White House was severely criticized by congressional Republicans, and together with Wright's willingness to win floor victories at the expense of comity within the House, it encouraged GOP legislators to mount an aggressive campaign against him that led to his resignation as Speaker (Barry 1989). I return to the subject of changing roles and duties of House Speakers since 1970, and the reasons for these changes, in the book's concluding chapter.

SERVING ONE'S DISTRICT, ENACTING ONE'S POLICY PREFERENCES, OR AIDING THE HOUSE

Concern with reelection to the House does not appear as a primary motivation for Speakers in any of the sweep-captured cases between 1971 and 1998, but three instances of leadership occurring during this twenty-eight-year period can be explained as a consequence of Speakers seeking personally preferred policy outcomes or serving the House as a whole. The first two involved legislator salaries, a matter of great concern to all representatives and one where legislators' views usually do not match those of the voting public. In both of those cases, the Speaker was clearly an important player in bringing about the final legislative outcome. The third case illustrates that even an aggressively partisan Speaker may openly exercise leadership to achieve a personal policy goal, regardless of the preferences of others in his or her congressional party.

Wright and the Congressional Pay Raise, 1989

As a general rule, members of Congress are partial to increasing their official salaries, usually over the objections of voters. As a consequence, legislators are typically loath to have an open vote on a congressional pay raise, because it can easily become a lightning rod of public protest, and instead prefer more "hidden" ways of increasing their paychecks. In early 1989, congressional pay raises became a major national issue. Speaker Jim Wright acknowledged the Congress-wide nature of the matter, but he failed to recognize how its politically sensitive nature meant that his fellow Democrats would want to completely distance themselves from it. Instead, he sought legislators' explicit support to pass a salary increase, in effect embracing a principal-agent leadership model—albeit for the entire House, not just for his party—and as a consequence committed a significant failure of legislative leadership.

For decades, members of Congress had struggled to identify a reliable mechanism that would provide regular congressional pay raises without approval via recorded floor votes. In 1985, Congress established a bipartisan Commission on Executive, Legislative, and Judicial Salaries to periodically recommend salary increases for legislators, federal judges, and senior executive branch employees. By law, the president could accept, reject, or modify any proposal made by the commission, which would then go into effect automatically unless both the House and Senate passed a resolution rejecting it and the president signed the resolution into law. The commission's first proposal, in 1987, recommended an increase in salary for members of Congress from $77,400 to $135,000, and although President Reagan reduced the raise to $89,500, public criticism of the proposal was intense. The Senate voted to kill the raise, but Speaker Wright (together with minority party leaders) decided to delay any vote on the increase until after it had gone into effect.

In December 1988, the commission once more proposed raising legislative salaries to $135,000. This time Reagan supported the recommended raise in full, and he included it in his budget proposal in early January 1989. With the Senate threatening to again vote against an increase, it would be up to Wright to decide whether or not to have a recorded vote on the proposal (Barry 1989, 112–16, 669–70; *Congressional Quarterly Almanac* 1989, 54, 59; Oreskes 1989a).

Given that the pay raise would affect all members Congress, the issue was, in principle, a bipartisan matter involving the House as a whole, not just the majority party. President Reagan and President-elect Bush, both Republicans, publicly endorsed the raise, although they may have done so on behalf of its noncongressional recipients (federal judges and employees) and perhaps to force House and Senate Democrats to accept or reject it. Furthermore, although the House Republican minority leader, Bob Michel of Illinois, publicly opposed the size of the raise, both he and the GOP minority deputy whip, Richard Cheney, were reportedly working behind the scenes with House Democrats to enact it into law. Though Wright himself was unenthusiastic about the size of the raise, which was more than three times larger than the previous increase, the general belief among lawmakers was that the Speaker would allow it to take effect without a vote on the floor, just as he had done two years before (Barry 1989, 669–72; *Congressional Quarterly Almanac* 1989, 59).

Because the 1989 raise was considerably bigger than the one adopted in 1987, it proved especially objectionable to voters and galvanized anti-raise activists. National polls showed that the vast majority of Americans opposed it; newspaper editorials and reformers like Ralph Nader condemned it; and talk-radio hosts initiated letter-writing and telephone campaigns that connected Wright's delay strategy to the raise.[5] Individual House Democrats as well as Republicans began openly criticizing the salary proposal and urging that it be subject to a floor vote, though most legislators privately preferred that nothing be done until after the increase had taken effect. The Senate then announced that, as it had in 1987, it would indeed vote on (and almost certainly reject) the pay raise before its automatic implementation, meaning that only the House stood in the way of those hoping to kill the raise. Wright began feeling increasingly isolated and helpless to protect his colleagues from mounting public demands to allow such a vote (Barry 1989, 670–74; *Congressional Quarterly Almanac* 1989, 56; Rasky 1989a; Wright 1994, 244–45).

The Speaker's solution was to solidify internal support for a raise by identifying the preferences of a majority of the House, then acting on behalf of those preferences. He suggested an alternative plan: a smaller, 30 percent pay increase, coupled with a ban on honoraria (such as payment for outside speeches). This, he believed, would both appear less extravagant and allow the raise to be framed as ethics reform. Suspicious of internal whip counts showing that Democrats wanted the original salary hike, Wright sent out a private, anonymous survey on January 30 to all members of the House, asking twelve questions about possible salary increases and when (or whether) to vote on such increases. To underscore his position as the agent of legislators, he prefaced the poll by writing, "I have been given the privilege and responsibility to represent the members and this institution to which each of us belongs. In that capacity, I want to be faithful to the wishes of the membership." Informing the press of the survey, he declared that if it showed majority support among legislators for allowing the raise to take effect, it was "not something Bob Michel or I am imposing on them" (Barry 1989, 673; Jim Wright Collection, Confidential Letter to Members of Congress, 30 January 1989, box 16–7).

With a majority of the House responding to the poll (326, or 75 percent), the results revealed that legislators preferred Wright's alternative proposal, with 56 percent agreeing that the current raise was too big. The survey also showed that 57 percent of legislators did not want a floor vote on the raise until after it had gone into effect,[6] and that 61 percent wanted to vote on the Wright plan after the first pay hike was implemented, which would allow them to appear opposed to a large salary increase while guaranteeing a raise of some sort. When Wright revealed the results to the public, legislators who had publicly opposed the raise were accused of hypocrisy, and the media began asking individual representatives how they had responded to the survey. Instead of protecting members of Congress with political cover, Wright had subjected them to additional criticism while implying that he was a directionless, survey-driven leader. Wright's move also cost him the support of House Republican leaders. Both Michel and Cheney told Democrats that when the House reconvened, before the salary increase would go into effect, they would vote against adjournment in order to force a floor vote on the pay raise (Barry 1989, 673–74; Toner 1989a; Wright Collection, Poll Results, box 3–8).

When the House returned from its recess on February 6, Democrats prevented an immediate floor vote on a resolution from California Republican Bill Dannemeyer approving the raise. On a subsequent motion to adjourn, however, Dannemeyer moved for a roll call vote. Given the procedural nature of Dannemeyer's motion, Wright hoped Democrats would uniformly vote to adjourn and thus end debate on the matter, but the anti-raise campaign had successfully labeled any procedural vote as a referendum on the raise itself. According to one press account, "the atmosphere in the House chamber had grown poisonous" (Rasky 1989b). More than enough House Democrats (108) defected and voted against adjournment, which failed, 88–238. Wright, "visibly shaken" (according to one reporter), then addressed the floor and agreed to have a vote on the salary increase the next day. On that vote, the raise was rejected, 48–380 (Barry 1989, 674–75; *Congressional Quarterly Almanac* 1989, 55; Rasky 1989b).

In retrospect, given both the Senate's action and the ferocity of public opposition to the pay raise, it is quite possible that the House would have killed the raise even without Wright's use of the internal House poll. But although Wright correctly understood the issue as Congress-wide in nature, associated with his duty to represent the entire House rather than his caucus, his decision to act as an explicit agent set him up for failure when members of Congress could not provide him with an open directive to act.

Foley and the Congressional Pay Raise, 1989

When the House considered increasing congressional salaries a second time in 1989, it did so under a new Speaker, Tom Foley. Foley's ultimate success on an issue where Wright had failed reflected in part his differing approach to leadership. Even before he was Speaker, Foley was known for having a more consensus-oriented, "conciliatory style" than Wright, and he made several efforts early in his Speakership to improve relations with the minority party (Peters 1997, 288; quote from Toner 1989b). Foley also succeeded by recognizing that active, assertive leadership on behalf of all House members' interests without being their explicit agent was necessary to pass a pay increase.

Foley's strategy, like Wright's, was to improve the chances of securing higher salaries for legislators by recommending a smaller raise and combining it with ethics legislation. In theory, this required the support of a majority of the House, but in practice Foley would need unanimous (or near unanimous) support to prevent a minority from using floor debate or procedural motions to politicize the raise and thereby encourage legislators to reject it.[7] Potential opposition to a salary increase came from at least three sets of legislators. First, congressional Republicans could renew their criticism of it, hoping to tarnish Democrats in the 1990 elections. Second, freshmen and other vulnerable Democrats might prefer to take a stand against a pay raise to avoid any negative electoral consequences. Finally, senior members, accustomed to the perks and benefits curtailed by Foley's ethics proposals, might vote to reject it (Biggs and Foley 1999, 140; *Congressional Quarterly Almanac* 1989, 57).

Throughout the year, both Foley and Minority Leader Bob Michel "put the full weight and prestige of their offices" behind a salary increase bill (*Congressional Quarterly Almanac* 1990, 51). As a first step, Foley announced during his first month as Speaker that he supported a pay raise, at least for the judges and executive employees who would have benefited from the earlier measure. He also encouraged a bipartisan task force on ethics, formed by Michel and then-Speaker Wright, to draft an ethics proposal in a timely fashion that could be tied to a future pay raise bill.[8] The final bill that emerged possessed three elements designed to ease its passage: the raise was implemented in increments, the largest of which would not occur until the next Congress; the total raise was smaller than the initial proposal ($125,000, rather than $135,000); and it was tied to ethics reforms suggested by the task force, including a ban on honoraria (*Congressional Quarterly Almanac* 1989, 57; Oreskes 1989b; Rasky 1989d; Sinclair 1995, 190–91).

Foley's efforts did not end there. Neither he nor the congressional task force disclosed the details of the package publicly until near the day of the vote, so as to discourage grassroots lobbying against the bill. Foley also opted to have the raise be implemented by a straight up-or-down vote. This strategy, while risky, avoided potential controversy if the raise went into effect automatically. Furthermore, although President Bush had endorsed a raise for legislators in June, Foley and Michel sought and obtained Bush's explicit endorsement for the new proposal as well. Finally, to emphasize the bipartisan nature of the measure, leaders from each party attended meetings of the other party to promote the legislation (*Congressional Quarterly Almanac* 1989, 57; Rasky 1989d).

In the end, Foley's pay raise passed by a fairly wide margin, 252–174, with a majority of Democrats supporting it and a slight majority of Republicans opposing it. Most important, Foley had succeeded in muting the partisan attacks that could have cowed legislators into voting against the raise, with the floor debate itself being relatively calm. Passage of the measure thus reflected Foley's greater emphasis on the House-wide duties of the Speakership (*Congressional Quarterly Almanac* 1989, 57).[9] But even Foley's leadership style could not overcome external factors, like divided government and an aggressive minority party, which would later lead him to exercise more partisan leadership.

Gingrich and Endangered Species Funding, 1995

As partisan a Speaker as Gingrich could be, he was not unwilling to exercise leadership on behalf of outcomes less closely associated with the preferences of fellow Republicans in Congress. An opportunity to do so arose in 1995 and involved an especially ardent fiscal conservative from his party's freshmen class. Early that year, Rep. Mark Neumann (R-WI) proposed a budget bill that would have made dramatic cuts in a variety of federal spending programs. When it failed to pass the House, Neumann changed his strategy, seeking instead to amend major appropriations bills with significant spending cuts (Killian 1998, 154–55). It was one of these floor amendments that received the ire of Speaker Gingrich.

At the end of June, the House Appropriations Committee passed a spending bill for the Department of the Interior that funded a variety of environmental and environment-related programs. Neumann decided to try cutting $800,000 from one program, a federal initiative to help protect endangered African animals. There was no clear reelection or policy stake for House Republicans in the conservation program, and more than a few members of the party supported deficit reduction through nonmilitary spending reductions. Gingrich, however, endorsed the program, which he saw as his "pet project" (in the words of journalist Linda Killian) and which reflected his wide-ranging interest in wildlife issues and animal conservation that went back, by some accounts, to his childhood.[10] Gingrich informed Neumann that he would personally oppose such a cut, but when the bill came to the House floor in July, Neumann ignored the Speaker's warning and offered his amendment anyway. Keeping his word, Gingrich went to the floor and, in a move unexpected by his colleagues, delivered a speech against Neumann's proposal, arguing that it represented an effort "to cut [the budget] mindlessly" and that animal conservation had important symbolic value (Cloud 1995b; Killian 1998, 155–56).

Because Neumann's amendment failed easily, 132–289, and because it is not clear that Gingrich did much beyond delivering a floor speech, it is difficult to attribute much credit to the Speaker for the vote outcome. The amendment was unpopular with both parties in the House, receiving the votes of only thirty-nine Democrats and ninety-three Republicans. Nonetheless, it was an example of how even a highly party-oriented Speaker may act to achieve a policy outcome he or she desires, trying to shape a legislative result on or near the House floor on an issue of limited salience to the majority party.

Neumann's failure did not keep the congressman from continuing to support spending cuts. His assertive and independent style made him a continual irritant to party leaders, eventually costing him his position on an important appropriations subcommittee (Killian 1998, 156–59).

FULFILLING PRESIDENT-ORIENTED ROLES
OR DUTIES

Post-1970 Speakers sometimes exercised legislative leadership to carry out the preferences of the White House, even if doing so provided little or no direct benefit to their party in Congress. In this section, I discuss the two cases in the data set that involved one or both of the Speaker's role-fulfillment goals related to the president: supporting the presidential party and aiding the institutional presidency. As in chapter 3, these cases involved defense and foreign affairs matters, policy areas usually ceded to chief executives by modern Speakers. In both instances, additional Speaker goals may have also been at play, albeit secondarily—illustrating how the Speaker can consider the preferences and desires of multiple individuals, groups, and institutions when choosing to exercise legislative leadership.

Albert and Vietnam Withdrawal, 1971–72

During his first term as Speaker, Carl Albert was forced to deal with an issue that severely divided his party: the war in Vietnam. Albert's predecessor, John McCormack, had openly supported the war and tried to minimize interparty dissent against it (see chapter 3). But opposition to the conflict had increased in the late 1960s, and after the 1970 election "the peace forces had greatly increased [in number] in the House" (Josephy 1979, 363).[11] Nonetheless, until mid-1972, Albert exercised legislative leadership on behalf of the war and President Richard Nixon's conduct of it. This was particularly remarkable given that by the early 1970s, a majority of Americans opposed the war; voters in Albert's district may have no longer shared the Speaker's enthusiasm for either the war or the military draft (Weaver 1971); and many—by some estimates, a majority—of House Democrats wanted to end U.S. troop deployment in Vietnam.[12] Even if Albert had initially feared that Democratic opposition to the conflict would tarnish his party as weak on national security issues and alienate conservative Democrats who were still behind the war effort, these fears were overshadowed by broader antiwar sentiments both within and outside Congress.

Albert's position on the war, like John McCormack's, is best explained not by a desire to implement the preferences of his party in Congress but by an effort to support the institutional presidency. Four months into Albert's speakership, one reporter wrote that the Oklahoman "is a traditionalist. He believes in deferring to Presidential leadership when it comes to the making of war and peace" (Shannon 1971). In his autobiography, Albert explained that early Democratic support for the war exemplified how "both parties in both houses had stood united behind the critical policy decisions of four presidents" since World War II, and that because of such bipartisanship, "peace had prevailed." Even as opposition to the war continued to grow within his congressional party, the Speaker met personally with President Nixon, who urged Albert as late as 1971 to, as one author later put it, "hold the line" on Vietnam. Like McCormack, Albert may have also had a secondary motive: to achieve a personal policy goal. Political scientist Ronald Peters argues that Albert was, in his words, a "hawk" on Vietnam. To be sure, Albert was a less strident anticommunist than McCormack, and he later claimed he had had "no great enthusiasm" for the war from its earliest stages. But Albert did admit that he opposed early withdrawal of U.S. troops because, he argued, it would not end conflict in the region, would endanger America's security and reputation, and would potentially hinder a diplomatic solution to the conflict (Albert 1990, 296, 335–37; Farrell 2001, 301; Peters 1997, 173; Sinclair 1995).[13]

Albert's opposition to legislative action against the war manifested itself on several occasions. The first was in early 1971, away from the House floor, when party liberals made several attempts to pass a caucus resolution advocating an end to troop deployment in Vietnam. Their efforts were bolstered when Senate Democrats endorsed a similar resolution in late February, and when the Democratic Policy Council in March advocated troop withdrawal by year's end. Attempts to pass such a measure in the House caucus, however, were met with resistance from Albert and other party leaders. After antiwar Democrats scheduled a caucus meeting at the end of March to consider the resolution, Albert and Majority Leader Hale Boggs (LA) tried to dissuade enough Democrats from attending to deny the caucus a quorum. When this failed, Albert endorsed an alternative resolution by Missouri Democrat Richard Bolling that imposed no firm deadline for troop withdrawal but supported the "initiatives of the President, the House committees and members, and the Senate, which may be pertinent to" ending the war. The caucus voted 120–81 to add language urging that troops be withdrawn by the end of that Congress, but an effort to impose an even earlier deadline lost by a narrow 100–101 vote. *New York Times* journalist William Shannon wrote that the resulting compromise, though more strongly antiwar than what Albert had hoped for, "exactly pleased no one—except the Speaker" (*Congressional Quarterly Almanac* 1971, 354–55; Maney 1998, 248; Shannon 1971).

Following this meeting, a series of war-related actions took place on the House floor. Throughout 1971, several Senate bills and House floor amendments offered by antiwar Democrats included provisions to end U.S. military involvement in Indochina. Working with Boggs, Albert "continued to muster a majority" on the floor against the approval of these measures, even when a majority of his party supported them (Josephy 1979, 363). Although sources do not clearly specify when or how Albert exercised such leadership, the House did indeed consider, and often block, legislative language mandating troop withdrawal. This legislation included:

- in late March and early April 1971, several amendments to a bill extending military conscription, all of which were defeated (*Congressional Quarterly Almanac* 1971, 266);
- in June 1971, a motion to instruct conferees (also on a conscription bill) to accept Senate language that set a deadline for troop withdrawal, which was tabled by a vote of 219–175;
- also in June 1971, five amendments on Vietnam offered to a defense procurement authorization bill, all of which failed;
- and in December 1971, on a foreign aid authorization bill, a motion to instruct conferees to protect bill language mandating the removal of U.S. troops within six months, which was tabled 130–101 (*Congressional Quarterly Almanac* 1971, 24, 408).

Of these, perhaps the most notable example of Albert's leadership involved the June 1971 floor amendments to the defense procurement authorization bill. One of the amendments, sponsored by Lucien Nedzi (D-MI) and Charles Whalen (R-OH), would have ended the war by stopping all funding for military operations in the region by the end of that year. Albert himself spoke briefly against it on the House floor, arguing that "I do not believe we should undertake by legislative fiat to settle the war at a time certain or to tie the hands of the President in any way" (*Congressional Record,* 17 June 1971, 20521). Though it failed by a fairly one-sided vote of 158 to 254, it marked the first time that a majority of Democrats (135 of the 240 casting ballots) voted against further funding of the war and, by implication, Albert's support for its conduct (*Congressional Quarterly Almanac* 1971, 310).[14]

A third instance of Speaker leadership on Vietnam, as with the first, occurred in the House Democratic Caucus. In early 1972, antiwar Democrats wanted the caucus to require the Foreign Affairs Committee to pass legislation mandating U.S. troop withdrawal. Albert opposed the move, but recognizing that he stood against the firm majority of his party, he agreed to go along, provided that the caucus also condemned a recent military offensive by the North Vietnamese Army. A resolution including both Albert's language and the directive to the committee passed, 135–66, with Albert voting in favor. After initial resistance, the Foreign Affairs Committee did approve a bill including troop withdrawal language, although it was later struck from the bill in a floor vote (*Congressional Quarterly Almanac* 1972, 123, 468–70; Evans and Novak 1972; Peters 1997, 160). The caucus vote was by secret ballot, but it mirrored the 153–80 Democratic vote against eliminating the withdrawal provision. In that vote, most northerners voted to withdraw troops (133 of 157), and a majority of southern Democrats did not (35 of 55). Interestingly, Democrats with current or future leadership positions also voted in favor of removing the provision, including Albert, Boggs, later Rules Committee chairman Bolling, future Armed Services Committee chairman Mel Price (IL), future majority whip John McFall (CA), and later Speaker Tom Foley.

Albert could not ignore the shift in his party's ideological preferences indefinitely. In mid-1972, with Nixon rapidly decreasing U.S. military presence in Indochina and war opponents in the party continuing to grow in size and assertiveness, the Speaker no longer resisted Democratic efforts to end troop deployment. By early 1973, the issue of Vietnam had finally ended its long prominence on the national agenda.

Foley and the North American Free Trade Agreement, 1993

Since the early 1980s, the White House and proponents of free trade had actively sought ways to expand bilateral trading relations among North American nations. In 1988, the United States signed a free trade agreement with

Canada that reduced or eliminated many tariffs and nontariff barriers to trade and investment between both countries. Two years later, Mexico, convinced in part by the apparent success of the agreement and led by pro–free trade president Carlos Salinas, sought to establish a trade agreement of its own with the United States. Eventually, all three countries began negotiations toward establishing a broader free trade area, in what would become the North American Free Trade Agreement (NAFTA). Despite opposition to NAFTA from labor unions and other important Democratic constituencies, Bill Clinton endorsed the agreement as a presidential candidate, although he also endorsed stronger labor and environmental protections for any agreement reached between Mexico and the United States (Grayson 1995, 49, 51–52, 121; Mayer 1998, 38–41, 49–50, 139, 144–45, 165).

Thus when the new Democratic Congress convened in early 1993, it was faced with a same-party president seeking to pursue a similar policy objective as that of his defeated predecessor. But while Republicans were generally supportive of free trade, congressional Democrats were less so, and they were particularly wary of extending free trade privileges to Mexico. During the previous Congress, a majority of the party had voted against extending so-called fast-track presidential authority, which allowed the negotiation and congressional approval of trade agreements under an expedited process. Much of the debate surrounding the fast-track extension had involved the NAFTA negotiations with Mexico, and although the extension did pass the House, it did so only with significant Republican support and after President Bush agreed to address environmental and labor matters as part of trade negotiations with Mexico. Even after approval of fast-track authority for the president, many House Democrats were still opposed to NAFTA: they viewed the agreement's environmental and labor protections as insufficient, feared possible manufacturing and blue-collar job losses in the United States, and faced strong pressure from interest groups and labor unions in their districts to reject the agreement. Their opposition was so widespread that in April 1993 Clinton's director of the Office of Management and Budget remarked that NAFTA was, at least at that moment, "dead" (Grayson 1995, 64–65, 68–69; Mayer 1998, 78, 89–90, 92, 203–4, 224–29, 238–41).

Foley's decision to support NAFTA is therefore not adequately explained by a desire to support the congressional party's policy preferences. Furthermore, given that many opinion polls showed a plurality, if not a majority, of the public opposed NAFTA, its passage was unlikely to help the immediate election chances of House Democrats.[15] But Foley could possibly achieve other leadership goals by helping pass the trade agreement. First, although deference to the institutional presidency on foreign affairs matters had arguably declined since the 1970s and the Vietnam War, it had not vanished entirely. Second, as Barbara Sinclair has noted, support for the agreement by Foley and others reflected the belief that party leaders should stand behind the initiatives of their party's president (Sinclair 1995, 88). Both of these president-related role-fulfillment goals seem to have been particularly salient to Foley with respect to NAFTA, given that Clinton not only endorsed the agreement but eventually dedicated considerable efforts to push it through Congress. Foley may have hoped to satisfy a third goal—reelection to Congress—by backing NAFTA because the economic interests of Foley's export-oriented state (if not his largely agricultural district) would likely benefit from the trade agreement; perhaps unsurprisingly, Foley had generally supported free trade as a member of Congress (Biggs and Foley 1999, 278; Mayer 1998, ch. 8).[16]

Although Speaker Foley stood behind NAFTA, much of what he may have done to ensure its enactment in the House remains hidden from view. This is probably no accident, given the opposition of many House Democrats and even some of his fellow party leaders to the agreement. Foley even made some initial moves (such as assuring that the vote would not be a party vote) to suggest that his involvement would be minimal at best, leading several White House officials to complain that the Speaker's efforts to pass NAFTA legislation were too tepid. Foley could initially do so because the Clinton White House was willing and able to lobby Capitol Hill.

When the date of the floor vote on NAFTA neared, however, Foley took a more assertive role. In September 1993, he appeared on national television to advocate for the agreement, and when a number of freshmen Democrats voted in the party caucus against NAFTA, the Speaker "worked to limit the damage" of the vote (Kondracke 1993). On the day of the vote, he may have also provided space for lobbyists and Democrats in favor of the bill to meet in what one account described as a "pep rally" in a House office building (MacArthur 2000, 272). Later, Foley delivered the final closing speech on the bill's behalf. "Our leadership is divided, our Members divided," he noted, but argued that he supported NAFTA because "it will be to the benefit of those neighbors, north and south, on both sides of the border" and because "I believe passionately, it is good for our country, and good for our future." The bill passed 234–200, but with a minority of Democratic votes (102, versus 156 against) (Cloud 1993; Connelly and Hansen 1993; *Congressional Record*, 17 November 1993, H10047; MacArthur 2000, 253; Sinclair 1995, 88). Nonetheless, Foley had succeeded.

HELPING THE PARTY IN CONGRESS AND
THE PRESIDENTIAL PARTY

As with Rayburn and McCormack, Speakers who served after 1970 sometimes exercised legislative leadership not just to serve the House majority party but also to fulfill their duties to the presidential party. Acknowledging the significance of these duties reveals the contributions that presidents have made in enacting legislation and also helps explain why Speakers have occasionally acted forcefully against key coalitions within their congressional party to achieve legislative outcomes. In the five cases reviewed below, aiding the majority House party (an electoral goal) and aiding the presidential party (a role-fulfillment goal) together motivated the Speaker to exercise leadership on behalf of a significant legislative initiative.

O'Neill and Energy Legislation, 1977–78

President Jimmy Carter's proposal to revise the nation's energy policy was perhaps the most important of his presidency. The energy bill that eventually became law failed to accomplish most of Carter's initial objectives and proved insufficient to guarantee him reelection. It did, however, serve to showcase the leadership skills of the newly selected Speaker, Tip O'Neill, who managed to overcome numerous procedural and ideological roadblocks in the House to pass the bill.

A major impetus for O'Neill in his support of the measure was the interests of his party in the House. Regional concerns divided Democrats on important aspects of energy regulation, but partisans generally agreed that proactive legislation was needed to respond to national concerns over energy costs and supply.[17] Energy reform would also enhance the congressional party's national reputation by demonstrating that it could accomplish important policy goals under unified government.[18] A second important explanation for O'Neill's leadership, however, was to fulfill the expectation that he support his presidential party. Republican presidents Ford and Nixon had suffered from the effects of a severe oil embargo and growing American reliance on overseas sources of energy, and Carter had proposed energy reform legislation during his presidential campaign. Though energy reform was less salient to voters after the oil crisis abated in 1976, Carter pledged early in his presidency (including in a televised speech, in which he famously wore a cardigan sweater) to introduce such legislation. Thus O'Neill recognized that the passage of energy reform would likely enhance the president's reputation and improve Carter's chances of reelection (Cochrane 1981, 547–49, 551, 578; Farrell 2001, 463–65).

The reform bill, which was drafted in the White House and formally introduced by Carter in April 1977, instituted a series of statutory changes designed to reduce energy consumption generally and fuel imports in particular. O'Neill quickly realized that the bill's complexity and size were serious liabilities. Many House committees had potential jurisdiction over the measure, and a number of their Democratic members had parochial and policy biases that could lead them to undermine various aspects of the legislation, like the establishment of fuel efficiency requirements for new cars, a new price mechanism for oil and gas, and the imposition of energy taxes. Those same biases could also encourage legislators to form cross-party coalitions on the House floor to amend or kill the bill. As a consequence, much of O'Neill's leadership involved controlling the content of the proposal and limiting what could be considered on the floor rather than shaping voting outcomes. Most notably, O'Neill formed a special ad hoc committee to revise, alter, and merge elements of the energy bill that had been approved by standing committees, and he later successfully persuaded the Rules Committee to pass a restrictive rule governing consideration of the measure. By doing so, the Speaker was able to build support for the legislation within his party while hindering attempts to weaken the bill's provisions (Cochrane 1981, 551–57, 564–77; Farrell 2001, 463, 465–69; Kraft 1974; O'Neill 1987, 383–84).

On at least two key occasions, however, O'Neill did exercise legislative leadership on the floor. The first took place during consideration of the House version of the bill in August 1977. The floor rule for the bill permitted only a handful of amendments, but one of them—related to the perennial issue of deregulation for the natural gas industry (see chapter 3)—posed a major threat to the legislation. To appeal to domestic gas producers without alienating Democrats from fuel-consuming districts in the North and Midwest, the House bill eased pricing restrictions for natural gas from new sources. But as they had in the 1940s and 1950s with Speaker Rayburn's support, legislators from energy-producing states sought to deregulate prices for the gas industry more broadly and drafted an amendment that would do so. If it were added to the energy package, it would upset the delicate balance within the legislation between oil-producing and energy-using constituencies, and northern Democrats would likely reject the legislation (Farrell 2001, 465, 468, 470). One O'Neill aide wrote to the Speaker at the end of July that "this is the key amendment that we must hold to keep the bill together" (O'Neill Papers, Legislative files, box 70, folder 10).

If southern Democrats united with Republicans, who otherwise opposed the energy bill, the deregulation proposal could pass. To prevent that outcome, members of a special task force created by O'Neill began whipping fellow Democrats, with coordination by O'Neill and additional lobbying from the White House, and congressional party leaders designated the natural gas amendment to be a "key vote" for Democrats (29 July 1977 memo to Speaker, O'Neill Papers, Legislative files, box 70, folder 10; list of key votes, O'Neill Papers, Party Leadership files, box 6, folder 13). The ad hoc committee also offered another amendment, which passed the House by voice vote, to expand the definition of "new" gas in the hopes of winning over would-be supporters of deregulation (*Congressional Quarterly Almanac* 1977, 1626–27; Lyons 1977). When the deregulation amendment came to the floor on August 3, O'Neill gave the last speech before the vote, arguing that the amendment would increase gas prices for consumers, that its passage would kill the bill, and that therefore "the future of America in 1985, the economy of this country, the defense of this Nation, are at stake" (*Congressional Record,* 3 August 1977, 26482). O'Neill's efforts were successful, and the amendment failed by a vote of 199–227. [19] Although state delegations representing major natural gas industries voted almost unanimously for the amendment (including legislators from Kansas, Louisiana, Mississippi, Oklahoma, and Texas), a W-NOMINATE analysis of the vote reveals that O'Neill may have persuaded the ten members of the North Carolina and Georgia delegations to vote contrary to their ideological preferences and oppose it.[20]

O'Neill's efforts at legislative leadership proved critical again when the House considered the conference version of the measure in late 1978. By this time, Carter's popularity was lower than it had been the previous summer,[21] and the press had begun questioning his earlier claims that conservation was urgently needed. The Senate had passed a version of the legislation that was more favorable to the energy industry, and the conference committee had altered the House bill considerably by omitting a variety of its conservation provisions and permitting greater natural gas deregulation (Cochrane 1981, 579, 582; Farrell 2001, 505–7).

Although the resulting legislation represented little of what O'Neill or liberal Democrats wanted, the Speaker knew that it represented the only chance to pass energy reform in the foreseeable future. Together with administration officials, O'Neill put intense pressure on House Democrats for their votes, and in a meeting with the party's Steering and Policy Committee in late September, he emphasized that "I want and need your all out help" and that the bill was both "the symbol and substance of our program in this Congress" (Notes from 26 September 1978, Democratic Steering and Policy Committee meeting, O'Neill Papers, Legislative files, box 61, folder 5). Majority party leaders also designated the vote on the floor rule to consider the conference report a "key vote," signaling its importance to fellow Democrats.[22] By contrast, bill opponents hoped to change the floor rule to allow a separate vote on the conference report's remaining natural gas regulations. If a vote were permitted on that portion of the legislation, enough southern Democrats might vote with Republicans to successfully remove it, thus encouraging bill supporters to return the measure to conference. This would delay, if not kill, the energy reform package (*Congressional Quarterly*, 14 October 1978, 2920; Farrell 2001, 506–8).

As an indication of how difficult the floor fight would be, the House Rules Committee at first failed to approve a rule that prohibited a vote on the natural gas provision. Only after what one Republican bill opponent later called "the most pressurized arm twisting we have seen since President Carter took office," the committee reversed itself, with one Rules Democrat switching to support the rule and two others voting present. The final vote on the rule proved extremely close. With Carter's help, the Speaker lobbied individual legislators even as the vote was underway and continued to do so in the final minutes of the vote when the bill seemed destined to lose. At one point, New Jersey Republican Millicent Fenwick switched from voting "yea" to "present," and the vote stood at a 206–206 tie until Michigan Democrat Robert Carr voted for the rule; at that point, O'Neill immediately closed the vote (*Congressional Quarterly Almanac* 1978, 2920; Farrell 2001, 507; Peters 1997, 219). It is not known if Carr was a direct recipient of leadership pressure, but a W-NOMINATE analysis of the roll call shows that Carr (and twenty-nine other Democrats) voted contrary to predicted behavior based on their own estimated preferences.[23]

Foley and Budget Reconciliation, 1993

Despite House passage of a rescission bill in 1993 that was designed to ease presidential cuts in spending (see table 4.1), the national deficit remained a major issue for Clinton and House Democrats. Significant deficit reduction would be difficult without major changes to tax rates and/or mandatory spending programs like Medicare. Thus Democrats focused on passing legislation to impose such changes and developed a so-called budget reconciliation bill that would cut between $400 and $500 billion from the deficit over five years with a combination of spending cuts and tax increases. As with the rescission legislation, reconciliation could yield political benefits for both congressional Democrats and the president, who jointly sought to establish a reputation for reducing the deficit. Clinton had also originated many of the details of the measure, placing it high on his legislative agenda and tying his reputation closely with the bill's fate, and he needed a decisive legislative victory after suffering setbacks in trying to pass an economic stimulus bill earlier that year. By helping pass the reconciliation bill, Foley would thus address a leadership re-election goal (by helping his party in Congress) and a role-fulfillment goal (by enacting the desired policy of a same-party incumbent president) (*Congressional Quarterly Almanac* 1993, 107–9).

To keep the bill alive, Speaker Foley was forced to employ floor-related legislative leadership on two separate occasions. The first was passage of the House version of the measure in May 1993. Since virtually no Republicans appeared willing to vote for reconciliation, Foley had to win the support of both Democratic conservatives, who were resistant to tax increases and thought the measure did not cut enough spending, and liberals who wanted no more cuts to social welfare entitlement programs than were already in the bill. The former group proved more difficult to persuade, and in mid-May three influential Democratic deficit hawks—David McCurdy from Oklahoma, Tim Penny from Minnesota, and Charles Stenholm from Texas—threatened to reject the bill without a chance to impose spending limits on entitlement programs, raising the specter that other party conservatives would join them. After further negotiations with members of both wings of his party, Foley agreed to include a requirement in the bill that the White House place firm limits on future entitlement spending and, if the limits were exceeded without proper justification, offer additional spending cuts or tax increases. This still left Foley shy of a majority, however, and he joined party leaders and the president in calling or meeting with individual Democrats, particularly those worried about the electoral consequences of supporting tax increases. Nonetheless, "a few hours before the vote," House leaders "were uncertain of the outcome. But they decided to go ahead, in part because they concluded that delay would not work in their favor" (Cohen 1994, 113). Finishing the day's floor debate, Foley delivered a lengthy speech on the legislation's behalf, acknowledging that "this is not an easy bill to vote for" but that "this bill, the President's plan, contains the most effective budget controls ever put in a Budget Reconciliation Act. . . . This is a time to justify your election and the confidence the American people have given in sending you to this chamber to carry on their business." The efforts of Foley and others paid off: they had managed to recruit a small but solid majority of legislators, and the bill passed on May 27, 219–213 (Cohen 1994, 113–14; *Congressional Quarterly Almanac* 1993, 111; *Congressional Record,* 27 May 1993, H3298–99; Krauss 1993a; Rosenbaum 1993).

The second occasion arose three months later, when the House had to pass the conference version of reconciliation. Clinton gave a televised address advocating the budget plan, and he and congressional leaders lobbied hard for votes among the House rank and file, privately warning some that failure to pass the conference report would convince voters that Democrats could not govern. But party conservatives were still unhappy with the measure's tax increases and limited spending cuts. In an attempt to keep fiscal conservatives in the "pro" camp and with the vote one day away, Foley tried to convince Representative Penny to publicly endorse the bill. He agreed to but on the condition that Clinton would propose further spending cuts in the near future. Nonetheless, key supporters of the original bill, including McCurdy, Bill Brewster of Oklahoma, and Ray Thornton of Arkansas all decided to oppose it at the last minute (Cohen 1994, 207, 209; Drew 1994, 264–66, 268; Krauss 1993b).

On the day of the vote, the conference report was lacking enough support, and Foley petitioned resistant Democrats throughout the day. In addition, the Speaker again delivered the closing speech on the House floor. Acknowledging that the bill "will not by itself accomplish what we need to do" to balance the federal budget, he argued that "it is a crucial beginning that we must make. . . . The Republican Party will march in lockstep, so we on this side of the aisle must bear the burden of responsibility. We are ready to do it. We are anxious to do it, and we will do it" (*Congressional Record,* 5 August 1993, H6271).

When the voting started, party leaders were still not sure that the measure would pass. At first, supporters outnumbered opponents in the running vote tally, but the margin shrank as time passed. After the standard fifteen-minute voting period had ended, the vote was tied, 210–210. A handful of additional legislators then cast their ballots, and the count stood at 216–214—but the House awaited the votes of four more Democrats, at least two of which were expected to vote no. Marjorie Margolies-Mezvinsky of Pennsylvania, a freshman Democrat who had voted against the earlier House bill and publicly opposed the conference report, had been reluctantly convinced by President Clinton to support the measure if it were absolutely necessary. Together with Montana Democrat Pat Williams, she went to the well of the House and voted yes; their two votes cancelled out the no votes of Democrats Thornton and David Minge (MN), and the conference report passed, 218–216. The measure later passed the Senate, with Vice President Al Gore casting the tie-breaking vote (Cohen 1994, 210–12; *Congressional Quarterly Almanac* 1993, 123; Drew 1994, 268; Wines 1993).

While Foley and Clinton had succeeded, the close House vote would come back to haunt at least one Democratic legislator. Representative Margolies-Mezvinsky's last-minute vote was highlighted by her opponent in the 1994 elections, and she lost in what would be a big year for Republican congressional candidates.

Gingrich and Welfare Reform, 1996

In August 1996, President Clinton signed into law a bill that would dramatically shift the nation's welfare system from a national entitlement program to one run by states, with more restrictive eligibility limits. Although Clinton claimed that by doing so he had met his 1992 promise to "end welfare as we know it," most of the efforts behind the measure came from Republicans in Congress, and Speaker Newt Gingrich in particular.[24]

By early 1996, Gingrich had at least two distinct goals in mind that could influence legislative strategy on welfare reform. The first was achieving his party's electoral and ideological objectives. Welfare reform was a major policy objective of the Republican Party, and it was also tied to the party's electoral fate: reform of the welfare system was included in the "Contract with America," and its enactment would help to shore up the GOP's reputation for legislative productivity, particularly after the unpopular government shutdowns of the previous year. Yet because Clinton had already vetoed two earlier welfare reform bills, avoiding a third veto would probably require Gingrich and fellow Republicans to compromise with the president. The second goal was to help the party's presumptive presidential candidate, Senator Bob Dole of Kansas. Dole was already criticizing Clinton for his two previous vetoes of welfare reform, and he could continue this line of attack if Clinton were to veto a third reform bill (Espo 1996; Seelye 1996; Strahan 2007, 153–57). Congressional Republicans would therefore best assist Dole if they sent Clinton a bill less palatable to the president.

Gingrich was faced with conflicting strategies. He initially leaned toward following the second path and pushed for a reform bill that also converted Medicaid into a state-run block grant program with a cap on its future growth —something Clinton would likely veto, thus helping Dole (or, in the unlikely case that Clinton signed it into law, achieving a much-desired legislative objective). But Gingrich was forced to change his position when freshman Rep. John Ensign (R-NV) spearheaded a successful lobbying effort within the Republican Party Conference to pass a bill that would face a more realistic chance of getting Clinton's signature. In July 1996, the Speaker and other party leaders announced that the next welfare reform bill would not include the changes to Medicaid, greatly increasing the chances of Clinton's approval as a consequence. Although congressional Republicans would later credit Dole with requesting this change, both Gingrich and the Dole campaign had really been compelled by the demands of Ensign and like-minded House Republicans (Clymer 1996; Drew 1997, 97–98; Espo 1996; Killian 1998, 346–47; Koszczuk 1996).[25]

Republicans had dropped Medicaid restructuring from the welfare reform measure, but Clinton and several moderate Republicans argued that the revised bill was still too draconian. They began coalescing around a different plan, introduced by Michael Castle (R-DE) and John Tanner (D-TN), that would impose fewer restrictions on welfare benefits and dedicate more resources for child care, food stamps, and job training. The Castle-Tanner bill gave Gingrich and other party leaders some worry, since there were enough Republican moderates in the House to join with a unanimous Democratic Party to pass it (Killian 1998, 347–48; Pear 1996).

Despite growing support for the Castle-Tanner plan, Gingrich chose neither to delay consideration of welfare reform nor to try blocking a floor vote on the alternative bill. Instead, he sent an "extremely strongly worded" letter to fellow Republicans on the day of the vote, writing, "I consider this to be the most important issue we will face between now and the end of the session," and urging would-be defectors to speak with him or Majority Leader Dick Armey before voting (Killian 1998, 348). Also, in an effort to gain support from moderates, the official Republican bill was modified to allow states to provide more funding for certain welfare programs. Although the Speaker did not advocate against the Castle-Tanner bill when it came to the floor in mid-July, he "personally worked the floor" in opposition and cast a rare vote against the measure. In the end, the alternative reform bill failed, 168–258, with only nine Republicans voting for it and thirty-six Democrats—plus seven Republicans who had sponsored the bill—voting no. Since the vote was not particularly close, Gingrich's lobbying efforts may not have been crucial to the outcome, but it seems likely that the Speaker did prevent at least some defections (Killian 1998, 349; Koszczuk 1996; Vobejda 1996).

The final welfare bill passed the House, 256–170, and the conference version of the measure passed later that month by a vote of 328 to 101. With Clinton's signature, the 104th Congress had successfully made one of the most significant changes to the federal welfare program in many years. Unfortunately for the Republican Party, however, Clinton used the bill to inoculate himself from criticism by Dole during his presidential campaign, and he won reelection that November.

HELPING THE PARTY IN CONGRESS

The majority of post-1970 cases in the data set (seventeen of twenty-seven) are best explained as Speakers acting to further their congressional party's electoral or policy objectives, thus ensuring their own status as Speaker. But some of these cases also reflected other, albeit secondary, goals of the Speaker (see table 4.1). Rather than discuss all seventeen cases of legislative leadership in detail, I focus on the eight examples that provide some of the stronger evidence of Speaker influence on or near the House floor. These eight also represent a cross section of Speakers and a diversity of legislative topics: three involved Albert, two O'Neill, one Wright, and two Gingrich, and they cover issues ranging from tax law and budget policy to welfare, economic aid, and foreign affairs.

Albert and Economic Legislation (three cases), 1971–72

Political scientist Ronald Peters argues that Speaker Carl Albert played an important role in the consideration of three major economic bills in the 91st and 92nd Congresses (1969–72). One bill would create federal jobs for the unemployed, the second would fund public works development in poorer regions of the United States, and the third would increase the minimum wage. Albert's support for these bills can be explained as stemming from his concern for the policy preferences of his party caucus. All three measures reflected the Democratic Party's basic support for an active federal role in social welfare; they focused attention away from more divisive issues for the congressional party, like the war in Vietnam; and they allowed Democrats to address economic concerns of the broader public (Peters 1997, 161–73).[26]

Albert supported all of these proposals, but his use of legislative leadership on or near the House floor was most apparent during the 1971 consideration of the job creation bill. Nixon had vetoed a jobs bill in the previous (91st) Congress, but after the 1970 elections an employment bill was reintroduced in the House, and it passed the House Education and Labor Committee in the spring of 1971. The biggest threat to the bill's passage on the floor came from the traditional "conservative coalition" of Republicans and southern Democrats, which, while weaker than it had been under Speakers Rayburn and McCormack, was still a significant presence in the House in the early 1970s. The coalition, less supportive of federal job creation programs than liberal Democrats, was expected to try to amend or defeat the legislation (Orfield 1975, 220–22; Peters 1997, 162–63).

To head off this possibility, Albert met with the party's Steering and Policy Committee to urge unified party support for the bill, and he lobbied Democrats following a leadership whip count. But when the rule allowing consideration of the measure came to the floor in mid-May, more than forty southern Democrats voted with House Republicans to defeat the previous question to the rule, 182–210, giving Republicans temporary control of the House floor. The same cross-party coalition then joined together to allow a second employment bill to come to the floor. By a vote of 210–177, the House amended the original floor rule, permitting consideration of legislation (endorsed by congressional Republicans and President Nixon) to provide job creation funding directly to state governments. The revised rule passed by an even wider margin. Initially confident of success, Albert and other party leaders were reportedly "shocked" by this major setback (Orfield 1975, 217–18, 223; Peters 1997, 164).

The Speaker and fellow Democratic leaders quickly swung into action. They delayed further debate on job creation legislation for two weeks, giving them time to lobby legislators and mobilize outside advocates to help. Together with Majority Leader Hale Boggs, Albert "personally made the rounds of southerners' offices to shake loose their support" of the Republican bill (Davidson 1972, 89). Albert's efforts paid off: on June 2, when the alternative Republican job creation measure came up for a vote, it failed 182–204. Only twenty-one southern Democrats voted for it, while fifty-one southern Democrats and six Republicans, along with all but two northern Democrats, voted against it. Comparing this vote with the earlier 210–177 vote to allow consideration of the amendment reveals that eighteen Democrats, all southerners, had switched their votes from opposing to supporting the Democratic leadership (as well as six Republicans). Most legislators' W-NOMINATE scores successfully predict their vote choice for the second vote, but Albert's lobbying had recruited enough Democrats to effectively "shift" the cut line separating supporters and opponents (see figure 4.1). The original job creation bill later passed the House, 245–141, and Nixon ultimately agreed to sign a compromise version of the legislation into law (Orfield 1975, 223; Peters 1997, 163).

With respect to the other two bills, on public works development and a minimum wage increase, Albert had mixed success. The former measure was passed in both the House and the Senate but was vetoed by the president in 1971. The

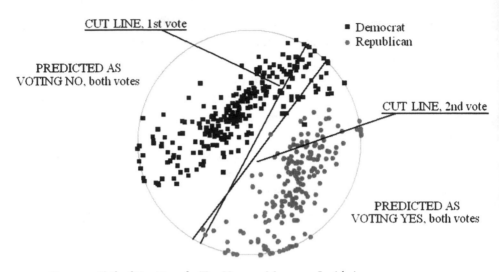

CUT LINE, 1st vote

■ Democrat
● Republican

PREDICTED AS
VOTING NO, both votes

CUT LINE, 2nd vote

PREDICTED AS
VOTING YES, both votes

Figure 4.1 Shift of Cut Lines for Two Votes on Manpower Legislation, 1971
Note: The first vote was to revise Democratic floor rule (210–177, 18 May); the second vote was to approve the alternative Republican bill (182–204, 2 June).

latter measure, however, did eventually become law. Both the Ways and Means Committee and the Rules Committee initially opposed a more liberal version of the bill supported by Albert; party dissidents then joined with Republicans in voting on the floor to reduce the scope and coverage of the plan, which never made it to the president's desk in the 92nd Congress. But after the 1972 elections, Congress eventually succeeded in getting Nixon to sign a minimum wage bill (Peters 1997, 165–72).

O'Neill and the Gramm-Latta Budget Resolution, 1981

One of Ronald Reagan's first major policy objectives as president was to cut federal taxes and social welfare spending while providing more funding for national defense. Although Republicans controlled the Senate, Democrats held a majority in the House, and they could be expected to reject or drastically alter the spending bills Reagan would need to achieve his fiscal goals. The Reagan White House, however, saw a possible route to success via the annual budget resolution process, which required Congress to pass a resolution each year setting spending and revenue caps for appropriations legislation. If the president could somehow persuade a majority in the House to pass a budget resolution that reflected his policy priorities, Congress's tax and spending bills for that year would have to comply with the White House's fiscal objectives. Doing so would also signal Democratic committee chairmen that legislation not conforming to Republican spending priorities would risk losing on the floor (Stockman 1986, 186).

The chances of success for this gambit seemed slim. A number of moderate House Republicans supported some federal spending programs, and conservative Democrats were as worried about the budget deficit that might result from the loss of federal revenue as they were about high tax rates. As a result, according to Reagan's director of the Office of Management and Budget, David Stockman, the president was initially "at least one hundred votes short of the House majority needed" to pass a Republican-sponsored budget resolution. But Reagan forged ahead, pushing for passage of a resolution ultimately named after its Budget Committee cosponsors, conservative Democrat Phil Gramm (D-TX) and Republican Delbert Latta (R-OH) (Stockman 1986, 184–85, 190).

Speaker O'Neill resisted the Gramm-Latta resolution in many ways, faithfully representing the policy interests of his congressional party. But some would later argue that the Speaker did not fight it as vigorously as he could have. While Reagan lobbied heavily for the resolution, for instance, O'Neill failed to seriously recruit Republicans to oppose it. Even more helpful to the president, O'Neill allowed the Rules Committee to let both the Democratic budget and Gramm-Latta be subject to separate floor votes, which Stockman later claimed "virtually ensured easy passage of our budget" (Barone 1990, 614; Farrell 2001, 552; Stockman 1986, 190).[27]

Some, including Ways and Means Committee Chairman Dan Rostenkowski and O'Neill advisor Gary Hymel, have suggested that O'Neill initially limited his resistance to Reagan's budget proposal out of deference to the executive branch. To be sure, Reagan was newly elected; the public expected the White House to act swiftly to address current economic problems; and shortly after the November 1980 elections, O'Neill declared he would cooperate with Reagan on policy making, noting that "it's America first and party second." As Hymel put it in an interview with the author, O'Neill believed that "the people elected him, so you've got to give him a chance" at governing (Farrell 2001, 545–46; O'Neill 1987, 412; Smith 1988, 511; Gary Hymel interview, May 2003). However, not only were the Speaker's actions plausibly motivated by the needs of his congressional party, but it is not clear that O'Neill actually wanted to give Reagan much, if any, help. Texas Democrat Jim Wright, who was the majority leader at the time, noted in an interview that he had worked closely with the Speaker to defeat Gramm-Latta and that if O'Neill's plan had been to let the bill pass, "he left me out on a damn limb" (interview with the author, May 2003). Furthermore, by not committing all of his efforts to blocking or defeating Gramm-Latta, O'Neill would help House Democrats by avoiding open opposition to a popular president. If the budget's cuts proved unpopular, it would also tarnish the reputation of Reagan and congressional Republicans. It may even be that O'Neill's apparent surrender to Reagan was actually a consequence of the Speaker underestimating the president, a sentiment that led him to travel to Australia and New Zealand as Reagan continued lobbying aggressively for votes. In short, rather than using his agenda-setting authority to increase the chances of a legislative victory but jeopardize the electoral status of vulnerable House Democrats, the Speaker deferred the legislative schedule—but not a policy victory—to the newly elected president (Farrell 2001, 546, 554–55; Remini 2006, 458; Safire 1981; Sinclair 1983, 194).[28]

Despite his initially unclear chances of success, Reagan adroitly exploited every advantage he had. Perhaps most important, the president focused on winning over conservative (so-called boll weevil) Democrats who might be willing to form a majority coalition with Republicans on the House floor. Reagan had won in many of their districts, and they were sympathetic to the idea of more spending on defense and less on social programs. Speaker O'Neill, recognizing the boll weevils' critical importance to a floor vote on the budget, sought to keep them from voting for Gramm-Latta by endorsing a Democratic budget resolution that contained many of Reagan's proposed spending cuts. But majority party leaders admitted that they would have to support much higher increases in defense spending than they wanted in order to prevent boll weevil votes for the president's bill. After March 30, when President Reagan was nearly assassinated, sympathy for the president and, by extension, his budget proposal seemed to negate the public's earlier concerns about Gramm-Latta's extensive spending cuts. By the end of April, as Wright later described it, Reagan "was [not only] a new president, he had [also] just risen from an attempt on his life" and was therefore "just immensely popular" (interview with the author, July 2003). O'Neill soon acknowledged publicly that Gramm-Latta was likely to pass (Dewar 1981a; Dewar and Lyons 1981; Farrell 2001, 544, 552–54, 556; Kaiser 1981; Stockman 1986, 184, 187).

Yet the Speaker and fellow party leaders still made some efforts to defeat the resolution. Floor deliberation was delayed for a week while Democrats considered altering their own budget resolution to attract more swing voters. The Democratic whip's office, which was conducting vote counts to gauge support for the Gramm-Latta measure, issued briefing papers to aid other party members who were helping whip for the party's budget resolution. O'Neill tried to halt Gramm-Latta's momentum by claiming it was losing the support of legislators, including many Republicans. The vote to pass Gramm-Latta was also designated a "key vote" for the party and thus an important test of Democrats' loyalty. These efforts in the face of an increasingly likely floor defeat are further evidence of the Speaker's strong partisan opposition to Reagan's budget. Meanwhile, the White House was pushing extensively for Gramm-Latta: for example, administration aide Elizabeth Dole enlisted hundreds of outside lobbyists to contact key persuadable Democrats (Dewar 1981b; 1981c; 1981d; Evans 2007; whip issue paper, O'Neill Papers, Kirk O'Donnell file, box 6, folder 9; Democratic Study Group memo, O'Neill Papers, Kirk O'Donnell file, box 6, folder 11; list of key votes from 97th Congress, O'Neill Papers, Party Leadership file, box 7, folder 6).[29]

Reagan's victory was virtually assured a few days before the scheduled vote when the number of Democrats publicly endorsing the Reagan budget reached thirty-three—seven more than needed to pass the bill, assuming no Republicans voted against it. When the Gramm-Latta resolution came to the floor, it passed, 253 to 176, with sixty-three Democrats joining a unanimous Republican Party in support. Both political momentum and White House lobbying made the difference. Some nineteen Democrats may have voted for Gramm-Latta once it was clear it would pass, and perhaps ten to twelve others did so in response to strong White House pressure (Sinclair 1983, 196–97; Tolchin 1981).

This event arguably represented an important turning point in Tip O'Neill's Speakership. O'Neill's initial instinct may have been to give some deference to the newly elected president, but he did not expect such a dramatic defeat, and as Jim Wright succinctly put it, "Tip and I got rolled." The Speaker continued to lose important floor votes against Reagan throughout 1981: for example, on a measure imposing the tax cuts specified in Gramm-Latta, which passed by a vote of 217 to 211, and on another major tax bill, which passed 238–195 (Peters 1997, 235–36; quote from Farrell 2001, 547). By the end of 1982, however, O'Neill had become more successful in fighting the White House's agenda, even successfully overriding a presidential veto on a supplemental spending bill (see table 4.1).

O'Neill and Contra Funding, 1983–86

In 1979, communist rebels overthrew the right-wing Somoza government of Nicaragua. Newly elected president Ronald Reagan was concerned by both the presence of communism in Latin America and reports that the new Sandinista communist regime was lending military support to like-minded rebels in neighboring El Salvador. In response, Reagan secretly authorized the Central Intelligence Agency to conduct covert operations against the Sandinistas, including providing assistance to former government soldiers and other Sandinista opponents who, collectively, came to be known as the "Contras" (Farrell 2001, 612; LeoGrande 1998, 14–27, 53, 86–89, 114–18).

Support for the Contras developed into a major partisan issue in Congress, dominating the legislative agenda throughout the 1980s. Democrats were skeptical of the Reagan administration's view that the Sandinistas posed a major threat to the region and were alarmed by reports of human rights abuses by security forces in neighboring (and anticommunist) El Salvador. A number of Democrats also feared that aid to the Contras would lead to a Vietnam-like quagmire for the United States, and news leaks about Reagan's secret military aid program did little to ease their concerns. Thus Speaker O'Neill's opposition to funding the Contras represented his congressional party's preferences: liberals became strong opponents of Contra aid while Reagan and House conservatives supported it. Evidence also points to another leadership goal, of secondary importance, that factored into O'Neill's position: passage of personally desired policy. The first prominent House "stalwart" in the 1970s to openly endorse withdrawing troops from Vietnam, O'Neill was particularly sensitive to the possibility of entering a similar conflict. The Speaker also had close ties to members of the American Catholic clergy, who expressed strong concerns to the Speaker about assaults and murders of local church members in the region (Farrell 2001, 245, 611–14; LeoGrande 1998, 59–62, 91–93; O'Neill 1987, 443; Smith 1984).

This case of legislative leadership encompasses a number of bills considered over several years. Ronald Peters argues that O'Neill was a consistent and active opponent of Contra military assistance, with seven of eight significant votes on military aid from 1983 to 1986 going in his favor (1997, 250). The outcome of most of these votes depended on a small number of moderate legislators from both parties.[30] They involved such measures as:

- in July 1983, legislation containing a provision authored by Edward Boland (D-MA) to prohibit covert funding for Contra operations, which passed 228–195 (LeoGrande 1998, 312–14, 321);
- in October 1983, an intelligence authorization bill containing similar prohibition language authored by Boland, which also passed the House (Farrell 2001, 614);[31]

- in May 1984, the conference version of a supplemental spending bill, which had been amended on the floor to cut $21 million in Contra aid added by the Senate (*Congressional Quarterly Almanac* 1984, 429);
- in August 1984, an intelligence authorization bill that prohibited secret operations in Nicaragua (Farrell 2001, 620; LeoGrande 1998, 344–45);
- in April 1985, legislation to authorize $14 million in military funding for the Contras, which was later rejected;
- in March 1986, a Contra funding resolution that also lost on the floor, 210–222;
- and in June of that year, in a loss for O'Neill, an appropriations bill providing $100 million in funding for the Contras, which passed 221–209 (Farrell 2001, 671; O'Neill 1987, 441–42).

O'Neill exercised floor leadership on at least two of these measures. One was the $14 million Contra aid bill from 1985. Congress had approved the funding the year before but made its release contingent on passage of a joint resolution the following year. The 1984 elections yielded no clear majority in Congress for Contra aid, and the odds that the resolution would pass seemed poor. Nonetheless, Reagan used public appearances to criticize the Sandinistas and urge support for the Contras; sent Secretary of State George Shultz to petition Capitol Hill; and, in an effort to win over moderate Democrats, offered to develop a peace plan for the region in exchange for the military aid (*Congressional Quarterly Almanac* 1985, 63–64; LeoGrande 1998, 417; O'Neill 1987, 440).

In response, O'Neill tasked two senior Democrats to draft an alternative to Reagan's peace proposal. O'Neill also put much more energy into killing the resolution than he had against Contra funding in the past. With the Speaker meeting personally with freshmen and swing Democrats, as O'Neill aide Kirk O'Donnell later put it, "you could hear the sound of elbows crunching." Once he believed he had the votes to win, the Speaker curtailed the president's ability to lobby Congress by scheduling the vote earlier than expected. O'Neill's lobbying was so extensive and personal in nature that it drew complaints from the president and made the vote in effect a referendum on the Speaker himself (Arnson 1989, 181; *Congressional Quarterly Almanac* 1985, 65–66; Omang and Shapiro 1985; O'Neill 1987, 440; Shapiro 1985).

When the resolution came to the floor, the House rejected an amendment version of the Reagan proposal, 180–248, but votes on two other amendments remained. The first was a Democratic alternative plan restricting the $14 million to nonmilitary humanitarian purposes; the second, a Republican amendment to that alternative, would also restrict the aid to nonmilitary purposes but give it to the Contras more directly. The Democratic alternative passed the following day but by a fairly close 219–206 vote. The vote on the Republican substitute proved even closer: when the regular time allowed for casting ballots had passed, the vote count was 205 to 205. The vote was held open while enough legislators cast last-minute votes to kill the substitute, and it lost, 213–215. O'Neill, however, suffered an unexpected defeat on the final vote to pass the bill, which now contained the Democratic language. Republican supporters of the Contras, dissatisfied with the Democratic amendment, joined liberals who were happy to vote against any Contra funding, and the resolution lost, 123–303. This meant no funds for the Contras, it but also left Democratic moderates without an alternative they could support, putting pressure on House leaders to pass some sort of Contra funding bill later that Congress (*Congressional Quarterly Almanac* 1985, 72; LeoGrande 1998, 423–26).

The second clear example of O'Neill's leadership on Contra funding occurred in March 1986. Under the provisions of a law passed the previous year, President Reagan could request nonlethal Contra assistance, which would get special consideration in Congress. Reagan went much further than many expected, however, asking for $100 million in funds (far larger than any previous request by the White House), the ability to spend $70 million of it at his discretion, and an end to statutory bans on Pentagon and CIA involvement in anti-Sandinista operations. Fortunately for Reagan, existing statute required that his proposal be considered on the House floor within as little as twenty legislative days, so Democrats could not use their usual control over the agenda to block the bill. In addition, the president made use of a televised national address, phone calls to legislators, and lobbying and media campaigns by outside interest groups to persuade undecided House members to support his plan (*Congressional Quarterly Almanac* 1986, 395, 397–99, 400; LeoGrande 1998, 443; Walsh 1986).

O'Neill fought back, mounting an "extensive personal lobbying" campaign and using "personal, emotional pleas" to secure votes (Boyd 1986; Evans and Novak 1986). The Speaker was leaving the House at the end of the year, and he framed the vote as a final personal favor to him as part of what one historian described as "the final epic battle between Reagan and Speaker Tip O'Neill." The president's funding plan also suffered from key weaknesses, including its size, its inclusion of military aid, and the tepid support it garnered from Central American leaders hoping to end the guerilla war. Democratic moderates tried to persuade Reagan to temper his proposal, but he agreed only to delay some spending for a few months while peace negotiations were underway, an offer that failed to persuade more than a small number of uncommitted legislators (*Congressional Quarterly Almanac* 1986, 398–400; LeoGrande 1998, 454).

Two events just before the vote also helped O'Neill. Reagan's press secretary, Pat Buchanan, suggested in a *Washington Post* editorial that bill opponents were aligning themselves with the Nicaraguan communists, an argument that alienated moderate Democrats. Then, two days before the vote, O'Neill made an important concession: meeting with key swing Democrats, he promised a future vote on Contra aid if Reagan's bill was defeated. O'Neill's offer reportedly cost Reagan the support of Oklahoman David McCurdy, a key leader of the party's moderates, and between four and twenty floor votes altogether (Arnson 1989, 192–93; Buchanan 1986; Boyd 1986; *Congressional Quarterly Almanac* 1986, 401).

O'Neill also took action by giving a speech during floor deliberation of the bill. Drawing a contrast between himself and Buchanan, the Speaker argued that the vote "is not a matter of partisanship." "All of you know that I have stood with the President on some tough foreign policy questions," he said, but claimed that arming the Contras "takes us . . . further toward a situation where our country's own troops become involved" (*Congressional Record,* 20 March 1986, 5768). O'Neill went against custom by casting a rare, early vote on the bill, presumably to further sway legislators (Farrell 2001, 671; see also chapter 5). The House rejected the resolution, 210–222, with most Democrats opposing the bill, along with six more Republicans than expected and twenty-four swing legislators who had voted for Contra aid the previous June (Boyd 1986; Parry 1986).

O'Neill did not always win on Contra-related votes: for example, the House passed a $100 million Contra funding package later in 1986 (LeoGrande 1998, 469–71). Nonetheless, such aid was losing support among House moderates, and O'Neill's successor, Jim Wright—who also had both personal and majority party incentives to oppose money for the Contras (see table 4.1)—would ultimately try to forge a solution to the regional conflict.

Wright and Budget Reconciliation, October 1987

Perhaps the most infamous example of Speaker Jim Wright's legislative leadership occurred in October 1987, when the House considered a major deficit-reduction reconciliation bill. The bill imposed tax increases and cut various mandatory spending programs, with the goal of reducing the deficit and avoiding automatic budget cuts otherwise required by existing anti-deficit law. Wright's reasons for supporting the measure were related to the majority sta tus of his party in Congress. Public perception of inaction on federal budget im- balances could, Democrats feared, hurt their reputation among voters. The deficit had also created enough jitters with investors to lead to a precipitous fall in the stock market at the end of October. And although the reconciliation bill included cuts in social welfare programs that liberals disliked, it also contained tax increases on wealthier Americans endorsed by House Democrats (Barry 1989).

Some individual Democrats had particular concerns with the reconciliation package, and Republicans generally opposed its tax increases, but the greatest initial threat to the measure's passage came from a decision to combine it with a major welfare reform bill. Support for changes to the federal welfare system came from state governors and leaders from both parties, who hoped to reduce welfare's costs and increase its effectiveness. Congressman Tom Downey (D-NY) had proposed a relatively expensive welfare reform bill, but expecting that its passage would be difficult, he convinced Ways and Means Committee Chair- man Dan Rostenkowski (D-IL) to include his welfare plan in the reconciliation bill. Speaker Wright agreed to the maneuver, perhaps in the hope that, if noth- ing else, welfare reform could later be removed in exchange for Republican support for the budget bill. Wright endorsed a special floor rule that would automatically enact the welfare bill without subjecting it to a separate vote, but Republicans refused to go along with the gambit, and even some Democrats ex- pressed concern with Wright's strategy (Barry 1989, 398–99, 401, 404–5, 412, 428–29).

What came next put Wright's leadership skills to a severe test. The Speaker asked Democratic whips to spread the word that passage of the rule would be a "leadership" or "party" vote and thus a possible basis for determining the al- location of future party benefits. Nonetheless, early whip counts revealed siz- able opposition to the rule. In response, Wright briefly considered dropping welfare reform from the reconciliation bill, but he and other leaders instead lobbied freshmen and other Democrats, and subsequent whip counts suggested that both reconciliation and welfare reform could pass as a single measure. To improve the bill's chances, party leaders tried to persuade more Democrats when the rule came to the House floor, and Wright spoke on the floor on its behalf (Barry 1989, 424, 429, 432–51, 457–58).

Unfortunately, as Wright himself would later describe it, "a miscount of vote commitments . . . precipitated a parliamentary crisis." The whip polls had been inaccurate: when the vote on the rule concluded, the rule had lost, 203–217, with forty-eight Democrats voting against it and not a single Republican voting in favor. Wright immediately decided to save the budget bill by jettisoning the welfare reform portion of the bill. This would require drafting and passing a new floor rule, which Wright wanted to do immediately—before legislators left for the weekend—to avoid losing momentum. House rules, however, required a minimum one-day interval between approval of a floor rule in the Rules Committee and its consideration on the floor. The rule could be suspended, but only with a two-thirds floor vote, which would be virtually impossible to achieve (Barry 1989, 458–61; Connelly and Pitney 1994, 82; Wright 1994, 238).

Wright then made a series of moves that, in the words of political scientist Ronald Peters, "set a modern precedent in the assertive use of the powers of the chair" (Peters 1997, 268). First, he undertook a creative use of the House calendar by officially adjourning the House but then reconvening for a "new" legislative day. While this clever maneuver was not technically prohibited by House rules, nor entirely unprecedented,[32] it infuriated Republicans. Wright and other leaders had briefed moderate and left-leaning Democrats about the plan and asked them for their support, and the revised floor rule for considering the trimmed-down reconciliation bill passed, 238–182. But the Speaker had failed to gauge the full level of Democratic opposition to the bill itself, including its tax increases and additional defense spending. After the normal fifteen minutes of voting time had expired, it was losing by a single vote, 205 to 206. Wright held the vote open while one of his aides tried to get Texas Democrat Jim Chapman, a bill opponent who was hiding in the Democratic cloakroom, to switch his vote. After ten minutes, Chapman reluctantly did so, and the reconciliation bill passed 206–205, with one Republican supporter and forty-one Democratic opponents. Chapman would later get a coveted seat on the Appropriations Committee, presumably in exchange for his last-minute vote (Barry 1989, 460–72; Peters 1997, 268; Sinclair 1995, 97).

The Speaker had undoubtedly made the difference in the final outcome, but his victory proved Pyrrhic. Republicans were deeply angered by how Wright and House Democrats had ignored the norms of the House to pass reconciliation. Even some Democrats felt that the process had been flawed and that party leaders, focusing solely on winning on the floor, had dismissed or ignored their individual concerns—or, as one Democrat put it, "the leadership is not listening" to us (Barry 1989, 480; Connelly and Pitney 1994, 83; Peters 1997, 268–69). Wright's aggressive legislative leadership had not only hurt his standing in the Democratic Caucus, but it helped further empower the vocal and assertive wing of the House Republican Party, led by Congressman (and later Speaker) Newt Gingrich. This dangerous combination contributed to the Speaker's resignation from the House less than two years later.[33]

Gingrich and the Balanced Budget Amendment, 1995

Late in the congressional election campaign of 1994, Republicans announced their legislative agenda, the Contract with America, which called for floor votes on a series of policy initiatives within the first one hundred days of the new Congress. When Republicans subsequently won control of the House, newly chosen Speaker Newt Gingrich and fellow GOP leaders immediately began working to implement it.

The Contract's first item included a constitutional amendment to balance the budget and therefore "restore fiscal responsibility to an out-of-control Congress." As later drafted, the amendment mandated a balanced budget every year, beginning no later than 2002 (or two years after its ratification), and that to do otherwise required a three-fifths vote in both the House and Senate.[34] Reflected by its place in the Contract, the proposal satisfied a major policy objective of House Republicans: many were self-described fiscal conservatives, and a balanced budget amendment to the Constitution, properly worded, had become a favored means of the party to end federal deficits.[35] In addition, its passage could help the party's reputation among the public (which, opinion polls suggested, supported the amendment), whereas its failure might signal that it was unable to enact the top proposal of the Contract. Gingrich would thus be aiding his congressional party in not only bringing the measure to the House floor but seeing it pass (*Contract with America* 1994; Taylor 1995b; Wines 1995b).[36]

Yet even with the momentum of his party's huge electoral success behind him, Speaker Gingrich could not assume an easy floor victory. Since a constitutional amendment required the support of two-thirds of voting House members for passage, the Speaker needed the votes of as many as 30 percent of all congressional Democrats. Some Republicans also disagreed over the wording of the amendment. The original proposal included a requirement that any tax increase must be approved by a supermajority (three-fifths) of the House and Senate, but many of the House's forty or so Republican moderates, less resistant to tax increases and more wary of giving the minority party too much power, opposed the provision. They were joined by Democrats, who feared the provision would lead to legislative stalemates and sharp cuts in social welfare programs; one vote count suggested that keeping the tax limitation requirement in the amendment would limit the number of Democratic supporters to no more than forty. On the other hand, the large Republican freshmen class wanted to remain faithful to the Contract and make it harder to raise taxes. Neither side seemed prepared to surrender their position (Killian 1998, 28; Salant 1995; Taylor 1995a; 1995b).

Gingrich and his leadership colleagues first tried to win support for the original amendment with the tax limitation language, and with that goal in mind, they delayed a floor vote on the matter until the end of January. But meetings between GOP leaders and moderates, including a mid-January session convened by the Speaker, failed to produce enough votes. Assuming that their party's freshmen members would vote for a balanced budget amendment even without the tax limitation requirement, the Republican leadership decided that the provision had to be dropped. Gingrich and other party leaders remained publicly in favor of the provision, but privately they supported an alternative measure (proposed by Texas Democrat Charlie Stenholm and Colorado Republican Dan Schaefer) which excluded the tax reduction provision, and also endorsed a plan to allow votes on both amendments (Killian 1998, 28; Salant 1995; Wines 1995a).

Unfortunately, Gingrich had miscalculated the sentiment of Republican freshmen, and his unexpected change in legislative strategy surprised and alienated many of them. Two first-term Republicans, John Shadegg (AZ) and Mark Souder (IN), quickly spearheaded a campaign of their own. Making phone calls and circulating a "dear colleague" letter in the House, they gathered pledges from around forty legislators to vote against a balanced budget amendment that excluded the tax reduction proposal. Even with the votes of Republican moderates and conservative Democrats, this would be enough to kill it (Killian 1998, 28–29).

Meanwhile, under the direction of Republican leaders, the House Rules Committee crafted an unusual "queen of the hill" floor rule. The rule allowed votes on several balanced budget amendments but permitted a final vote only on the amendment that had garnered the most votes (Taylor 1995a). The original amendment, which included the tax limitation language, would be voted on first, allowing Gingrich to estimate its chances of passing the House (Wines 1995c). This procedure gave both conservatives and moderates a chance to vote their sincere preferences, but it was no guarantee that the two groups would unify behind whichever amendment would get a final floor vote.

With Republican moderates still unwilling to support the tax limitation proposal, Gingrich and other leaders began asking the proposal's most ardent enthusiasts—the Republican freshmen—to vote for the Stenholm-Schaefer plan. Shadegg eventually told the Speaker that the freshmen would drop their opposition to the plan only if the House held a floor vote on the supermajority tax reduction proposal at some future point. On the morning before floor votes were to be held, Gingrich and other party leaders mounted a day-long intensive lobbying blitz in which, as one GOP staffer commented, "The leadership squeezed them [the freshmen] pretty hard." Finally, one hour before the first vote, Gingrich met personally with about a dozen conservative Republicans, agreed to Shadegg's compromise, and managed to convince a number of them to also agree to Shadegg's deal (Gray 1995a; Killian 1998, 29–30; Taylor 1995b; Wines 1995d).

Gingrich was soon proved right in his decision to abandon the original amendment: it received 253 votes, 31 votes shy of the necessary two-thirds, with only thirty-three Democrats in favor and eight Republicans against.[37] By contrast, the Stenholm-Schaefer amendment received the most votes: 293, including those of seventy-two Democrats, with just nine Republican opponents, five of whom were freshmen. In the final floor vote, it passed with 300 affirmative votes (including those of seventy-two Democrats), while only two Republicans, both freshmen, opposed the measure (Killian 1998, 30; Taylor 1995b).

The amendment's passage, along with significant changes to House rules proposed in the Contract with America and enacted earlier in January, was the beginning of a flurry of legislative activity in the first few months of the 104th Congress. Yet it also was a sign that the House Republican majority was not entirely unified around its legislative agenda. The ultimate fate of the amendment—failure in the Senate by a single vote—also illustrated that House passage of Contract items did not ensure their success in the other legislative chamber (Cloud 1995a).

Gingrich and Income Tax Reduction, 1995

Near the end of the first one hundred days of the 104th Congress, Gingrich faced a major intraparty battle over another Contract item: income tax reduction. Tax cuts would satisfy important policy and election goals for congressional Republicans. They were a central tenet of the Republican Party and particularly important to its major constituencies, including conservative religious and family-oriented interest groups. In addition, many GOP congressional candidates had endorsed tax reduction during their 1994 campaigns and had criticized President Clinton's unmet promise two years before to reduce income taxes for the middle class (Gingrich 1995, 134; Killian 1998, 73; Pianin 1995a).

After a bill cutting federal taxes on individuals passed the Ways and Means Committee, however, three groups of congressional Republicans emerged that opposed different elements of the bill. First, Republicans from districts with large numbers of federal employees criticized a provision in the legislation that required more pension contributions by government workers, thus reducing their salaries.[38] Two House Republicans, Greg Ganske (IA) and Pat Roberts (KN), organized a second coalition in opposition to the bill's relatively high family annual income limit ($200,000) for eligibility to receive a $500-per-child tax credit. Fearing that the limit was unfairly high, or would at least allow Democrats to make such an accusation, Ganske and Roberts sought to reduce the limit to $95,000, and they obtained signatures from more than one hundred other Republicans (including the chairman of the House Rules Committee) endorsing the change.[39] Finally, a third group of thirty or so fiscally conservative Republicans and twenty-three like-minded Democrats urged that the tax cuts be postponed until the deficit had been reduced, and they seemed particularly adamant in refusing to compromise their position.[40] Even with some crossover in membership between these three coalitions, it was clear that, at best, only a slim majority of House Republicans supported the tax bill as written, and if it drew the expected opposition of most Democrats, it would probably not pass on the floor (Gray 1995b; Killian 1998, 74; Rubin 1995b; Wines 1995e).

Nonetheless, as Randall Strahan and Daniel Palazzolo note in their analysis of his speakership, Gingrich refused to drop the plan or even change it significantly and instead sought to pass the measure with as few modifications as possible. His strategic choice of action serves as an example of how the Speaker may represent other party objectives besides enacting desired policy; in this case, Gingrich was particularly attentive to the electoral consequences for the GOP if it failed to pass the bill. Opinion polls suggested that the broader voting public was largely unfamiliar with the details of the Contract just before the 1994 election, and surveys in early 1995 showed that people were more concerned with the deficit than with tax reduction. Conservative constituents, however, strongly desired tax reduction. They had provided funding and grassroots organizing, as well as votes, for Republican candidates in 1994 and had felt betrayed when the last Republican president, George H. W. Bush, failed to carry through on his promise not to increase taxes (Apple 1995; Killian 1998, 6, 73; Pianin 1995a; Strahan and Palazzolo 2004).

The Speaker used several tactics to quell the burgeoning revolts within his party. He expressed strong support for the bill in a variety of open forums, including public speeches, a "satellite town meeting," and an editorial in the *Wall Street Journal*. To give dissidents a reason to not vote against the bill, Gingrich threatened to delay the House's first scheduled recess if the bill failed. The Speaker and other party leaders also petitioned would-be bill opponents directly, recruiting outside groups to help their lobbying effort. For example, meeting with a number of moderate Republicans just days before the scheduled vote on the bill, the Speaker won additional votes by promising to delay the tax cut's implementation until Congress passed a budget eliminating the deficit within seven years (Killian 1998, 74–75; Pianin 1995b; Rubin 1995a; Wines 1995e).

The real threat was not to the bill but to the floor rule for the bill, because the rule's procedural nature made it easier to oppose without alarming supportive constituencies, and because it did not permit an amendment to reduce the income cap for the child tax cut. To buy additional time, the House Rules Committee delayed meeting for several hours before passing the rule; but by the morning of the vote, the party's whip count showed that there were still at least twenty Republicans planning to vote no. During the day of the scheduled vote, party leaders and committee chairmen continued to put pressure on wavering Republicans. The final outcome was a nail-biter for bill supporters. After voting on the rule began, the number in favor climbed steadily, but then froze at 217, one vote fewer than necessary for passage. Finally, a handful of hesitating Republicans cast their votes for the rule, and it passed, 228–204. Eleven Republicans had voted against it, and nine Democrats had voted in favor (Killian 1998, 76, 79; Rubin 1995c).

Although the rule had come close to losing, the probability that the actual bill would fail was more remote. Nonetheless, Gingrich did not take its passage for granted, and he delivered the closing speech during the subsequent debate on the tax cut, "goading his troops on to final passage" (Killian 1998, 80; Pianin 1995c). With only eleven Republicans opponents and twenty-seven Democrats in favor, the bill passed, 246–188. Its passage represented a significant victory for Gingrich: as he had promised, a floor vote had been held on every item in the Contract within one hundred days, with many of them—including the tax cut, one of its signature elements—passing the House.

CONCLUSION

The cases examined in this chapter reveal that despite their greater formal powers, Speakers from 1971 through 1998 continued to turn to the floor at times to exercise consequential leadership on behalf of major legislation. They are also evidence that the theory of goal-driven leadership best explains when and why Speakers have done so.

The first prediction of the theory—that the modern Speaker exercises legislative leadership to achieve other goals besides reelection to leadership—is valid for the five Speakers who served between Carl Albert and Dennis Hastert. These goals include reelection to Congress (by advocating one's district's preferences), enacting personally desired policy, and satisfying important leadership responsibilities or duties (including support for the presidential party, the institutional presidency, or the House as a whole). Focusing on just the goal of reelection to leadership as motivating Speaker behavior, as party-based leadership theories do, fails to adequately explain several important instances of Speaker leadership.

Second, data in this chapter support the claim that Speakers may exercise leadership for a particular bill or measure to achieve more than one goal. The most common combination of goals found in these cases was the leadership re-election goal (that is, exercising leadership on behalf of congressional party preferences) and the role-fulfillment goal of support for the presidential party. But other goals mattered at times as well; sometimes Speakers sought to fulfill their responsibility to support the institutional presidency (for example, debt limit legislation and NAFTA) or, secondarily, wanted to achieve a personal policy goal (as occurred with flag-burning legislation and Contra funding).

Third, since 1970 Speakers have continued to exercise leadership most often to aid the policy objectives and electoral concerns of their party in Congress. Indeed, a much larger proportion of cases in this chapter, compared to the previous chapter, can be explained by this single goal. The nature of the data (cases derived from sweeps of histories) makes a direct quantitative comparison between historical periods somewhat suspect, but this difference nonetheless suggests that the majority party in Congress has become an increasingly important influence on congressional leader behavior, while other individuals and institutions have become less so. In chapter 7, I discuss this apparent trend and its implication for leadership in Congress.

The sweep-based data make it difficult to test whether the two factors hypothesized in chapter 1—issue saliency and party unity—increased the likelihood of leadership by Speakers Albert through Gingrich. But the evidence suggests that saliency, and to a lesser extent unity, were both important. First, when certain issues were highly salient to the Speaker's presidential party candidate or were strongly supported by the White House, the Speaker proved willing to exercise leadership to assist the executive branch. The same also occurred for issues of great importance to the Speaker personally (for example, Gingrich and funding for endangered species protection), the party in Congress, or the House as a whole. Second, the House majority party, particularly under Gingrich, was often highly unified on issues that commanded the attention of the Speaker. Speakers did, however, sometimes exercise legislative leadership when their party was not unified. In some of these cases, Speakers did so on behalf of a long-standing or well-understood party plank or to carry water for a sizable majority with strong preferences. Other times, Speakers acted not on behalf of their party's policy goals but to help their party's reputation or otherwise maximize its electoral safety (as with, for example, the 1979 debt limit legislation, budget reconciliation in 1993, and the vote on Everglades protection in 1995).

Finally, it is worth noting that in several cases in this chapter, the Speaker incorrectly predicted or estimated the preferences (or at least voting behavior) of members of his caucus. These instances include the two Wright examples discussed in detail (budget reconciliation and the congressional pay raise), the passage of the 1995 Balanced Budget Act, and two other cases shown in table 4.1 (Wright and Contra funding in 1988, and Speaker Gingrich and a committee funding bill in early 1997). An important assumption of most congressional leadership theories is that party leaders are able to adequately assess the concerns or preferences of those they represent, be it their party in Congress or some other individual or group. As these cases demonstrate, such an assumption cannot always be made, and the consequences can be profound for legislative results or even security of the Speaker's position as party leader.

Chapter 5 Leadership beyond the Floor, 1941–1998

Speakers of the House do not limit themselves to influencing legislative outcomes on or near the House floor. They may also exercise influence in other ways, such as by manipulating the agenda, crafting legislation, or strategically referring bills (for example, Shepsle and Bonchek 1997, 390–92). Unlike floor-related behavior, these kinds of leadership techniques are often difficult to observe and have a less certain causal relation to legislative outcomes, but they are no less important. In this chapter, I examine whether the theory of goal-driven leadership can explain such methods of influence. The evidence suggests that in many cases it does: Speakers often exercise non-floor leadership to satisfy not only their reelection goals but their policy and/or role-fulfillment goals as well.

Using the same literature sweep method employed in chapters 3 and 4, I collected and examined all instances of non-floor legislative leadership from 1941 to 1998 to test the broader applicability of my theory. (Cases involving Speaker Dennis Hastert are discussed in chapter 6.) Because of the large number of cases, rather than discussing them all, in this chapter I provide an in-depth case study analysis of a subset. I then briefly discuss a relatively recent form of Speaker leadership, "going public," which may also influence legislative results. I show that because of its very nature, going public is usually employed to benefit the majority party in Congress rather than other individuals, entities, or institutions.

CASES OF NON-FLOOR
LEGISLATIVE LEADERSHIP

Speakers are not restricted to the floor as the only sphere in which to exercise legislative leadership. Other categories of leadership include (1) setting or shaping the agenda, to determine what (or when) bills, amendments, or resolutions may be brought to the House floor; (2) influencing the specific content of legislation, that is, proposing, drafting, or altering legislation before or after floor deliberation; (3) influencing committee consideration of legislation, such as by referring bills to particular committees, creating "special" committees or task forces, or urging committees to (not) undertake an investigation or pass a bill; and (4) miscellaneous legislative leadership that does not fall into the other categories, such as influencing presidential behavior or appointing representatives to summit talks with the White House.[1]

To capture cases of such Speaker behavior, I used the literature sweep methodology outlined in chapter 1, looking for references to activity that fell into one of the four categories above. The sweeps uncovered ninety-five specific incidents of legislative leadership committed by Speakers Sam Rayburn through Newt Gingrich (see tables 5.1 through 5.4). Note that in several of these instances Speakers also used floor leadership that was captured in the sweeps in chapters 3 and 4. A cursory review of these ninety-five cases suggests certain patterns and commonalities. For example, agenda setting was the most frequent type of non-floor leadership, and the primary method of agenda setting was to influence the Rules Committee, which serves as the "traffic cop" for most major legislation in the House before it is scheduled for a floor vote.

There are good reasons to refrain from broad comparisons using these data, however. First, since the number of sources mentioning recent Speakers is necessarily fewer than those mentioning earlier ones, the sweeps may undercount the number of cases involving more contemporary Speakers. Second, the literature sweeps capture specific and concrete instances of Speaker activity but not general allegations of influence (see also appendix A). As a result, some important references to the non-floor behavior of Speakers were excluded,[2] giving a potentially misleading impression of the amount of assertive legislative leadership certain Speakers exercised. Third, I do not examine leadership activity involving the opportunity structure of Congress, such as who is given committee seats or chosen to chair standing committees, even though this activity can (if indirectly) influence the legislative process.

What drove Speakers to exercise non-floor legislative leadership in these ninety-five instances? To answer to this question, I drew from secondary literature and other evidence to identify the likely incentives that induced the Speaker to act in each case. The summary results of this analysis are listed in the last column of tables 5.1 through 5.4. As expected, a majority of cases (sixty-five of ninety-five, or 68 percent) involved the Speaker's goal of ensuring his congressional party's support as Speaker. While this can be seen as strong evidence for party-based leadership theories, the cases also show that multiple goals can motivate the Speaker to exercise leadership. Nearly a quarter of the cases involving the majority party (sixteen of sixty-five) also involved such role-fulfillment goals as supporting the presidential party (thirteen cases), the institutional presidency (one case), and the whole House (two cases). Furthermore, a majority of the remaining thirty cases were associated primarily with a role-fulfillment goal of the Speaker.[3] Interestingly, as with floor-related leadership, non-floor leadership cases motivated by the electoral or policy concerns of the majority party tend to appear more often for recent Speakers, a phenomenon I discuss further in chapter 7.

In short, a summary analysis lends further credence to the theory of goal-driven leadership. The seven cases discussed below were selected to provide a representative sample across Speakers, types of leadership activity, and Speaker goals. In each case study, I highlight how the Speaker's use of non-floor legislative leadership is best explained not (or not only) by the goal to remain in leadership but by other Speaker objectives as well.

Serving One's District, Enacting One's Policy Preferences, or Aiding the House

McCormack and the congressional recess, 1967 (committee activity). One case of non-floor leadership that reflected the Speaker's desire to serve the entire House involved the legislative calendar. Missouri Congressman Richard Bolling, prominent House Democrat and staunch critic of Speaker John McCormack, alleged that McCormack acted to kill legislation in the 90th Congress (1967–68) that would have established a regular congressional recess each August. By 1967, Bolling later wrote, "a large bipartisan majority" in the House supported a recess, which would guarantee legislators time in their districts and

Table 5.1 Agenda-Setting Legislative Leadership by the Speaker of the House

Speaker	Activity	Year(s)	Source(s)	Primary Goal (Relevant Individual/Entity)
Martin	Pressured Rules to report emergency funding for Greece and Turkey	1947	Galloway (1976)	Role fulfillment (inst. pres.)
Martin	Lobbied GOP steering committee for quick action on Marshall Plan	1948	Galloway (1976)	Role fulfillment (inst. pres.)
Martin	Pressured Rules to report a bill renewing Selective Service	1948	*Congressional Quarterly*	Reelection (majority party [MP]), role fulfillment (inst. pres.)
Rayburn	Threatened 21-day rule to compel Rules Committee to release housing bill	1949	Truman (1959)	Reelection (MP), role fulfillment (pres. party)
Rayburn	Threatened 21-day rule to compel Rules Committee to release Social Security bill	1949	Truman (1959)	Reelection (MP), role fulfillment (pres. party)
Rayburn	Refused to recognize Rep. Lesinski to consider FEPC repeal on House Floor	1950	Truman (1959)	Reelection (MP), role fulfillment (pres. party)
Martin	Had Rules block a tax reduction bill	1953	Remini (2006)	Role fulfillment (pres. party)
Rayburn	*Proposed a $20 tax credit*	*1955*	*Gould and Young (1998)*	*Reelection (MP), role fulfillment (pres. party)*
Rayburn	Helped delay passage of first civil rights bill (see chapter 3)	1956	Bolling (1964), Peters (1997)	Reelection (MP)
Rayburn	Refused to allow unilateral consideration of a tax cut by Democrats	1958	Mooney (1964)	Role fulfillment (inst. pres.)

Rayburn	Held off party liberals on Rules Committee reform, offered compromise (see chapter 3)	1959	Several[a]	Reelection (MP), role fulfillment (pres. party)
Rayburn	Used Calendar Wednesday to bypass Rules on public works bill	1960	Bolling (1968)	Reelection (MP)
Rayburn	Persuaded Rep. Cox not to speak on House floor against Truman	Unclear[b]	MacNeil (1963)	Role fulfillment (pres. party)
McCormack	Allowed Rules to report bill without committee approval	1964	Bolling (1964)	Other (committee deference)
McCormack	Failed to keep controversial civil rights, labor bills from floor	1965–66	Bolling (1968)	Role fulfillment (pres. party)
McCormack	Pushed quick approval of civil rights bill	1968	Thurber (2004)	Reelection (MP), role fulfillment (pres. party)
Albert	Pursued anti-impoundment bills	1973	Peters (1997)	Reelection (MP), role fulfillment (House-wide)
Albert	Supported impeachment of Pres. Nixon but not Vice President Agnew	1973	Peters (1997), Remini (2006), Sinclair (1998)	Reelection (MP)
Albert	*Initiated congressional committee reform*	*1973–74*	*Peters (1997)*	*Role fulfillment (House-wide)*
Albert	Endorsed seven-point economic program	1975	Peters (1997), Sinclair (1995)	Reelection (MP)
O'Neill	Prioritized ethics reform, coupled it with pay raise	1977	Josephy (1979), Sinclair (1998)	Role fulfillment (House-wide)
O'Neill	Pulled consumer protection agency bill from calendar	1977	Barone (1990), Kafman (1993)	Reelection (MP), role fulfillment (pres. party)

(continued)

Table 5.1 (*continued*)

Speaker	Activity	Year(s)	Source(s)	Primary Goal (Relevant Individual/ Entity)
O'Neill	Delayed consideration of welfare reform	1978	Kaufman (1993)	Reelection (MP)
O'Neill	Pushed Rules Committee to deny floor vote on tax proposal	1978	Peters (1997)	Reelection (MP)
O'Neill	Allowed Pres. Reagan's budget plan to come to House floor (see chapter 4)	1981	Remini (2006)	Reelection (MP)
O'Neill	Announced Democratic economic plan	1981	Sinclair (1995, 1998)	Reelection (MP)
O'Neill	Chose Social Security as election-year issue	1981–82	Several[c]	Reelection (MP)
O'Neill	Let Equal Rights Amendment be considered under suspension of the rules	1983	Connelly and Pitney (1994)	Reelection (MP)
O'Neill	Blocked tax reform bill until Pres. Reagan recruited more votes	1985	Mervin (1990)	Reelection (MP)
O'Neill	Decided against impeachment proceedings for Pres. Reagan	1986	Remini (2006)	Other (deference to opp. party pres.)[d]
Wright	Proposed broad domestic policy agenda for House Democrats	1987	Sinclair (1995, 1998)	Reelection (MP), role fulfillment (pres. party)

Wright	Decided House should enact drug bill	1988	Sinclair (1995)	Reelection (MP), role fulfillment (pres. party)
Wright	Allowed Rep. Pepper to bring major health care bill to floor	1988	Peters (1997)	Reelection (MP)
Wright	*Pushed minimum wage bill, gave it low bill number*	*1989*	*Sinclair (1995)*	*Reelection (MP)*
Foley	Led fiscal summit with President Bush to write reconciliation bill	1990	Patashnik (2004), Peters (1997)	Other (cooperative divided government)
Foley	*Pushed Rules to alter some anti-China floor amendments*	*1990*	*Sinclair (1995)*	*Role fulfillment (inst. pres.)*
Foley	Resisted campaign finance reform legislation	1993–94	Peters (1997)	Reelection (MP)
Gingrich	Tried to limit the number of term limits bills on floor	1995	Killian (1998)	Reelection (MP)
Gingrich	Would not schedule bill altering Endangered Species Act	1996	Sinclair (1999a, 1999b)	Reelection (MP)

Note: Cases in italics are discussed in this chapter.

[a] Bolling (1964), *Congressional Quarterly* (1976), Galloway (1976), MacNeil (1963), and Peters (1997).

[b] Occurred at some point under President Truman (1945–52) (MacNeil 1963, 77).

[c] Barone (1990), Connelly and Pitney (1994), Peters (1997), and Remini (2006).

[d] Perhaps more accurately, O'Neill was concerned by the negative consequences of potentially divisive impeachment proceedings (Remini 2006, 469).

limit the uncertainty of the legislative calendar. McCormack, however, was concerned about the impact a recess would have on the reputation of Congress as a whole. He may have feared that institutionalizing a legislative recess would convey the impression that legislators were working less diligently, particularly in the context of a deepening military conflict in Vietnam and continuing domestic urban unrest. If so, such worry was not without merit: one *New York Times* editorial, for example, criticized the House over rumors of a possible August break along with a week-and-a-half Labor Day recess (Bolling 1968, 246; *New York Times,* 21 August 1967).

By Bolling's account, Speaker McCormack helped defeat the congressional recess proposal in May 1967. Earlier that year, a set of freestanding bills that mandated some type of August recess had been referred to the Rules Committee. When Rules held an open hearing in early May on the measures, Speaker McCormack and Minority Leader Gerald Ford (R-MI) asked to address the committee in a private session. With the public excluded, both leaders testified that the recess would suggest a poor legislator work ethic and that it was particularly ill timed given the war in Vietnam. According to Bolling, a Rules Committee member at the time, "a substantial majority within the Rules Committee . . . favored the recess." But the testimony of McCormack and Ford, together with the Speaker's promise to arrange a short vacation in late summer, apparently convinced the committee to take no further action on any of the recess bills for the remainder of that Congress (Bolling 1968, 246; *Congressional Quarterly Almanac* 1967, 516).

The recess proposal did not disappear, however. A broad congressional reform measure, which passed in the Senate in early 1967, mandated an August recess unless the United States was engaged in a military conflict or faced a national emergency. The bill also contained broad institutional changes to Congress designed to increase its efficiency and openness, such as requiring open committee hearings, changing committee jurisdictions, and compelling more lobbying groups to register under federal law. In fact, the recess was largely a "sweetener" proviso designed to mitigate the more controversial aspects of the bill, like establishing standard rules for all committees, ending proxy voting in committees, and dividing the House Education and Labor Committee into two separate entities. McCormack's objection to this bill was probably grounded less in the desire to protect Congress's reputation than out of deference to powerful Democrats, particularly House chairmen, who strenuously objected to several elements of the bill (see table 5.3). McCormack ultimately signaled support for the measure but not before referring the bill to the Rules

Committee, which never acted on it (*Congressional Quarterly Almanac* 1967, 515–17; *Congressional Quarterly Almanac* 1968, 657–58; Evans and Novak 1968; Lyons 1967).

In the following congress, McCormack dropped his resistance to an annual August recess. After facing a serious leadership challenge from within his party after the 1968 elections and after reconsidering his concerns about the plan, the Speaker relented: an agreement was reached with the Senate in early January to schedule an August break, and a congressional reform bill was passed later in that congress.

Albert and committee reform, 1973–74 (agenda setting, committee activity). Speaker Carl Albert exercised considerable legislative leadership in the 93rd Congress (1973–74) on behalf of a bill to reform the House committee system.[4] In early 1973, the Speaker and many of his colleagues saw an urgent need for significant structural changes to congressional committees. The legislative process had become hindered by the presence of several standing committees with overlapping responsibilities and a recent proliferation of subcommittees, and these inefficiencies were exacerbated by a powerful, assertive, and centralized Nixon White House. A strong push for change also came from newly elected legislators and outside reform groups. Albert believed that internal reform could potentially increase his authority over the affairs of congressional committees—particularly the powerful and independent Ways and Means Committee—and, by extension, the House's agenda. But he also supported reform because, as Ronald Peters describes it, "he appreciated his responsibility as speaker to defend the prerogatives of the House and attend to the health of its internal system of governance" (Davidson and Oleszek 1977, 60–67, 105, 179; Peters 1997, 178).[5]

Legislative leadership would be critical to bring about any changes to the House's committee system, and Albert's efforts occurred principally in the early stages of the reform attempt. In late 1972, the Speaker met with Representative Richard Bolling (D-MO), an influential proponent of reform who had been frustrated by previous failed reform efforts (see above), to gain his support for drafting legislation in the following Congress. Following Albert's urging, Bolling and fellow Rules Committee member David Martin (R-NE) introduced a resolution in January 1973 to create a select committee tasked with proposing changes to the committee system. When the resolution passed the House shortly thereafter, Albert appointed the Democratic members of the select committee, making Bolling the chairman, and appeared before the committee with Minority Leader Gerald Ford (as the committee's first two wit-

Table 5.2 Bill-Drafting Legislative Leadership by the Speaker of the House

Speaker	Activity	Year(s)	Source	Primary Goal (Relevant Individual/ Entity)
Rayburn	*Aided passage of Lend-Lease by shaping content of proposal*	*1941*	*Peters (1997), Barone (1990)*	*Role fulfillment (inst. pres.)*
Rayburn	Held congressional reorganization bill until key provisions were dropped	1946	Remini (2006)	Other (personal power)
Rayburn	Asked for increase in foreign aid funding by House conferees	1958	MacNeil (1963)	Role fulfillment (inst. pres.)
Rayburn	Tasked Rep. Ikard to draft amendment on trade bill	1958	MacNeil (1963)	Role fulfillment (inst. pres.)
McCormack	Lobbied for increase in foreign aid	1962	MacNeil (1963)	Reelection (MP), role fulfillment (pres. party)
O'Neill	Met with Carter to develop budget	1980	Sinclair (1995)	Reelection (MP), role fulfillment (pres. party)
O'Neill	Got conference committee to amend Gramm-Rudman budget bill	1985	Barone (1990)	Reelection (MP)
O'Neill	Met with Reagan to develop budget	1985	Sinclair (1995)	Other (cooperative divided government)
Wright	Proposed adding drug payments to Reagan health care bill	1987	Peters (1997), Sinclair (1995)	Reelection (MP)
Wright	Told conference committee to keep anti-pornography language in education bill	1988	Sinclair (1995)	Reelection (MP)

				Role fulfillment (House-wide)
Foley	Helped draft House reforms on self-appointed bipartisan task force	1992	Sinclair (1995)	Reelection (MP)
Gingrich	Intervened in negotiations on agriculture bill, removed dairy provisions	1995	Deering (1999)	Reelection (MP)
Gingrich	Threatened to remove abortion language on appropriations bill (see chapter 4)	1995	Sinclair (1999a, 1999b)	Reelection (MP)
Gingrich	Influenced content of Medicare reform legislation drafted by task force (see chapter 4)	1995	Several[a]	Reelection (MP)
Gingrich	Instructed committee to negotiate with governors on job training bill	1995	Sinclair (1999a, 1999b)	Reelection (MP)
Gingrich	Proposed blanket gift ban for legislators	1995	Killian (1998)	Reelection (MP)
Gingrich	Set seven-year budget timetable, bound fellow leaders to support it	1995	Several[b]	Reelection (MP)
Gingrich	Ordered DC Appropriations Subcommittee to rewrite bill	1995	Deering (1999)	Reelection (MP)
Gingrich	Rejected portions of telecommunications bill	1995–96	Deering (1999)	Reelection (MP)
Gingrich	Demanded drinking water bill be bipartisan	1996	Sinclair (1999a, 1999b)	Reelection (MP)
Gingrich	Pulled controversial language from disaster relief bill	1997	Killian (1998)	Reelection (MP)

Note: Cases in italics are discussed in this chapter.

[a] Deering (1999), Killian (1998), Peters (1999), and Sinclair (1999a, 1999b).

[b] Critchlow (2004), Fenno (1997), Sinclair (1999), and Strahan and Palazzolo (2004).

nesses). Indeed, Ford's support for the reform effort was a further sign of the House-wide nature of the issue, as both he and the Speaker believed that "the House's capacity to function depended upon bringing order to a committee system that had grown chaotic" (Davidson and Oleszek 1977, 67–68, 71, 83–85; Peters 1997, 178, 183).

Albert did not remove himself entirely from the legislative process once the select committee began its deliberations; for instance, he occasionally helped the committee publish its transcripts in a timely fashion. Nonetheless, Albert committed a strategic error in not sufficiently following through on his initial leadership efforts, particularly in failing to dictate or influence the content of the reform proposal as developed by the committee. When it released its recommendations in March 1974, the proposed changes proved too broad and controversial for Democrats. Opposition soon developed among three groups: chairmen whose committees would be weakened or eliminated by the reforms; Democrats who, because of a specific proposal to further restrict the number of permissible committee assignments, would be kicked off at least one committee; and partisans opposed to the plan's allocation of greater resources to committee minorities. Bolling believed that obtaining early caucus endorsement of the reforms would ease floor approval, but Albert further erred when he agreed to a request from concerned Democrats to delay caucus consideration. This gave opponents time to campaign against the recommendations, and although Albert lobbied his Democratic colleagues to support the measure, the caucus voted 111–95 to send it to the party's Committee on Organization, Study, and Review for further changes. This so-called Hansen committee, named after its chairman, Julia Butler Hansen (WA), subsequently reported a more moderate bill that was missing many of the original proposals.

The Speaker exercised additional leadership when the initial reforms, along with the Hansen bill, came to the House floor late in September; nonetheless, reform supporters viewed his actions as tepid at best. Albert spoke on the floor on behalf of four floor amendments, but the original plan itself failed, and the Hansen substitute passed the House in what was later characterized by Peters as a significant loss for the Speaker (Davidson and Oleszek 1977, 115, 192–214; Peters 1997, 184).[6]

Fulfilling President-Oriented Roles or Duties

Rayburn and Lend-Lease, 1941 (legislative content). An important example of the Speaker influencing the content of legislation occurred in early 1941 when Sam Rayburn made key modifications to a bill granting military aid to countries (England in particular) fighting Nazi Germany (Barone 1990, 146–47; Peters 1997, 124). In this case the Speaker also acted on behalf of the institutional presidency, and in doing so he had to persuade the members of his own party in the House to do the same.

In January 1941, seeking to provide the British with more military supplies in their efforts against the Germans, President Franklin Roosevelt proposed a "Lend-Lease" program to allow the production and shipment of military equipment to any country he determined was essential to America's national security, with or without repayment. The tremendous grant of authority the program would delegate to the executive branch gave pause to some Democrats, however. If they joined with congressional isolationists and many House Republicans, these legislators could derail the bill in the House (Hardeman and Bacon 1987, 257–58; Steinberg 1975, 167).

Rayburn viewed Roosevelt as the right person to possess such authority and recognized the need to help an important American ally without entering into the war directly. But the Speaker, evaluating the mood of Congress, determined that Lend-Lease had no chance of passing the House without major changes. Though a bill codifying Roosevelt's proposal had already been introduced by Majority Leader John McCormack,[7] Rayburn met privately with Roosevelt and urged him to permit several changes to the initiative to protect congressional prerogatives and ease resistance among Democrats. The Speaker recommended, among other things, that Lend-Lease be limited to two years of operation, receive explicit funding through appropriations committees, require regular reports from the White House on its implementation, and prohibit U.S. convoys from shipping Lend-Lease equipment. Roosevelt eventually assented, and the bill was modified accordingly before it came to the House floor in early February (Dorough 1962, 309; Hardeman and Bacon 1987, 257–58; Steinberg 1975, 167).

These changes appeared to have greatly improved the bill's chances of passage, but Rayburn and other party leaders also exercised some floor leadership to help win a majority for the plan. Democratic leaders assisted in defeating nineteen amendments to the bill, with Rayburn speaking on the House floor on several of them and even scolding one Democrat (Jerry Voorhis of California) for trying to amend the legislation with further limits on the program's scope. After surviving these attempts to alter the bill, Lend-Lease passed the House, 260–165, with 236 Democrats and 24 Republicans voting for it. Although Rayburn's efforts on the floor helped assure the bill's passage, his success in altering it early in the legislative process was the necessary first step, giv-

Table 5.3 Committee-Related Legislative Leadership by the Speaker of the House

Speaker	Activity	Year(s)	Source(s)	Primary Goal (Relevant Individual/ Entity)
Rayburn	Pushed Banking Committee to report resolution granting power to President Roosevelt	1942	Gould and Young (1998)	Role fulfillment (inst. pres.)
Martin	Used threats to force committee to report Eisenhower tax extension bill	1953	MacNeil (1963), Peters (1997), Remini (2006)	Reelection (MP), role fulfillment (pres. party)
Rayburn	Urged Commerce Committee to investigate operations of executive agencies	1957	MacNeil (1963)	Reelection (MP), role fulfillment (House-wide)
Rayburn	Delayed referral of labor bill (see chapter 3)	1958	Bolling (1964), Gould and Young (1998)	Reelection (MP)
McCormack	Failed to resolve House-Senate Appropriations Committee dispute	1962	Bolling (1964, 1968)	Reelection (MP), role fulfillment (House-wide)
McCormack	Kept congressional reform bill in committee	1967–68	Bolling (1968), Remini (2006)	Other (committee deference)
McCormack	*Worked with GOP to have Rules Committee kill August recess bill*	*1967*	*Bolling (1968)*	*Role fulfillment (House-wide)*
McCormack	Chose legislators to serve on Hansen congressional reorganization committee	1970	Peabody (1976)	Role fulfillment (House-wide)
Albert	Referred impeachment to Judiciary Committee rather than create a select committee	1973	Peters (1997), Remini (2006)	Role fulfillment (House-wide)

Albert	Appointed task force to draft economic recovery program	1974	Sinclair (1995)	Reelection (MP)
Albert	Created select committee on outer continental shelf	1975	Peters (1997)	Reelection (MP)
Albert	Formed task force to draft energy legislation	1975	Peters (1997)	Reelection (MP)
Albert	Used credible threats to get Appropriations to pass jobs bill	1975	Sinclair (1995)	Reelection (MP)
O'Neill	Convinced Democrats on Rules Committee to support ethics reform	1977	Sinclair (1998)	Role fulfillment (House-wide)
O'Neill	Created special ad hoc committee to draft President Carter's energy bill (see chapter 4)	1977	Several[a]	Reelection (MP), role fulfillment (pres. party)
O'Neill	Extended committee deadline to report hospital cost bill	1979	Peters (1997)	Role fulfillment (pres. party)
O'Neill	*Pushed for consensus in Budget Committee on budget bill*	*1983*	*Peters (1997)*	*Reelection (MP)*
O'Neill	Used multiple referral for Republican bill but not Democratic one	1985 or 1986	Young and Cooper (1993)	Reelection (MP)
Wright	Pushed Ways and Means Committee to pass progressive tax bill	1987	Sinclair (1995)	Reelection (MP)
Wright	Limited committee consideration of trade bill, brokered conference compromise	1987–88	Young and Cooper (1993)	Reelection (MP)

Table 5.3 (*continued*)

Speaker	Activity	Year(s)	Source(s)	Primary Goal (Relevant Individual/ Entity)
Wright	Appointed task force to create ethics and pay raise bill (see chapter 4)	1989	Sinclair (1995)	Role fulfillment (House-wide)
Foley	Brokered deal on child care bill between committees	1990	Sinclair (1995)	Reelection (MP)
Foley	Pushed conferees to agree on transportation bill	1991	Sinclair (1993, 1995)	Reelection (MP)
Foley	Pressed Ways and Means Committee to enact unemployment legislation	1991	Sinclair (1995)	Reelection (MP)
Foley	Created task force to draft campaign finance legislation	1991	Sinclair (1995)	Reelection (MP)
Gingrich	Threatened committee members who rejected agriculture bill	1995	Evans and Oleszek (1997), Fiorina (2001)	Reelection (MP)
Gingrich	Obtained loyalty pledge from Appropriations Committee Republicans	1995	Several[b]	Reelection (MP)
Gingrich	Formed task force to bring assault weapons bill to floor	1995	Killian (1998)	Reelection (MP)

Note: Cases in italics are discussed in this chapter.

[a]Barone (1990), Kaufman (1993), Peters (1997), and Sinclair (1998).

[b]Aldrich and Rohde (2001), Fenno (1997), Patashnik (2004), and Sinclair (1999a, 1999b).

ing it a fighting chance at passage if not earning a floor majority outright (*Congressional Record*, 6 February 1941, 746, 788, 809; Hardeman and Bacon 1987, 258–59).

Foley and MFN for China, 1990 (agenda setting). Less than a year after the Tiananmen Square massacre in June 1989, in which the Chinese Communist government used force to end pro-democracy protests in Beijing, Democrats and Republicans remained eager to impose economic sanctions on the country in retaliation. An opportunity to do so appeared in mid-1990, when China's temporary nondiscriminatory trading status with the United States (known as most favored nation, or MFN) came up for renewal. The president could renew China's MFN status without congressional approval, and did so in May, but representatives and senators from both parties sought to use the program to punish the Chinese government, and bills were soon introduced to suspend MFN for China (*Congressional Quarterly Almanac* 1990, 764–65).

Given the bipartisan support in Congress for sanctions, any bill to limit or repeal MFN for China would likely pass the House floor by a simple, if not veto-proof, majority. Speaker Thomas Foley, however, chose to try to prevent the passage of sanctions. Deference to the White House on trade issues may best explain his choice of action. With President George H. W. Bush, a Republican, supporting MFN renewal and administration officials urging Congress not to limit or revoke China's trade status, the Speaker decided to permit only modest punishments against China to pass the House and to prohibit more severe anti-China measures from being considered on the floor. A secondary, but perhaps also significant, goal for Foley in hindering anti-China sanctions was to help his constituents, since Washington State benefited from overseas trade with China and other Asian countries (which may also have contributed to his leadership on NAFTA; see chapter 4). Foley was supported by other leaders, including Minority Leader Robert Michel (R-IL) and Ways and Means Chairman Dan Rostenkowski (D-IL), who believed that withdrawing China's MFN status would do more harm than good (*Congressional Quarterly Almanac* 1990, 765, 766; Krauss 1990).

Reflecting Congress's concerns with human rights in China, the House Ways and Means Committee approved a bill in July renewing the country's MFN status but included some conditions for renewal, including progress toward greater freedom of the press and information on the status of those arrested in Tiananmen Square. At the same time, reflecting the preferences of Foley and other congressional leaders (including the committee's chairman), Ways and Means rejected more stringent conditions for MFN. In addition, the committee voted

Table 5.4 Other Non-Floor Legislative Leadership by the Speaker of the House

Speaker	Activity	Year(s)	Source(s)	Primary Goal (Relevant Individual/ Entity)
O'Neill	Sided with Rep. Pickle over Rep. Pepper on changing Social Security retirement age	1983	Barone (1990)	Other (legislator deference)
Wright	Appointed key legislators to budget summit	1987	Sinclair (1995)	Other (cooperative divided government)
Foley	Appointed Rep. Hoyer to lead passage of disabilities bill	1989	Sinclair (1995)	Other (cooperative divided government)
Foley	Asked Rep. Gray to oversee drafting a substitute civil rights bill	1991	Sinclair (1995)	Reelection (MP)
Foley	Appointed legislators to agenda-setting "policy development" group	1993	Sinclair (1995)	Reelection (MP)
Gingrich	Threatened to sanction Rep. Neumann for vote on defense spending bill	1995	Killian (1998)	Reelection (MP)
Gingrich	Worked with, then against, President Clinton on fast-track bill	1997–98	Connelly and Pitney (1999), Destler (2001)	Reelection (MP), role fulfillment (inst. pres.)

to request that the Rules Committee not allow any floor amendments to the legislation (*Congressional Quarterly Almanac* 1990, 766).

The Speaker stepped in when the Rules Committee did not follow that request. According to one insider, Foley "said very clearly that he wanted no [floor] amendments allowed" by Rep. Nancy Pelosi, a strong advocate for sanctioning China. But a majority of the Rules Committee's members, persuaded by legislators seeking to alter the bill, agreed to permit floor votes on a number of tough anti-China amendments, including one from Pelosi.[8] Facing the real danger that these amendments would pass, Foley worked to get the committee to reverse its position. The Speaker first met with the chairman of Rules, Joe Moakley (MA), then addressed the committee's other Democrats in a private meeting, urging them to drop or modify the amendments. Foley's tactics of persuasion proved successful, and he "worked out some changes to the amendments with Pelosi" (*Congressional Quarterly Almanac* 1990, 766; Krauss 1990; quotes from Sinclair 1995, 154).

Nonetheless, Foley had not been able to stop all amendments to the MFN renewal bill. Pelosi's amendment, which required China to release those arrested as a result of the prodemocracy protests, passed by a wide margin, 347–74. The bill itself passed by a veto-proof 384–30, but the Senate failed to consider legislation on the matter, and the president's one-year renewal of MFN status for China remained in place (*Congressional Quarterly Almanac* 1990, 768; Farnsworth 1990; Krauss 1990).

Helping the Party in Congress and the Presidential Party

Rayburn and the income tax cut, 1955 (agenda setting). An example of non-floor legislative leadership used to achieve both congressional and presidential party objectives took place in early 1955. It illustrates not only how Sam Rayburn could use his agenda-setting power to build support for specific legislation, but also how partisan differences sometimes colored the relationship between Rayburn and President Eisenhower—a relationship traditionally depicted as cooperative and bipartisan (Gould and Young 1998, 191–97).

The 1954 congressional elections ended Republicans' short-lived, two-year majority in the House. Sam Rayburn suddenly had an opportunity to use his regained authority as Speaker both to strengthen Democratic control of Congress and to increase his party's chances of winning the White House in 1956. To accomplish these two objectives, Rayburn decided to propose a uniform, twenty-dollar reduction in federal income taxes for every taxpayer (plus a twenty-dollar reduction for each dependent) and place it at the top of the congressional agenda (Drury 1955b; Egan 1955; Gould and Young 1998, 192–93).

Although tax reduction was generally closer to Republican policy preferences, Rayburn's bill would satisfy both ideological and electoral interests of House Democrats. Unlike a tax cut bill passed by the House GOP in 1954, which congressional Democrats criticized for benefiting wealthy individuals more than poorer citizens, the twenty-dollar tax reduction would apply to all taxpayers and thus disproportionately benefit those with lower incomes. Democrats had made the GOP tax cut a major campaign issue, and they could gain credit by being the first party to initiate tax relief after the midterm elections. But the Speaker also saw advantages for his presidential party in pursuing the legislation. Despite Eisenhower's expressed reluctance to reduce taxes, it was widely believed that Republicans would propose a tax cut in 1956, timed to help win votes for the president's reelection. Sharing this view, Rayburn hoped that his bill could give similar credit to the Democratic presidential nominee in 1956 or at least dilute the political capital Eisenhower might otherwise gain from the GOP's strategy. Opponents of Rayburn's tax bill feared as much; *New York Times* reporter Charles Egan wrote that Republicans saw Rayburn's proposal as "an obvious attempt to take the play away from the Administration in any claims for individual tax reductions next year, a Presidential election year" (Egan 1955; Gould and Young 1998, 192–93; White 1955c).[9]

Rayburn's most important leadership on behalf of the bill was to prioritize it on the legislative agenda. The Speaker, a sharp critic of the 1954 tax cut, suggested to the press in early January that Democrats might respond with their own tax plan. The $20 tax cut bill was officially introduced after members of the Ways and Means Committee met with Speaker Rayburn in mid-February, and while one committee member (Arkansas Democrat Wilbur Mills) had sponsored the bill, Rayburn strongly endorsed the measure and may have cosponsored or even written the proposal himself.[10] The bill was passed by the committee within a week, and to maximize its chances of survival, it was sent to the floor in late February as part of an unrelated proposal desired by Eisenhower (Drury 1955b; Egan 1955; Gould and Young 1998, 192–94; Lawrence 1995).

Democratic leaders also exercised some floor leadership on behalf of the bill, although the full extent of Rayburn's participation in this respect is not known. Since few Republicans would support the bill, and many southern conservative Democrats expressed concerns over its impact on the federal budget, passage of the legislation was not assured. Party leaders whipped their rank and file and urged their attendance, and Rayburn endorsed the bill in a House floor speech.

On the critical vote to recommit (and thus effectively kill) the bill, the final vote tally was delayed while both parties' leaders whipped their members, but Democrats prevailed: the motion lost, 205–210, with sixteen Democrats and five Republicans defecting from their parties' ranks (Drury 1955b; 1955c; Gould and Young 1998, 195; Lawrence 1955).

Rayburn's tax proposal did not get far, however. The Senate Finance Committee rejected it outright, and a modified version of the tax cut, offered on the Senate floor by Majority Leader Lyndon Johnson (D-TX), was defeated by a coalition of Republicans and southern Democrats (Gould and Young 1998, 196). Nonetheless, Rayburn's point had been made: House Democrats were prepared to support tax reduction—if on their terms—and had perhaps helped inoculate themselves and their future presidential candidate on a potential campaign issue.

Helping the Party in Congress

O'Neill and the budget resolution, 1983 (committee activity). Following a series of defeats on budget policy at the hands of President Reagan,[11] the Democrats gained twenty-six seats in the House in the 1982 midterm elections. Speaker O'Neill seized the opportunity to unite his party around legislation reflecting Democrats' budgetary policy goals.[12] O'Neill's first—and perhaps most important—step toward achieving this objective was to ensure that House Budget Committee Democrats unanimously approved a budget resolution that would reflect the majority caucus's fiscal priorities. Doing so would erase the image of the party as divided and ineffective on budgetary matters, create momentum for passage of the resolution, and discourage would-be conservative Democrats from defecting on any floor votes (as they had on budget bills in the previous Congress) (Cowan 1983a; Peters 1997, 245–46).

Together with committee chairman Jim Jones (OK), O'Neill worked to build broad support behind a budget resolution that would be more leftward leaning than the committee's 1981 or 1982 budget proposals. First, to increase unity and minimize intraparty dissent, the Speaker convened a series of party caucus meetings where rank-and-file Democrats were invited to discuss and debate budget policy. He and other party leaders also distributed a questionnaire to all House Democrats requesting their opinion on spending and revenue priorities. Using these sources of input, O'Neill and Jones crafted a budget resolution that they believed would both garner a majority of votes on the floor and be relatively close to the Democratic Party median member's preferences. O'Neill aligned himself closely with the resolution when it was introduced, publicly endorsing the measure and leading the press conference at which it was formally announced. The resolution called for tax increases to reduce the deficit, slight increases in defense spending, and funding for a variety of social programs that had been reduced in previous years. Only two days later, with both the Speaker and the committee chairman reportedly "pressing for consensus," Budget Committee Democrats voted unanimously for what one newspaper story called an "old-fashioned Democratic budget" (Broder 1983; Cowan 1983a; Dewar 1983; Peters 1997, 245–46).

The budget resolution ultimately passed, 229–196, with four Republicans voting for it and thirty-six Democrats opposing it—three fewer Democrats than party leaders had expected. In May, the Senate passed its version of the resolution after weeks of wrangling among its majority Republicans, and both chambers agreed to a compromise budget the following month (Broder 1983; Cowan 1983b; 1983c; Roberts 1983).

Wright and minimum wage legislation, 1989 (agenda setting). During what would be his final year as Speaker, Jim Wright used his influence over the legislative agenda to pass a new minimum wage bill. Most House Democrats were traditional supporters of a higher minimum wage, as was organized labor, and House Republicans were generally opposed to wage increases on economic and philosophical grounds. The Speaker's use of legislative leadership to enact a wage increase in early 1989 can thus be best viewed as representing the policy preferences of his own party in the House.

Wright's move came after nearly a decade of no change in the federal minimum wage. President Ronald Reagan had expressed no interest in altering the then-existing wage of $3.35 an hour. The political climate appeared to shift in the 101st Congress (1989–90) when Republican George H. W. Bush, newly elected to the White House, expressed greater sympathy toward the idea of a minimum wage hike. But Bush and House Democrats differed on important elements of such a plan: in particular, Bush endorsed a smaller wage increase than was proposed by House Democrats ($4.25 versus $4.65), and he wanted businesses to have the option of giving a reduced salary to new employees (*Congressional Quarterly Almanac* 1989, 333).

The president's position, plus the usual competition for attention among the myriad bills and legislative initiatives facing a new Congress, meant that enactment of a minimum wage increase would not be easy sailing. Wright and fellow party leaders began by deciding to give the measure precedence in the 101st Congress. The Speaker described a wage hike as a major concern in several public statements and speeches; then, when a Democratic wage bill was introduced early in the first session of that Congress, Wright gave the measure a low number (H.R. 2) to further highlight its importance. Taken together, these efforts by Wright gave the legislation a prominent place in the House's agenda and eased its early passage. The president announced his own minimum wage proposal in early 1989, but the House Education and Labor Committee approved the Democratic bill on a party-line vote. A version of that measure, which increased the wage to $4.55 and permitted a more generous subminimum wage for new workers than Bush wanted, passed on the House floor in March, 248–171. Bush's alternative plan failed by a closer floor vote of 198–218 (*Congressional Quarterly Almanac* 1989, 337–38; Rasky 1989c; Sinclair 1995, 287).

Wright's use of agenda setting on the minimum wage was followed by an act of floor-related leadership two months later. Negotiators from the House and Senate agreed on a conference version of the minimum wage bill in early May, and Wright went to the floor during deliberation of the conference report. Since Bush continued to oppose the bill, the Speaker sought a veto-proof, two-thirds vote of approval, though the chances of getting it seemed slim. In a ten-minute speech, which he (as he later described it) "saw as a test of my leadership," Wright urged both Republicans and Democrats to support the bill. The subsequent 247–172 vote, however, was well shy of the two-thirds majority needed; President Bush vetoed the bill shortly thereafter, and a cursory attempt to override the veto failed on June 14. Finally, in November of that year, with a new Speaker in office, the House passed a minimum wage bill more to Bush's liking, which the president signed into law (*Congressional Quarterly Almanac* 1989, 333–35, 339–40; Wright 1996, 487).

SPEAKERS GOING PUBLIC

The ability of the president to make public appearances in order to achieve policy victories in Washington has been widely studied. One political scientist, Samuel Kernell, calls this tactic "going public" and defines it as acting in the public sphere to announce preferences, set a public agenda, or encourage specific behavior from other political actors (Kernell 1997). Although going public by the president has been widely examined, less well studied is the degree to which the Speaker of the House does the same.[13] Such activity on the part of the Speaker could influence legislative outcomes in several ways, including:

- *Setting the legislative agenda.* The Speaker could use press conferences or public addresses to declare a specific policy agenda, sending a signal to other members of Congress of the Speaker's intent. When the president is of the opposite party, the official response to the annual State of the Union address can be a particularly useful opportunity to do this. Speaker Jim Wright, for example, used such a forum in January 1987 to argue that the House would address "three of our most urgent problems . . . the trade deficit, the farm crisis, and the education crisis." In his response the following year, Wright promised that "your national Congress will complete this agenda that we began last year."[14]

- *Persuading influential legislators.* Well-placed comments during a Speaker's public appearance could increase pressure on key members of Congress to take a certain action contrary to their preferences. For instance, Speaker Tom Foley expressed confidence in a 1993 press conference that an expedited rescission bill would pass the House, putting the onus on influential opponents of the bill to end their resistance (Sinclair 1995, 267; see also chapter 4). Similarly, Newt Gingrich publicly announced in 1995 that Congress would enact a resolution balancing the federal budget within seven years, helping convince less enthusiastic party leaders and the chairman of the House Budget Committee to support that outcome (Sinclair 1999a, 439; Strahan and Palazzolo 2004, 104).

- *Pressuring the president.* If the Speaker advocates a position contrary to that expected from the White House, he might put the president on the defensive or encourage voters to petition the president themselves (Sinclair 1995, 266–67). This would primarily, but not necessarily always, be of use to Speakers serving with opposite-party presidents.

Tip O'Neill is often credited with being the first Speaker of the House to aggressively exploit media appearances for political gain (for example, Harris 1998). In fact, the Speaker's use of electronic mass communication dates back to at least June 1933, when Henry Rainey (D-IL) delivered a radio address touting the achievements of his party in Congress (*Congressional Record,* 7 June 1933, 5197–98). Twenty-six years later, Sam Rayburn used a radio address to advocate for a Democratic labor bill and to counter an earlier speech by President Eisenhower criticizing the legislation (see chapter 3).[15] Rayburn also met daily with reporters to discuss the activities of the House. Carl Albert was willing to use television as well as radio, making public statements in support of economic legislation in 1971 (see chapter 4) and critical of President Nixon's budgetary reduction proposals in early 1973, and delivering the on-air reply to Ford's State of the Union speech in January 1975 (Dorough 1962, 325–26; Peters 1997, 162, 176; Sinclair 1995, 37).

O'Neill occasionally utilized mass communication in his early years as Speaker, but he did so much more often after the 1980 elections. With the help of a newly hired media advisor, Chris Matthews, O'Neill appeared in press conferences and on Sunday talk shows and other television programs to improve the reputation of House Democrats and put President Reagan on the defensive. Since the end of O'Neill's term as Speaker in 1986, both press conferences and appearances on television have become much more common for House Speakers. O'Neill did not appear on a single Sunday news show between 1978 and early 1981; by contrast, between February 1990 and the end of 1994, Tom Foley appeared four times on CBS's *Face the Nation,* was interviewed on ABC's *Nightline* seven times, and delivered the Democratic response to President George H. W. Bush's State of the Union address in 1990 and 1992. His successor, Newt Gingrich, appeared on *Face the Nation* six times and *Nightline* five times between 1995 and 1998 (Farrell 2001, 563–70, 572–73).[16]

Going public has become fairly common for Speakers, but determining its intent and influence on legislative results is not straightforward. A Speaker's use of the media may be intended to sway public opinion; however, its impact will vary widely based on media coverage and may be considerably diffuse (such as improving citizens' perception of the majority party generally) or narrowly targeted (such as persuading particular voters to view a certain issue, action, or individual positively or negatively). Even if visible public appearances do change the opinions of voters, those opinions must usually be translated into direct action to have an effect—action (for example, phone calls or letters directed to the president or members of Congress) that is often difficult to gather or measure systematically. In addition, the Speaker may go public for varying reasons, for example, to improve Congress's national reputation or garner favor with Capitol Hill reporters. An aide to Tom Foley asserted that his appearances on national shows like *Face the Nation* were "an opportunity for the leadership . . . to speak to the other members of [the] caucus" or to the president at least as much as to address the public directly (interview with the author, March 2003). Thus, going public is a less clear form of legislative leadership than action taken within the House itself.

Nonetheless, if we assume that the Speaker uses the media to alter legislative outcomes, can it be explained by the theory of goal-driven leadership? The examples mentioned above, and the fact that going public has become more common with the increased frequency of divided government, suggest that meeting the objectives of the majority party in the House is the primary reason for this behavior. Rayburn's criticism of the Landrum-Griffin labor bill; Albert's response to the Republican presidential agenda in 1973 and 1975; O'Neill's embrace of Sunday talk shows after 1980; the frequent use of the media by Speakers Wright, Foley, and Gingrich—all appear to have been driven primarily by a desire to contest the policies of the opposite party and advocate the House majority party's agenda. Certain Speakers, particularly O'Neill and Gingrich, are noteworthy for having used public press events to provide national leadership for their parties against an opposite-party president. Thus the partisan model of congressional leadership may best explain the use of going public.

The television appearances of recent Speakers seem particularly driven by this objective. For instance, Foley's *Face the Nation* guest spots included discussions about foreign policy (Bosnia, a summit with the Soviet Union) and House-wide matters (the check-bouncing and post office scandals). But he also discussed bills associated with the House Democratic agenda, such as flood relief legislation and a controversial gas tax bill, and he appeared frequently on *Nightline* episodes that focused on the 1991 Persian Gulf War, which Foley (and a majority of House Democrats) opposed. On *Face the Nation,* Gingrich regularly emphasized policy positions contrary to those of the Clinton White House or focused on major partisan legislation enacted in the House (such as Medicare reform, budget cuts, and a tax bill).

There are two plausible explanations for why other Speaker goals would fail to motivate this particular behavior. First, some concerns and objectives may be more difficult to address by going public. Internal House-wide matters, policy interests of the Speaker, or similar issues are probably of little interest to the broader voting public and thus are much less amenable to a strategy of going public. Second, the president's stature, perceived authority, and selection through direct elections give him inherent advantages over the Speaker in using these leadership techniques. If a certain legislative outcome will benefit the president (of either party), Speakers who also want that outcome may defer to him in public appearances; but if the president takes a policy position contrary to that of the majority party in Congress, the White House can more easily drown out the Speaker's attempt to gain media attention. Going public could still be a useful strategy in these cases: for example, if the Speaker and the opposite-party president both desire a particular result, the Speaker can use the media to defend the White House and defuse possible criticism of the president. Nonetheless, the president's power and higher public profile may limit the Speaker's use of going public on matters salient to the president (Kernell 1997, 262; Sinclair 1995, 268–69).

In short, going public is a potentially critical tool of legislative leadership at the modern Speaker's disposal. While its intended and actual effects on outcomes may be difficult to ascertain, the tactic appears most amenable to achieving the objectives of the Speaker's party in the House, and it is therefore better thought of as a partisan technique than one driven by multiple goals.

CONCLUSION

Looking more broadly at the leadership behavior of modern Speakers, the evidence presented in this chapter reveals that the Speaker can influence the legislative process away from the House floor in important ways and has done so to satisfy a range of leadership goals. Speakers set agendas, shape the content of legislation, and direct committee activity not always on behalf of their party in the House, but to help presidents, defend the interests of the whole House, or achieve other purposes. In addition, even when Speakers are seeking to help their party in the House through non-floor leadership, they can have another objective as well. Most commonly, this second goal is to support the presidential party. This, too, indicates that party-based theories of congressional leadership miss the importance of nonparty goals in explaining Speaker leadership. Although agenda setting, shaping legislation, and influencing committees may be best explained by the theory of goal-driven leadership, Speakers seem to go public primarily to defend congressional party interests and concerns.

Chapter 6 The Hastert Speakership

Serving between two historic Speakers—Newt Gingrich, the first Republican Speaker in forty years, and Nancy Pelosi, the first woman Speaker in American history—the more low-key Dennis Hastert may suffer from relative neglect by future historians. But Hastert not only achieved a "first" of his own, serving longer as Speaker than any Republican had before, but also presided over the House during enactment of a broad range of significant legislative initiatives, including a major reduction of federal taxes, the creation of a new national education program, a revision of federal campaign finance laws, an expansion of the Medicare health care program, and the establishment of a new cabinet-level agency.

Hastert was suddenly and unexpectedly promoted to the highest office in the House in late 1998. As the chamber debated whether to impeach President Bill Clinton, Gingrich's expected successor, Robert Livingston of Louisiana, resigned in the face of a looming sex scandal. Support quickly coalesced around Hastert, the chief deputy Republican whip who had also been a (reluctant) candidate for majority leader weeks earlier (Hastert 2004, 161–69). Hastert, a former wrestling coach, was amicable, subdued, and largely unknown outside the Beltway—a refreshing contrast to Gingrich, whose unpredictability, polarizing presence, and high negatives among the public had alienated many congressional Republicans.

Speaker Hastert proved capable of keeping his small and sometimes divided party unified, thanks to his personal skills, persuasive abilities, willingness to negotiate, and help from fellow GOP leaders (most notably, whip and later majority leader Tom DeLay of Texas). Sometimes Hastert used intensive lobbying and aggressive leadership to bring Republicans together on specific bills, aided after 2000 by a same-party president in the White House. Other times he maintained party unity by intentionally avoiding conflict, occasionally revising or even abandoning specific goals in the face of deep intraparty divisions. Hastert's eight-year reign as Speaker ended when Republicans lost control of the House after the 2006 elections; he left the Party leadership completely and resigned from the House the following year.

Relevant to this book is not Hastert's leadership style or abilities per se, but whether the Speaker exercised consequential legislative leadership and if the theory of goal-driven leadership explains such behavior. Conventional wisdom strongly suggests that the answer to both questions is no. Tom DeLay, the strong-willed and highly skilled party leader who served with Hastert, was often described by congressional observers as exercising more power and influence than the Speaker (for example, Dubose and Reid 2004; Hohler 1999). Furthermore, Hastert not only served over a highly partisan chamber but was famous for adopting the so-called Hastert doctrine, declaring that only the wishes of the majority of the majority party should be followed when approving legislation (Broder 2006). In 2005, political scientist and congressional observer Norman Ornstein told a reporter that when faced with a choice between helping his congressional party and aiding the House as a whole, Hastert had never chosen the latter over the former (Stolberg 2005). Hastert's speakership thus presents an especially stringent test of the claims I have made in this book.

Nonetheless, a closer look at Hastert's Speakership indicates that he, like his predecessors, made critical contributions to the passage of legislation both on and away from the House floor and was sometimes willing to do so for reasons other than to secure reelection as Speaker. The evidence I draw on to support this claim differs somewhat from the evidence used in earlier chapters. As of this writing, the Hastert Speakership is too recent to be the subject of many major historical studies, so I cannot employ my sweep method to identify instances of Hastert's legislative leadership. But journalistic accounts of the period turn up several reasonably plausible candidates for a future historian's set of significant cases of legislative leadership by Hastert, both on the House floor and away from it. I analyze these cases in this chapter in the order I have used elsewhere in the book: (1) cases involving the Speaker's district, his personal policy goals, or the House as a whole; (2) cases related to president-related roles; (3) cases involving the Speaker's party in both Congress and the White House; and (4) cases in which Hastert exercised leadership on behalf of his party in the House.

SERVING ONE'S DISTRICT, ENACTING ONE'S POLICY PREFERENCES, OR AIDING THE HOUSE

Media accounts provide little evidence of consequential legislative leadership by Speaker Hastert on behalf of either his own district or the entire House, though he did recognize the importance of both.[1] In at least one instance, however, Hastert exercised significant legislative leadership to enact personally preferred policy. During his first term as Speaker, Congress passed an emergency spending bill that included more than $1 billion in aid to combat drug production in Colombia and neighboring countries. Hastert played an important part, both on and off the House floor, in determining the bill's content and ensuring its passage, and he did so primarily to satisfy his own policy preferences.

Antidrug assistance to Central America and Colombia had been a long-term concern of Hastert's. As one of his staffers told a reporter (in somewhat awkward prose), the fight against drug trafficking was the "one issue that radiates out of him a true sense of passion." He was familiar with the region, having taken a number of trips to Colombia as the chairman of a House Government Reform and Oversight subcommittee, and his worries about drug trafficking in the region led him (two years before becoming Speaker) to openly criticize the Clinton White House in a *Chicago Tribune* op-ed piece for failing to stop the influx of illegal narcotics from Colombia (Pomper 1999c). By contrast, Congress and the White House played a much smaller role in motivating the Speaker to halt drug trafficking. Drug enforcement was neither a uniquely Republican issue nor one either party pursued with extreme passion at the time. In fact, a number of congressional Republicans were skeptical about the utility of providing more antidrug funding to Colombia. In September 1999, the GOP chairmen of both the Committee on International Relations and the Committee on Government Reform expressed concern with the tactics used by Colombia's president against domestic rebels who allegedly had ties to local drug traffickers

(Pomper 1999d). And although President Clinton would eventually ask Congress for increased spending to stop illegal narcotic trafficking, he did so only after Hastert had petitioned the White House to do so.

Hastert's initial strategy was to persuade President Clinton to propose greater federal funding for antidrug trafficking programs in Colombia. He and the Senate majority leader, Trent Lott (R-MS), jointly sent a letter to Clinton asking for additional aid to the country to combat illegal drug cultivation and export. The same year, Hastert asked like-minded House Republicans to bring attention to the issue with press events and committee hearings, and in early January 2000 Hastert delivered a speech in Chicago urging the White House to request more assistance. The Speaker's efforts apparently worked: the day after his speech, Clinton expressed support for lending more help to Colombia, and in February he sent a $4.4 billion supplemental spending proposal to Congress that included $1 billion in antidrug trafficking money to Colombia (Pomper 1999c; 2000a; 2000b).[2]

It soon became clear that Hastert would also have to win over legislators if Colombia was to receive more anti-narcotic assistance. At a House Appropriations Committee hearing at the end of February, several key committee members expressed reservations about the proposal, including how the South American country would spend the funds and how it would pay for the additional $4 billion it was required to provide as part of the initiative. They included not only Democrats but Sonny Callahan of Alabama, the Republican chairman of the subcommittee with jurisdiction over the money. According to Callahan, many legislators were skeptical of the plan: "If we were to bring it [the spending bill] up before the House today," he declared at the hearing, "it would not pass" (Towell 2000). To overcome these doubts, Speaker Hastert sought to increase the funding to include three other countries in the region. More money was also added for other purposes, and a small percentage of the Colombia anti-narcotic aid was transferred from the often criticized Colombian military to the nation's police forces (Pianin and DeYoung 2000).

Another roadblock emerged in March when Lott and fiscal hawks in the House objected to the bill's expanded price tag and inclusion of funding that was arguably nonemergency in nature. Hesitation about aid to Colombia also remained. Tom Campbell (R-CA) indirectly referenced the Vietnam War when he openly worried that the bill would fund "a civil war in a jungle setting." Such dissension forced the bill to be pulled quickly from the House floor, albeit only temporarily. The Speaker endorsed an amendment to the bill adding another $4 billion for a variety of defense-related expenses, and with more support for the measure from the House rank and file as a result, it quickly returned to the floor (Pianin 2000a; *Washington Post,* 28 March 2000).

Hastert also gave one of his few floor speeches that year on behalf of the bill. David Obey, the ranking member of the Appropriations Committee, offered an amendment to strike out $500 million in drug-eradication funding from the measure. In defending the amendment, Obey pleaded to his colleagues, "We are not to be agents of the President; we are not to be the agents of the Speaker." Hastert, however, responded that "thousands of families are destroyed because of what Colombian drugs and others, but mainly Colombian drugs, are doing in this country," and that "I could tell Members stories from my own experience" of observing the damaging effects of illegal drug use (*Congressional Record,* 29 March 2000, H1522–23). The Obey amendment failed, 186 to 239, and the next day the House approved the full bill—now totaling over $13 billion in size—by a vote of 263 to 146 (Parks 2000). Despite Hastert's leadership, both votes reflected some disagreement within his party: the Obey amendment received the yea votes of fifty-eight Republicans, and sixty-one Republicans voted against the bill's final passage.

Even after the measure went to the Senate, Hastert continued to lobby for it. Lott steadfastly opposed any appropriations made outside of the regular budget process, particularly one as expensive as this bill, and the Speaker began negotiating with him to try to move the legislation forward (Parks 2000). After more than two months had passed, Lott finally relented, agreeing to bring the spending bill to the Senate floor. As the chairman of the Senate Appropriations Committee, Ted Stevens of Alaska (who also supported the bill), told a reporter, "The speaker is the speaker . . . and if in the final analysis, he says he has to have it, as far as I'm concerned, he'll have it" (Pianin 2000a; 2000b; Pianin and Dewar 2000). The final bill, which in the end had a price tag of more than $11 billion, passed the House and Senate at the end of the month and was signed into law in July 2000.

FULFILLING PRESIDENT-ORIENTED ROLES
OR DUTIES

As partisan as Congress may have been during the Hastert speakership, there is at least one noteworthy example of Hastert exercising legislative leadership for an opposite-party president on a matter unpopular with his congressional party. But Hastert exercised such leadership reluctantly, defending the president's agenda only after being publicly criticized for failing to do so.

In 1991, after the end of the cold war, the former communist state of Yugoslavia began to divide into independent states. Tensions between Serbia, the state that inherited what remained of Yugoslavia, and the breakaway republics of Bosnia and Croatia led to years of violent conflict. The war ended after member nations of the North Atlantic Treaty Organization (NATO) initiated a bombing campaign against Serbia and the Clinton White House brokered a major peace agreement in 1995 in Dayton, Ohio. Yet new problems emerged when Kosovo, a province within Serbia, made moves to achieve its own independence. Serbian leader Slobodan Milosevic responded with violent counterinsurgency tactics that led to civilian massacres and the displacement of hundreds of thousands of Kosovars. By early 1999, peace talks had failed to resolve the dispute. Fearing a spread of the conflict to neighboring countries, the Clinton administration threatened NATO air attacks against Serbian targets and suggested that several thousand U.S. peacekeeping soldiers could be sent to the region to prevent further violence (Central Intelligence Agency 2009; Pomper 1999a).

Many members of Congress had doubts about the president's proposed strategy, and Hastert himself professed "mixed feelings" about the campaign. A number of House Republicans opposed the deployment of any U.S. troops to the region; some advocated for an open debate in Congress on Clinton's plans before they could be implemented (Eilperin and Claiborne 1999; Pomper 1999a). Other Republicans, seeing the situation as an opportunity for partisan gain, believed the party should distance itself from a military intervention in Kosovo, allowing the GOP to blame the president if it went badly (for example, VandeHei 1999).

Hastert initially offered some cooperation with the White House but preferred not to directly challenge his own party. The Speaker told the president that the House would "work with" him on the matter, but he also insisted to the president and his staff—over White House objections—that Congress vote on any troop deployment in advance (Alvarez and Schmitt 2000; Gugliotta and Eilperin 1999a; Pomper 1999a). While not offering to whip the vote for Clinton, he did pledge (as one reporter described it) to "try not to influence any House debate" and to "frame the issue as a positive vote endorsing Clinton's policy, rather than a negative vote opposing it" (Pomper 1999a).

At first, Hastert's more limited deference to Clinton did not appear to jeopardize the president's objectives. In mid-March, the House passed a resolution authorizing the deployment of peacekeepers in Kosovo, with the House GOP leadership taking no official position on the measure. Nonetheless, the outcome was not an overwhelming endorsement of the White House. The vote was fairly close (219 to 191), and a majority of Republicans not only voted against the authorization but also supported an amendment (which failed) prohibiting any use of American ground troops in Kosovo. Hastert spoke on the floor but urged only that the House pass the rule for considering the resolution, remaining neutral on the resolution itself. He told the House that he had informed Clinton, "I personally have reservations regarding the wisdom of deploying the additional U.S. troops to the former Yugoslavia, but I have not made up my mind and I will listen intently and closely to this debate" (*Congressional Record,* 11 March 1999, H1180). One House Republican, Peter King of New York, later expressed concern about the sentiments of his party, noting, "We have to forget Bill Clinton is the president and think about the office of the presidency" (Eilperin and Claiborne 1999).

Meanwhile, American military involvement in the Kosovo crisis escalated. With no significant progress being made to end the conflict, NATO began a bombing campaign in Serbia on March 24. Clinton gave a televised speech the same day, defending the bombing and assuring the public that U.S. troops would not be sent into combat (Pomper 1999b). In response, Hastert continued his "middle of the road" approach. On one hand, he did the White House a favor by refusing to schedule immediate votes or floor debate on the NATO attacks, avoiding any open challenge or repudiation by the House of Clinton's military strategy. Instead, he allowed only a vote on a resolution expressing support for U.S. troops in the region, which he endorsed on the House floor. On the other hand, he opted not to pursue a bipartisan resolution supporting Clinton's policy, out of apparent deference to Republicans who "did not want to sanction what Clinton was doing in Kosovo" (Dewar and Eilperin 1999). He also promised floor votes at some future point on two resolutions, both sponsored by Republican Tom Campbell of California, which would assert greater congressional authority on U.S. military policy in the region and potentially challenge the president's own policy decisions. The first required troop withdrawal from the Balkans, and the second declared a state of war between the United States and the former Yugoslavia. Campbell, though, had forced Hastert's hand: the Speaker was not eager to allow consideration of either measure, but the War Powers Act gave Campbell the authority to call for votes on both (Tyson 1999; VandeHei 1999).

The Speaker's hands-off approach finally backfired in late April when the House brought Campbell's resolutions to the floor, plus two other measures: a bill requiring congressional authorization in advance of any troop deployments in the Balkans, and a Democratic resolution (already approved in the Senate) authorizing NATO's use of air strikes in Serbia and Montenegro (Dewar and Eilperin 1999). Besides opposing the first three measures, the White House presumably wanted to ensure that the last resolution would pass, in order to demonstrate congressional support for the bombing operation in Serbia. Unfortunately for the president, while Hastert kept largely distant from the vote on that resolution, Republicans who opposed the president would prove to be less reticent about influencing its outcome.

The legislation mandating Congress's advance approval for American military deployment came up for a vote first. It passed, 249 to 180, with all but sixteen Republicans voting for it (and Hastert also voting yes). Campbell's two resolutions were next. The Clinton administration was against them both, as were House GOP leaders, who feared that passage of either measure would force their party to take greater responsibility for the U.S. and NATO military operation. Both were rejected by the House: the withdrawal resolution lost, 139–290, and the declaration of war received a scant two yes votes (Lee 1999; VandeHei 1999). The fourth and final vote would be on the measure granting congressional approval for the NATO air campaign. Hastert voted in favor, but he did so after many legislators had already voted—too late to serve as a signal to wavering Republicans—and otherwise remained "near the back rail of the chamber as [voting] time elapsed," according to one account. Majority Whip Tom DeLay and Deputy Whip Roy Blunt, however, actively lobbied legislators to oppose the measure, and they were successful: it lost by a tie 213–213 vote, rejected by 187 Republicans (86 percent of all voting GOP legislators) and 26 Democrats (Eilperin 1999; Welch 1999a).

The last vote may have reflected the ideological preferences of the House Republican Party, but it was a policy victory that would prove damaging to the new Speaker. Hastert was roundly criticized for what many interpreted as an open rejection of the president's defense policy during a U.S. military campaign. Not surprisingly, congressional Democrats criticized the Speaker: Minority Leader Richard Gephardt (D-MO), for example, declared, "The Republican leadership has shown an amazing lack of leadership" (Eilperin 1999). But complaints also came from the media as well. The *New York Daily News* ran a story with the headline "Hastert Can't Cut It, Some Republicans Say," and according to Hastert, even his local newspaper ran stories with headlines questioning his leadership (Burger 1999; Hastert 2004, 197).

Hastert quickly changed course. In a private meeting with fellow House Republicans, he admitted he had been mistaken in not pushing harder for passage of the resolution. The next week, the House considered a $13 billion funding bill to pay for immediate military operations in Yugoslavia, which Hastert used as an opportunity to act more assertively. Addressing the House from the floor, he urged approval for both the measure itself and the procedures governing its consideration. "To my colleagues who disagree with the President's policy," he said, "let me say simply, you had your vote last week. . . . Now is the time to rise above the partisanship and vote for the good of the country as a whole" (*Congressional Record,* 6 May 1999, H2822). The Speaker prevailed, with the measure passing 311 to 105, the majorities of both parties (and Hastert himself) voting in favor. He also employed direct lobbying to kill an amendment prohibiting money from being spent to send troops to the region without congressional approval. And later he and Minority Leader Gephardt both requested that a congressional delegation visiting Russia allow the White House to take the lead on setting U.S. policy toward Kosovo (Dealey 1999; Gugliotta and Eilperin 1999b; Welch 1999a).

Hastert did retreat somewhat from his pro–White House position later in May. An impending defense authorization bill contained language that would have cut off funds for the conflict after September. Hastert first agreed to remove the provision after Clinton threatened to veto the bill, but when doing so threatened its passage, he decided to keep the bill as written. The language was later stricken from the bill by a Democratic floor amendment, which Hastert voted for; however, he and other party leaders had refrained from lobbying on the matter, and Republicans rejected the amendment by a nearly 2 to 1 margin. But by this time, a peace agreement had already been reached with Serbia, and peacekeepers were about to be deployed to Kosovo (Pianin and Eilperin 1999a; Welch 1999b). When Serbian military forces had fully withdrawn from the breakaway region, the United Nations took responsibility for its future status. Kosovo finally declared itself an independent state in February 2008.

HELPING THE CONGRESSIONAL PARTY AND
THE PRESIDENTIAL PARTY

From 2001 though 2006, GOP President George W. Bush and congressional Republicans displayed a remarkable level of cooperation and coordination. Bush vetoed only one bill during that time, a paucity of vetoes unseen since the nineteenth century, and Republicans in the House and Senate seldom openly challenged their party's president. This six-year lack of dissent between the executive and legislative branches of government was interrupted only when, in May 2001, the departure of Vermont Senator Jim Jeffords from the GOP gave Democrats control of the Senate until the end of 2002.

Why did this apparent unity happen? Did House and Senate Republicans find a like-minded president with whom they could jointly accomplish shared policy goals? Or did they acquiesce to presidential power and enact legislation they would not otherwise have passed? Given the variety of issues and bills Congress considered during this period, the answer is probably "it depends." But two major legislative initiatives considered during this period seem to illustrate the first dynamic: that is, the Speaker acting both to help his congressional party and to fulfill a duty to help the same-party president. They are also prime candidates for inclusion in any history of the Hastert Speakership, illustrating the important role Hastert could play in influencing the legislative process.

The first initiative would expand Medicare to include coverage for prescription drugs. Both House Republicans and President Bush hoped such an expansion would allow them to take credit for a major new federal program to assist seniors. It was important to Hastert, who had a strong personal interest in health care policy; but in addition, it was a priority for the president, who had proposed a prescription drug plan during his 2000 campaign, along with his opponent, Vice President Al Gore (Bruni 2000; Franzen 2003).

Speaker Hastert's dramatic attempt to pass a prescription drug bill on the House floor in 2003, described in chapter 1, is perhaps the most noteworthy example of his leadership on the issue. But his efforts on behalf of prescription drug coverage for seniors had begun several years before. Congressional Republicans first tried to pass legislation providing such a benefit in the 106th Congress (1999–2000), in response to President Bill Clinton's proposal for a new Medicare drug benefit and after hearing many constituents' complaints about rising prices of prescription drugs. The Speaker asked several legislators to draft a bill on the issue, participated in their deliberations when his help was needed, and promised a floor vote when they wrote up their final proposal. The measure was strongly opposed by Democrats and Clinton for being overly free market oriented; it passed the House in the summer of 2000, but by a slim three-vote margin (217 to 214), and it never became law (Adams 1999; Carey 2000; Eilperin 2000).

A similar prescription drug bill was brought to the floor two years later. In a preview of the problems that would face House GOP leaders in 2003, several rank-and-file Republicans opposed various elements of the legislation: some viewed the bill as too stingy, and others disliked the creation of a new federal entitlement program, particularly if it proved to be expensive. Though Democrats remained hostile to the legislation, the Speaker worked hard to pass it in his chamber—even after Republicans lost control of the Senate in May 2001 —"hoping," if nothing else, to protect his party "from Democratic criticisms on the issue during an election year" (*Congressional Quarterly Almanac* 2002, 10-4). Along with sympathetic interest groups, White House officials, and other House leaders, he lobbied dozens of reluctant Republicans, postponing the bill's passage until the early morning hours of June 28 while gathering votes for the plan. According to *Congressional Quarterly*, "at one point" the Speaker even "threatened to hold the House in session into the weekend," if necessary, "to ensure action on the bill" (Carey 2002; *Congressional Quarterly Almanac* 2002, 10–4 to 10–6, quote p. 10-6). That measure also passed the House, but it would not be until the following Congress that Hastert and other Republicans would manage to create a new drug coverage element of Medicare, albeit with an aggressive use of the voting clock in the House.

The second initiative, also health care related, would extend certain protections to patients in managed health care plans. These health care plans, such as health maintenance organizations (HMOs), were designed keep medical expenses low by placing limits or restrictions on the type of treatment patients could receive. By the late 1990s, however, managed care patients increasingly complained about struggling with excessive bureaucracy to get medical treatments approved, and also about overly restrictive limits that jeopardized their ability to get needed care in a timely fashion (*Congressional Quarterly Almanac* 2001, 12–5).

Congressional Republicans, generally wary of government regulation of private enterprise and concerned about excessive litigation against businesses, were hesitant to enact legislation that might do both. But with greater public demand for action against HMOs and President Clinton and congressional Democrats pushing the issue, the GOP could protect themselves electorally by taking action of some sort.[3] Enacting managed care reform, also known as "patients' rights" legislation, would address the concerns of others besides just House Republicans. In the 2000 presidential campaign, the issue was highly salient—the first question asked at an October debate was on the topic—and George W. Bush made note of his support for a similar initiative while governor of Texas. Bush continued to call for managed care patient protection legislation after entering the White House, and in February 2001 he detailed what such reform should entail (Abraham 2000; Lardner Jr. 2000; Pear 2001). In addition, though it was probably not his primary motivation, a managed care bill did complement Hastert's own personal interest in health care policy.

Hastert was involved extensively with the two major attempts to enact a patients' rights bill during his tenure as Speaker. In mid-1999, after the Senate approved a managed care measure but two House committees failed to develop acceptable legislation, he asked several Republicans to draft a conservative-leaning bill that could pass with GOP votes. Doing so would not be easy. Although a majority of House Republicans had voted for a managed care bill in the previous Congress, it had passed narrowly, 216 to 210, with only three Democrats voting in favor. Since then, the party had lost five House seats, meaning that Republican leaders would almost certainly have to find a way to get more Democratic votes to pass a similar bill (Eilperin and Goldstein 1999; Mitchell 1999c).

The biggest source of disagreement in Congress on managed care reform would revolve around liability: whether patients could sue their HMOs for damages if they had received poor medical treatment or had been denied necessary care. Republican leaders and a majority of the party wanted liability protections for the managed care industry, but some Republicans and most Democrats felt differently. Hastert hoped to win over at least some members of the second group by passing a bill with, as one reporter described it, only a "limited approach to health care regulation." But he faced a significant setback when the task force he had formed unexpectedly wrote a bill permitting some (though restricted) legal action by patients against health maintenance organizations. At the same time, support was growing for a bipartisan measure, written by Rep. Charlie Norwood (R-GA) and Rep. John Dingell (D-MI), which would expand the power of patients to sue managed care organizations. These moves threatened to alienate House Republicans and pass a bill closer to the preferences of the Democratic minority (Goldstein and Dewar 1999; Mitchell 1999c).

Given pressure from both his own task force and supporters of the Norwood-Dingell bill, Hastert had to relent somewhat on the question of legal liability, and he stood behind the task force's plan as the lesser of two evils. Facing what one news report called "a budding rebellion within his own party" by legislators who wanted a floor vote on a patients' rights measure, the Speaker agreed to let the task force legislation and the Norwood-Dingell measure both come to the floor (Goldstein and Dewar 1999). But during debate on the House floor in October, he spoke in favor of only the task force bill, warning that the Norwood-Dingell proposal meant "trial lawyers will be given unprecedented new rights to sue any time for any reason in any venue" (*Congressional Record,*

7 October 1999, H9601). Hastert's speech was not enough to ensure a win. In a rare floor defeat for the Speaker, the task force bill lost, 193–238, and the Norwood-Dingell measure passed, 275–151 (with sixty-eight Republicans and all but two Democrats voting in favor). To prevent the Norwood-Dingell bill from becoming law, Hastert appointed legislators who had opposed the measure to the conference committee, and it failed to survive conference negotiations with the Senate (Goldstein and Dewar 1999; *New York Times,* 5 November 1999; *Congressional Quarterly Almanac* 2000, 12–3).

At the start of the next Congress, Republicans enjoyed a unified GOP government for the first time in fifty-four years. With President Bush pushing for managed care reform, yet having "long been convinced that frivolous lawsuits [were] a serious public policy problem," the environment seemed ideal for the passage of a bill that would reflect more conservative policy principles. Nonetheless, a number of Republicans still supported expanded legal liability for managed care organizations. The party also had extremely narrow seat margins in Congress, controlling exactly half of the seats in the Senate and 221 of 435 seats in the House, making it challenging to pass a bill with only Republican votes (Balz and Harris 2001).

The Republican-favored margin in the Senate proved short-lived when Senator Jeffords left the GOP five months into 2001. The new Democratic majority in the Senate quickly passed a managed care reform bill that, like the earlier Norwood-Dingell plan, gave patients the power to sue managed care plans under broader conditions and for more damages than conservatives wanted. Furthermore, attempts by Bush and Hastert to agree on a compromise bill with Norwood failed, and the Georgia congressman again lent his name to the legislation that had passed the House in 1999. President Bush now faced the real possibility that he would either have to sign a managed care bill he and other Republicans opposed or veto a popular measure passed with bipartisan congressional support (Balz and Harris 2001).

The Speaker and the president undertook considerable efforts to prevent both outcomes. Hastert assigned three committee chairmen to draft an alternative to the Norwood-Dingell bill. Reportedly "weary beyond belief" of dealing with the issue, the Speaker relented to some degree on the question of liability; the resulting bill (sponsored by Republican Ernie Fletcher of Kentucky) permitted HMOs to be sued in state courts—but for limited damages and only if a patient's insurance company had not followed the guidelines of an outside reviewing agency. Bush and Hastert lobbied House Republicans to support the plan. The president met with Republican legislators at the White

House and on Capitol Hill, spoke to the House GOP Conference, and openly suggested he would veto the Norwood-Dingell bill if Congress passed it instead (Balz and Harris 2001; *Congressional Quarterly Almanac* 2001, 12–3; Goldstein and Eilperin 2001; Goldstein and Milbank 2001). A decision to renew discussions with Norwood proved to be the most fruitful course. When the independent-minded legislator finally reached an agreement with the president, the Fletcher bill (with modifications) quickly passed the House, 218–213, and Hastert followed up with an op-ed in the *Boston Globe* praising the bill (Hastert 2001; McQueen 2001; Rosenbaum 2001).

In the end, managed care reform would fall victim to changing circumstances. The terrorist attacks of September 11, 2001, drastically altered Washington's political priorities. Meanwhile, many HMOs had begun expanding medical options for patients, and in June 2002 the Supreme Court ruled that states could allow an outside review of an HMO's decision to refuse payment for particular treatment. These developments lessened the perceived necessity of a legislative remedy, and as in the previous Congress, managed care reform died (*Congressional Quarterly Almanac* 2002, 10–7 to 10–8).

HELPING THE PARTY IN CONGRESS

As Speaker, Hastert often seemed especially attentive to the objectives and concerns of his own party in the House. This arguably made Hastert closer to the classic "party agent" model of congressional leadership than perhaps any Speaker in this study. Many examples of this attentive sort of leadership occurred after 2000, when close cooperation between congressional Republicans and President Bush make it difficult to separate the independent influence of each. For at least two important legislative proposals, however, Hastert clearly exercised assertive leadership principally on behalf of his party in the House.

The first proposal was considered during Hastert's first year as Speaker. In summer 1999, the Clinton White House estimated that the federal budget would have a $1 trillion surplus over the next ten years, more than $300 billion above what had been previously estimated. For congressional Republicans, this represented a chance to pursue one of their top legislative priorities—a cut in federal taxes—without creating large budget deficits. Speaker Hastert immediately took the lead on exploiting this opportunity. Hastert spoke at a large public rally at the Capitol with fellow Republicans, endorsing new cuts that could reduce taxes by nearly $800 billion, and perhaps as much as $1 trillion, over the following decade (Eilperin and Pianin 1999; Pianin 1999a).[4]

But just as Newt Gingrich had faced pivotal dissenters in his party over his 1995 income tax cut (see chapter 4), Hastert would have to deal with a sizable number of skeptics among House Republicans while recognizing the likelihood that few Democrats would probably go along with the bill. Initially, Hastert later admitted, "it wasn't even close. I didn't have the votes" for the tax reduction package (Hastert 2004, 198). A moderate Republican, Michael Castle of Delaware, sought backing for a smaller tax cut of $500 billion, and GOP leaders looked for ways to reduce the cost of the bill to allay the fears of a significant number of Republicans who were concerned about the size the measure. Some party conservatives were also disappointed that the bill did not abolish the so-called marriage tax penalty that increased taxes for married couples (Mitchell 1999b; Pianin and Eilperin 1999b).

Although the tax cut was reduced in size somewhat, resistance remained. But the Speaker remained a strong advocate for passing a major tax bill. It would, he argued, give Congress a stronger position to negotiate with the White House on a final tax reduction proposal; but also, its failure would threaten Hastert's reputation as a new Speaker and mean the loss of what one news story called "a potent campaign issue" (Pianin and Eilperin 1999c). Hastert spoke to the full Republican Conference on behalf of the measure, asked party officials and donors to lobby legislators, and personally met with the "10 to 20 moderate[s]" whose votes would affect the outcome if Democrats were to uniformly oppose the measure (Kiely 1999). On July 20, two days before the scheduled vote on the plan, Majority Whip DeLay still did not have a majority of Representatives counted in favor of the bill. But the next day, Ways and Means Committee Chairman Bill Archer agreed to the request of a group of Republicans that the measure's income tax cuts be contingent on a decline in interest on the federal debt. When the finalized bill came to the floor on July 22, Hastert spoke on its behalf, and it passed 223 to 208, with near unanimous Republican support. Appreciative Republicans began chanting "coach" on the House floor in recognition of Hastert's efforts (Boyer 1999; Hastert 2004, 199; Kiely 1999; Mitchell 1999b; Pianin and Eilperin 1999b; 1999c).

In early August, the Senate passed a final version of the bill, and the House followed suit. Rather than send the bill to the president, Hastert and other party leaders first tried to rally public support for tax reductions. In a version of the "going public" technique (see chapter 5), Hastert joined other House Republicans in holding public events in local districts during the August congressional recess, touting the cuts and urging voters to ask Clinton to sign the bill into law. The effort failed to persuade the White House to support the legislation, however, and congressional Republicans soon gave it up for that congress (*Boston Globe,* 12 August 1999; Pianin 1999b).

The other proposal was one that a majority of Republicans opposed: greater federal regulation of campaign finance. Under Speaker Gingrich, the House had been forced to deal with a major campaign reform measure sponsored by Chris Shays (R-CT) and Martin Meehan (D-MA) that would, among other things, have prohibited so-called soft-money—unregulated donations to political parties—which had increased significantly in the 1996 election campaigns. Their bill had passed in 1998, over the voting opposition of a majority of the GOP, but had failed to become law. Shays and Meehan reintroduced their legislation the following February, shortly after the new Congress had convened and with Hastert as the new House Speaker (Dwyre and Farrar-Myers 2001, 21–24, 28; Kornblut 1999).[5]

Views on the Shays-Meehan bill primarily followed party lines. Democrats generally favored it, but most Republicans remained opposed, fearing it would end their fund-raising advantage over Democrats. Many Republicans also believed that limits on campaign spending imposed restrictions on the constitutional right to free expression. Thus Hastert's decision to exercise leadership on the measure would primarily derive from the policy preferences and electoral concerns of his party in the House. In the 106th Congress, with the 2000 presidential election looming, Hastert might have also been concerned with how changes to campaign finance law might affect the race for president. But at least one GOP presidential candidate, John McCain, supported a ban of soft money, and though George W. Bush was less enamored with such a prohibition, he felt the need to endorse a reform package of his own (Dwyer and Farrar-Myers 2001, 17; Kornblut 2001).

In the previous Congress, Speaker Gingrich had refused to allow Shays and Meehan to schedule their bill for a vote, relenting only when it appeared likely that a majority of legislators would sign a discharge petition to force the bill to the floor. Hastert, not wanting to face a similar loss of agenda control, promised the two Representatives a vote on their measure, which diminished enthusiasm among Republicans for another discharge petition—as did the fear that doing so would be a rebuke of the new Speaker. Nonetheless, three months later a group of restless pro-reform Republicans met with Hastert to ask for a timely floor vote on the legislation. The Speaker would not agree to have the vote sooner than September 1999, greatly increasing the odds it would be filibustered successfully in the Senate; and even if it did pass the other chamber and was signed into law, it would probably be too late for the bill to apply to the upcoming congressional elections (Drinkard 1999; Dwyre and Farrar-Myers 2001, 83–84, 202–4; Kornblut 1999; Mitchell 1999a).

When the bill was finally sent to the floor (after a failed attempt to force an earlier vote by using a discharge petition), the procedures for considering it allowed votes on three other substitute bills and a variety of so-called poison pill amendments—any of which, if passed, would either gut the bill or make it more likely to fail in a final floor vote. Despite these challenging conditions set by the Republican-controlled Rules Committee, the Shays-Meehan bill passed largely unchanged, with none of the substitute amendments winning and only two relatively minor amendments being approved. The final measure passed, 252–177, with fifty-four Republicans voting in the affirmative and the Speaker casting a vote against. Hastert and other leaders had failed to stop the legislation in the House, but it was filibustered successfully in the Senate and died in the 106th Congress (Dwyre and Farrar-Myers 2001, 202–21).

Shays and Meehan tried again in the next Congress. Newly elected president George W. Bush did not support their bill's broader prohibition on soft money, but he did suggest that he could sign a reform bill into law—and as the Senate debated the bill in March, Bush did not issue a veto threat against it. Hastert again promised a vote in the full House on the Shays-Meehan bill, though he remained opposed to it (Farrar-Myers and Dwyre 2008, 76–77, 80–81; Shenon 2001).

When a reform bill passed the Senate that differed slightly from Shays-Meehan, the two congressmen faced a tricky decision. On one hand, they could try to pass the Senate version of the measure, which would avoid a conference committee that could delay or kill the proposal. But they also needed to make changes to the bill that would solidify, if not expand, support in the House for the legislation. Shays and Meehan chose the latter approach and tried to convince the Speaker to permit a single floor amendment incorporating the fourteen changes they wanted. Hastert turned down their request, however, after facing resistance from conservative party members. Democrats and pro-reform Republicans responded by rejecting the floor rule for considering the Shays-Meehan bill—the first time a rule had failed under Hastert—and the Speaker then declared that he had "no plans to bring up" the bill again (Dewar and Eilperin 2001; Farrar-Myers and Dwyre 2008, 81).

The bill's authors did not give up, and in January 2002 they had gathered 218 signatures on a discharge petition, enough to bring the legislation back to the floor (Eilperin and Dewar 2002). Hastert now openly and adamantly opposed the measure. In a strongly worded speech before a meeting of the Republican

Conference, he announced that "this is Armageddon," and a Hastert staffer told one reporter that the Speaker would urge fellow Republicans to vote against the Shays-Meehan bill (Eilperin 2002). Hastert "held strategy meetings as his aides made calls," and other party leaders also lobbied rank-and-file members (Mitchell 2002). In addition, Hastert and GOP leaders planned to use the same floor tactics as in 1999, offering alternative bills and politically attractive amendments that, if any of them passed, would either require a conference committee or make Shays-Meehan unpalatable to a majority of representatives (Farrar-Myers and Dwyre 2008, 84; Mitchell 2002).

The Speaker had hoped that the White House would lend a hand in trying to defeat Shays-Meehan, but Bush wanted to keep distant from the issue—especially in the wake of a financial scandal involving the Texas oil company Enron, whose executives had donated considerable sums to the president's election campaign (Milbank 2002). Following the pleas of Hastert, the White House reportedly gave the national Republican Party permission to lobby persuadable House Republicans. But Bush remained officially neutral, if not slightly sympathetic, toward the measure: his press secretary, to Hastert's chagrin, suggested at one point that the bill would "improve the [campaign finance] system," and that Bush should perhaps take credit if it passed Congress (Allen and Milbank 2002; Berke and Mitchell 2002).

In a marathon session, the House cast sixteen recorded votes on a variety of amendments and alternative measures designed by the GOP leadership to kill Shays-Meehan. But the attempt by Hastert and other House Republican leaders to stop the measure was unsuccessful: at 2:30 on the morning of February 14, the bill passed, 240–189. Forty-one Republicans and 198 Democrats had voted in favor of the measure. The Senate approved the bill without changes, avoiding a conference committee, and it was later signed into law by President Bush (Farrar-Myers and Dwyre 2008, 85–86; Johnson 2002).

CONCLUSION

Dennis Hastert was a partisan Speaker who often seemed most comfortable pushing for legislative outcomes that clearly met the objectives of the majority of his party in Congress. But as partisan as Hastert may have been, he, like his predecessors, was willing to exercise legislative leadership to achieve other goals besides reelection as Speaker by his party. His initial abdication of leadership on the issue of military operations in Yugoslavia also illustrated the negative consequences that could befall a Speaker who neglected important Speaker-related roles. And after the 2000 elections Hastert demonstrated how the objectives of a same-party president could also motivate a Speaker's legislative leadership in concert with the desires or preferences of the majority party in the House.

Hastert elucidated his dual view of the Speakership in a symposium on the office of Speaker held at the Library of Congress in 2004. At one point he remarked: "The job of the Speaker is to rule fairly, but ultimately to carry out the will of the majority. Unlike some other parliamentary bodies, the Speaker in the U.S. House of Representatives is the leader of his party . . . the hallmark of an effective leadership is one that can deliver the votes." But in the same speech, Hastert observed that this partisan dimension of the Speakership is bounded by other considerations. He acknowledged the "unique tension within the Office of the Speaker" between its partisan and nonpartisan roles and noted that "if the chair is seen as being unfair, the likely result is a breakdown in parliamentary comity" (Hastert 2003).

Another important aspect of the Hastert speakership is that, on more than one occasion, Hastert formulated or even altered his strategy or legislative objectives in response to demands by members of his own party. For instance, the Speaker hesitated to support Clinton's Kosovo policy because many House Republicans opposed it on policy or electoral grounds, and he ended negotiations on campaign finance reform with Chris Shays and Martin Meehan when his party objected. In another example, not discussed in this chapter, Hastert kept a major intelligence bill from the House floor in late 2004 when, in a meeting with his caucus, a number of Republicans voiced opposition to it—even though it was supported by President Bush and a majority of the House (Allen 2004).[6] This is a noteworthy contrast to two earlier Speakers, Jim Wright and Newt Gingrich, who each demonstrated failure to accurately assess the preferences of their respective parties in Congress. By avoiding these kinds of mistakes, Hastert steered clear of creating open and possibly durable divisions in the GOP Conference while buying time to build consensus within his party around contentious legislation and, as described by one reporter in the context of the intelligence bill, "[keeping] his political capital in the bank" (Allen 2004). This seemed to be a particularly effective strategy for Hastert since, for most of his tenure, Republicans possessed very narrow seat margins in the House and sometimes seemed chronically divided between conservatives and moderates. But the strategy was also not without risks, including the danger of being perceived as insufficiently strong or as abdicating leadership to others.

Chapter 7 Goal-Oriented Leadership: Trends and Implications

The central claim of this book is that the Speaker of the House of Representatives is a strategic actor who uses legislative leadership to achieve goals central to his or her position in the House. Most Speakers want to remain Speaker, and to ensure this objective they frequently exercise leadership on behalf of their congressional party. But this is not their only important goal. Since Speakers are also representatives, they share two goals with their colleagues in Congress: to get reelected to the House and to enact preferred public policy. Furthermore, Speakers have important duties and roles related to the Speakership that they may seek to fulfill. These duties include supporting the presidential party, aiding the institutional presidency, and defending matters of concern to all members of the House. As a consequence, Speakers may at times use the leadership tools at their disposal to achieve legislative outcomes irrespective of the preferences of the majority party in Congress. Furthermore, since these objectives are not necessarily mutually exclusive, Speakers may exercise leadership to satisfy more than one of them simultaneously.

Previous chapters have provided both qualitative and quantitative evidence for this claim, which I call the theory of goal-driven leadership. In this chapter, I explore this theory further. First, I examine the extent to which it helps us understand when the Speaker of the House will most likely exercise legislative leadership. Next, I discuss a historical trend suggested by this book: the declining frequency of modern Speakers acting to fulfill particular leadership duties or roles. I then review other possible reasons Speakers may exercise leadership and whether they discount the validity of the theory. Finally, I conclude with a discussion of some broader implications of this book and the theory's applicability to the Speakership of Nancy Pelosi.

PREDICTING LEGISLATIVE LEADERSHIP

In chapter 1, I offered a possible hypothesis stemming from the theory of goal-driven leadership: when the Speakers' party is more unified or when highly salient legislative issues are under consideration in the House, the Speaker is more likely to exercise legislative leadership. The case studies in chapters 3 and 4 suggested that the latter factor does matter and that the former may be less important if (1) a critical majority of the majority party desires a legislative outcome or (2) the Speaker seeks to secure an important electoral objective of his or her divided party. (This second finding seems to further confirm the claim of C. Lawrence Evans and Walter Oleszek that policy divisions within congressional parties, at least in committee, can increase the probability of leadership activity; see Evans and Oleszek 1999a.)

To more systematically determine what factors increase the probability of Speaker leadership on legislation, one would ideally compare instances of legislative leadership against the universe of all possible opportunities for such behavior. The case studies in earlier chapters do not readily lend themselves to this sort of comparative analysis, but the Speaker's use of floor speeches, analyzed in chapter 2, does. These data are not an ideal test of the hypothesis, since floor advocacy is not always used to exercise influence on legislation, but because it is more quantitative in nature, it does at least allow for a rough determination of the validity of the hypothesis. Thus I used a logit regression model with a dependent variable measuring whether the Speaker delivered a floor statement on a "key vote"—a recorded vote deemed by the journal *Congressional Quarterly* (*CQ*) as significant or controversial—from 1945 (when *CQ* began compiling such votes) to 1988 (when presidential request data is last available, see below).[1] Key votes are not a perfect representation of all voting activity,[2] but they are a useful benchmark because very few floor statements are delivered in proportion to all of the votes cast on the House floor, and because not every roll call is the same: some occur on major initiatives and others on routine or minor bills. It also allows one to control for the behavior of more loquacious Speakers who have delivered a number of speeches on relatively minor legislation (that is, John McCormack; see chapter 2).

Explanatory variables were used to test competing hypotheses of when legislative leadership, at least with respect to floor advocacy, may be exercised by the Speaker (regardless of the Speaker's actual position on the given vote). To capture the possibility that majority party unity matters, I measured the degree of the party's voting cohesion on each key vote. The variable "Rice score" measures every vote's Rice cohesion score, calculated by dividing the difference between the yes and no votes of the majority party on a vote by the total number of majority party votes cast. To be sure, this variable is limited in important ways: it cannot capture the strength of party preferences or the extent that a key vote aids the party's electoral (if not its policy) objectives.[3] Nonetheless, smaller values of "Rice score" do indicate a more divided majority party, at least on the actual vote, and imply the absence of clear party policy objectives. If this factor is positive and significant in the logit analysis, it suggests that greater party division deters the Speaker from using floor advocacy.[4]

I also hypothesize that certain issues related to the Speaker's goals are more likely to attract his attention. (See chapter 1, table 1.3 for a summary of these issues.) To test these, I included variables that approximate the salience of particular legislative matters. To determine if a vote was associated with the Speaker's goals of reelection to Congress or passage of personally desired policy, I used a dichotomous variable equal to 1 if a key vote was on a matter of special importance to the Speaker's district or to the Speaker personally (see chapter 2, table 2.2). The relation of a vote to the Speaker's goal of fulfilling leadership duties and roles was estimated with several variables. For issues relevant to the presidential party, I included an interaction of two dichotomous variables: "presidential request", coded 1 if a vote outcome was explicitly requested by the president (from the Michael Malbin data set of presidential requests, coded through 1988; see chapter 2); and "unified government", coded 1 if the Speaker and president were of the same party. This measurement is imperfect since it does not capture votes that might aid a potential presidential candidate or identify whether a presidential request also reflects similar support among legislators.[5] Nonetheless, it does indicate the potential salience of a measure for an incumbent same-party president. To capture institutional presidency concerns, I interacted the "presidential request" variable with dichotomous variables measuring whether the vote was on a foreign policy, defense, or trade matter (according to the Policy Agendas Project coding system; see chapter 2).[6] (Note that this takes into account neither the party's nor the Speaker's position on each measure, which may be important in predicting whether Speakers will talk on the floor.[7]) Another dichotomous variable was also included to identify if a vote was on a House-wide matter (code 2011 in the Policy Agendas Project coding scheme). These matters are closely associated with the Speaker's role as an officer of the entire chamber.

These variables are used to test the hypotheses I set forth in chapter 1, but there are two other possible explanations of when Speakers will exercise leadership. First, Speakers might be more likely to use floor advocacy on high-priority measures for which failure would have significant and negative policy repercussions. This includes appropriations bills, required to keep the government in operation; debt limit increases, necessary to prevent default on the national treasury; and annual budget resolutions, required by the congressional budget process since 1976. To test this "agenda-pressure" hypothesis, I used a dichotomous variable, "must-pass measure", equal to 1 if a key vote was cast on one of these measures. Second, Speakers may talk on behalf of a vote if the threat of a legislative defeat is high (for example, Sinclair 1995, 57–59, 206). I approximated such a threat by examining the narrowness of the final vote outcome, using the variable "vote margin" to measure the absolute difference between yes and no votes for the key vote in question.[8] It should be noted that the effect of this variable may wash out of the logit analysis since both key votes in general and those subject to floor advocacy tend to be relatively close (Shull and Vanderleeuw 1987).[9]

I also account for other possible factors that may be significant. A vote to override a presidential veto may increase the likelihood of floor advocacy—not only because the vote is related to the president's agenda but also because it is harder to pass (requiring a two-thirds vote) and may thus require additional floor leadership. I thus included a dichotomous variable, "veto override", which equals 1 if a key vote would override a veto. Since veto overrides are more likely to occur when the president is of the opposite party, I also interacted this variable with the "unified government" variable. If the interaction term is negative, it suggests that the Speaker is acting as a partisan officer by challenging an opposite-party president's veto. Finally, the nature of the data implies two possible "fixed effects" in the model: factors constant within individual congresses, like the formal powers of Speakers and the majority's overall homogeneity (Cooper and Brady 1981; Sinclair 1995); and factors unique to particular Speak-

Table 7.1 Determinants of Whether the Speaker Addresses
a Key Vote, 1945–88

Hypothesis	Variable	Model 1: Full Dataset, Controlling for Speakers	Model 2: Full Dataset, Controlling for Congresses
Goal-driven leadership	Rice score	−.37	−.64
		(.68)	(.73)
	Speaker personal/district issue	.85^	.89^
		(.49)	(.50)
	Presidential request × unified government	.01	−.08
		(.65)	(.66)
	Presidential request × defense issue	−.99	−1.25
		(1.02)	(1.04)
	Presidential request × foreign affairs issue	−.17	−.36
		(1.09)	(1.11)
	Presidential request × trade issue	1.30	1.37
		(1.67)	(1.88)
	Issue: House	2.34***	2.60***
		(.64)	(.68)
Agenda pressure	Must-pass measure	−.34	−.52
		(.46)	(.48)
Threat of floor loss	Vote margin	−.00	.00
		(.00)	(.00)
Other variables	Veto override	1.96**	2.55***
		(.59)	(.68)
	Veto override × unified government	−.89	−1.75
		(1.31)	(1.40)
	Presidential request	0.00*	0.00**
		(.00)	(.00)
	Unified government	.18	(i)
		(.47)	
	Issue: defense	.60	.58
		(.61)	(.61)
	Issue: foreign affairs	.49	.62
		(.66)	(.65)
	Issue: trade	−.36	−.20
		(1.10)	(1.09)
	Chi-square	34.20**	42.17**
	N	548	509

Note: Model 1 includes fixed effects for each Speaker of the House from Rayburn to Wright. Model 2 includes fixed effects for each Congress; two congresses were dropped because they produced all negative outcomes. (i) Dropped due to lack of within-group variance.

^p < .10, *p < .05, **p < .01, ***p < .001 (two-tailed test)

ers, such as leadership style or personal traits, that may influence their use of floor speeches. I ran two separate logit analyses controlling for each of these fixed effects.

The results of both statistical models are shown in table 7.1.[10] Intriguingly, the data indicate that some issues related to actors and institutions besides the Speaker's party predict floor advocacy. Key votes on matters affecting the whole House are more likely to be subject to floor speeches by the Speaker, as are votes on issues of particular importance to the Speaker or his district. But the other variables related to the theory of goal-driven leadership are not significant, including same-party presidential requests and party unity (measured by Rice cohesion scores)—though, as noted above, the case studies suggest that voting unity alone may not be the only way of measuring a vote's salience to the majority party. Two other conditions increase the probability of floor advocacy: bills on the president's agenda (albeit with a very small substantive effect) and veto overrides. Since the "veto override $\times$ unified government" interaction term is negative (albeit not statistically significant), it implies that veto overrides attract Speaker floor advocacy primarily when issued by an opposite party president.[11]

It may also be that the variables predicting the Speaker's use of floor speeches are themselves conditional on some other factor, like the unity of the majority party. This so-called bounded rationality model posits that under divided parties, congressional leaders are more likely to exercise leadership for non-party-related reasons (Vega and Peters 1996). Alternatively, Speakers may be more likely to talk on the floor if a measure is expected to pass by a wide margin, in which case they might feel safer speaking on behalf of institutions or individuals besides the majority party without fear of alienating too many of their fellow partisans. To test these two related possibilities, I reran the logit analysis, splitting the data in two ways: by the degree of party unity (using the benchmark of a Rice cohesion score under .75) and by the closeness of the key vote (the breakpoint being a vote margin less than twenty).[12]

The results, displayed in table 7.2, show that party unity, if not vote margin, might dictate the salience of other factors in determining Speaker floor advocacy. When the majority party is divided, House-wide and Speaker-specific issues predict floor advocacy, but they do not when the party is unified. This distinction is less clear when looking at close versus one-sided votes, however: Speaker-specific matters fail to predict floor advocacy in either case, and legislation related to the whole House predicts floor advocacy regardless of the closeness of the vote (though for close votes, that variable is just barely significant

Table 7.2 Testing the Bounded Rationality and Vote Margin Hypotheses

Hypothesis	Variable	Unified Party (Rice Score ≥ .75)	Divided Party (Rice Score < .75)	Closer Votes (Margin ≤ 20)	Less Close Votes (Margin > 20)
Goal-driven leadership	Rice score	.35	.48	.40	−.52
		(4.84)	(.91)	(1.49)	(.71)
	Speaker personal / district issue	.61	1.11*	1.77	.79
		(1.20)	(.51)	(1.34)	(.54)
	Presidential request × unified government	.40	.29	−.71	.55
		(1.97)	(.76)	(1.57)	(.78)
	Presidential request × defense issue	(i)	−1.16	(iii)	−1.70
			(1.04)		(1.25)
	Presidential request × foreign affairs issue	(i)	−.92	(i)	−.35
			(1.15)		(1.26)
	Presidential request × trade issue	(i)	(iii)	(iii)	(i)
	Issue: House	1.58	3.57***	3.29^	2.82***
		(1.39)	(.87)	(1.99)	(.69)
Agenda pressure	Must-pass measure	.75	−.32	1.10	−.45
		(1.06)	(.55)	(1.19)	(.60)
Threat of floor loss	Vote margin	−.00	.00	−.03	−.00
		(.00)	(.00)	(.07)	(.00)
Other variables	Veto override	2.99*	1.05	.63	2.33**
		(1.30)	(1.36)	(1.41)	(.69)
	Veto override × unified government	(ii)	−.29	(i)	−1.58
			(1.92)		(1.46)
	Presidential request	.00	.00*	.00^	.00^
		(.00)	(.00)	(.00)	(.00)
	Unified government	1.76	.12	−.25	.47
		(1.18)	(.54)	(1.19)	(.50)
	Issue: defense	(i)	.72	(iii)	.88
			(.64)		(.64)
	Issue: foreign affairs	(i)	.92	−.50	1.03
			(.76)	(2.78)	(.81)
	Issue: trade	1.77	(iii)	(iii)	.18
		(1.23)			(.99)
	Constant	−4.58	−3.55***	−3.49**	−3.11**
		(3.90)	(.54)	(1.15)	(.51)
	Chi-square	19.73*	39.90*	20.93*	37.36**
	Pseudo-R^2	.22	.13	.18	.14
	N	87	447	122	419

Note: All models calculated with robust standard errors.

(i) dropped due to lack of variation; (ii) dropped due to collinearity; (iii) could not be estimated by the regression.

^p < .10, *p < .05, **p < .01, ***p < .001 (two-tailed test)

at the p < .10 level). The models also had difficulty estimating several predictors for unified parties and close votes, particularly trade and defense-related variables. Nonetheless, the findings suggest that the congressional party can matter in driving legislative leadership but that Speakers may stray from serving as strict party agents when their party is not unified, at least when using floor advocacy.

The statistical analysis done here is, at best, an incomplete test of the factors dictating when Speakers will exercise legislative leadership on the floor of the House. It studies only one kind of floor activity, and some of the variables are approximate measures of hypothesized factors. Several variables expected to matter proved unexpectedly insignificant, and much of the variance in the dependent variable is unexplained by the models (as indicated by the rather low pseudo-R^2 fit statistics reported in table 7.2). In addition, the analysis does not fully account for the possibility that different Speaker goals have varied in importance over time; for example, dividing the data into pre-1971 and post-1970 sets and running the logit analysis for each (results not shown) reveals that Speakers serving before 1971 were more likely to talk on personal policy interests, matters salient to their district, and House-wide matters than later Speakers. Nonetheless, the analysis does intimate that Speakers consider other actors and institutions besides their congressional party when deciding whether to use floor advocacy.

THE DECLINING IMPORTANCE OF SPEAKER ROLES AND DUTIES

The theory of goal-driven leadership posits that Speakers may exercise legislative leadership to satisfy certain duties or roles associated with their unique leadership position. The evidence reviewed in this book indicates that one such duty, to aid a same-party president, has remained salient to Speakers from 1941 through 2006. But two other roles—to aid the institutional presidency and support the whole House—explain fewer instances of legislative leadership in recent years than cases from earlier in House history.[13] Why is this so, and does it mean that this facet of the theory is no longer valid?

Perhaps the best explanation for this shift is that the rise in partisanship in Congress, particularly starting in the 1980s, led to changing demands and expectations by the Speaker's party in the House. The increase in partisan voting, and the strengthening of party control over House rules and procedures, has been widely documented elsewhere (for example, Nivola and Brady 2006; Rohde 1991; Theriault 2006). But in addition to directing voting behavior and influencing the rules of the chamber, growing partisanship may have had more subtle and profound effects in the House. If legislators are more partisan, they may come to value the passage of party policy more highly. And they may in turn put greater pressure on their leaders to help enact such policy and to abandon leadership goals that are unrelated to party objectives. Furthermore, party conflict may emerge on issues related to the president or the whole House, meaning that Speakers may feel compelled to ignore or oppose presidential or chamberwide concerns unless doing so helps their own party.

An important, and possibly influential, example of the latter was Speaker Albert's leadership on the Vietnam War, examined in chapter 4. At first Albert supported President Nixon's conduct of the war (as had his predecessor, John McCormack) in order to achieve personal policy goals and aid the institutional presidency. But he was ultimately forced to abandon that support because of the strong policy preferences of a majority of his own party. His initial deference to an opposite-party president on a national defense issue does not seem to have been taken up with the same degree of conviction by his successors. Some openly challenged opposite-party presidents on these kinds of issues (for example, O'Neill and Central America), and others endorsed presidential policy but balked at helping presidents implement it (such as Speakers Gingrich and Hastert with respect to President Bill Clinton's use of the military in the former Yugoslavia).

The behavior of the minority party in Congress matters too. For example, if the House minority (which in most cases examined in this book was the Republican Party) pursues more ideologically extreme outcomes, or does so more assertively, there is less opportunity for the Speaker to exercise leadership on behalf of the whole House. Speaker Jim Wright faced this problem when he endorsed a major pay raise for representatives, which House Republicans successfully exploited for partisan gain (see chapter 4).

Close competitiveness between both parties (the norm in the House for the last twelve years of this study) can further encourage party conflict and, with it, differing views between parties of the proper roles and duties of the presiding officer, further hindering the Speaker's ability to serve the common objectives of both parties (Wahlke et al. 1962, 152, 183–84). For instance, in a polarized legislature, the minority party may have greater need for leadership that protects their procedural rights; but at the same time, the majority may seek stronger leadership to minimize party defections and win policy victories on the floor, discouraging the Speaker from helping the minority. A sort of "feedback" dynamic could also be at work (Pierson 2004): if Speakers, in response to pressures from their party, exercise leadership in a certain partisan fashion, the consequent reaction from the minority party may reduce comity and further increase party conflict and division within the legislature.[14]

In addition to party polarization in Congress contributing to a partisan Speakership, presidents may also further push Speakers away from pursuing nonpartisan goals. In particular, during long periods of divided government with assertive chief executives, there is less opportunity for Speakers to find common ground with presidents and defend presidential interests. One possible turning point in this regard was when Speaker O'Neill failed to prevent passage of President Reagan's budget proposals in early 1981 (see chapter 4). O'Neill and his successors may have drawn a lesson from this failure: deference of any kind to an assertive opposite-party president, intentional or otherwise, can easily lead to major policy defeat for one's party in Congress.

Besides internal partisanship and the behavior of presidents, one other factor may have shaped Speaker leadership. Recall from chapter 1 that the roles and duties of the Speaker can derive not just from the expectations of other actors but from Speakers themselves. It could be that independent of divided government or party conflict in Congress, recent Speakers have simply not believed that they have significant responsibilities to the House at large or to the executive branch. Speakers without long prior service in the legislature, in the majority party, or in leadership may be less cognizant or more dismissive of these sorts of nonpartisan duties or roles. This possibility seems most plausible in explaining the party-oriented legislative leadership of Newt Gingrich, who had served nine terms in the minority and only one term as a leader (minority whip) before becoming Speaker of the House. By contrast, his three predecessors had all served in the majority party leadership structure and been in the House longer; and one of the three, Tip O'Neill, had also served as Speaker in a state legislature (as did an earlier Speaker, Sam Rayburn).

Regardless of the reasons for Speakers to seemingly turn away from nonpartisan leadership roles, this apparent decline in importance of such roles should not be seen as conclusive proof that the theory of goal-driven leadership is merely historical. Although recent Speakers may be less willing to exercise decisive legislative leadership on behalf of the entire House or some presidential concerns, these aspects of the role-fulfillment goal have not disappeared completely, as I documented in chapter 4 and discuss further below.

ALTERNATIVE EXPLANATIONS OF
SPEAKER BEHAVIOR

In chapter 1, I outlined three goals that Speakers will seek to achieve through the exercise of legislative leadership: reelection (to the House and to the Speakership), passage of personally desired policy, and fulfillment of key leadership roles (to support the presidential party, the institutional presidency, and the House as a whole). In subsequent chapters, I have provided evidence that pursuing these goals, individually or in combination, accounts for most major cases of leadership by the Speaker between 1941 and 2006. But a few cases and examples do not seem adequately explained by these three goals. Do these instances of leadership serve as evidence that other objectives motivate Speakers' legislative leadership? And do they show that the theory of goal-driven leadership is incomplete or even incorrect?

The data suggest three possible exceptions to the theory of goal-driven leadership. First, the Speaker may exercise leadership to assist an opposite-party president on a policy matter unrelated to defense, foreign affairs, or trade. Speakers sometimes did so with coincident support of their party, which I la beled "cooperative divided government" (appearing four times in chapter 2 and four times in chapter 5). Other times, they did so without such support, which I labeled "broad deference to opposite party president" (appearing twice in chapter 2 and once in chapter 5).

Some of these instances indicate not that the theory is wrong, however, but that Speakers can occasionally be driven by a variant of one of the three goals: enactment of desired public policy. Speakers, perhaps with the cooperation of opposite-party presidents, may work to resolve difficult *national* issues even if the Speaker's party in the House does not agree. For instance, one "cooperative divided government" case involved the refusal of Speaker O'Neill to support impeachment proceedings against President Ronald Reagan because of his concern with its possible long-term impact on national politics (Remini 2006, 469; see chapter 5). Other examples were related to budget and tax revenue matters and occurred in a particular historical context: expanding budget deficits, shrinking Social Security surpluses, and a consequent fear of a major national fiscal crisis. These cases can be explained as Speakers seeking particular policy outcomes for the national good. (They may also be rooted in Speakers' concern that inaction would severely threaten the reputation of their congressional party in the long term.) Though occurring rarely, they indicate that Speakers can think quite broadly about policy even if they are not elected by the nation at large, a tendency more likely among party leaders generally than among rank-and-file legislators (Davidson 1969, 134–35; Strahan 2007).[15] This "national policy" concern may be more salient when Speakers exercise leadership on issues that lend themselves to this perspective, such as national security, though the expectation that Speakers should defer to the president can explain these instances as well.

The remaining cases in which the Speaker helped an opposing party's president on nonexecutive issues can be understood as driven by the objectives of the majority party in Congress, but on an issue that is bipartisan in nature. For instance, in 1985 and 1986, Speaker O'Neill delivered floor speeches on behalf of tax reform, which was supported by many key House Democrats as well as the Reagan White House; and Speaker Foley later spoke on behalf of equal access for the disabled, a policy supported by both political parties. On these issues, cooperation between the president and the congressional majority party was possible, but it was not necessarily presidents pushing the Speaker to exercise legislative leadership. Such examples illustrate how legislative cooperation is achievable under divided government, at least under select conditions or for certain issues (Mayhew 1991).

A second alternative to the theory of goal-driven leadership is that Speakers may act to protect or aid congressional committees or individual legislators. For example, Rayburn opposed a 1944 floor rule that was unpopular with many Democratic committee chairmen (see table 3.1). Three cases of floor advocacy from chapter 2 also suggest that this motivation can matter: McCormack's speech in defense of a 1969 tax bill, O'Neill's 1977 floor speech supporting a budget resolution, and O'Neill's 1983 speech on the Social Security retirement age (see also chapter 5, table 5.4). In addition, two instances of non-floor leadership seem to fall into this category: in 1964, McCormack allowed the Rules Committee to report a bill without committee approval, and in 1967–68 he delayed a major congressional reform initiative opposed by committee chairmen (see chapter 5).[16]

Most of these examples do seem to have been driven by a desire to protect the legislative output or preferences of a committee or legislator. This may in turn be contingent on both the relative power and autonomy of committees and the likelihood that a committee's product will be altered or rejected on the House floor. Two of the examples, however, can still be explained by the theory of goal-driven leadership. In the Rayburn instance, the 1944 floor rule that the Speaker opposed would have undermined the independence of legislative committees, and in 1964 McCormack was seeking to defend the Rules Committee's right to discharge legislation. Both can be seen as the Speaker protecting the general *powers* of a committee or legislator, which is arguably part of the Speaker's responsibility as an officer of the whole House.

The third potential exception to the theory is that Speakers may act in order to protect their own power or reputation (Strahan 2007). In 1946, Rayburn opposed a major congressional reform proposal because he feared that its creation of party policy committees and a special legislative-executive council would weaken his power (Remini 2006, 347; Schickler 2001, 145–46; see chapter 5). But this instance, I would argue, is the only one in which this concern clearly explained Speaker behavior.[17] In the seven other possible cases from chapters 3 and 4—Rayburn and the Rules Committee fight of 1944, Albert and three economic bills from 1971 and 1972, O'Neill and passage of an energy bill, Wright and Contra aid in 1988, and Foley and flag burning legislation—the Speaker had other goals that were at least as important, if not more so, in driving his behavior. Interestingly, though, six of the seven cases involved Speakers serving in their first year as Speaker. This implies that such a goal, to the extent it is salient, matters especially to newly selected Speakers, who may be the most sensitive to initial perceptions and evaluations of their abilities.

In short, many of the seeming exceptions to the theory of goal-driven leadership, on closer inspection, serve as further evidence of its validity. The most persuasive contrary examples are Speakers seeking either to defend the preferences of powerful legislators or committees or to protect their own power and authority. Yet these constitute a tiny fraction of the cases examined: less than 1 percent of floor advocacy cases (3 of 400) and 1.4 percent of the cases captured in the literature sweeps (2 of 145). When compared with other models of congressional leadership, the goal-driven approach remains far more successful in explaining the behavior of the modern Speaker of the House.

GOAL-DRIVEN LEADERSHIP: IMPLICATIONS AND EXTENSIONS

The theory of goal-driven leadership could also be applied more broadly than it is in this study. In general, it suggests the utility of institutionally based perspectives of political leadership. More specifically, it provides important and useful insights into how and why political leaders in other institutions, like the U.S. Senate, behave as they do and how future Speakers will exercise leadership. I conclude this chapter with a discussion of these two implications of the model.

Applying the Theory to the Senate

The theory of goal-driven leadership intimates that every legislative leader, not just the Speaker, has more than one goal he or she wishes to achieve. If this is so, the behavior of legislative leaders should not be defined solely by an electoral connection, as many party-based theories posit, or by individual commitments or preferences. These leaders should also be defined by their *position:* that is, the formal and informal definitions of their office, the duties and responsibilities that are included in those definitions, and expectations of the office's proper functions. Furthermore, such leaders should be understood as driven by the *broader contextual environment* that surrounds them, including other formal and informal leaders that must be contended with and demands and expectations from the electorate and other political actors and institutions. They will therefore exercise independent leadership not just to reward constituents (and thereby remain in office) but also because their role and position within the political realm establishes multiple salient goals they wish to satisfy. In other words, by committing independent leadership for different (or at times conjoining) reasons, political leaders fulfill the true nature of their leadership position.

This dynamic is especially apparent with the Speaker of the House, given the Speaker's unique constitutional, partisan, and electoral position. But could it also apply to the top party leader in the other chamber of the legislature, the Senate majority leader? If so, the majority leader should be motivated to exercise legislative leadership on behalf of multiple goals, and the political context should indicate the nature and salience of those goals. In fact, that context does suggest the presence of multiple leadership goals: for example, the majority leader is also an individual senator, is chosen by his party at the start of every Congress from among his fellow senators, and must also work with the president. Comments by Senator Olympia Snowe (R-ME) in a recent interview seem to support the idea that the majority leader has more than one goal. "As majority leader," she said, "you can't be single-minded. You've got to deal with a confluence of challenges and priorities, on behalf of the president, on behalf of the overall party and on behalf of the institution" (Babington 2006). More important, differences between the majority leader of the Senate and the Speaker of the House suggest that the former is much closer to being a party leader, and further from being a chamber-wide officer, than is the latter.

The Constitution specifies two officers for the Senate: the vice president, who serves as "president" of the Senate but can cast a ballot only to break tie votes; and the president pro-tem(pore), who serves in the vice president's absence (Article I, section 3). Neither officer evolved into the chamber's party leader. The vice president's electoral independence from senators, and the possibility of divided government, made him too distant and unreliable to serve as the head of the Senate majority party; and the ambiguous position of president pro-tem led senators to gradually transfer important powers, like committee assignments, from that office to the party caucus organization.

The position of majority leader first appeared in the early twentieth century. Selected by the party caucus and not a Senate-wide vote (as with the Speaker), the majority leader became the top party leader in the chamber, gaining important formal and informal powers over bill referral and legislative scheduling. Parliamentary and tie-breaking voting duties, however, remained associated with the president pro-tem and vice president, respectively (*Congressional Quarterly* 1976; Gamm and Smith 2000; Riddick 1988). Thus the office's separation of partisan and nonpartisan responsibilities should lead contemporary majority leaders to commit greater partisan leadership and less nonpartisan chamber-wide leadership, while president-related, district, and personal policy interests should also be salient.

Some prominent examples of leadership intimate that this is the case. First, since *reelection* (to Congress and to leadership) is determined in the same manner as for the Speaker of the House, it should matter as a leadership goal. The preferences of the party in the Senate do appear to have a strong pull on the Senate majority leader. In interviews with political scientist Barbara Sinclair, for example, aides to Majority Leader Trent Lott (R-MS) argued that the primary duties of the position, including influencing the agenda and determining the party's position, were partisan in nature (Sinclair 2001, 71). There have even been instances in which the Senate majority leader pushed for partisan outcomes on particular legislation when the Speaker did not. For example, in the case from chapter 5 involving the 1991 renewal of most favored nation status (MFN) for China, Majority Leader George Mitchell (D-ME) argued strenuously against granting MFN without imposing strong human rights–related conditions for renewal, whereas Foley was more willing to defer to the president's position in favor of MFN (Krauss 1990).[18] As far as the interests of the majority leader's state are concerned, they too have probably driven his behavior, since he is elected to the Senate, and past leaders have lost reelection before (such as Democrat Scott Lucas of Illinois, who lost his seat in 1950, and Tom Daschle, who lost in 2004). As one scholar has observed, the majority leader can sometimes face a difficult dilemma when his party's agenda conflicts with the policy needs of his home constituents (Riddick 1988, 24).

Second, Senate majority leaders may be driven by the goal of *enacting policy* they desire, since they are individual legislators as well as party leaders. For example, in 1995, Senate Majority Leader Bob Dole (R-KS) blocked a House Republican proposal to let states operate the federal school lunch program, in part because he personally supported the program and had helped expand it in the 1970s. More recently, Majority Leader Bill Frist (R-TN), a doctor and heart surgeon, played an active role in finalizing the 2003 Medicare prescription drug bill, perhaps motivated in part (like Speaker Hastert) by his own interest in health care (Cloud 1995c; Cochran 2003).

The third goal, *role fulfillment*, also matters to majority leaders in the Senate, though to a different extent than for Speakers. The majority leader does operate in an environment in which certain presidential-related duties are salient. As with the Speaker, one important role of this sort is to support the presidential party. Donald Matthews, a famous observer of the Senate, noted that "Senate leaders of the president's party accept considerable responsibility to serve as his spokesmen," though they do have other roles and constituencies as well (Matthews 1973, 142). Senator Richard Russell (D-GA), a conservative southerner with no particular affection for President Truman, decided not to run for majority leader when the office became vacant in 1951 because, he believed, "a Majority Leader had an obligation to give at least a modicum of support to a President of his own party." Furthermore, the majority leader's relative lack of formal authority, at least until the 1950s, has meant a greater reliance on the president to ensure legislative success, giving him an additional incentive to support a same-party president's program (Caro 2002, 354–63, quote p. 364).[19]

In addition to supporting the presidential party, some evidence indicates that Senate majority leaders act on behalf of institutional presidency demands, though perhaps less so than Speakers. As leader in the 1950s, for example, Lyndon Johnson (D-TX) sought to help President Eisenhower pass his foreign policy agenda, lobbying his caucus extensively to persuade them of the wisdom of the strategy. Johnson's successor, Mike Mansfield (D-MT), remarked in late 1963, "I have always felt that the president of the United States—whoever he may be—is entitled to the dignity of his office and is worthy of the respect of the Senate." At the same time, Mansfield was much more willing than Speakers John McCormack or Carl Albert to openly oppose the White House, particularly on the war in Vietnam. This, and the above example of George

Mitchell's leadership on MFN for China, does suggest that because the majority leader is a more partisan officer, support for the institution of the presidency on his behalf may be more easily trumped by the preferences of his caucus in the Senate (Caro 2002, 521–23; Farrell 2001, 211–12; quote from Byrd 1994, 696).

Finally, though some Senate majority leaders, such as Robert Byrd (D-WV), have been particularly cognizant of the institutional authority and history of the Senate, chamberwide concerns or demands appear to be much less salient for majority leaders than for Speakers. With no parliamentary responsibilities or electoral connection with all senators, majority leaders can focus more of their attention to their party's objectives and policy preferences. As Mansfield remarked in the speech cited above: "The constitutional authority and responsibility [of the Senate] does not lie with the leadership. It lies with all of us individually, collectively, and equally" (Byrd 1994, 697). In one case from chapter 4—the congressional pay raise proposal considered in early 1989—Majority Leader Mitchell agreed to hold a vote on the matter, knowing it would lead to a rejection of a pay raise for members of Congress, to help enhance the reputation of Senate Democrats among angry voters. When Byrd, his "institutionalist" predecessor, did the same for an earlier raise proposed in January 1987, House Majority Whip Tony Coelho (D-CA) remarked that senators "are supposed to have the luxury of taking care of the institution. . . . [But] those of us with the two-year terms end up taking care of the institution" (Barry 1989, 114, 670).[20] When bipartisan leadership is committed by the majority leader, it seems to be due primarily to the nature of the Senate itself: unless his party controls a supermajority of seats, the leader must contend with the considerable power of the minority to hinder or obstruct legislation, encouraging consensual leadership to ensure legislative success.

Though the theory of goal-driven leadership seems to have some utility in explaining the behavior of the Senate majority leader, it should be noted that any comparison between that office and the Speaker of the House is complicated by the differing institutional rules and norms of their respective chambers, the ways in which those rules have changed, and the timing of these changes. The Senate, unlike the House, grants considerable autonomy and authority to individual senators, who also serve longer terms than House member. This limits the ability of the majority leader to exert influence over fellow partisans and requires greater compromise and cooperation between both parties and among individual senators. As a result, the majority leader must be more familiar with every individual senator's parliamentary rights, which may contribute to more frequent bipartisan leadership (Riddick 1988, 24). Furthermore, the power of the majority leader has derived more from custom and party rules than from Senate rules or the Constitution, and it has thus evolved in different ways from that of the Speaker. In the 1950s, under Majority Leaders Robert Taft (R-OH) and Lyndon Johnson, the office accrued greater authority, suggesting that an analysis of the Senate majority leader should treat that period as a distinct breakpoint in time, rather than the 1940s. In any event, even the contemporary majority leader remains dependent upon the goodwill of all members of the Senate to ensure some degree of agenda control and influence over legislative output, which in turn constrains his ability to exercise leadership.

Speaker Leadership after Hastert: Is It Driven by Multiple Goals?

As Speakers of the House continue to act in partisan ways and be less attuned to nonparty goals, one may wonder if the theory of goal-driven leadership will still explain the behavior of future occupants of the office. An examination of the early tenure of the first Speaker to follow Dennis Hastert, Nancy Pelosi, suggests that she also recognizes other concerns or demands besides those of her party in the House and is capable of acting on behalf of those concerns to achieve varying goals.

Pelosi became the first female Speaker in American history when Republicans lost control of the House in 2006. In her opening speech to the House as a newly elected Speaker, Pelosi suggested that she would be a more bipartisan leader than Speakers before her. At one point, looking largely to the Republican side of the chamber, she said, "My colleagues elected me to be Speaker of the House, *the entire House*. Respectful of the vision of our Founders, the expectation of our people, and the great challenges that we face, we have an obligation to reach beyond partisanship to work for all Americans" (*Congressional Record* 4 January 2007, H5; emphasis added).

Despite her public statement, in her first term—and especially her initial year as Speaker—Pelosi followed a largely partisan pattern of leadership, pushing legislation that would aid her party and/or reflected the policy preferences of her own caucus. Major Democratic legislative initiatives considered in the 110th Congress that arguably fell into this category included expansion of the federal child health insurance program (known as SCHIP), a raise in the minimum wage, the establishment of deadlines to end the war in Iraq, and the creation of incentives for greater energy conservation and development of renewable energy sources (Stanton and Dennis 2008).

Pelosi did openly reject one of Hastert's party-oriented principles of leadership, the so-called Hastert doctrine. On more than one occasion during her first term, the Speaker allowed the House to pass bills, including measures funding U.S. troops in Iraq and the authorization of intelligence surveillance programs, over the opposition of a majority of her party. She stood behind this rejection of the doctrine, declaring in one news story, "I'm the Speaker of the House. I have to take into consideration something broader than the majority of the majority in the Democratic Caucus" (Davis 2007). Pelosi likely pursued this option not in spite of her party, however, but because of it: that is, the policy preferences of her party were less important with regard to these bills than the electoral reputation of House Democrats. For troop funding measures, for instance, Pelosi—who also voted against the measures—probably knew that the legislation would pass regardless, because Republicans were going to vote for it, and that its enactment could shield Democrats from being criticized for failing to support U.S. troops deployed overseas.

Nonetheless, Pelosi was not a uniformly party-driven Speaker, and other nonparty goals manifested themselves occasionally during her first two years in the Speaker's chair. For example, in early 2007, the Speaker promised a floor vote in April on a resolution condemning Turkey for the death of millions of native Armenians in the early twentieth century. Though the resolution would eventually garner a majority of representatives as cosponsors, Pelosi had more personal reasons for supporting its passage. An advocate of human rights in the past, she was a "longtime backer" of the resolution and one of its "dedicated proponents" (Hulse 2007), echoing her opposition to extending trade preferences to China after the 1989 Tiananmen Square massacre (discussed in chapter 5). It also resonated with her own state's politics: California was home to many Americans of Armenian descent, and several members of the state delegation supported the bill. Only in late October, after months of warnings from the White House and others that its passage would harm United States–Turkey relations and jeopardize military operations in Iraq, did Pelosi and the resolution's chief sponsors agree to delay its consideration (Arsu and Knowlton 2007; Hulse 2007; Williamson 2007).

Another example, also from her first year as Speaker, occurred when the House considered legislation to revise the nation's energy policy. John Dingell, the chairman of the House Energy Committee, proposed legislation that would, among other things, prevent states from regulating vehicle emissions. That would have ended California's unique authority to set its own standards for such emissions—not only running counter to House Democrats' general inclination toward greater environmental protection, but also targeting (intentionally or not) the Speaker's home state. As one reporter put it, Pelosi "stopped [the proposal] cold," having not only partisan but also district-related reasons for doing so (Davenport 2007; Dennis 2007).

Finally, Pelosi was willing to work with Republicans—in Congress, the White House, or both—on issues of major national import. Early in 2008, she negotiated with the House GOP to enact an economic stimulus package, even though it did not contain some provisions, like more money for food stamps, that Democrats wanted (Hulse 2008). And later that year, she cooperated with the Bush White House to bring a $700 billion Wall Street rescue package to the floor, despite opposition from both liberals and fiscal conservatives in her party (Kronholz, Lueck, and Hitt 2008). Although these cases are not necessarily examples of the theory of goal-driven leadership—they may instead reflect the Speaker acting out of concern with "national policy"—they do illustrate the limits of the standard, party-oriented view of congressional leadership.

In short, while partisan goals remain dominant for the Speaker of the House, Speakers have yet to abandon completely their other objectives, including reelection to the legislature, passage of desired public policy, assistance to the presidential party, support for the institutional presidency, and support for the demands of the House as a whole. As long as constitutional text, presidential power, and Beltway beliefs persist, these goals will remain. Indeed, should the political environment change—say, the electorate becomes less polarized, the margins between the House majority and minority parties grow, or someone with a dramatically new perspective becomes Speaker—we could see a shift in the emphasis of some goals over others, perhaps bringing the Speaker back toward a more balanced and less partisan leadership role in Congress.

Appendix A

Sources and Use of Data

Two basic types of data were used in this study. The first is floor statements in the *Congressional Record,* used to identify cases of floor advocacy (see chapters 2 and 7). The second is sweeps of historical works on Congress and congressional leadership, used to capture all other types of legislative leadership by the Speaker (examined in chapters 3, 4, and 5).

The Congressional Record. For each annual index of the *Congressional Record,* I identified all citations in which the sitting Speaker made a floor speech on a legislative bill, resolution, or amendment.[1] I then examined each speech to determine if it was an act of floor advocacy (as defined in chapter 2). Extensions of remarks, general praise of individual members, eulogies, positions on general policy, and clarifying questions or comments were not counted as floor advocacy; nor were comments that were of a technical nature or that did not clearly indicate a position on the particular bill or amendment. To avoid measuring verbosity rather than distinct occurrences of leadership, a single "instance" of Speaker advocacy could include multiple statements delivered on behalf of one vote. If a Speaker used one state-

Table A.1 List of Sweep Sources

Category	Source	Years Covered	Chapter Authors
Leadership histories	Bolling 1968	1941–1960s	
	Connelly and Pitney 1994	1970s–1990s	
	Davidson, Hammond, and Smock 1998	1941–1980s	—Gould and Young —Maney —Sinclair
	Dodd and Oppenheimer 1993	1941–1990s	—Sinclair —Young and Cooper
	Jones 1970	1941–1960s	
	Mooney 1964	1941–1961	
	Peabody 1976	1941–1970s	
	Peabody and Polsby 1977	1941–1970s	—Dexter —Peabody
	Peters 1997	–1990s	
	Ripley 1964	1960s	
	Ripley 1967	–1960s	
	Sinclair 1995	–1990s	
	Sinclair 1999a	1990s	
	Strahan and Palazzolo 2004	1990s	
	Truman 1959	1949–1951	
Histories of Congress	Bolling 1964	1941–1960s	
	Congressional Quarterly 1976	–1970s	
	Dodd and Oppenheimer 2001	1990s	—Aldrich and Rohde —Destler —Evans —Fiorina —Groseclose and King
	Fenno 1997	1990s	
	Galloway 1976	1941–1970s	
	Josephy 1979	1941–1970s	
	Killian 1998	1990s	
	MacNeil 1963	1941–1960s	

(continued)

Table A.1 (*continued*)

Category	Source	Years Covered	Chapter Authors
	Rae and Campbell 1999	1990s	—Connelly and Pitney —Deering —Evans and Oleszek —Peters —Sinclair
	Remini 2006	1941–1990s	
	Riddick 1949	1940s	
	Truman 1973	1941–1960s	—Fenno
	Zelizer 2004	1990s	—Critchlow —Patashnik —Sinclair —Thurber
General histories	Barone 1990	1941–1980s	
	Grantham 1976	1945–1970s	
	Grantham 1987	1945–1980s	
	Kaufman 1993	1976–1980	
	Mervin 1990	1980–1988	

ment to advocate positions on several votes for one measure (for example, "reject all amendments and approve the bill as is"), it was counted as a single case of floor advocacy; if a Speaker gave many speeches for the same bill but on substantively different votes (such as an amendment vote and a vote on final passage), each speech was counted as a distinct event under the assumption that they represented discrete instances of leadership.[2]

One possible concern with using the *Congressional Record* in this way is its accuracy. Legislators traditionally have had the ability to alter their speeches prior to publication of the *Record* or to add entirely new unspoken remarks. Identifying "true" floor statements before 1978, when extensions of remarks were not noted as such in the *Congressional Record* (U.S. Congress 2005, Rule 6 § 692), is more difficult. If a Speaker's remarks were delivered but altered after the actual floor debate, it does not pose a major problem for my analysis, since these sorts of statements still likely convey the Speaker's intent in addressing the floor. To avoid counting remarks that were never actually made on the floor, however, I examined the context in which each speech appeared: if other legislators did not respond to the floor statement or if time was not yielded to the Speaker for debate, I considered the speech to have been inserted post hoc and did not count it.[3]

Literature Sweeps. To identify cases in which Speakers have committed acts of legislative leadership other than floor advocacy, I constructed a data set of historically significant acts of leadership by "sweeping" historical sources related to congressional leadership activity. The thirty-three sources (forty-eight if one counts separately each chapter cited from an edited volume), which are listed in table A.1, are of three kinds: general histories of Congress, histories of congressional leaders, and histories of American politics that reference the Speaker of the House.[4] As with Schickler (2001, 19), I sought variation in these sources to avoid bias either toward or away from reporting particular kinds of leadership behavior. The index of each work, if available, was reviewed to identify and record any instance in which the Speaker was described as having acted to alter legislative outcomes. An act of the Speaker was recorded as an attempt to alter legislative outcomes if at least one[5] of the sources in table A.1 noted it to be so. (General claims of leadership influence over a broad range of issues or institutions were excluded; as I note in chapter 5, this omitted some important references to some Speakers, particularly Newt Gingrich.)

Since much of the Speaker's leadership activity may be difficult to verify, I used multiple sources when possible to support claims that an individual instance of leadership took place. These include statements by members of Congress and the Speaker, accounts from reporters and legislators, and analyses of floor statements, floor votes, and archival material. To estimate the reasons for the Speaker's use of leadership, I drew from a variety of sources for three kinds of evidence: first, what individual, group, or institution would have principally benefited from, or been harmed by, the desired outcome; second, where the particular legislative proposal originated, such as the White House, congressional committees, or party leaders in Congress; and third, whether the issue was closely associated with the Speaker's district or personal policy interests.

Other scholars have collected and analyzed different data on congressional leadership; most notably, Barbara Sinclair reviewed references to leadership on major votes and legislation in select congresses from 1969 through 1990 from the journal *Congressional Quarterly* (Sinclair 1995). While Sinclair's method is in some ways more thorough, the sweep approach that I use has at least two advantages. First, it covers a much broader range of history. Even using *Congressional Quarterly* as a primary source, as Sinclair does, limits the analysis to 1945 (when the journal was first published). Second, my methodology avoids dependence on the editorial or journalistic biases of a single source and possible changes in those biases over time. *Congressional Quarterly*'s identification of key votes, for example, has been critiqued for emphasizing certain topics over others (for example, Shull and Vanderleeuw 1987), and its early issues may have given less coverage of leadership activity than more recent ones.

The citation must mention a specific act of leadership, or specific bill or measure, to be included; general claims of leadership influence were excluded. Other data, like caucus records, press accounts, or material from Speaker archives were also used (when available) to supplement these sources. The literature sweeps also frequently netted references to significant Speaker floor speeches, providing a useful check of the floor advocacy data collected from the *Congressional Record*.[6] Not all actions need to have been positive or successful to be counted; "failed" actions—that is, events when the Speaker instigated some important act or behavior but failed to achieve his goal(s)—were also considered acts of legislative leadership. Legislative leadership could also include "negative" leadership, or a lack of action on the part of a Speaker, though this kind of phenomenon is more difficult to observe and thus less likely to appear in the sources.

I used several techniques to mitigate potential measurement problems with these sweeps. One problem is distinguishing group leadership from that of the Speaker, since the modern Speaker shares several important leadership responsibilities with other legislators, and an alleged act of leadership may have actually been committed in conjunction with a broader effort by other House party leaders. I therefore coded only those leadership actions attributed primarily to the Speaker, and I did not count acts credited to party leadership or a leadership "team" generally or that passively attributed an act to the Speaker (such as "under Speaker Rayburn, such-and-such occurred"). Another potential problem is false credit-claiming: a source (including the Speaker himself) incorrectly attributing responsibility to the Speaker for an action. This is a particular danger with claims of "negative" leadership, since the occurrence and effects of such leadership are hard to verify. Although identifying false credit-claming is difficult, I used the statements of observers, drawing from multiple sources when available, to determine whether a Speaker should be properly credited with committing the alleged action. A third measurement problem, closely related to the second, arises when the Speaker falsely denies an act of leadership (for example, giving credit to the "will of the majority"). Regardless of the Speaker's claims, an instance of leadership was counted if a source attributed it to the Speaker.

The sweeps methodology could also conceivably omit important acts of legislative leadership if they were hidden from, downplayed, or even ignored by historians or other observers. I acknowledge this possibility but note that leadership on or near the House floor, the primary focus of this book, is among the least likely to be hidden or neglected. I also drew from an array of sources, where available, to further document cases of leadership, employing some degree of skepticism for older cases when warranted. Finally, a historical source may simply be inaccurate or incorrect. One cannot always have absolute certainty that a documented action did, in fact, happen; but I use multiple sources with variation in theoretical or normative biases and perspectives, as well as data from the *Congressional Record* and other materials, to minimize this possibility.[7]

Appendix B

Categorizing Instances of

Floor Voting

The following table lists all recorded floor votes by Speakers from 1977 through 1990 referenced in chapter 2. "Pivotal" votes are those for which the Speaker's vote changed the outcome (that is, made or broke a tie). "Possible attempted influence" votes are those in which the final tally was within three votes, the Speaker was known to be unsure of outcome, and/or the Speaker voted early. "Salient to majority party" votes are those which are known to have been important to the party in Congress, based on the party's platform or legislative agenda. "Salient to Speaker" votes are those on issues coded as highly important to the Speaker personally or to his district (see chapter 2). A "key vote" is a vote categorized as such by the journal *Congressional Quarterly*.

Table B.1 Recorded Floor Votes by Speakers, 1977–90

Speaker	Date	Measure	Total	Speaker Vote	Pivotal?	Possible Attempted Influence?[a]	Salient to Majority Party?	Salient to Speaker?	Key Vote?
O'Neill	9/15/77	Minimum wage, amendment	209–211	No		✓			Yes
O'Neill	12/6/77	Supplemental appropriations, amendment	182–181	Yes	✓				No
O'Neill	6/4/80	Smithsonian funding	262–131	Yes					No
O'Neill	6/25/81	Budget, rule (previous question vote)	219–208	No	✓[b]		✓		No
O'Neill	6/25/81	Budget, amendment to rule	216–212	No[c]			✓		No
O'Neill	6/26/81	Budget, amendment	217–211	No[c]			✓		Yes
O'Neill	6/26/81	Budget (previous question vote)	215–212	No[c]		✓	✓		No
O'Neill	7/29/81	Tax bill, amendment	238–195	No[c]			✓		Yes
O'Neill	8/5/82	Nuclear freeze, amendment	204–202	No[c]		✓			Yes
O'Neill	9/9/82	Supplemental, veto override	301–117	Yes			✓		Yes
O'Neill	12/14/82	House pay raise	208–208	No	✓				Yes
O'Neill	3/9/83	Social Security bill	228–202	No[c]			✓	✓	Yes
O'Neill	7/28/83	Intelligence bill, amendment (Contras)	213–214	Yes[c]		✓	✓	✓	No
O'Neill	9/14/83	Plane downing by USSR	416–0	Yes					No
O'Neill	11/15/83	ERA amendment	278–147	Yes		✓	✓		Yes
O'Neill	5/31/84	MX bill, 2nd degree amendment	199–197	Yes		✓			Yes
O'Neill	5/31/84	MX bill, amendment	198–197	Yes	✓				No
O'Neill	3/20/86	Contra aid	210–220	No		✓	✓	✓	No

O'Neill	6/26/86	Troops in Nicaragua	215–212	Yes	✓	✓		No
O'Neill	8/6/86	Textile bill, veto override	276–149	Yes			✓	Yes
O'Neill	9/29/86	S. Africa sanctions, veto override	313–83	Yes			✓	Yes
O'Neill	10/9/86	Immigration bill, amendment	197–199	Yes	✓			No
Wright	4/23/87	Appropriations, Walker amendment (1st vote)	209–194	No[c]			✓	No
Wright	4/23/87	Appropriations, Walker amendment (2nd vote)	204–184	No[c]				No
Wright	4/29/87	Trade bill, Gephardt amendment	218–214	Yes		✓		No
Wright	9/16/87	Textile bill	263–156	Yes				No
Wright	9/17/87	Japanese internment	243–141	Yes			✓	No
Wright	10/29/87	Set time for House to reconvene	243–166	Yes		✓		No
Wright	10/29/87	Adjourn	236–171	Yes		✓		No
Wright	10/30/87	Approve journal	81–74	Yes		✓		No
Wright	3/3/88	Contra aid, Bonior amendment	215–210	Yes		✓	✓	No
Wright	3/29/88	Shipwreck bill	263–139	Yes				No
Wright	4/19/88	INF Treaty	393–7	Yes				No
Wright	4/19/88	Pornography ban	380–2	Yes				No
Wright	4/19/88	Education bill, motion	397–1	Yes				No
Wright	5/24/88	Trade bill, veto override	308–113	Yes		✓	✓	Yes
Wright	5/26/88	Intelligence bill, Contra amendment	190–214	No		✓	✓	No

(continued)

Table B.1 (continued)

Speaker	Date	Measure	Total	Speaker Vote	Pivotal?	Possible Attempted Influence?[a]	Salient to Majority Party?	Salient to Speaker?	Key Vote?
Wright	8/9/88	O'Neill library	158–239	Yes[c]				✓	No
Wright	9/9/88	Pledge of Allegiance resolution	226–168	Yes					No
Foley	11/16/89	Ethics bill	252–174	Yes					Yes
Foley	6/22/90	Flag burning	254–177	No			✓		Yes
Foley	7/26/90	Frank censure, recommittal	141–287	No					Yes
Foley	7/26/90	Frank censure, passage	406–17	Yes					No
Foley	10/5/90	Budget resolution	179–254	Yes[c]					Yes
Foley	10/6/90	Budget resolution, veto override	260–138	Yes			✓		No
Foley	10/7/90	Budget resolution, conference report	250–164	Yes			✓		No
Foley	10/7/90	Appropriations, sequester amendment	186–24	No					No
Foley	10/7/90	Appropriations, pass	305–105	Yes					No
Foley	10/17/90	Foreign aid, UNITA amendment	207–206	Yes	✓				No
Foley	10/26/90	Budget reconciliation, conference report	228–200	Yes			✓		No
Foley	10/27/90	Scenic river designation	157–95	Yes					No

[a]The final tally was within three votes, the Speaker was known to be unsure of outcome, or the Speaker voted early.
[b]Considered under the suspension calendar, which requires a two-thirds vote for approval
[c]The Speaker was on the losing side of the vote.

Notes

CHAPTER 1. "AN OFFICE OF GREAT HONOR AND INFLUENCE"

1. Five months after passage of the House version of the Medicare bill, Hastert kept the voting clock open for nearly *three hours*—a House record—while he and other party leaders lobbied for votes to pass the conference version of the same bill. The length of the vote—and allegations of improper lobbying on its behalf—became a source of considerable controversy (Broder 2003; Committee on Standards of Official Conduct 2004; Hastert 2004). I discuss Hastert's legislative leadership in more detail in chapter 6.

2. Some congressional scholars have demonstrated that institutional change within the House can also result from Speakers' independent, consequential leadership actions (Schickler 2001, 39–40; Strahan 2007).

3. As perhaps an additional sign of its relative significance, the office of Speaker has been in close succession to the presidency for most of its history: third in line from 1947 to the present day, and fourth (behind the Senate president pro-tem) from 1792 to 1885. The Speaker was absent from the line of succession between 1886 and 1946 (Stathis 1994; 3 USC 19(a)(1)).

4. The Senate's constitutional officers either are chosen outside of the chamber (i.e., the vice president) or never developed beyond a figurehead position (e.g., the president pro-tem). See chapter 7 for further comparisons between the Speaker and the Senate majority leader.

5. Some political scientists also disagree over how consequential congressional leadership is for legislative outcomes. Keith Krehbiel (2000), for example, has argued that party leaders' impact on the legislative process is, or may be, much less than it appears, and that examples of their influence may in fact be legislators acting sincerely on their personal preferences. By contrast, Steven Smith (2007) points to circumstantial evidence that parties do have influence. Though I do not address directly the question of whether leaders influence member behavior—only when and why they seek to do so—I provide evidence that suggests Speakers can, in fact, play an important role in determining legislative outcomes.

6. Legislative leadership on or near the House floor can include other, less common activities as well, such as endorsing legislation just before its consideration, issuing helpful rulings from the chair, and helping defend against procedural tactics by bill opponents. See, for example, the leadership of Sam Rayburn on behalf of civil rights in 1956 and 1957, discussed in chapter 3.

7. One may argue that Speakers with more formal powers have stronger informal powers as well; for example, they can credibly impose greater sanctions or provide more benefits as a means of persuasion. On the other hand, formal powers may be neither necessary nor sufficient to exercise strong informal powers, as suggested by examples of floor-related leadership failures by Speakers with more formal authority, such as Jim Wright and Newt Gingrich. I discuss cases involving Wright in more detail in chapter 4.

8. My focus on the floor means that the cases I examine are generally biased toward *positive* action by the Speaker and toward legislation that, for whatever reason, is "must-pass" in nature (see appendix A).

9. See also Edinger 1964, 437; Strahan 2002, 262–64; Strahan, Moscardelli, Haspel, and Wike 2000; and Weisberg, Heberlig, and Campoli 1999, ch. 20.

10. In an early article based on this research (Green 2007), I relied on a somewhat different theoretical approach, focusing more on expectations for Speaker behavior than on Speaker goals. The article also did not include four cases of Speaker leadership found in the literature sweeps conducted for this book, nor did it contain an analysis of the Hastert Speakership.

11. Strahan argues that Speaker goals include reelection to leadership, policy enactment, institutional (or House-wide) matters, and personal (e.g., reputation or ambition) objectives. My model includes the first and third goals and divides the second into party policy (satisfying the leadership reelection goal) and personally preferred policy. I discuss the possible role of national policy concerns and the Speaker's personal power/ambition objectives in the concluding chapter.

12. See also Rohde and Shepsle 1987, 118, and Smith and Gamm 2001. Note that Weisberg et al. use the term "context" more broadly to include the legislative agenda and the norms and rules of the legislature (1999, 320–22).

13. There have been some important exceptions to this rule in the history of Congress; see, for example, Stewart (2000).

14. Although I generally treat these two party-related interests as part of a single Speaker goal, the electoral and policy concerns can come into conflict, forcing the Speaker to reconcile or choose between them. For more on this potential conflict, see Smith 2007.

15. One could argue that this goal applies to the Speaker as a congressional leader as well

as a representative: that is, the Speaker may seek to enact what he or she views as good *national* policy, regardless of the views of his or her district or party. In chapter 7, I examine the possibility that this may explain, in a select few cases between 1941 and 2006, instances of Speaker leadership. The third Fenno goal, securing influence in Congress, is not usually relevant for Speakers since they have already achieved the highest possible leadership position in the House of Representatives. In chapter 7 I do discuss how variants of this goal—to maintain one's power or secure a reputation for influence—may help explain legislative leadership by the Speaker in occasional situations (Cox and McCubbins 1993, 126; Dodd 1977). Fenno notes in passing that two other goals may motivate legislators: achieving higher political office and earning personal profit (Fenno 1973a, 1). Because these will vary widely in salience with individual Speakers, I do not consider them here. The former may have been salient in one case examined in this book, that involving Speaker Sam Rayburn in 1944 (see chapter 3), when Rayburn might have hoped to improve his chances of winning a vice presidential nomination by publicly siding with Democratic liberals against the conservative Rules Committee (Hardeman and Bacon 1987, 293–95).

16. For more about the origins of legislators' personal preferences, see Burden 2007. In looking at personal motivations for congressional leadership, some scholars have examined leader intelligence, character, or political acumen (e.g., Fuller 1909; Ornstein 1990). I do not do so here. One problem with the psychological or personality-based approach is that it is unclear what a generalizable theory of legislative leadership based on personal traits would be. Indeed, an emphasis on personal traits, particularly after the end of a Speaker's career, can commit the fallacy of attributing successful leadership to good personal qualities and failed leadership to bad ones without demonstrating convincingly a clear causal relationship between certain traits and particular leadership behavior. The psychological or character-based approach to political leadership is more common in presidential studies; see, e.g., Barber 1972; Greenstein 2000; and Renshon 1996.

17. For an (older) review of political science research that use role theory explicitly, see Magid 1980 and Meller 1960, 144.

18. Barbara Sinclair, for example, argues that congressional Democrats "expect" their leaders to set the agenda, the public "expects" Congress to support newly elected presidents, and legislators have an "expectation" that leaders will support the policy goals of a same-party president or the majority of the majority party (1995, 88, 272–73).

19. Another actor of this sort is the House parliamentarian. One former staffer for Speaker Jim Wright noted in an interview how it would "drive the parliamentarians nuts" when Wright cast nonpivotal floor votes (interview with the author, May 2003). For more on floor voting, see chapter 2.

20. David Truman argues that party leaders in Congress may also downplay the influence or preferences of the White House, but for a strategic reason: to reduce expectations that they will achieve the president's desired outcome (1959, 300–4).

21. The latter scenario occurs rarely but does appear at least once in the cases of floor-related legislative leadership examined in this book. Speaker Rayburn's decision to support civil rights bills in 1956 and 1957 came in part from his recognition that it would improve his party's chances for winning the White House, even though southern House Democrats

strongly opposed such legislation (see chapter 3). Some scholars emphasize the president's inability to influence same-party congressional activity; see, e.g., Pious 1979, 122, 180–83.

22. In my case studies, I draw an important distinction between a *motive* for leadership based on the presidency and the *mechanisms* of leadership the president can employ. The president may not initiate or even strongly support a particular piece of legislation but may still play an active role in helping the Speaker enact it; in those circumstances, I do not consider the president's policy or electoral objectives to be motivating Speaker leadership.

23. Another issue that could be associated with the institutional presidency is the statutory federal debt limit. On one hand, the debt limit falls under the purview of the White House, presidents generally initiate legislative changes to the limit, and there are important international consequences if the limit is breached (i.e., default on the federal treasury). On the other hand, the failure of debt limit legislation can harm the reputation of the majority party in Congress. As a result, I generally consider the passage of debt limit legislation to be important to Speakers for both role-fulfillment and electoral reasons.

24. On the potential gains associated with forcing an opposite-party president to veto legislation, see Groseclose and McCarty, 2001.

25. As part of the research for this book, more than a dozen interviews were conducted with current and former party leaders in the House, other members of Congress, and leadership staff. Most of the interviews were provided on condition of anonymity, unless the interviewee permitted otherwise.

26. Scott James further argues that the influence of the executive will make Electoral College–related considerations drive congressional party priorities (2000, 15–16).

27. When the president of the same party requests congressional support for a measure related to the institutional presidency, it can be difficult to identify whether the partisan or institutional presidency (or both) is driving the Speaker's subsequent leadership. I discuss this potential identification problem in the empirical chapters that follow.

28. Earlier Speakers also noted the importance of this role of the Speakership. For example, Speaker Thomas Reed (R-ME), who served in the late nineteenth century, argued that "whoever at any time . . . attempts to lower the prestige of that office, by just so much lowers the prestige of the House itself, *whose servant and exponent the Speaker is*" (Hinds 1907, 870, emphasis added).

29. Others have acknowledged this potential problem. Ronald Peters has pointed out possible conflicts between the institutional and individual roles of the Speaker, particularly over whether to cast votes or deliberate on the floor (Peters 1997, 23; see also chapter 2). In an interview, one former staffer for Speaker Tom Foley noted that an election challenger to the Speaker argued to voters that "we [the district] need someone who votes" in Congress, given that the Speaker traditionally does not vote on the floor (interview with the author, March 2003). In chapter 5, I discuss in more detail the use of Speaker voting as a tool of legislative leadership. Individual legislators who are not leaders may face conflict among duties or goals as well, such as between personal policy goals and desire for higher office (e.g., Fenno 1973a). For more about role conflict among representatives, see Wahlke et al. 1962 and Sigel and Pindur 1973.

30. There could be additional reasons for partisans to tolerate wayward behavior by their leaders. For instance, leaders can be difficult to remove, and they may even "buy" loyalty from partisans by providing them with scarce benefits in exchange for their support.

31. In this respect, the Speaker of the House is similar to other leadership offices in American government that share multiple institutional drives and limitations for action, such as the presidency (Skowronek 1993) and, though to a lesser extent, the Senate majority leader—a matter I turn to in the final chapter of the book.

32. As noted in footnote 8, above, a study of floor leadership will generally be biased toward measuring positive action by the Speaker rather than negative action (which usually occurs off the floor). But circumstances can force the Speaker to exercise negative leadership on the House floor as well. In cases of this sort, the eight outcomes discussed below can be reframed as follows: the "status quo" is a particular policy proposal that the Speaker opposes, and the Speaker's own "proposal" or legislative alternative is the actual status quo point. For more on agenda control, see chapter 5.

33. One possibility not considered here is that the Speaker needs to sway a supermajority of the majority party. This applies most readily under the rules of the Democratic binding caucus, which requires all party members to vote for a measure following a two-thirds approval in caucus; these rules fell into disuse after the 1910s, however (Green 2002). The only case in this analysis that might apply is passage of the 21-day rule in 1949 (chapter 3), but the fact that many Democrats voted against the rule in caucus and again on the floor suggests that the binding caucus rule was not in operation.

CHAPTER 2. SPEAKING AND VOTING ON THE HOUSE FLOOR

1. I define floor advocacy as any instance in which a Speaker of the House addressed the floor on a pending legislative matter (a bill, amendment, or motion) advocating a specific vote position. Excluded are extensions of remarks, special order speeches, eulogies, tributes, informational queries by the Speaker, and statements that do not advocate a particular position. Speakers seldom use extensions of remarks or special order speeches; eulogies and tributes, however, are more common. See appendix A for a more detailed discussion of the methodology used to capture instances of floor advocacy.

2. Today the Speaker rarely serves as presiding officer, apart from opening the daily session of the House. This job of the Speaker has been relatively muted since at least the 1920s, when the House usually met in the Committee of the Whole (over which the Speaker does not preside), rules of recognition were well established, and the Rules Committee often structured the order of debate (Chiu 1928, 175–79).

3. Figure 2.1 suggests that the continuous use of floor advocacy may technically have begun slightly earlier, in the 74th Congress (1935–36) with Speaker Joseph Byrns (D-TN).

4. I define a "personal" statement as one either made in response to personal criticism or prefaced with a remark that the Speaker is talking as an individual member and not as Speaker. Statements that do not advocate a position on a vote or measure are excluded from this category.

5. In 1878, Randall was again criticized (by Representative Omar Conger, R-MI) for his appearances on the floor (*Congressional Record,* 30 April 1878, 2988).

6. See, e.g., Rep. Champ Clark to Speaker Cannon, *Congressional Record*, 24 March 1909, 218.

7. For an analysis of Senate party leadership that uses floor statements as a measure of influence, see Rhodes 1997.

8. These claims were not always entirely accurate. In January 1940, Speaker Bankhead prefaced his floor remarks on an amendment by declaring, "It has only been on very rare occasions that I have felt impelled to participate in the debate in the Committee of the Whole" (*Congressional Record*, 18 January, 505). By then Bankhead had already spoken on nine separate bills since 1937 (five of which while in the Committee of the Whole), more than any Speaker over a similar time span since Champ Clark two decades earlier.

9. As one former party leader from the post-reform House noted in an interview, if a Speaker loses on the House floor, "it implies the Speaker doesn't have any influence" (interview with the author, December 2002).

10. Each sample consists of approximately 10 percent of all legislators elected at the start of the given Congress. The results in figure 2.2 should be treated with some caution, especially as an indicator of trends over time. Since the number of statements is estimated from the *Congressional Record* index, changes in the accuracy and comprehensiveness of the index could bias the sample average. In general, the index is less comprehensive before the 80th Congress (1947–49) and is less clear about when a floor statement was delivered on behalf of a particular bill or measure (as opposed to being made on behalf of general policy, for instance, or during special orders).

11. In the chapters that follow, I provide evidence that Speakers' other methods have often occurred in tandem with their floor statements. At least one example of Speaker floor advocacy did explicitly link a specific vote outcome with future benefits: Sam Rayburn's promise in a November 1941 speech to permit consideration of antistrike legislation if the House adopted changes to the Neutrality Act (Hardeman and Bacon 1987, 272).

12. Although it seems highly unlikely, one cannot rule out from these data alone the possibility that a Speaker's floor statement contributes to the close margin of a final vote. Recorded whip counts, though often unavailable, can be a means of determining the uncertainty of an impending vote. See, e.g., Burden and Frisby (2002); Evans (2007); Evans, Roscoe, Deering, and O'Neill (2003); and the case studies in chapters 3 and 4.

13. Presumably, including voice votes—which are omitted in both figures 2.3 and 2.4—and coding them as unanimous would show a somewhat greater proportion of one-sided voting. Including supermajority votes in figure 2.4 has minimal effect on vote distribution but doing so for figure 2.3 shows a spike in votes decided by a larger margin (260 to 280 votes).

14. From 1941 through 1970, recorded votes subject to floor advocacy tended to be close (as in figure 2.4), but *unrecorded* votes subject to floor advocacy (such as votes by voice or by unanimous consent) made up a disproportionate number of the total. This was probably not because floor advocacy had no influence but rather due to how these votes were conducted. Just over two-thirds of all votes subject to legislative advocacy in that thirty-year period took place in the Committee of the Whole, where legislators' identities were usually not revealed. This provided party leaders with an important advantage, since members of Congress could be more easily persuaded to vote against their

districts with no electoral penalty for doing so (Froman and Ripley 1965, 59–60). As a result, these lopsided unrecorded votes may still have been uncertain in their outcome, but the Speaker might have convinced opponents not to request a head count after the announced result.

15. Statements that reference multiple floor votes are counted only once in table 2.2, coded by the primary issue the Speaker discussed. Two Speaker floor statements were delivered on multiple roll call votes on different issue topics: a speech by Carl Albert in June 1972 on an agriculture appropriations bill (coded as agriculture), and a statement by Tip O'Neill in September 1977 on a series of amendments to a minimum wage bill (coded as labor/employment/immigration). The data itself, originally collected by Frank R. Baumgartner and Bryan D. Jones with the support of National Science Foundation grant number SBR 9320922, was obtained from the Center for American Politics and Public Policy at the University of Washington (http://www.policyagendas.org/index .html). The author thanks the Policy Agendas Project for its use. Neither NSF nor the original collectors of the data are responsible for the analysis conducted with the data.

16. One issue not coded in this fashion is the federal debt limit. As I note in chapter 1, the debt limit can be seen as both an institutional presidency matter and a congressional party concern. To err on the side of assuming that the Speaker acts on behalf of the majority party, I do not count debt limit bills as institutional presidency matters in this chapter, though I do so for cases in chapters 3 and 4.

17. Issues of personal interest to Speakers include: for McCormack, foreign affairs (Vietnam and anticommunism generally) and education (particularly parochial education); for O'Neill, foreign policy (Central America); for Wright, foreign policy (Central America); and for Hastert, health care. Matters of high salience to Speakers' districts include: for Rayburn, energy and agriculture (due to his rural district and the importance of natural gas for his state); and for Albert and Foley, agriculture (based on the major industry of their rural districts).

18. Specifically, I used the estimated standard error of every proportion of Speaker-addressed roll calls for each issue to construct 90 percent and 95 percent confidence intervals. If the percentage of all roll calls on the same issue fell outside either interval, it strongly suggested that the Speaker chose to use (or not use) floor advocacy on that subject above and beyond its prevalence on the agenda.

19. Votes subject to floor advocacy were seldom decided by voice after 1970.

20. The totals in tables 2.3 through 2.6 do not match the number of statements for the three Speakers in figure 2.1 because these tables count the number of *votes,* not the number of *statements.* Some Speaker statements addressed more than one recorded vote, and others addressed unrecorded votes. Thus multiple roll call votes subject to a single floor statement were counted separately rather than being merged together.

21. In the 99th Congress, O'Neill spoke twice on "macroeconomics" issues, once on a defense matter, and once on an international affairs–related bill. None of the differences from the entire total voting agenda of that Congress were statistically significant.

22. Foley addressed four roll call votes in two speeches in the 103rd Congress, but the difference remains statistically significant (at $p < 0.1$ for the 103rd Congress, and $p < .05$ overall) if one counts each speech only once.

23. The first two years of Hastert's speakership, not shown here, reveal that the percentage of his statements on macroeconomics-related votes is greater than the proportion of all floor votes on these kinds of measures, and the difference is statistically significant. These were generally high-profile party measures, such as the repeal of the estate tax, removing the marriage tax penalty, and requiring a supermajority vote in Congress to raise taxes.

24. Since the unit of this analysis is floor statements, not roll call votes, statements delivered on multiple floor votes are counted only once. In nearly all cases, multiple roll call votes subject to a single floor speech were on substantively similar issues, subject to the same presidential preferences (if any), and delivered on similarly divided floor votes.

25. Data on presidential positions for more recent roll call votes have been collected by David Rohde and the Political Institutions and Public Choice Program at Michigan State University. The Rohde data, however, appear to use a broader definition of presidential position taking than the Malbin data, which rely on formal requests published and issued directly from the president. In order to ensure that only those votes for which the president has strong preferences are measured as White House–desired, I used the Malbin data.

26. As I discussed in chapter 1, the theory of goal-driven leadership also considers support for a same-party presidential *candidate* as an important duty-related goal of the Speaker. The analysis here does not measure this since it is difficult to identify its presence in the aggregate, so I may be underestimating its importance for floor advocacy.

27. The coding scheme does not take into account the possibility that this sort of issue, if endorsed by a same-party president, could also be salient to the presidential party. It may thus overstate the influence of presidential institutional concerns over partisan ones, even if both satisfy the same general goal (i.e., leadership role fulfillment). I distinguish the two concerns more carefully in the case study analyses in chapters 3 and 4.

28. Note that table 2.7 does not capture other combinations, such as both the enactment of personal policy preferences and the fulfillment of a leadership role. The case studies in the subsequent chapters, however, do consider these combinations.

29. For example, the Speaker may have been acting at times on behalf of a future presidential candidate as 70.4 percent of these "congressional party only" cases took place with a president of the opposite party in the White House.

30. Eight of the ten institutional presidency/majority party instances involved a same-party president urging action on a defense, trade, or foreign policy matter, and the remaining two were associated with an opposite-party president: a 1955 resolution granting Eisenhower the authority to defend the island of Formosa China (see chapter 3), and a 1957 Eisenhower resolution to delay British repayment of war loans. Excluding the garrulous McCormack from the analysis only slightly changes the proportions in each category: e.g., 71.1 percent of statements by all Speakers except McCormack involved just the party in Congress, 12.6 percent involved the party in Congress and presidential party, and 5.2 percent involved the party in Congress and the institutional presidency.

31. Deference to the House in passing revenue-raising measures is taken seriously in both chambers. Of the thirty-five *Congressional Quarterly* "key votes" in the House on tax matters from 1945 to 1998, only one was cast on a bill first passed in the Senate: a 1982

measure increasing taxes. In that case, O'Neill probably saw a strategic advantage in neglecting his chamber's constitutional obligations, because the House's failure to take action forced the Republican-controlled Senate to act first on an unpopular bill. This rare deferral of congressional authority was challenged by a Republican on the House floor in August of that year on constitutional grounds, but a motion to return the bill to the Senate was tabled (*Congressional Quarterly Almanac* 1982, 37). Another twenty-five *CQ* key votes in the same period occurred on House versions of bills not yet enacted in the Senate; six others were cast on conference reports; and three occurred on veto overrides.

32. As noted above and in chapter 1, debt limit legislation could be defined as an institutional presidency issue, though it is not coded in that way here.

33. This means that presidential motivations for Speaker leadership could be present for other cases in table 2.7 as well.

34. It should be noted that the original effort to restore the supersonic vehicle funding may have come from within the House (*Congressional Quarterly Almanac* 1971, 147). Prior to the second 1974 vote (in October) on aid to Turkey, Albert stated: "I have not had one call from the President. . . . I have not discussed this matter with the President or the Secretary of State since before the continuing resolution was passed" (*Congressional Record,* 11 October 1974, 35421).Other legislators, however, did claim to have observed such pressure, and Secretary of State Henry Kissinger as well as the White House publicly opposed cutting aid to Turkey (*Congressional Quarterly Almanac* 1974, 548, 122-H, 138-H). Albert also cited deference to the Foreign Affairs Committee as justification for not banning United States aid to Turkey.

35. President Bush also wanted the expanded authorization proposal to pass, but Wright seems to have soured on his original position before being lobbied by the White House. Also, Wright did not combine his speech with additional efforts to win, unlike others who opposed the proposal (Barry 1989, 239–40). This rejection may have also been due in part to the diminished influence of the Banking Committee's chairman, Fernand St. Germain (RI), because of ethics problems (Nash 1987).

36. For a contrary view of O'Neill's position on the Pepper amendment, see Barone 1990, 629. In the same floor speech, O'Neill also advocated passage of the Social Security reform bill even if the Pepper amendment failed; the House did pass it, 282–148, with Democrats in favor 185 to 79. If this were counted in table 2.7 as a separate case, it would increase the number of floor statements motivated by a "cooperative divided government" goal to five, because the bill was the result of a bipartisan task force created by House Democrats and President Reagan to address growing financial shortfalls in the Social Security trust fund.

37. Of the twenty-four cases of nonparty support in table 2.7, nineteen involved the majority party voting against the Speaker's position rather than narrowly supporting it; table 2.8 adds two cases from Foley's Speakership.

38. These include Rayburn's leadership on natural gas deregulation (discussed in chapter 3), Foley's on the passage of NAFTA (see chapter 4), and O'Neill's on Social Security (see chapter 5). These and other cases discussed in subsequent chapters illustrate that Speakers do not use floor advocacy only when their party is too divided to exercise additional kinds of legislative leadership.

39. In none of the floor statements did the Speaker give explicit permission for partisans to vote their conscience. Only one was framed as a nonleadership matter: in his 1993 speech on NAFTA, Speaker Foley said, "I stand here tonight . . . as a Representative of my constituents" (*Congressional Record,* 17 November 1993, p. H10047). Although Foley no doubt supported the measure personally, his comments belie his other efforts to pass the measure; see chapter 4.

40. See chapter 5, table 5.1. Foley's initial drive for budget negotiations with the Republican White House did reflect concerns of his party in the House; see footnote 15 in chapter 7.

41. This norm may have also derived from the constitutional limitations imposed on the head officer of the Senate, the vice president, who "shall have no vote, unless [the Senate] be equally divided" (Article I, section 3).

42. Balloted voting was discontinued after the 1860s (Chiu 1927, 59n1).

43. Some have objected to the increasing ubiquity of floor voting by Speakers. As mentioned in footnote 19 in chapter 1, Speaker Wright's floor voting was apparently an annoyance to the House parliamentarian (interview with the author, May 2003). It has also at times been met with opposition from minority party members: some Republicans, for example, saw Jim Wright's vote on the Gephardt amendment to the trade bill in 1987 as an unnecessarily partisan move (Barry 1989, 278).

44. Ronald Peters argues that Albert's voting "was intended to signal his position" (Peters 1998, 354n68) but does not specify to whom Albert was signaling. Albert could have been following a tradition of Speakers voting on formerly unrecorded votes in the Committee of the Whole, though it is not known if that practice existed. This poses another measurement problem: it is possible that Speakers before 1971 voted on the floor in the Committee of the Whole (see, e.g., instance the 1949 Taft-Hartley case in chapter 3), but since these votes were cast by teller—a head count of total votes in favor or against a measure as legislators walked past vote counters, or "tellers"—it is impossible to confirm whether they did.

45. Ronald Peters argues that the establishment of an electronic voting system in 1973 deterred Albert from casting votes with such frequency (Peters 1997, 354n68).

46. This confirms the observation of one Wright aide, who recalled in an interview that the Speaker usually voted when he "cared deeply" and personally about the matter at hand, and said he could not recollect any instance in which Wright's vote "made the difference" in persuading others (interview with the author, May 2003).

47. Wright voted only once in the 101st Congress, on the vote for Speaker (voting for Foley). Foley also voted in the first four roll calls after his election as Speaker, three times on that day (June 6) and once the following day, all on routine measures; those instances are not counted here.

CHAPTER 3. SAM RAYBURN AND JOHN MCCORMACK

1. For more on this time period, see Peters 1997 (ch. 3), Polsby 2004 (esp. ch. 1), and Remini 2006 (chs. 14–16).

2. Contrast Barbara Sinclair's depiction of pre-1970s House leadership as weak with Randall Ripley's description of the multiple leadership techniques available to party leaders

in 1963–65 (Ripley 1969, 41–44; Sinclair 1995). One might argue that the Speaker's very use of the floor was due to his weaknesses as party leader (see, e.g., Cooper and Brady 1981), but as I discuss in chapters 4 and 5, this activity was also used by Speakers with greater formal powers.

3. One case of legislative leadership, cited by a single source, is insufficiently documented to be analyzed: Rayburn's lobbying on the floor for funding of a Texas dam (Peabody 1976, 46).

4. The literature sweeps failed to capture any cases of floor-related legislative leadership by Joe Martin (R-MA), who served two nonconcurrent terms as Speaker (1947–48 and 1953–54). But it did capture other types of legislative leadership he committed; see chapter 5. Note also that the majority of cases presented here are acts of a positive, rather than negative, nature; as I discuss in chapter 5, other kinds of Speaker authority, such as agenda control, lend themselves more toward leadership based on preventing outcomes rather than promoting them.

5. This means the Speaker's congressional party may not be fully homogeneous on a policy issue—that is, the party may suffer from significant defections or dissent on the matter—yet the issue may still be related to the Speaker's desire to retain support of his party in Congress. I discuss this further in the conclusion of this chapter.

6. Table 2.2 in chapter 2 lists a number of issues of general salience to the Speaker or his district, but the case studies also reveal that specific bills or initiatives were sometimes of particular importance to the Speaker or his district. If an issue is considered both salient to the Speaker's district and of personal policy interest to the Speaker, I code the issue as being only the former, in order to weigh on the side of "common wisdom" that the reelection goal drives Speaker leadership.

7. Rayburn especially was more comfortable acting privately and behind the scenes than openly exercising his power as Speaker (e.g., Bolling 1964, 219; Goodwin 1970, 213).

8. This quote refers to a 1955 exemption bill, but the content of the measure, and the politics surrounding it, were similar (Carper 1962). Though not captured by the literature sweeps, the 1955 vote also represents an act of legislative leadership: Rayburn scheduled the vote for a day when many liberals would be absent, and it passed "with Rayburn calling in all his IOU's" (Hardeman and Bacon 1987, 394).

9. For more on the connection between the natural gas industry and Rayburn's electoral interests, see Champagne 1984, 151–55; see also Lapham 1988, 268. One plausible counterargument is that Rayburn was working on behalf of Democrats on the Interstate and Foreign Commerce Committee, which had cleared the exemption bill and which he had once chaired. The evidence does not preclude this possibility, though it seems unlikely that Rayburn would exercise such extensive leadership to enact a bill, against the policy preferences of his own party, solely in support of a committee.

10. Despite Rayburn's appeal to House-wide concerns about congressional power, there is no evidence that this role-fulfillment goal was particularly salient to Rayburn or other bill supporters.

11. According to the *Congressional Record,* four legislators changed their vote from nay to yea at the end of the vote: Henry Latham (R-NY), Morgan Moulder (D-MO), Paul Shafer (R-MI), and Earl Wilson (R-IN). See also Lapham 1988, 268.

12. One story postulated that the expansion would end an ongoing deadlock in Massachusetts over redistricting, which if left unresolved, would have forced McCormack to run as an "at-large" representative (*Newsweek,* 19 March 1962).

13. Speaker leadership on foreign affairs might suggest that Speakers are pursing a variation of the "enact policy" goal: to send a signal overseas of strong domestic support for American foreign policy. For more on this possibility, see chapter 7.

14. Even thirty years later, in an interview with Dorothy and William F. McSweeny, McCormack described the vote vividly and extensively (McCormack Papers, McSweeny interview, box 195, tape 6).

15. Roosevelt may have been much less enthusiastic about the extension than others in his administration (Sherwood 1948, 367).

16. Recent research has suggested that isolationism among the public was less widespread at the time. Nonetheless, the perception of public isolationism by House leaders was at least as important, and the military draft was probably much less popular among voters than other foreign aid and military-related programs (Berinsky 2004).

17. Although I do not consider such activity to be legislative leadership "near" the House floor, I note it here as an important element of Rayburn's overall efforts to enact the draft extension bill. For more on leadership exercised beyond the House floor, see chapter 5.

18. Rayburn's attempt to sway minority party members speaks not just to his influence with Republicans, but more generally to the willingness of Speakers to lobby minority party legislators in order to win on the House floor. Also, in the 1970 McSweeny interview, McCormack suggests that his "pocket" votes consisted of legislators willing to switch from nay to yea and were not true "live pairs," or legislators opposed to the bill but paired with an absent member voting in favor and thus willing to change their vote to "absent" if needed (*McCormack Papers,* McSweeny interview, box 196, tapes 6 and 11).

19. These twelve included seven from Ohio (Harold Claypool, Jacob Davis, Greg Holbrock, John Hunter, Lawrence Imhoff, Robert Secrest, and Stephen Young), plus Congressmen John Cochran (MO), Harry Haines (PA), Lucien Maciora (CT), John McIntyre (WY), and John Tolan (CA).

20. Specifically, I use W-NOMINATE scores, which are unique to each Congress and do not allow for cross-Congress comparisons. The W-NOMINATE scores and graphs were generated using the W-NOMINATE software package in R (version 2.5.0), written by Keith Poole, Jeffrey Lewis, James Lo, and Royce Carroll. I thank the authors for the software and Dr. Poole for the roll call data used to calculate the scores.

21. Another possible effect of leadership influence would be to shift the yes-no cut line by persuading similarly arrayed legislators to vote against their preferences; see chapter 4.

22. Note that some of the solid circles in figure 3.1 are obscured. The six Democrats who were correctly predicted to vote against recommittal, but incorrectly predicted to vote against the bill itself, were Joseph Casey (MA), Herman Eberharter (PA), Henry Jackson (WA), Michael Kirwan (OH), James O'Connor (MT), and William Sutphin (NJ).

23. Leaders were later successful in overturning both amendments on subsequent votes (Belair 1950; *Congressional Quarterly Almanac* 1950, 212). On Rayburn's leadership against the Burleson amendment, see footnote 25 below.

24. The relatively partisan nature of the vote on the motion to recommit (Democrats

against, 31–190; Republicans in favor, 118–29) suggests that Rayburn was acting to help his party in Congress, thus securing a leadership reelection goal. As discussed earlier, however, the vote belies the lack of salience the issue had for Rayburn's party in the House, particularly in contrast to the White House. Since the vote was on a motion to recommit, which is often considered a test of party loyalty, it may also give a false impression of House Democrats' support for the actual Point Four program.

25. Rayburn may have exercised leadership on another element of the bill as well. In the same floor statement, Rayburn sharply criticized the Burleson amendment, and in a dramatic reversal from the previous day, the House voted 70–198 by division to reject it (Belair 1950). Although neither vote on the Burleson amendment was conducted by roll call, thus precluding the identification of vote switchers, the dramatic difference in vote totals suggests how unrecorded voting could give party leaders great advantages in influencing vote outcomes.

26. In this respect, Rayburn may have also had his party's electoral viability in mind. Similarly, the Speaker might have been worried about conveying an image that Democrats opposed the military policy of a popular president and former military commander. In a January poll, a majority of Americans, albeit not an overwhelming majority (56 percent), believed the United States should defend Taiwan from China (Foreign Affairs Survey, National Opinion Research Center, USNORC.550366.R13).

27. Since both Jones and Holifield had initially voted to end debate, it is possible that their last-minute votes were due to an error on their part rather than last-minute lobbying by party leaders.

28. Republicans were important vote switchers in this case: four switched from voting against ending debate to voting against Brown, and eight (different) Republicans went from voting against ending debate to voting for the original rule. Fewer than three Democrats had switched the opposite way, i.e., voting against Rayburn after having initially supported ending debate.

29. Josephy suggests that McCormack's support actually originated with Rivers, who he claims "had a considerable hold over" the Speaker (1979, 361). This may mean that McCormack was also motivated to exercise leadership on Vietnam matters to protect the legislative output of the Armed Services Committee.

30. This suggests another motive for McCormack: to aid the war effort by signaling to the enemy that Americans were unified. As McCormack noted on behalf of the March 1966 military authorization bill, "We will convey to the actual and potential enemy and also the rest of the world that America is united" (*Congressional Record,* 1 March 1966, 4429). For further discussion of this possibility, see footnote 13 and chapter 7.

31. One study has shown that the frequency of congressional floor votes on Vietnam was positively affected by the number of large, nonviolent anti-Vietnam protests (McAdam and Su 2002). This suggests that McCormack's strategy was to use floor votes to keep wavering Democrats in support of the war, while countering the impression that these protests might give to the North Vietnamese. Unfortunately, McAdam and Su do not distinguish between House and Senate voting in their analysis, even though the Senate arguably had more aggressive advocates of U.S. troop withdrawal than did the House.

32. Though the vote was technically "binding," thirty-one Democrats later supported the

motion on the floor to recommit the measure, suggesting that significant defections from the binding caucus, apparent as early as the 64th Congress (1915–17), were still a problem (Green 2002).

33. One potential source of influence for Rayburn was to prevent recorded roll call votes on legislation. This suggests the limitations of looking only at recorded floor votes to determine leadership influence and party unity, at least through 1970 (after which recorded floor votes became the norm). See also chapter 2.

34. A variable measuring presidential voting behavior at the district level cannot be included because such data exist at the county level only, and some districts were composed of subunits of counties (most notably, urban districts). However, running the regression for only those districts where this voting behavior data are available ($n = 310$) shows that Truman vote percentage has a statistically significant and positive effect on the likelihood of support for the rule (in 1949: B = .016, se = .008; in 1950: B = .032, se = .011), and Thurmond vote percentage has a statistically significant and negative effect (in 1949: B = −.015, se = .008; in 1950: B = −.028, se = .011).

35. Even if Rayburn had opposed an open floor rule, it is unclear if he could have overcome the conservative coalition's dominance of the Rules Committee during this period (see above).

36. See Rayburn Papers, letter to Harry, John, and William Porter, 7 May 1949; telegram to Jay C. Stilley, 6 May 1949, box 3R353. Since the vote was conducted by teller, Rayburn's claims of having cast a vote cannot be independently verified.

37. The Speaker's efforts to recommit the bill suggest he was not simply acting to protect the output of the Education and Labor Committee from being amended or rejected. Joining Rayburn in lobbying for the recommittal were White House and labor representatives (Pomper 1959, 168).

38. It is cited by eighteen sources, more than any other in the data set.

39. The vice president, Lyndon Johnson, also reportedly lobbied House members on the expansion proposal (Hardeman and Bacon 1987, 459). The Speaker's role to support the presidential party also helps explain why Rayburn did not push for Rules Committee expansion in 1958: he worried that, by empowering party liberals, committee expansion would cause less moderate legislation to pass the House, jeopardizing the Democrats' presidential chances in 1960 (Bolling 1964, 206).

40. Given that Rayburn was the most senior Texan in the House (first elected in 1912) and had previously served as Speaker of the Texas House, his effective lobbying of Texas Democrats (in this case and in others discussed in this chapter) seems quite plausible. Younger Texans may have been particularly susceptible, as suggested by the lesser seniority of some unexpected supporters of the 1957 civil rights bill (John Young, first term; J. T. Rutherford, second term) as well as the 1961 Rules Committee expansion (Robert Casey, second term, and Rutherford, fourth term).

41. The other nine Democrats were: Thomas Dale Alford (AR), Walter Baring (NV), Herbert Bonner (NC), Overton Brooks (LA), Oren Harris (AR), William Hull (MO), Richard Ichord (MO), Theo Thompson (LA), and Edwin Willis (LA). Five Republicans were also falsely predicted to oppose the resolution, and six Democrats and four Republicans had unexpectedly voted against the rules change.

42. Although not cited in the literature sweeps, material from the McCormack papers suggests that the Speaker was involved in the Agriculture Committee's deliberations as well. In a letter to the Speaker in January 1963, South Carolina Democrat John McMillan cited his vote for the bill in the Agriculture Committee as an example of how he had agreed to help McCormack, even if doing so ran contrary to the sentiments of his district (McCormack Papers, letter from Rep. John McMillan, 14 January 1963, box 162, folder 2). This suggests that the Speaker was motivated by more than a desire to protect a committee chairman's bill on the floor, but also to get the committee to approve particular legislative language.

43. Republican support for civil rights legislation suggests a "cooperative divided government" model of Speaker leadership (see chapter 2) rather than a partisan-oriented one. Pressure for the civil rights measure, however, came principally from actors within Rayburn's own party, as discussed below.

44. The 1956 Republican Party platform emphasized its "impressive record of accomplishment in the field of civil rights," whereas the Democrats' statement on the topic remained near the end of their platform (Johnson and Porter 1973, 487, 541–42, 554). In another potentially ominous sign, Rep. Adam Clayton Powell, a leading black Democrat from Harlem, endorsed Eisenhower for reelection. Concern by Democrats about securing black votes to maintain their party's majority coalition dated back at least to 1948 (Valelly 2004).

45. Bolling later noted that Rayburn also had in mind one Democratic aspirant for the White House in particular: Texas Senator Lyndon Johnson. Johnson, fearing that turmoil in the Senate surrounding civil rights legislation would kill his presidential nomination chances in 1956, asked Rayburn to wait on the legislation until the following year (Caro 2002, 790–91).

46. Both in 1956 and 1957, Rules Committee Chairman Howard Smith (VA) employed many tactics to prevent floor consideration of civil rights legislation (Bolling 1964, 180, 183–84). Smith, however, allowed the bill to reach the floor in 1956, and in 1957, "under more than the usual pressure to grant a rule for" the measure, Smith relented again (Phillips 1957). Assuming Rayburn was responsible for Smith's behavior, it suggests that Rayburn exercised significant influence over the agenda, as well as the Senate's handling of civil rights, in this particular case (Bolling 1964, 179–80; Bolling 1968, 193–94). See also chapter 5.

47. This included a young Jim Wright, who recalled an encounter with Rayburn at the Speaker's dais on the day of the vote in both his memoirs and in an interview with the author (Wright 1996, 54; interview with the author, July 2003). The other five Texans were Frank Ikard, W. R. Poage, J. T. Rutherford, Albert Thomas, and John Young. Albert Burleson and Olin Teague remain as unknowns on Rayburn's list, while six other Texans were noted as willing to support the conference report and seven as being opposed.

48. Those four were Poague, Rutherford, Thomas, and Young. The other four unexpected bill supporters from Texas were already listed on Rayburn's work list as agreeing to vote for the measure: Wright Patman, William Thornberry, Joe Kilgore, and Clark Thompson. For more on Rayburn's lobbying of the Texas delegation, see previous footnote.

49. As Charles O. Jones notes, although Eisenhower played an active role in the passage of labor reform legislation, "the action was primarily in Congress, with the president as one of the important players" (Jones 2005, 273).

50. Gallup Polls, April 1957, August 1957, and October 1958 (USGALLUP.57–581.Q006, USGALLUP.57–588.Q005A, and USGALLUP.58–606.R028), accessed from the Roper Center iPoll databank (http://www.ropercenter.uconn.edu/data_access/ipoll/ipoll.html).

51. This loss was hardly a surprise to the Speaker. Rayburn wanted Democratic legislators to have a chance to vote on union reform of some sort before the upcoming election but had brought the bill to the floor via the suspension calendar, which required a two-thirds vote of approval for legislation to pass (Bolling 1964, 158).

52. Fifty percent of those surveyed by Gallup in January 1959 believed "the laws regulating labor unions" were "not strict enough" (USGALLUP.59–609.Q006, accessed from the Roper Center iPoll databank). The results of another poll, sent to House members in June 1959, showed majority support for additional regulation of unions (Patterson 1966, 21–22).

53. This was particularly remarkable because Rayburn, representing a relatively conservative district, had largely concealed his other leadership efforts on the matter (Peters 1997, 135).

54. Interestingly, W-NOMINATE analysis of legislator voting patterns shows that of the thirteen Democrats who voted for the bill contrary to estimated preferences, four were from Rayburn's home state of Texas (Lindley Beckworth, Paul Kilday, William Thornberry, and Frank Ikard). Another four were from Maryland (Daniel Brewster, George Fallon, Thomas Johnson, and Richard Lankford).

CHAPTER 4. SPEAKER LEADERSHIP IN THE REFORM AND POST-REFORM HOUSE

1. Toward the end of the pre-reform period, McCormack acquired important new authority over agenda setting that Rayburn had lacked. However, he was often reluctant to use it, preferring to negotiate quietly with power brokers in his party to achieve legislative outcomes. See chapter 3.

2. Three additional cases of legislative leadership that appeared in the literature sweeps are not discussed here. In early 1971, Carl Albert reportedly tried to protect a cap on the interest rates of government bonds, but evidence of Albert's specific action could not be identified (Peters 1997, 167–68). Albert also reportedly lobbied for votes on behalf of committee reform legislation in 1974 but mostly did so away from the floor (Peters 1997, 184; see chapter 5). And Speaker O'Neill's strong push for a resolution removing American Marines from Lebanon, approved in his party's caucus in early 1985, was abandoned when President Reagan agreed to withdraw the troops (*Congressional Quarterly Almanac* 1984, 22; Peters 1997, 248–49).

3. As a sign of the growing importance of party leaders and leadership organizations after 1970, whip counts were taken in many of the 1971–98 cases captured in the literature sweeps. Instances where this occurred that are not mentioned in the text include the public works, job creation, and minimum wage bills from 1971–72; the 1977 energy bill; the 1979 debt limit increase; the 1982 appropriations veto override; and funding for the Contras (Evans 2007).

4. Changing voter beliefs about the proper degree of deference to the president on national security matters may also explain this development (Lindsay and Ripley 1992).

5. Republican National Committee Chairman Lee Atwater sent a fundraising letter criticizing the raise, signaling that his party might use it as an issue in the next election (Barry 1989, 672).

6. The question was followed by this warning: "If the majority respond affirmatively [to have a vote], there will be a vote."

7. See Representative Dannemeyer's floor tactic on the first pay raise proposal (above) as an example. In effect, legislators preferred a no vote on a pay raise to any salary increase at all; the status quo of no raise was thus closer to legislators' expressed preferences than was Foley's proposal.

8. For more on this type of committee-related leadership, see chapter 5.

9. As noted chapter 2, Foley also demonstrated an inclination toward the less partisan, more House-wide role of his office by delivering floor speeches less often than other Speakers, and by sometimes prefacing his floor remarks as coming from him as a member of Congress, not as Speaker (see, e.g., *Congressional Record,* 21 June 1990, H4086; and 12 January 1991, 1085).

10. Gingrich's position may have been further reinforced by lobbying from a pro-hunting organization that supported wild animal conservation (Cloud 1995b).

11. Doug McAdam and Yang Su argue that the size and nature of antiwar protests affected the number of "pro-peace" votes cast in the House and Senate, which might also explain the growing congressional opposition to the war during this period (McAdam and Su 2002).

12. For example, responses to a Gallup survey question in January 1967 showed that a majority of respondents (52 percent) believed the decision to send troops to Vietnam was not a "mistake," yet another Gallup poll taken two years later reported that the same percentage said it was (USGALLUP.740.Q011 and USGALLUP.774.Q006, accessed from the Roper Center iPoll databank [http://www.ropercenter.uconn.edu/data_access/ipoll/ipoll.html]).

13. As with McCormack, Albert may have also been concerned that partisan opposition to the president during wartime would send a negative signal to potential and actual enemies of the United States. One cannot rule out another possibility: that Albert wanted to help committee chairmen who opposed withdrawing troops from Vietnam. But Albert's efforts to modify or kill antiwar caucus resolutions, as well as legislation restricting troop deployment, suggest that he was concerned with Vietnam policy more broadly, not just with protecting the legislative output of congressional committees. Interestingly, Albert (along with the party caucus) was able to persuade at least one chairman, Thomas Morgan of the Foreign Affairs Committee, to switch from opposing troop withdrawal to actually endorsing and voting for a floor amendment that included such a requirement (*Congressional Quarterly Almanac* 1972, 123).

14. The Senate's tenacity on the issue led to some success for antiwar Democrats despite Albert's resistance. The conference report of the military conscription extension bill, for example, contained language urging the removal of U.S. troops from Vietnam by a "date certain," and its approval on the House floor in early August 1971 represented the

first time that the House passed legislation endorsing troop withdrawal (*Congressional Quarterly Almanac* 1971, 305).

15. See, e.g., Time/CNN/Yankelovich Partners Poll, June 1993, USYANKP.062693.R15, and ABC News Poll, November 1993, USABC.111193.R02.

16. Ironically, Foley would later cite his support for NAFTA as contributing to his 1994 election loss because of "a disenthralling reaction" by would-be supporters (Biggs and Foley 1999, 278). This illustrates how seeking to achieve a reelection goal by acting on behalf of one state/district interest (economic) can threaten the same goal by working against another interest or constituency. Foley may have had a personal policy motivation for supporting NAFTA, but following my conservative coding rule for classifying Speaker goals (discussed in chapter 3), I do not code it that way here.

17. Some of the public's support for energy reform had been enhanced by the Carter administration itself, which issued a series of reports in early 1977 warning of dire consequences for failure to revise U.S. energy policy (Cochrane 1981, 558–64).

18. While probably not as salient, it is possible that O'Neill, newly sworn in as Speaker, had his own reputation in mind, as well as the image of the House. As O'Neill would later tell the Democrats on the ad hoc House energy committee, "My reputation, our party's reputation, and reputation of the Congress are all tied up with this legislation" (O'Neill 1987, 386; see also Peters 1997, 219).

19. Though other floor amendments to the bill passed by close votes, the literature sweeps did not capture any acts of legislative leadership associated with them. At least one Democrat, Richard Ottinger (NY), did later suffer retaliation from O'Neill for casting a wayward vote on the energy bill (Farrell 2001, 437).

20. Seven other Democrats—from Alabama, Florida, Mississippi, Missouri, Ohio, and Tennessee—also voted against the amendment (contrary to prediction) as well as eight Republicans. Three Republicans and twenty-seven Democrats voted for the amendment, contrary to estimated preferences.

21. Compare, e.g., the results of the Cambridge Reports National Omnibus Survey asking about presidential performance in July 1977 (USCAMREP.77JUL.R257) with the results from October 1978 (USCAMREP.78OCT.R258).

22. The vote was one of thirty-two key votes on a computerized list from the 95th Congress, 2nd session. It is unclear whether the votes were explicitly used in determining committee assignments, but the data are located in the O'Neill papers together with steering committee ballots on committee appointments (Rep. Jim Mattox voting record, O'Neill Papers, Party Leadership files, box 7, folder 1).

23. One source claims that a Republican legislator, Thomas Evans of Delaware, cast the decisive vote to break the tie (*Congressional Quarterly Almanac* 1978, 2920). Evans also voted for the rule contrary to what the W-NOMINATE procedure predicts, as well as nine other House Republicans.

24. One might argue that this case can be explained by the "cooperative divided government" leadership model discussed in chapter 2, since both Gingrich and Clinton publicly endorsed welfare reform. But Clinton's reform proposal, introduced late in the 103rd Congress, differed in important ways from the Republican plan: most notably,

Clinton's plan did not convert the existing federal welfare program, known as Aid to Families with Dependent Children (AFDC), into a block grant program, and it had fewer limits on eligibility (*Congressional Quarterly Almanac* 1995, 7–36). Clinton's support for the congressional Republican plan seems to have tepid at best, and his decision to sign the bill after two previous vetoes was probably motivated at least as much by concerns about his own reelection as it was by agreement with the provisions of the Republican-written bill. Randall Strahan also suggests that welfare reform was a personal policy goal of Gingrich, as he had advocated restructuring the federal welfare program for many years (2007, 155).

25. This suggests that, at least in this decision, Gingrich was forced to act more as an agent of his party than as an assertive and independent party leader (Sinclair 1999a; Strahan 2007, 161).

26. By instigating a policy conflict with the Republican White House, Albert may have also had the presidential party in mind, though there is no clear evidence of this. In addition, by pushing this trio of legislation early in his Speakership, Albert may have hoped to establish a reputation for legislative activism, in contrast to his more staid predecessor, John McCormack (Peters 1997, 162, 166).

27. O'Neill may have feared that the rule would otherwise be defeated. Procedural votes, however, are both less visible and more important to party leaders and are thus usually less susceptible to defections (Froman and Ripley 1965, 59).

28. Although one scholar claims that O'Neill intentionally took his ill-timed overseas trip to distance himself from an expected defeat (Peters 1997, 234), the trip had been planned well in advance of the subsequent budget battle (Farrell 2001, 554–55; Sinclair 1983, 194). For more on the use of the agenda by Speakers to influence legislative outcomes, see chapter 5.

29. One former Democratic whip staffer later noted that O'Neill hoped, if nothing else, that fighting Gramm-Latta would help clearly define his party's policy position and aid its morale (interview with the author, June 2003). House Democrats tried to head off Dole's campaign by contacting the legislators in advance, but fifteen of the twenty-four who were lobbied ultimately voted for Gramm-Latta.

30. O'Neill did not always win on other House votes regarding Contra or Contra-related funding. For example, in a series of votes on a foreign aid authorization bill in May 1984, the House approved the president's request for $62 million in military funding for El Salvador and rejected attempts to restrict or reduce it (Shapiro and Reid 1984). For an analysis of the characteristics of Contra-related "swing" legislators and the factors that influenced vote choice on Contra funding and the likelihood such funding would pass the House, see LeoGrande and Brenner 1993.

31. In addition to any floor leadership that O'Neill exercised on this measure, the Speaker also instructed conferees to keep the Boland restriction language in the conference report (LeoGrande 1998, 324).

32. Speaker John Carlisle (D-KY) similarly manipulated legislative time in 1887, when he twice turned back the House timepiece to pass appropriations legislation before the adjournment of Congress (Barnes 1967, 111; Follett 1896, 254). O'Neill may have com-

mitted a move similar to Wright's on at least one occasion (Barry 1989, 460). Later, Speaker Dennis Hastert would twice keep the House voting clock open for an even longer period of time to reverse vote outcomes (see chapter 1).

33. Wright's tactical errors, both in this case and with the pay raise case discussed above, suggest the importance of Speakers' ability to gauge the preferences of their party when exercising leadership on behalf of their interests. I discuss this in more detail in the conclusion.

34. The Contract also called for giving "a legislative line-item veto" power to the president (*Contract With America* 1994). That proposal was enacted separately in the 104th Congress, but was later ruled unconstitutional by the Supreme Court.

35. House Republicans had previously gone on record in favor of a balanced budget amendment to the Constitution; in the 103rd Congress, for example, such an amendment received the votes of all but one Republican on the House floor in March of 1994.

36. Randall Strahan argues that Gingrich also supported a balanced federal budget as a strong personal goal, as well as federal tax reduction (discussed below) (Strahan 2007, 140–41).

37. Six of the eight were relatively moderate Republicans, including Doug Bereuter (NE), Sherwood Boehlert (NY), Amo Houghton (NY), Nancy Johnson (CT), John Porter (IL), and Marge Roukema (NJ).

38. The actual size of this group is unclear. Not surprisingly, it included three Republicans from the Washington, D.C. area: Thomas Davis (VA), Constance Morella (MD), and Frank Wolf (VA). But at least one source claimed that as many as a dozen Republicans were members of the group (Killian 1998, 75; Rubin 1995c).

39. Interestingly, Roberts claimed that Gingrich himself had suggested the $95,000 limit and encouraged Roberts to circulate the letter to determine the degree of legislator interest in the proposal (Rubin 1995a). If true, it suggests a tactical error on Gingrich's part, foreshadowing problems with Gingrich's leadership style that would appear later in the 105th Congress. See further discussion at the end of this chapter.

40. Estimates of the number of Republicans in this group ranged from twenty to forty (Gray 1995b; Rubin 1995b).

CHAPTER 5. LEADERSHIP BEYOND THE FLOOR, 1941–1998

1. Agenda-setting activity could also, in principle, involve committee-related leadership. I define it here, however, as including only specific involvement by the Speaker in the activity of the Rules Committee (when it acts as a control committee for the House floor, not as a policy committee on matters within its jurisdiction). Agenda setting also includes Speakers allowing certain legislators to offer particular amendments and Speakers proposing or prioritizing legislation. Influence over the specific content of legislation includes committee activity only when the Speaker makes specific requests or suggestions to committees on bill content, or if the Speaker helps draft legislation while serving on a task force. It also includes Speakers persuading legislators to amend (or not amend) legislation. Speaker influence over committee consideration of legislation includes all other kinds of Speaker leadership directed at task forces or at standing, spe-

cial, or conference committees. It also includes brokering deals between committees or within conference committees. I make these distinctions with the understanding that one kind of activity can often have an impact on another (e.g., getting a committee to pass a bill may then affect the House's floor agenda).

2. This is especially true of Newt Gingrich, who sources noted had committed actions like adding policy riders to appropriations bills, shaping bills in the Rules Committee, participating in conference committee negotiations, and directing committee activity on elements of the Contract with America (Deering 1999, 104; Dodd and Oppenheimer 2001, 26; Evans 2001, 232; Evans and Oleszek 1999b, 124; Fenno 1997, 31; Peters 1999, 43; Smith and Gamm 2001, 260). Many sources also cited Gingrich's creation of various task forces to draft legislation (Deering 1999, 105–6; Evans 2001, 217; Fenno 1997, 31; Groseclose and King 2001, 205; Peters 1999, 43; Rae and Campbell 1999, 3, 12; Sinclair 1999a, 429; 1999b, 27). One source mentions fifteen such task forces; adding each as a separate case of leadership would, of course, increase the number of Gingrich cases in the data set (Deering 1999, 105–6).

3. One Speaker goal, reelection to the House, is not a primary explanation of any of the cases related to non-floor leadership, though that objective could be a secondary factor (see the discussion of Speaker Foley and the renewal of China's MFN status, below). Another goal, enacting personally desired policy, also does not appear as a primary explanation. Nine cases are not adequately explained by the theory of goal-driven leadership. Speakers in these instances were motivated by a desire to help an opposite-party president on a major domestic issue, defer to a committee, or achieve some other objective. I discuss these exceptions to the theory further in chapter 7.

4. This case is categorized as primarily agenda-setting behavior (table 5.1), but it includes committee-related activity as well.

5. Eric Schickler notes that one of the institutional innovations ultimately adopted by the House, multiple bill referrals, was most salient to legislators' desire to improve the capacity of Congress (Schickler 2001, 201).

6. Political scientist Ronald Peters argues that Albert may have sought to distance himself from the original plan when he realized it was too controversial to pass on the floor. Peters, however, notes that the Speaker could have used other tactics, such as insisting on a direct vote on the Bolling proposal in caucus before sending it to the Hansen committee, to improve the original bill's chances and avoid a public defeat (Peters 1997, 184–85).

7. Rayburn had played a part in the introduction of this bill as well, insisting that the measure be referred to the House Foreign Affairs Committee in deference to normal House procedures and to avoid complaints from other legislators (Kimball 1969, 262, 264).

8. The House considered controversial China-MFN legislation in both 1990 and 1991, and Barbara Sinclair does not specify in which year this particular case took place. Press accounts confirm that the Speaker played a role in influencing the Rules Committee's behavior in 1990 but not in 1991.

9. A secondary consideration for Rayburn may have been the authority of the House, since the House is constitutionally required to initiate all tax measures (White 1955c).

10. If the latter is true, this would also be an example of the Speaker influencing the content of legislation. But the extent of Rayburn's activity in this regard is not known since the bill was formally drafted and approved by the Ways and Means Committee.

11. They included, in 1981, passage of the so-called Gramm-Latta budget resolution (see chapter 4), and, in 1982, rejection of the Democratic budget resolution on the House floor (Dewar 1982; Tolchin 1982a; 1982b).

12. The Speaker's desire to support the presidential party may have also mattered in this case. Ronald Peters suggests that O'Neill had an eye toward the upcoming presidential elections in passing legislation that "would clarify the differences between the two parties on major domestic and foreign policy issues" (Peters 1997, 244).

13. Kernell defines going public as including three kinds of activity: public addresses, appearances in public, and strategic trip-taking (Kernell 1997, 106–23). The latter two are not the focus of this discussion: while Speakers may make appearances or conduct travel to influence public opinion, such activity more likely serves as campaign devices for fellow partisans (e.g., travel to legislators' districts in an election year). For a more thorough treatment of the "public Speakership" and reasons for its increased importance in recent decades, see Harris 1998.

14. Response to the State of the Union address, January 1987 and 1988; Sinclair 1995, 271–72, 276–77.

15. This is often cited as the first use of public media by Rayburn to shape public opinion. This may be so for his tenure as Speaker, but not as party leader. In 1954, as House minority leader, Rayburn delivered at least two radio addresses criticizing President Eisenhower's tax agenda (Gould and Young 1998, 192–93; Morris 1954).

16. Data on Foley's and Gingrich's television appearances are taken from the Lexis-Nexis News Transcripts database and the Vanderbilt News Archives.

CHAPTER 6. THE HASTERT SPEAKERSHIP

1. There are some noteworthy examples of Hastert's *non*-legislative leadership falling into one of these two categories. For instance, Hastert lobbied for a federal loan guarantee for United Airlines, headquartered in his home state of Illinois, and even spoke directly with the secretary of the treasury on the matter (e.g., Maynard 2004). And in 2006, when the FBI removed documents from the House office of Democrat Bill Jefferson of Louisiana as part of a corruption investigation, Hastert and Minority Leader Nancy Pelosi jointly complained that the raid violated Congress's independence (Hulse 2006).

2. Clinton also felt pressure from within the executive branch: General Barry McCaffrey, the White House's so-called drug czar, had suggested more funding from the White House in July 1999 (Pomper 1999c).

3. The initial dynamics were thus somewhat analogous to the consideration of labor reform in 1959, when the House Democratic Party felt compelled to regulate labor unions even though a majority of their own members' preferences did not square well with a move of that sort (see chapter 3).

4. As presidential candidate, George W. Bush would later endorse the measure himself

(Hess 1999), and as president he successfully pushed for a similarly sized tax cut in his first year in office.

5. For a summary of the effort in Congress to change campaign finance laws before 1999, see Dwyre and Farrar-Myers 2001, chs. 1–3.

6. Hastert at least partially attributed his decision to pull the intelligence bill to the objections of the chairman of the Armed Services Committee (Allen 2004).

CHAPTER 7. GOAL-ORIENTED LEADERSHIP

1. An alternative approach would be to use a multinomial logit model to test the effect of independent variables on whether the Speaker supports, opposes, or has no opinion about a specific vote outcome. In predicting Speaker opposition to a vote (where the baseline value is the Speaker having no opinion), the results of that model show no statistically significant effects of any of the explanatory variables. In predicting Speaker support for a vote outcome, the results of this analysis largely mirror that of table 7.1, below: House-wide issues, matters of personal interest to the Speaker, veto overrides, and presidential requests have a significant ($p < .05$) and positive effect.

2. Since key votes were not identified by *Congressional Quarterly* before 1945, they cannot be used to study Rayburn's first two congresses (1941–45). Some scholars have criticized key votes for overemphasizing controversial matters, measuring congressional-presidential relations better than disputes internal to Congress, or varying in comprehensiveness over time (Shull and LeLoup 1981; Shull and Vanderleeuw 1987).

3. This variable does not measure whether the party supports the particular vote, only the degree of division within the party on the vote. As noted in chapter 2, using the final vote to determine prior party support is problematic because a floor vote may be affected by leadership influence (including floor advocacy) and not just reflect sincere voting preferences. Only three of the eight key votes through 1988 in which the Speaker's position was rejected by his own party had a Rice cohesion score below 0.1.

4. One might argue that intraparty division *increases* the likelihood of floor advocacy because it puts the passage of a measure in greater doubt (e.g., Sinclair 1995, 206). But since floor passage also depends on the voting behavior of the minority party, I used instead the closeness of the final vote as a measure of possible failure of passage.

5. If the "unified government" variable is negative and statistically significant, it could be interpreted to mean that Speakers use floor advocacy as national spokespersons for their party when the president is of the opposite party. The data suggest that partisan concerns motivate the Speaker with respect to presidential requests, but not uniformly so. From 1945 to 1990, when Speakers addressed the floor on a key vote for which a same-party president took a documented position, they agreed with the president's position 71 percent of the time (twelve of seventeen instances); under divided government, they concurred with the president 30 percent of the time (three of ten).

6. I did not include a separate measure of presidential requests to increase the debt limit. These requests may, as I suggest in chapter 1, invoke an institutional deference to the White House by the Speaker. They are not, however, as closely associated with the con-

stitutional authority of the president over defense, trade, or foreign affairs, and the consequences of inaction on that kind of legislation is sufficiently dire to likely compel legislative action regardless of the president's position. Debt limit matters are instead measured with the "must-pass measure" variable discussed below. Of the seven key votes on the debt limit cast between 1945 and 1988, the Malbin data indicate that five were requested by presidents (three by opposite-party presidents, two by same-party presidents).

7. A more fine-tuned test of presidency-related Speaker goals would also take into account the prior position of the House majority party, since such goals are presumably more salient if the majority party opposes the preferred outcome. Though using floor votes to measure prior preferences is approximate at best, I did rerun the regressions with two additional interaction terms, using the relative division of the majority party on the final vote as a rough test of the party's prior preferences ("Rice score × presidential request" and "Rice score × presidential request × unified government"). Both regressors proved statistically insignificant in the fixed effects models, and their inclusion left the original findings largely unchanged, apart from the "Presidential request" variable becoming statistically insignificant.

8. Including an interaction term between "vote margin" and "must-pass measure" did not substantively change the findings. Adding a dichotomous variable that measured if the Speaker was new and serving his first six months in the House also left the results unchanged.

9. Another potential problem with this variable is its heteroskedastic relation with the *Rice Score* variable discussed below. When the vote margin is small, the Rice cohesion score (i.e., majority party division) can be large or small, but when the vote margin is large, the Rice score can only be large. As a substitute for the "vote margin" variable, I reran the fixed effects logit models twice, each time using a different dichotomous variable to measure party division: one, measuring whether 75 percent of the majority party voted against 75 percent of the minority party; and a second, measuring whether 90 percent of the majority voted against 90 percent of the minority. Neither variable meaningfully changed the estimated coefficients or their statistical significance, whether controlling for Speakers or congresses.

10. Since the presidency variables are coded only through 1988, I also ran the two fixed effects models without those variables in order to include Speaker floor advocacy from 1989 through 1996. The "veto override" variable and the variable measuring House-wide matters remained statistically significant in both models; the result was the same if one excluded the presidency variables but used just data through 1988.

11. Nine of the ten Speaker floor statements on veto overrides from 1945 through 1998 occurred during divided government: in other words, the sitting Speaker used floor advocacy to oppose the policy actions of a president of the opposite party. But because veto overrides require a supermajority of votes—which majority parties have rarely commanded—they could, conceivably, also reflect a bipartisan action of the whole House to protect its legislative output against the wishes of the president. Only four of the ten veto override cases occurred when the majority party controlled two-thirds or more of House seats (between 1975 and 1979). The other six cases all took place under divided government, and they could have been motivated by partisan position taking against an

opposite-party president with no expectation of winning the vote. But the veto was successfully overridden in five of them, and the sole failure, a November 1991 override of a labor appropriations bill (276–156), was a measure advocated for by Speaker Foley in bipartisan terms (*Congressional Record,* 19 November 1991, 32863). For more on how presidential vetoes can be used by Congress to send signals to the public, see Groseclose and McCarty 2001.

12. Fixed effects were not used in these regressions because a number of variable coefficients were indeterminate in the results. For divided parties, including fixed effects (controlling for congresses) resulted in similar results as in table 7.1, except that veto overrides were not statistically significant. For one-sided votes (controlling for congresses or Speakers), House matters, veto overrides, and presidential requests remained statistically significant. Doing so for unified parties and close votes (controlling for Congresses or Speakers) generally resulted in no statistical significance for any of the predictors.

13. Another way of describing this shift is that the expectation to assist the whole House or the institutional presidency is not institutionalized. The institutionalization of certain behaviors tends to occur when the behaviors are anticipated by others, and sanctions will follow if they do not occur (Parsons 1951, 40). For an overview of how role theorists explain shifts in individuals' roles and duties, see Turner 1990.

14. The amount of conflict on the floor specifically may also matter. Increased floor fights after the 1820s required a strong parliamentarian to manage House proceedings, encouraging Speakers to abandon using the floor to, for instance, deliver speeches (Strahan, Gunning, and Vining 2006, 65–66). A decline in that conflict later in the nineteenth and early twentieth centuries may have contributed to the reverse outcome.

15. Some cases start as bipartisan in nature but lose support of the Speaker's congressional party. For example, Foley's push for bipartisan budget negotiations with President Bush in 1990 may have reflected House Democrats' concerns with failure to reduce the deficit, but by the time the agreement came up for a floor vote, it was opposed by a majority of the party (see chapter 2). Similarly, the 1985 and 1987 budget summits may have stemmed from congressional Democrats' general desire to reach a budgetary agreement with the White House, but the compromise proposals that resulted from the summits were not greeted warmheartedly by the party.

16. The same deference to Pepper that O'Neill demonstrated in his 1983 speech on Social Security may also help explain Speaker Wright's decision to allow a floor vote on a major health care bill in 1988 (chapter 5, table 5.1). In another case, Speaker Albert cited committee deference in his 1974 floor speech on foreign aid to Turkey. Lobbying from the White House, however, may have been at least as important to Albert's decision calculus. See chapter 2.

17. The Albert committee reform case from chapter 5 could also be thought of as satisfying this goal, but Albert's internal power status was probably secondary in concern to his bigger interest in the overall operation of the House.

18. This goal of reselection to leadership has probably become more important to majority leaders (as it has with Speakers), since some of the same factors contributing to increased partisanship in the House—the presence of younger, more ideological, and ambitious legislators, for example—are present in the Senate too (Sinclair 2001).

19. One political scientist has suggested that this role-fulfillment goal may even be more salient for Senate majority leaders than for Speakers because majority leaders are more conspicuous, though Speakers have also become more prominent in recent decades (Truman 1959, 306n30). For a more skeptical view of the argument that a same-party president has significant influence over the Senate majority leader, see White 1957, 98.

20. Byrd's explanation for permitting the vote, that Senate rules could not prevent him from allowing a senator to call for a vote on the pay raise, also indicates (if true) that the majority leader's limited ability to control the agenda can hinder him in exerting influence on behalf of multiple leadership-related goals (Barry 1989, 114).

APPENDIX A. SOURCES AND USE OF DATA

1. Citations in the *Congressional Record* index under the heading "Speaker of the House" were primarily instances in which the Speaker addressed the House from the chair in a nonadvocacy (i.e., judicial) manner.

2. This latter scenario rarely occurred: Speakers almost always spoke on the floor once per bill, though they sometimes advocated outcomes for several different votes. I also distinguished between the House and conference versions of a bill, since they were usually passed by separate votes and probably also differ in content.

3. In virtually all cases, Speakers' statements appeared to have occurred on the floor during debate rather than being added later, though they may have subsequently been amended or altered. In one case, the Speaker did imply that at least some of his remarks were not delivered on the House floor. On 23 May 1952, Speaker Rayburn prefaced his lengthy (two-plus-page) printed floor statement by saying, "I shall not ask the indulgence of the House to listen to all that I have committed to paper, but I will put it in the Record" (*Congressional Record,* 23 May 1953, 5885).

4. Seven other sources were examined but had no relevant references to Speakers: John Morton Blum, *V Was for Victory* (1976); Russell Buchanan, *The United States and World War II* (1964); George Galloway, *Congress at the Crossroads* (1946); Eric Goldman, *The Crucial Decade—and After* (1973); Allen Matusow, *The Unravelling of America* (1984); Michael Schaller, *Reckoning with Reagan* (1992); and Barbara Sinclair, "Congressional Leadership," chapter 7 in *Leading Congress: New Styles, New Strategies,* ed. John J. Kornacki.

5. Unlike other works using literature sweeps (Mayhew 2000; Schickler 2001), I do not discard citations from just one source. References to leadership activities tend to be relatively rare, and many cases were mentioned by only one or two distinct sources.

6. Cases that involved leadership on or near the House floor were counted if they (1) involved legislation and/or (2) involved internal institutional change. Because floor advocacy is analyzed more thoroughly in chapter 2, and (as I note in that chapter) not all cases of floor advocacy may be attempts to alter legislative outcomes, I only included cases from the sweeps that referenced just floor advocacy if the source at least suggested that the Speaker's intent, if not effect, was to shape legislative outcomes.

7. I excluded one case in chapter 3 and three in chapter 4 that were captured in the sweeps but whose existence could not be supported by secondary evidence.

Bibliography

Abel, Elie. 1955. "President to Set U.S. Defense Area in Formosa Policy." *New York Times,* 23 January.

Abraham, Yvonne. 2000. "Gore vs. Bush: The Last Debate." *Boston Globe,* 18 October.

Adams, Rebecca. 1999. "Clinton's Medicare Drug Subsidy Plan Is Criticized for Scope and Cost." *Congressional Quarterly Weekly Report,* 3 July, 1612.

Adams, Rebecca (with Mary Agnes Carey). 2003. "Compromise Will Come Hard in Medicare-Overhaul Conference." *Congressional Quarterly Weekly Report,* 28 June, 1611–17.

Albert, Carl. 1976. *The Duties of the Speaker.* U.S. House of Representatives, Doc. 94–582.

Albert, Carl (with Danney Goble). 1990. *Little Giant: The Life and Times of Speaker Carl Albert.* Norman: University of Oklahoma Press.

Albright, Robert C. 1949a. "Six Truman Men Elected to Ways, Means Committee; Rayburn Is Speaker." *Washington Post,* 2 January.

———. 1949b. "Truman Forces Win Significant Opening Battle." *Washington Post,* 4 January.

Aldrich, John H., and David W. Rohde. 2001. "The Logic of Conditional Party Government: Revisiting the Electoral Connection." Chapter 12 in Lawrence D. Dodd and Bruce I. Oppenheimer, eds., *Congress Reconsidered,* 7th ed. Washington, DC: Congressional Quarterly Press.

Allen, Jonathan. 2004. "In Abandoning Vote on Overhaul Bill, Hastert Stresses Keeping Caucus Happy." *Congressional Quarterly Weekly Report,* 27 November.

Allen, Jonathan, and Adam Graham-Silverman. 2003. "Hour by Hour, Vote by Vote, GOP Breaks Tense Tie." *Congressional Quarterly Weekly Report,* 28 June.

Allen, Mike, and Dana Milbank. 2002. "President's Politics of Pragmatism Helped Undermine GOP Opposition." *Washington Post,* 15 February.

Alvarez, Lizette, and Eric Schmitt. 2000. "Disarming Leader at Battle on the Hill." *New York Times,* 9 October.

Ambrose, Stephen E. 1984. *Eisenhower: The President.* New York: Simon and Schuster.

Apple, R. W., Jr. 1995. "Tax-Cutters Finish First." *New York Times,* 6 April.

Arnold, R. Douglas. 1990. *The Logic of Congressional Action.* New Haven: Yale University Press.

Arnson, Cynthia J. 1989. *Crossroads: Congress, the President, and Central America, 1976–1993.* New York: Pantheon Books.

Arsu, Sebnem, and Brian Knowlton. 2007. "Planned House Vote on Armenian Massacre Angers Turks." *New York Times,* 30 March.

Babington, Charles. 2006. "Senate GOP Fears Frist's Ambitions Split Party." *Washington Post,* 30 March.

Barber, James David. 1972. *Presidential Character: Predicting Performance in the White House.* Englewood Cliffs, NJ: Prentice-Hall.

Barnes, James A. 1967 [1931]. *John G. Carlisle, Financial Statesman.* Gloucester, MA: Peter Smith.

Barone, Michael. 1990. *Our Country: The Shaping of America from Roosevelt to Reagan.* New York: Free Press.

Barry, John M. 1989. *The Ambition and the Power: Jim Wright and the Will of the House.* New York: Viking.

Balz, Dan, and John F. Harris. 2001. "For Bush, Losing the Initiative on Patient's Rights." *Washington Post,* 23 July.

Bauer, Raymond A., Ithiel de Sola Pool, and Lewis Anthony Dexter. 1963. *American Business and Public Policy: The Politics of Foreign Trade.* New York: Atherton Press.

Baumgartner, Frank, and Bryan Jones. 2007. "List of Topic and Subtopic Codes." Policy Agendas Project, retrieved 1 September 2003 from http://www.policyagendas.org/Codebooks/topicindex.html.

Belair, Felix, Jr. 1950. "$3,102,450,000 Aid Is Voted By House: Irish Clause Out." *New York Times,* 1 April.

Berinsky, Adam J. 2004. "American Public Opinion and World War II: A Research Agenda and Some Preliminary Findings." Working Paper, Massachusetts Institute of Technology.

Berke, Richard L., and Alison Mitchell. 2002. "White House Is Backing Foes of Finance Bill." *New York Times,* 12 February.

Berman, Daniel M. 1964. *In Congress Assembled: The Legislative Process in the National Government.* New York: Macmillan.

Biddle, Bruce J. 1979. *Role Theory: Expectations, Identities, and Behaviors.* New York: Academic Press.

Biggs, Jeffrey R., and Thomas S. Foley. 1999. *Honor in the House: Speaker Tom Foley.* Pullman: Washington State University Press.

Binder, Sarah A. 1997. *Minority Rights, Majority Rule: Partisanship and the Development of Congress.* New York: Cambridge University Press.

Birnbaum, Jeffrey H., and Alan S. Murray. 1987. *Showdown at Gucci Gulch: Lawmakers, Lobbyists, and the Unlikely Triumph of Tax Reform.* New York: Vintage Books.

Blair, William M. 1962a. "GOP Challenged by Kennedy to Back Farm Bill in House." *New York Times,* 15 June.

———. 1962b. "Freeman Spurs Farm Bill Fight." *New York Times,* 19 September.

Bolling, Richard. 1964. *House Out of Order.* New York: E. P. Dutton.

———. 1968. *Power in the House: A History of the Leadership of the House of Representatives.* New York: E. P. Dutton.

Boyd, Gerald M. 1986. "President Turns to the Senate in Fight for Bill." *New York Times,* 21 March.

Boyer, Dave. 1999. "Compromise Persuaded GOP Centrists to Support Tax Cut." *Washington Times,* 23 July.

Broder, David S. 1968. "Congressional Reorganization Is Test of Chicago Warning." *Washington Post,* 3 September.

———. 1983. "Numbers and Discipline Contribute to Major Victory." *Washington Post,* 24 March.

———. 2003. "Time Was GOP's Ally on the Vote." *Washington Post,* 23 November, A1.

. 2006. "Immigration Deal? Don't Bet on It." *Washington Post,* 28 May.

Bruni, Frank. 2000. "Bush Pushes Health Plan to Attract Older Voters." *New York Times,* 12 September.

Buchanan, Patrick J. 1986. "The Contras Need Our Help." *Washington Post,* 5 March.

Burden, Barry C. 2007. *Personal Roots of Representation.* Princeton: Princeton University Press.

Burden, Barry C., and Tammy M. Frisby. 2004. "Preferences, Partisanship, and Whip Activity in the House of Representatives." *Legislative Studies Quarterly* 29, 569-90.

Burger, Timothy J. 1999. "Hastert Can't Cut It, Some Republicans Say." *New York Daily News,* 7 May.

Burns, James MacGregor. 1963. *The Deadlock of Democracy: Four-Party Politics in America.* Englewood Cliffs, NJ: Prentice-Hall.

———. 1978. *Leadership.* New York: Harper and Row.

Butterfield, Samuel Hale. 2004. *U.S. Development Aid—An Historic First: Achievements and Failures in the Twentieth Century.* Westport, CT: Praeger.

Byrd, Robert C. 1994. *The Senate, 1789–1989.* Vol. 3. Washington, DC: Government Printing Office.

Carey, Mary Agnes. 2000. "GOP Drug Plan Prevails." *Congressional Quarterly Weekly Report,* 1 July.

———. 2002. "GOP Bets on Private Insurers with Medicare Drug Bill." *Congressional Quarterly Weekly Report,* 29 June.

Caro, Robert A. 2002. *The Years of Lyndon Johnson: Master of the Senate.* New York: Alfred A. Knopf.

Carpenter, Daniel P. 2001. *The Forging of Bureaucratic Autonomy: Reputations, Networks, and Policy Innovation in Executive Agencies, 1862–1928.* Princeton: Princeton University Press.

Carper, Edith T. 1962. "Lobbying and Natural Gas Bill." Inter-University Case Program, Inc. #72. Alabama: University of Alabama Press.

Central Intelligence Agency. 2009. "Serbia: Introduction." *The World Factbook.* https://www.cia.gov/library/publications/the-world-factbook/geos/rb.html#Intro (accessed 28 January).

Champagne, Anthony. 1984. *Congressman Sam Rayburn: A Bio-Bibliography.* New Brunswick, NJ: Rutgers University Press.

Cheever, Daniel S., and H. Field Haviland, Jr. 1952. *American Foreign Policy and the Separation of Powers.* Cambridge: Harvard University Press.

Chiu, Chang-Wei. 1928. *The Speaker of the House of Representatives since 1896.* New York: Columbia University Press.

Clark, Albert. 1950. "Truman Placated Big City Areas, but He Now Risks Wrath of Aides in Congress Who Believed He'd Sign It." *Wall Street Journal,* 17 April.

Cloud, David S. 1993. "NAFTA Boosters Win in Court but Lose with Gephardt." *Congressional Quarterly Weekly Report,* 25 September, 2532.

———. 1995a. "GOP's Balancing Act Gets Tricky as Budget Amendment Sinks." *Congressional Quarterly Weekly Report,* 4 March.

———. 1995b. "Hunt Club Ahead of the Game in Gaining Power on Hill." *Congressional Quarterly Weekly Report,* 18 November.

———. 1995c. "Sen. Dole's Dual Challenge and Defining Moment." *Congressional Quarterly Weekly Report,* 25 November.

Clymer, Adam. 1996. "Republicans Shift Strategy in Bid to Avoid Welfare Bill Veto." *New York Times,* 12 July.

Cochran, John. 2003. "Frist Sheds Low-Key Style for High-Octane Finish." *Congressional Quarterly Weekly Report,* 15 November.

Cochrane, James L. 1981. "Carter Energy Policy and the Ninety-fifth Congress." Chapter 8 in Craufurd D. Goodwin, ed., *Energy Policy in Perspective: Today's Problems, Yesterday's Solutions.* Washington, DC: Brookings Institution.

Cochrane, Willard W., and Mary E. Ryan. 1976. *American Farm Policy, 1948–1973.* Minneapolis: University of Minnesota Press.

Cohen, Richard E. 1994. *Changing Course in Washington: Clinton and the New Congress.* New York: Macmillan College Publishing.

Collie, Melissa P. 1988. "Universalism and the Parties in the U.S. House of Representatives, 1921–80." *American Journal of Political Science* 32, 865–83.

Committee on Standards of Official Conduct. 2004. "Investigation of Certain Allegations Related to Voting on the Medicare Prescription Drug, Improvement, and Modernization Act of 2003." U.S. House of Representatives, Report No. 108–722.

"Congress: Close, but No Cigar, The" 1962. *Newsweek,* 19 March, 33–34.

Congressional Quarterly. 1976. *Origins and Development of Congress.* Washington, DC: Congressional Quarterly Inc.

Congressional Quarterly Almanac. Various dates. Washington, DC: Congressional Quarterly Press.

Congressional Quarterly. 1976. *Congress and the Nation.* Washington, DC: Congressional Quarterly Press.

"Congressional War Critics Threaten New Attack." 1969. *New York Times,* 1 November.

Conley, Richard S., and Richard M. Yon. 2007. "The 'Hidden Hand' and White House Roll-Call Predictions: Legislative Liaison in the Eisenhower White House, 83d–84th Congresses." *Presidential Studies Quarterly* 37, 291–311.

Connelly, Joel, and Christopher Hansen. 1993. "Support for NAFTA Is Scarce within State's Delegation." *Seattle Post-Intelligencer,* 13 September.

Connelly, William F., Jr., and John J. Pitney, Jr. 1994. *Congress' Permanent Minority? Republicans in the U.S. House.* Lanham, MD: Rowman and Littlefield.

———. 1999. "The House Republicans: Lessons for Political Science." Chapter 9 in Nicol C. Rae and Colton C. Campbell, eds., *New Majority or Old Minority? The Impact of Republicans on Congress.* Lanham, MD: Rowman and Littlefield.

Contract with America. 1994. Accessed at http://www.house.gov/house/Contract/CONTRACT.html.

Cooper, Joseph, and David W. Brady. 1981. "Institutional Context and Leadership Style: The House from Cannon to Rayburn." *American Political Science Review* 75, 411–25.

Corwin, Edward S. 1940. *The President: Office and Powers.* New York: NYU Press.

Cowan, Edward. 1983a. "Democrats Offer Budget That Cuts Military Growth." *New York Times,* 16 March.

———. 1983b. "Democratic Budget Is Adopted by House, 229–196." *Washington Post,* 24 March.

———. 1983c. "Senate Approves 1984 Budget Plan with Big Tax Rise." *New York Times,* 20 May.

Cox, Gary, and Mathew D. McCubbins. 1993. *Legislative Leviathan: Party Government in the House.* Berkeley: University of California.

———. 2005. *Setting the Agenda: Responsible Party Government in the U.S. House of Representatives.* New York: Cambridge University Press.

Critchlow, Donald T. 2004. "When Republicans Become Revolutionaries: Conservatives in Congress." Chapter 40 in Julian E. Zelizer, ed., *The American Congress: The Building of Democracy.* Boston: Houghton Mifflin.

Cummings, Milton C., Jr., and Robert L. Peabody. 1969. "The Decision to Enlarge the Committee on Rules: An Analysis of the 1961 Vote." Chapter 11 in Robert L. Peabody and Nelson W. Polsby, eds., *New Perspectives on the House of Representatives,* 2nd ed. Chicago: Rand McNally.

Davenport, Coral. 2007. "A Battle of House Titans, Reignited." *Congressional Quarterly Weekly Report,* 18 June.

Davidson, Roger H. 1969. *The Role of the Congressman.* New York: Pegasus.

———. 1972. *The Politics of Comprehensive Manpower Legislation.* Baltimore: Johns Hopkins University Press.

Davidson, Roger H., Susan Webb Hammond, and Raymond W. Smock, eds. 1998. *Masters of the House: Congressional Leadership over Two Centuries.* Boulder: Westview Press.

Davidson, Roger H., and Walter J. Oleszek. 1977. *Congress against Itself.* Bloomington: Indiana University Press.

Davis, Susan. 2007. "Pelosi Brings End to 'Hastert Rule.'" *Roll Call,* 29 May.

Dealey, Sam. 1999. "House Leaders Defer to Clinton on Kosovo Plan." *The Hill,* 26 May.

Deering, Christopher J. 1999. "Learning to Legislate: Committees in the Republican Congress." Chapter 5 in Nicol C. Rae and Colton C. Campbell, eds., *New Majority or Old Minority? The Impact of Republicans on Congress.* Lanham, MD: Rowman and Littlefield.

Dennis, Steven T. 2007. "An Evolving Relationship: With Panel Chairmen, Pelosi Picks Her Battles." *Roll Call,* 10 September.

Destler, I. M. 2001. "Congress and Foreign Policy at Century's End: Requiem on Cooperation?" Chapter 14 in in Lawrence C. Dodd and Bruce I. Oppenheimer, eds., *Congress Reconsidered,* 7th ed. Washington, DC: Congressional Quarterly Press.

Dewar, Helen. 1981a. "Fresh Momentum Given to Reagan's Austerity Budget." *Washington Post,* 28 April.

———. 1981b. "Democrats Try New Bait for Budget Votes." *Washington Post,* 29 April.

———. 1981c. "House Opens Budget Debate; Neither Side Sure It Can Win." *Washington Post,* 1 May.

———. 1981d. "Reagan Woos Budget Waverers; Democrats Bewail Favors Game." *Washington Post,* 2 May.

——— 1982. "Reagan Budget, Three Others Rejected." *Washington Post,* 28 May.

———. 1983. "Budget Panel, on Party Line, Defies Reagan." *Washington Post,* 18 March.

Dewar, Helen, and Juliet Eilperin. 1999. "Hill GOP Leaders Take Cautious Course on Kosovo." *Washington Post,* 28 April.

———. 2001. "Campaign Reform Bill Stalls." *Washington Post,* 13 July.

Dewar, Helen, and Amy Goldstein. 2003. "Medicare Expansion Reaches Last Hurdle." *Washington Post,* 28 June.

Dewar, Helen, and Richard L. Lyons. 1981. "Reagan Budget-Cut Plan Jolted as Panel Democrats Hold Firm." *Washington Post,* 8 April.

Dexter, Lewis Anthony. 1977. "The Representative and His District." Chapter 1 in Robert L. Peabody and Nelson W. Polsby, eds., *New Perspectives on the House of Representatives.* 3rd ed. Chicago: Rand McNally.

Dodd, Lawrence C. 1977. "Congress and the Quest for Power." From Lawrence C. Dodd and Bruce I. Oppenheimer, eds., *Congress Reconsidered,* 1st ed. New York: Praeger, 269–307.

Dodd, Lawrence C., and Bruce I. Oppenheimer, eds. 1993. *Congress Reconsidered,* 5th ed. Washington, DC: Congressional Quarterly Press.

———. 2001. *Congress Reconsidered,* 7th ed. Washington, DC: Congressional Quarterly Press.

Dorough, C. Dwight. 1962. *Mr. Sam.* New York: Random House.

Dubose, Lou, and Jan Reid. 2004. *The Hammer: Tom DeLay, God, Money, and the Rise of the Republican Congress.* New York: Public Affairs.

Drew, Elizabeth. 1994. *On the Edge: The Clinton Presidency.* New York: Simon and Schuster.

———. 1997. *Whatever it Takes: The Real Struggle for Political Power in America.* New York: Viking Press.

Drinkard, Jim. 1999. "Rebellious Republicans Call for Reform." *USA Today,* 27 May.

Drury, Allen. 1955a. "Tariff Bill Held Peril to New York." *New York Times,* 5 February.

———. 1955b. "Defections Mark Tax Cut Dispute." *New York Times,* 25 February.

———. 1955c. "$20 Tax Cut Wins Close House Vote; Senators Hostile." *New York Times,* 26 February.

Duscha, Julius. 1962. "Farm Bill Goes through House in 202–197 Vote." *Washington Post,* 21 September.

Dwyre, Diana, and Victoria A. Farrar-Myers. 2001. *Legislative Labyrinth: Congress and Campaign Finance Reform.* Washington, DC: Congressional Quarterly Press.

Edinger, Lewis J. 1964. "Political Science and Political Biography: Reflections on the Study of Leadership (I)." *Journal of Politics* 26, 423–39.

Egan, Charles E. 1955. "Democrats Plan Income Tax Slash of $20 per Person." *New York Times,* 20 February.

Eilperin, Juliet. 1999. "Democrats Blame Kosovo Resolution Failure on Hastert's Silence." *Washington Post,* 30 April.

———. 2000. "For House GOP, a New Prescription." *Washington Post,* 26 April.

———. 2002. "Hastert Pledges to Fight Campaign Finance Bill." *Washington Post,* 7 February.

Eilperin, Juliet, and William Claiborne. 1999. "Troop Deployment Narrowly Approved." *Washington Post,* 12 March.

Eilperin, Juliet, and Helen Dewar. 2002. "Campaign Bill Heads for a Vote in House." *Washington Post,* 25 January.

Eilperin, Juliet, and Amy Goldstein. 1999. "Bypassing Committees, Hastert Will Bring a Managed-Care Bill to Floor." *Washington Post,* 28 July.

Eilperin, Juliet, and Eric Pianin. 1999. "House GOP to Seek Bigger Tax Cut." *Washington Post,* 1 July.

Espo, David. 1996. "GOP Lawmakers Declare Independence from Dole." Associated Press, 12 July.

Evans, C. Lawrence. 2001. "Committees, Leaders, and Message Politics." Chapter 10 in Lawrence C. Dodd and Bruce I. Oppenheimer, eds., *Congress Reconsidered.* 7th ed. Washington, DC: Congressional Quarterly Press.

———. 2007. "The House Whip System and Party Theories of Congress." Research project (National Science Foundation).

Evans, C. Lawrence, and Walter J. Oleszek 1997. *Congress under Fire: Reform Politics and the Republican Majority.* Boston: Houghton Mifflin.

———. 1999a. "The Strategic Context of Congressional Party Leadership." *Congress and the Presidency* 26, 1–20.

———. 1999b. "Procedural Features of House Republican Rule." Chapter 6 in Nicol C. Rae and Colton C. Campbell, eds., *New Majority or Old Minority? The Impact of Republicans on Congress.* Lanham, MD: Rowman and Littlefield.

Evans, C. Lawrence, Douglas D. Roscoe, Timothy M. Deering, and Michael D. O'Neill. 2003. "The House Whip Process and Party Theories of Congress: An Exploration." Paper presented at the annual meeting of the American Political Science Association, Philadelphia.

Evans, Rowland, and Robert Novak. 1968. "Reform-Minded Young GOP Group Plotting Massive House 'Filibuster.'" *Washington Post,* 6 September.

———. 1972. "The Doves Jump the Gun." *New York Times,* 26 April.

———. 1982. "Reagan: Persuading Democrats . . ." *Washington Post,* 23 August.

―――. 1986. "A Divided House." *Washington Post,* 24 March.

Farnsworth, Clyde H. 1990. "Assailing Beijing, House Votes a Rise in China's Tariffs." *New York Times,* 19 October.

Farrar-Myers, Victoria A., and Diana Dwyre. 2008. *Limits and Loopholes: The Quest for Money, Free Speech, and Fair Elections.* Washington, DC: Congressional Quarterly Press.

Farrell, John A. 2001. *Tip O'Neill and the Democratic Century.* Boston: Little, Brown.

Fenno, Richard F., Jr. 1973a. *Congressmen in Committees.* Boston: Little, Brown.

―――. 1973b. "The Internal Distribution of Influence: The House." Chapter 3 in David B. Truman, ed., *The Congress and America's Future,* 2nd ed. Englewood Cliffs, NJ: Prentice-Hall.

―――. 1997. *Learning to Govern: An Institutional View of the 104th Congress.* Washington, DC: Brookings Institution Press.

Finney, John W. 1967. "McCormack Scores Foes of War Policy." *New York Times,* 12 October.

―――. 1969a. "House Cuts Off War Protest after Nearly 4 Hours." *New York Times,* 15 October.

―――. 1969b. "Democrats in Congress Block GOP Resolution on the Hanoi Moratorium Letter." *New York Times,* 16 October.

―――. 1969c. "House Leaders Push for Vote Next Week on Pro-Nixon Vietnam Resolution; Senate War Hearing Delayed." *New York Times,* 6 November.

―――. 1969d. "Backers of Nixon Win a House Test." *New York Times,* 2 December.

―――. 1969e. "House, 333 to 55, Backs Nixon Bid for 'Just Peace.'" *New York Times* 3 December.

Fiorina, Morris P. 2001. "*Keystone* Reconsidered." Chapter 8 in Lawrence C. Dodd and Bruce I. Oppenheimer eds., *Congress Reconsidered,* 7th ed. Washington, DC: Congressional Quarterly Press.

Fisher, Louis. 1995. *Presidential War Power.* Lawrence: University Press of Kansas.

Foley, Thomas S. 2004. Interview with Jim Lehrer. *The NewsHour with Jim Lehrer.* PBS. December 6.

Follett, Mary Parker. 1896. *The Speaker of the House of Representatives.* New York: Longmans, Green.

Franzen, Jonathan. 2003. "The Listener." *New Yorker,* 6 October, 85–99.

"Freeman Declares Farm Bill in Peril." 1962. *New York Times,* 13 June.

Froman, Lewis A., Jr., and Randall B. Ripley. 1965. "Conditions for Party Leadership: The Case of the House Democrats." *American Political Science Review* 59, 52–63.

Fuller, Hubert Bruce. 1909. *The Speakers of the House.* Boston: Little, Brown.

Galloway, George B. 1955. *The Legislative Process in Congress.* New York: Thomas Y. Crowell.

Galloway, George B. (with Sidney Wise). 1976. *History of the House of Representatives.* 2nd ed. New York: Thomas Y. Crowell.

Gamm, Gerald, and Steven S. Smith. 2000. "Last among Equals: The Senate's Presiding Officer." Chapter 6 in Burdett A. Loomis, ed., *Esteemed Colleagues: Civility and Deliberation in the U.S. Senate."* Washington, DC: Brookings Institution Press.

Gerth, Hans, and C. Wright Mills. 1964. *Character and Social Structure: The Psychology of Social Institutions.* New York: Harcourt, Brace and World.

Gingrich, Newt. 1995. *To Renew America.* New York: Harper-Collins.

Goldstein, Amy, and Helen Dewar. 1999. "House Vote on Patients' Rights Set." *Washington Post,* 18 September.

Goldstein, Amy, and Juliet Eilperin. 2001. "Bush Lobbies Hill On Patient Rights; President Seeks Compromise in House." *Washington Post,* 27 July.

Goldstein, Amy, and Dana Milbank. 2001. "Democrats, Pharmacists Criticize Bush Drug Proposal." *Washington Post,* 12 July.

Goodwin, George, Jr. 1970. *The Little Legislatures.* Amherst: University of Massachusetts Press.

Gosnell, Harold F. 1980. *Truman's Crises: A Political Biography of Harry S. Truman.* Westport, CT: Greenwood Press.

Gould, Lewis L. 2003. *The Modern American Presidency.* Lawrence: University Press of Kansas.

Gould, Lewis L., and Nancy Beck Young. 1998. "The Speaker and the Presidents: Sam Rayburn, the White House, and the Legislative Process, 1941–1961." Chapter 7 in Rogers H. Davidson, Susan Webb Hammond, and Raymond W. Smock, eds. *Masters of the House: Congressional Leadership over Two Centuries.* Boulder: Westview Press.

Grantham, Dewey W. 1976. *The United States since 1945: The Ordeal of Power.* New York: McGraw-Hill.

———. 1987. *Recent America: The United States Since 1945.* Arlington Heights, IL: Harlan Davidson.

Gray, Jerry. 1995a. "For GOP Freshmen in the House, Political Reality Arrives All Too Quickly." *New York Times,* 29 January.

———. 1995b. "GOP Bloc Seeks Delay in Tax Cuts." *New York Times,* 25 March.

Grayson, George W. 1995. *The North American Free Trade Agreement: Regional Community and the New World Order.* Lanham, MD: University Press of America.

Green, Matthew N. 2002. "Institutional Change, Party Discipline, and the House Democratic Caucus, 1911–19." *Legislative Studies Quarterly* 27, 601–33.

———. 2007. "Presidents and Personal Goals: The Speaker of the House as Nonmajoritarian Leader." *Congress and the Presidency* 34 (2), 1–22.

Greenstein, Fred I. 2000. *The Presidential Difference: Leadership Style from FDR to Clinton.* New York: Free Press.

Groseclose, Tim, and David C. King. 2001. "Committee Theories Reconsidered." Chapter 9 in Lawrence C. Dodd and Bruce I. Oppenheimer, eds., *Congress Reconsidered.* 7th ed. Washington, DC: Congressional Quarterly Press.

Groseclose, Tim, and Nolan McCarty. 2001. "The Politics of Blame: Bargaining before an Audience." *American Journal of Political Science* 45, 100–19.

Groseclose, Tim, and James M. Snyder, Jr. 1996. "Buying Supermajorities." *American Political Science Review* 90, 303–15.

Gugliotta, Guy, and Juliet Eilperin. 1999a. "Speaker Determined to Stay Low-Key." *Washington Post,* 18 April.

———. 1999b. "House Backs Balkan Funds." *Washington Post,* 7 May.

Hadwiger, Don F., and Ross B. Talbot. 1965. *Pressures and Protests: The Kennedy Farm Program and the Wheat Referendum of 1963.* San Francisco: Chandler Publishing.

Hansen, John Mark. 1991. *Gaining Access: Congress and the Farm Lobby, 1919–81.* Chicago: University of Chicago Press.

Hardeman, D. B., and Donald C. Bacon. 1987. *Rayburn: A Biography.* Austin: Texas Monthly Press.

Harris, Douglas B. 1998. "The Rise of the Public Speakership." *Political Science Quarterly* 113, 193–212.

Hart, John. 1995. *The Presidential Branch: From Washington to Clinton.* 2nd ed. Chatham, NJ: Chatham House.

Hastert, Dennis. 2001. "Putting Patients First." *Boston Globe,* 4 August.

———. 2003. "Reflections on the Role of the Speaker in the Modern Day House of Representatives." Speech delivered at the Cannon Centenary Conference, U.S. Congress, 12 November.

———. 2004. *Speaker: Lessons from Forty Years in Coaching and Politics.* Washington, DC: Regnery.

"Hastert Makes Appeal to Taxpayers' Pockets." 1999. *Boston Globe,* 12 August.

Hess, David. 1999. "Both Houses Pass GOP's Tax-Cut Plan." *Philadelphia Inquirer,* 6 August.

Hinds, Asher C. 1907. *Hinds' Precedents of the House of Representatives of the United States.* Washington, DC: Government Printing Office.

Hohler, Bob. 1999. "House's Quiet Speaker Forges a Reign by Committee." *Boston Globe,* 21 November.

"House Group Acts on Trade Treaty." 1955. *New York Times,* 10 February.

"House Passes Bill to Exempt from Control of FPC 'Independent' Natural Gas Producers." 1949. *New York Times,* 6 August.

Hulse, Carl. 2006. "House Leaders Demand Return of Seized Files." *New York Times,* 25 May.

———. 2007. "U.S. and Turkey Thwart Armenian Genocide Bill." *New York Times,* 26 October.

———. 2008. "For Speaker, Calculated Stimulus Steps." *New York Times,* 27 January.

James, Scott C. 2000. *Presidents, Parties, and the State: A Party System Perspective on Democratic Regulatory Choice, 1884–1936.* New York: Cambridge University Press.

Jim Wright Collection. Special Collections, Mary Couts Burnett Library, Texas Christian University. Fort Worth, TX.

Johnson, Donald Bruce, and Kirk H. Porter. 1973. *National Party Platforms, 1840–1972.* Urbana: University of Illinois Press.

Johnson, Glen. 2002. "Pivotal Moments United Coalition Despite Pressure." *Boston Globe,* 15 February.

John W. McCormack Papers. Special Collections, Boston University. Boston, MA.

Jones, Charles O. 1968. "Joseph G. Cannon and Howard W. Smith: An Essay on the Limits of Leadership in the House of Representatives." *Journal of Politics* 30, 617–46.

———. 1970. *The Minority Party in Congress.* Boston: Little, Brown.

———. 2005. *The Presidency in a Separated System.* 2nd ed. Washington, DC: Brookings Institution.

Josephy, Alvin M., Jr. 1979. *On the Hill: A History of the American Congress.* New York: Simon and Shuster.

Kaiser, Robert G. 1981. "House Budget Battle Reflects Rightward Shift of Center." *Washington Post,* 9 April.

Kaufman, Burton I. 1993. *The Presidency of James Earl Carter Jr.* Lawrence: University Press of Kansas.

Keegan, John. 1989. *The Second World War.* New York: Penguin Books.

Kernell, Samuel. 1997. *Going Public: New Strategies of Presidential Leadership.* 3rd ed. Washington, DC: Congressional Quarterly Press.

Kesselman, Mark. 1961. "A Note: Presidential Leadership in Congress on Foreign Policy." *Midwest Journal of Political Science* 5, 284–89.

Kiely, Kathy. 1999. "For Hastert, Tax Bill Quite a Workout." *USA Today,* 22 July.

Killian, Linda. 1998. *The Freshmen: What Happened to the Republican Revolution?* Boulder: Westview Press.

Kimball, Warren F. 1969. "'1776': Lend-Lease Gets a Number." *New England Quarterly* 42 (2), 260–67.

Kofmehl, Kenneth. 1964. "The Institutionalization of a Voting Bloc." *Western Political Quarterly* 17, 263.

Kornblut, Anne E. 1999. "Campaign Reform Awaits Day in House." *Boston Globe,* 25 February.

———. 2001. "Bush, McCain Meet on Finance Issue." *Boston Globe,* 25 January.

Kondracke, Morton. 1993. "Familiar Refrain on Foley: Get Tough." *Roll Call,* 20 September.

Koszczuk, Jackie. 1996. "For Embattled GOP Leadership, a Season of Discontent." *Congressional Quarterly Weekly Report,* 20 July.

Kraft, Joseph. 1974. "An Old Pol with a Touch of Class." *Washington Post,* 4 August.

Krauss, Clifford. 1990. "Democratic Leaders Divided on China Trade." *New York Times,* 9 October, A5.

———. 1993a. "House Democrats Rush to Extinguish Rebellion." *New York Times,* 19 May.

———. 1993b. "Undecided Feeling No Uncertain Heat." *New York Times,* 5 August.

Krehbiel, Keith. 2000. "Party Discipline and Measures of Partisanship." *American Journal of Political Science* 44, 212–27.

Krehbiel, Keith, and Alan Wiseman. 2001. "Joseph G. Cannon: Majoritarian from Illinois." *Legislative Studies Quarterly* 26, 357–89.

Kronholz, June, Sarah Lueck, and Greg Hitt. 2008. "'No' Votes Came from All Directions." *Wall Street Journal,* 30 September.

Lapham, Lewis J. 1988. *Party Leadership and the House Committee on Rules.* New York: Garland Publishing.

Lardner, George Jr. 2000. "Fact Check: On HMOs, a Reluctant Reformer." *Washington Post,* 17 February.

Lawrence, W. H. 1955. "President Scores $20 Tax Cut Move; Democrats Irate." *New York Times,* 24 February.

Lee, Jessica. 1999. "House Chooses Middle Ground in Balkans Votes." *USA Today,* 29 April.

LeoGrande, William M. 1998. *Our Own Backyard: The United States in Central America, 1977–1992.* Chapel Hill: University of North Carolina Press.

LeoGrande, William M., and Philip Brenner. 1993. "The House Divided: Ideological Polarization over Aid to the Nicaraguan 'Contras.'" *Legislative Studies Quarterly* 18, 105–36.

Light, Paul. 1985. *Artful Work: The Politics of Social Security Reform.* New York: Random House.

Lindsay, James M., and Randall B. Ripley. 1992. "Foreign and Defense Policy in Congress: A Research Agenda for the 1990s." *Legislative Studies Quarterly* 17, 417–449.

Linton, Ralph. 1936. *The Study of Man: An Introduction.* New York: D. Appleton–Century.

Loftus, Joseph A. 1949. "Wood's Draft of Labor Bill Dies in House." *New York Times,* 5 May.

"Look at Government's Top-Ranking Democrat, A." 1969. *U.S. News and World Report,* 8 September, 14–16.

Lyons, Richard L. 1967. "Scapegoats Raised on Reform Bill." *Washington Post,* 10 May.

———. 1977. "House Votes Down Gas Deregulation; Victory for Carter." *Washington Post,* 4 August.

MacArthur, John R. 2000. *The Selling of "Free Trade": NAFTA, Washington, and the Subversion of American Democracy.* New York: Hill and Wang.

MacNeil, Neil. 1963. *Forge of Democracy: The House of Representatives.* New York: David McKay.

Magid, Alvin. 1980. "'Role Theory,' Political Science, and African Studies." *World Politics* 32 (2), 311–30.

Maney, Patrick J. 1998. "Hale Boggs: The Southerner as National Democrat." Chapter 8 in Roger H. Davidson, Susan Webb Hammond, and Raymond W. Smock, eds. *Masters of the House: Congressional Leadership over Two Centuries.* Boulder: Westview Press.

Maslin-Wicks, Kimberly. 1998. "Two Types of Presidential Influence in Congress." *Presidential Studies Quarterly* 28, 108–26.

Matthews, Donald R. 1973 [1960]. *U.S. Senators and Their World.* New York: W. W. Norton.

Mayer, Frederick W. 1998. *Interpreting NAFTA: The Science and Art of Political Analysis.* New York: Columbia University Press.

Mayhew, David R. 1974. *Congress: The Electoral Connection.* New Haven: Yale University Press.

———. 1991. *Divided We Govern: Party Control, Lawmaking and Investigations, 1946–2002.* New Haven: Yale University Press.

———. 2000. *America's Congress: Actions in the Public Sphere, James Madison through Newt Gingrich.* New Haven: Yale University Press.

Maynard, Micheline. 2004. "United Airlines Is Turned Down in Bid for Loans." *New York Times,* 18 June.

McAdam, Doug, and Yang Su. 2002. "The War at Home: Antiwar Protests and Congressional Voting, 1965 to 1973." *American Sociological Review* 67, 696–721.

McCullough, David. 1992. *Truman.* New York: Simon and Schuster.

McQueen, Anjetta. 2001. "Norwood Strikes Deal with Bush." Associated Press Online, 3 August.

Mead, George H. 1934. *Mind, Self, and Society.* Chicago: University of Chicago Press.

Meller, Norman. 1960. "Legislative Behavior Research." *Western Political Quarterly* 13 (1), 131–53.

Merton, Robert K. 1968 [1957]. *Social Theory and Social Structure.* New York: Free Press.

Mervin, David. 1990. *Ronald Reagan and the American Presidency.* London: Longman.

Milbank, Dana. 2002. "Bush Is Quiet in Campaign Bill Fight." *Washington Post,* 10 February.

Milkis, Sidney M. 1993. *The President and the Parties: The Transformation of the American Party System since the New Deal.* New York: Oxford University Press.

Miroff, Bruce. 2004. "Leadership and American Political Development." Paper presented at "Political Action and Political Change: Agents, Entrepreneurs, and Leaders," a conference at Yale University, New Haven, CT.

Mitchell, Alison. 1999a. "Speaker Pressed to Expedite Vote on Campaign Finance." *New York Times,* 6 May.

———. 1999b. "A Speaker under Pressure Beseeches His Party's Members." *New York Times,* 22 July.

———. 1999c. "GOP Rebels Force a Delay on Health Vote." *New York Times,* 30 July.

———. 2002. "House GOP Proposes Rival to Campaign Finance Bill." *New York Times,* 13 February.

Moe, Terry M. 1987. "Interests, Institutions, and Positive Theory: The Politics of the NLRB." *Studies in American Political Development* 2, 236–99.

Mooney, Booth. 1964. *Mr. Speaker: Four Men Who Shaped the United States House of Representatives.* Chicago: Follett.

Morris, Brian. 1971. "Reflections on Role Analysis." *British Journal of Sociology* 22 (4), 395–409.

Morris, John D. 1954. "Democrats Take Tax Cut to Nation; Close Fight Seen." *New York Times,* 17 March.

———. 1962a. "Farm Bill Points Up Kennedy's Obstacles." *New York Times,* 24 June.

———. 1962b. "House Expecting Bitter Struggle on Rules Power." *New York Times,* 21 December.

"Mr. Truman's Blunder." 1949. *New York Times,* 29 April.

Nash, Nathaniel C. 1987. "Panel Says St. Germain Did Not Abuse Position." *New York Times* 16 April.

Nivola, Pietro S., and David W. Brady. 2006. *Red and Blue Nation? Characteristics and Causes of America's Polarized Politics.* Vol 1. Washington, DC: Brookings Institution Press.

"Oil Men Plan Finish Fight on Trade Act." 1954. *Washington Post,* 17 January.

Omang, Joanne, and Margaret Shapiro. 1985. "President Drops '85 Request for 'Contra' Arms." *Washington Post,* 19 April.

O'Neill, Tip (with William Novak). 1987. *Man of the House: The Life and Political Memoirs of Speaker Tip O'Neill.* New York: Random House.

Oreskes, Michael. 1989a. "House Plan to Assure a Raise: Prevent Floor Vote." *New York Times,* 7 January.

———. 1989b. "Foley Urges Raise for U.S. Judiciary and Top Officials." *New York Times,* 20 June.

Orfield, Gary. 1975. *Congressional Power: Congress and Social Change.* New York: Harcourt Brace Jovanovich.

Ornstein, Norman J. 1990. "Can Congress Be Led?" Chapter 1 in John J. Kornacki, ed., *Leading Congress: New Styles, New Strategies.* Washington, DC: Congressional Quarterly Inc., 13–25.

Palazzolo, Daniel J. 1992. *The Speaker and the Budget: Leadership in the Post-Reform House of Representatives*. Pittsburgh: University of Pittsburgh Press.

Parks, Daniel J. 2000. "House Sets a Costly Example for Senate's Supplemental." *Congressional Quarterly Weekly Report*, 1 April.

Parry, Robert. 1986. "Swing Votes Could Deliver Contra Aid." *Washington Post*, 21 March.

Parsons, Talcott. 1951. *Toward a General Theory of Action*. New York: Harper and Row.

Patashnik, Eric. 2004. "Congress and the Budget since 1974." Chapter 38 in Julian E. Zelizer, ed., *The American Congress: The Building of Democracy*. Boston: Houghton Mifflin.

Patterson, Samuel C. 1966. "Labor Lobbying and Labor Reform: The Passage of the Landrum-Griffin Act." Inter-University Case Program, Inc. #99. Indianapolis: Bobbs-Merrill.

Peabody, Robert L. 1963. "The Enlarged Rules Committee." Chapter 6 in Robert L. Peabody and Nelson W. Polsby, eds., *New Perspectives on the House of Representatives*. Chicago: Rand McNally.

———. 1976. *Leadership in Congress: Stability, Succession, and Change*. Boston: Little, Brown.

———. 1977. "Party Leadership Change in the United States House of Representatives." Chapter 13 in Robert L. Peabody and Nelson W. Polsby, eds., *New Perspectives on the House of Representatives*. 3rd ed. Chicago: Rand McNally.

Peabody, Robert L., and Nelson W. Polsby, eds. 1977. *New Perspectives on the House of Representatives*. 3rd ed. Chicago: Rand McNally.

Pear, Robert. 1996. "President Says Cuts Are Too Deep in Republican Welfare Plan." *New York Times*, 18 July.

———. 2001. "Bush Outlines His Principles for Protecting Patient Rights." *New York Times*, 8 February.

Peltzman, Sam. 1984. "Constituent Interests and Congressional Voting." *Journal of Law and Economics* 27, 181–210.

Peters, Ronald M., Jr. 1997. *The American Speakership: The Office in Historical Perspective*. Baltimore: Johns Hopkins University Press.

———. 1999. "Institutional Context and Leadership Style: The Case of Newt Gingrich." Chapter 3 in Nicol C. Rae and Colton C. Campbell, eds., *New Majority or Old Minority? The Impact of Republicans on Congress*. Lanham, MD: Rowman and Littlefield.

Phillips, Cabell. 1957. "Southern Forces Alter Strategy on Civil Rights." *New York Times*, 21 April, 167.

Pianin, Eric. 1995a. "House GOP Sticks with Tax Cut Plans, Despite Reagan-Era Memories." *Washington Post*, 2 April.

———. 1995b. "GOP Claims Accord on Tax Cut; House Leaders Persuade Moderates to Back Plan." *Congressional Quarterly Weekly Report*, 4 April.

———. 1995c. "Tax Cut Bill Passed by House, 246–188; $189 Billion Measure Caps 100-Day Dash." *Washington Post*, 6 April.

———. 1999a. "GOP Rally Celebrates Prospects for Tax Cut." *Washington Post*, 2 July.

———. 1999b. "Congressional Republicans Give Up on Huge Tax Cut This Year." *Washington Post*, 10 September.

———. 2000a. "Emergency Spending Bill Caught in GOP Whirlpool." *Washington Post*, 17 March.

———. 2000b. "Lawmakers Eye 'Emergency' Bill as a Vehicle for Pet Projects." *Washington Post,* 23 June.

Pianin, Eric, and Helen Dewar. 2000. "GOP, White House Clear Hurdle on Colombia Involvement." *Washington Post,* 28 June.

Pianin, Eric, and Karen DeYoung. 2000. "GOP Plans Funding Boost for Military, Drug War." *Washington Post,* 8 March.

Pianin, Eric, and Juliet Eilperin. 1999a. "Vote Delay Reflects Shaky House GOP." *Washington Post,* 28 May.

———. 1999b. "House GOP Moderate Offers Rival Tax Cut Plan." *Washington Post,* 20 July.

———. 1999c. "Hastert Pleads for GOP Unity on Taxes." *Washington Post,* 21 July.

Pierson, Paul. 2004. *Politics in Time: History, Institutions, and Social Analysis.* Princeton: Princeton University Press.

Pious, Richard M. 1979. *The American Presidency.* New York: Basic Books.

Pitkin, Hannah. 1967. *The Concept of Representation.* Berkeley: University of California Press.

Polsby, Nelson. 2004. *How Congress Evolves: Social Bases of Institutional Change.* New York: Oxford University Press.

Pomper, Gerald M. 1959. "Organized Labor in Politics: The Campaign to Revise the Taft-Hartley Act." Ph.D. diss.: Princeton University.

Pomper, Miles A. 1999a. "Congress Wants a Bigger Voice on Sending Troops to Kosovo." *Congressional Quarterly Weekly Report,* 27 February.

———. 1999b. "Members Rally Around Kosovo Mission Despite Misgivings About Strategy." *Congressional Quarterly Weekly Report,* 27 March.

———. 1999c. "Hastert Leads the Charge In Colombian Drug War." *Congressional Quarterly Weekly Report,* 11 September.

———. 1999d. "Colombian President's Aid Request Gets Favorable Response on Hill." *Congressional Quarterly Weekly Report,* 25 September.

———. 2000a. "Clinton's Billion-Dollar Proposal for Colombian Anti-Drug Aid Is a Good Beginning, Hastert Says." *Congressional Quarterly Weekly Report,* 15 January.

———. 2000b. "Clinton Seeks Extra $4.4 Billion to Fight Drugs, Keep Peace." *Congressional Quarterly Weekly Report,* 12 February.

Poole, Keith, and Howard Rosenthal. 1997. *Congress: A Political-Economic History of Roll Call Voting.* New York: Oxford University Press.

"Putting First Things First." 1967. *New York Times,* 21 August.

Rae, Nicol C., and Colton C. Campbell. 1999. "From Revolution to Evolution: Congress under Republican Control." Chapter 1 in Nicol C. Rae and Colton C. Campbell, eds., *New Majority or Old Minority? The Impact of Republicans on Congress.* Lanham, MD: Rowman and Littlefield.

Rae, Nicol C., and Colton C. Campbell, eds. 1999. *New Majority or Old Minority? The Impact of Republicans on Congress.* Lanham, MD: Rowman and Littlefield.

Rasky, Susan F. 1989a. "Fury over Lawmakers' Raise Finds an Outlet on the Radio." *New York Times,* 6 February.

———. 1989b. "Blow to Speaker." *New York Times,* 7 February.

———. 1989c. "House, Defying Threat of a Veto, Backs Increase in Minimum Wage." *New York Times,* 24 March.

———. 1989d. "Vote Likely on 33 Percent Raise for Congress." *New York Times,* 14 November.

"Rayburn Helps to Speed Kerr Bill to House." 1950. *Washington Post,* 31 March.

Reichard, Gary W. 1978. "Divisions and Dissent: Democrats and Foreign Policy, 1952–1956." *Political Science Quarterly* 93 (1), 51–72.

Remini, Robert V. 2006. *The House: The History of the House of Representatives.* New York: HarperCollins.

Renshon, Stanley A. 1996. *The Psychological Assessment of Presidential Candidates.* New York: New York University Press.

Reston, James. 1959. "Script for Congress." *New York Times,* 5 January.

Rhodes, Carl M. 1997. "Party Leadership in the U.S. Congress: The Role of a Leader's Reputation for Competence and Ideology." Paper presented at the annual meeting of the American Political Science Association, Atlanta.

Riddick, Floyd M. 1949. *The United States Congress: Organization and Procedure.* Manassas, VA: National Capital Publishers.

———. 1988. *Majority and Minority Leaders of the Senate.* Washington, DC: Government Printing Office.

Riker, William H. 1986. *The Art of Political Manipulation.* New Haven: Yale University Press.

Ripley, Randall B. 1964. "The Party Whip Organizations in the United States House of Representatives." *American Political Science Review,* 561–76.

———. 1967. *Party Leaders in the House of Representatives.* Washington, DC: Brookings Institution.

———. 1969. *Majority Party Leadership in Congress.* Boston: Little, Brown.

Roberts, Steven V. 1983. "Congress Adopts 1984 Budget Plan." *New York Times,* 24 June.

———. 1988. "The Foreign Policy Tussle." *New York Times,* 24 January.

Rohde, David W. 1991. *Parties and Leaders in the Postreform House.* Chicago: University of Chicago Press.

———. 2005. *Roll Call Voting Data for the United States House of Representatives, 1953–2004.* Compiled by the Political Institutions and Public Choice Program, Michigan State University, East Lansing, MI, 2004.

Rohde, David W., and Kenneth A. Shepsle. 1987. "Leaders and Followers in the House of Representatives: Reflections on Woodrow Wilson's *Congressional Government.*" *Congress and the Presidency* 14, 111–33.

Rosenbaum, David E. 1993. "Clinton and Allies Twist Arms in Bid for Budget Votes." *New York Times,* 27 May.

———. 2001. "How a Lawmaker Shifted Position on an Issue and Took a Majority with Him." *New York Times,* 3 August.

Rubin, Alissa J. 1995a. "Taxes: Unity Frays within House GOP over Family Tax Credit." *Congressional Quarterly Weekly Report,* 25 March.

———. 1995b. "Taxes: GOP Leaders Ready to Deal on Troubled Tax-Cuts Bill." *Congressional Quarterly Weekly Report,* 1 April.

———. 1995c. "Finishing the 'Contract' in Style, House Passes Tax-Cut Bill." *Congressional Quarterly Weekly Report,* 8 April.

Safire, William. 1981. "Tipper versus Gipper." *New York Times,* 11 May.

Salant, Jonathan D. 1995. "GOP Moderates Feeling Their Clout." *Congressional Quarterly Weekly Report,* 21 January.

Sam Rayburn Papers. Center for American History, University of Texas at Austin, Austin, TX.

Sanders, M. Elizabeth. 1981. *The Regulation of Natural Gas: Policy and Politics, 1938–1978.* Philadelphia: Temple University Press.

Sanders, Paul. 2001. "The Speaker and the Draft." *American History,* 42–46.

Schickler, Eric. 2000. "Institutional Change in the House of Representatives, 1867–1998: A Test of Partisan and Ideological Power Balance Models." *American Political Science Review* 94, 269–88.

———. 2001. *Disjointed Pluralism: Institutional Innovation and the Development of the U.S. Congress.* Princeton: Princeton University Press.

Searing, Donald D. 1994. *Westminster's World: Understanding Political Roles.* Cambridge: Harvard University Press.

Seelye, Katharine Q. 1996. "Dole Is Confronted on His View of Welfare." *New York Times,* 31 May.

Shannon, William V. 1971. "The Speaker's Plans." *New York Times,* 8 April.

Shapiro, Margaret. 1985. "House Votes Down 'Contra' Aid Plan." *Washington Post,* 25 April.

Shapiro, Margaret, and T. R. Reid. 1984. "House Rejects Rights Linkage." *Washington Post,* 11 May.

Shenon, Philip. 2001. "And in House, GOP Stalwart Will Fight a Finance Overhaul." *New York Times,* 30 March.

Shepsle, Kenneth A., and Mark S. Bonchek. 1997. *Analyzing Politics: Rationality, Behavior, and Institutions.* New York: W. W. Norton.

Sherwood, Robert E. 1948. *Roosevelt and Hopkins: An Intimate History.* New York: Harper and Brothers.

Shull, Steven A., and Lance T. LeLoup. 1981. "Reassessing the Reassessment: Comment on Sigelman's Note on the 'Two Presidencies' Thesis." *Journal of Politics* 43, 563–64.

Shull, Steven A., and James M. Vanderleeuw. 1987. "What Do Key Votes Measure?" *Legislative Studies Quarterly* 12, 573–82.

Sigel, Roberta S., and Wolfgang Pindur. 1973. "Role Congruence and Role Strain among Urban Legislators." *Social Science Quarterly* 54: 54–65.

Sinclair, Barbara. 1983. *Majority Leadership in the U.S. House.* Baltimore: Johns Hopkins University Press.

———. 1993. "House Majority Party Leadership in an Era of Divided Control." Chapter 10 in Lawrence C. Dodd and Bruce I. Oppenheimer, eds., *Congress Reconsidered,* 5th ed. Washington, DC: Congressional Quarterly Press.

———. 1995. *Legislators, Leaders, and Lawmaking: The U.S. House of Representatives in the Postreform Era.* Baltimore: Johns Hopkins University.

———. 1998. "Tip O'Neill and Contemporary House Leadership." Chapter 10 in Roger H. Davidson, Susan Webb Hammond, and Raymond W. Smock, eds., *Masters of the House: Congressional Leadership over Two Centuries.* Boulder: Westview Press.

———. 1999a. "Transformational Leader or Faithful Agent? Principal-Agent Theory and House Majority Party Leadership." *Legislative Studies Quarterly* 24, 421–47.

———. 1999b. "Partisan Imperatives and Institutional Constraints: Republican Party Leadership in the House and Senate." Chapter 2 in Nicol C. Rae and Colton C. Campbell, eds., *New Majority or Old Minority? The Impact of Republicans on Congress*. Lanham, MD: Rowman and Littlefield.

———. 2001. "The Senate Leadership Dilemma: Passing Bills and Pursuing Partisan Advantage in a Nonmajoritarian Chamber." Chapter 4 in Colton C. Campbell and Nicol C. Rae, eds., *The Contentious Senate: Partisanship, Ideology, and the Myth of Cool Judgment*. Lanham, MD: Rowman and Littlefield.

———. 2004. "Congressional Reform." Chapter 35 in Julian E. Zelizer, ed., *The American Congress: The Building of Democracy*. Boston: Houghton Mifflin.

Skowronek, Stephen. 1993. *The Politics Presidents Make: Leadership from John Adams to George Bush*. Cambridge: Harvard University Press.

Smith, Hedrick. 1967. "Pacification Foiled, Gen. Giap Declares." *New York Times,* 10 October, 1.

———. 1984. "Reagan Fighting to Win Aid for Anti-Sandinistas." *New York Times,* 27 May.

———. 1988. *The Power Game: How Washington Works*. New York: Ballantine Books.

Smith, Steven S. 2007. *Party Influence in Congress*. New York: Cambridge University Press.

Smith, Steven S., and Gerald Gamm. 2001. "The Dynamics of Party Government in Congress." From Lawrence C. Dodd and Bruce I. Oppenheimer, eds., *Congress Reconsidered,* 7th ed. Washington, DC: Congressional Quarterly Press.

Stanton, John, and Steven T. Dennis. 2008. "Promises, Promises: Record Mixed on Democrats' Follow Through." *Roll Call,* 22 September.

Stark, Louis. 1949. "Difficulties Faced in New Labor Law." *New York Times,* 3 January.

Stathis, Stephen W. 1994. "Succession, Presidential." From Leonard W. Levy and Louis Fisher, eds., *Encyclopedia of the American Presidency,* vol. 4.

Stavisky, Sam. 1949. "Administration Compromise Defeated by Coalition." *Washington Post,* 4 May.

Steinberg, Alfred. 1975. *Sam Rayburn: A Biography*. New York: Hawthorn Books.

Stewart, Charles, III. 2000. "Speakership Elections and Control of the U.S. House, 1839–1859." Paper presented at the annual meeting of the Midwest Political Science Association, Chicago.

Stockman, David A. 1986. *The Triumph of Politics: The Inside Story of the Reagan Revolution*. New York: Avon.

Stolberg, Sheryl Gay. 2005. "Quietly but Firmly, Hastert Asserts His Power." *New York Times,* 3 January, 1.

Strahan, Randall. 2002. "Leadership and Institutional Change in the Nineteenth Century House." Chapter 9 in David Brady and Mathew D. McCubbins, eds. *Party, Process and Political Change in Congress*. Stanford: Stanford University Press.

———. 2007. *Leading Representatives: The Agency of Leaders in the Politics of the U.S. House*. Baltimore: Johns Hopkins University Press.

Strahan, Randall, Matthew Gunning, and Richard L. Vining, Jr. 2006. "From Moderator to Leader: Floor Participation by U.S. House Speakers, 1789–1841." *Social Science History* 30, 51–74.

Strahan, Randall, Vincent G. Moscardelli, Moshe Haspel, and Richard S. Wike. 2000. "The Clay Speakership Revisited." *Polity* 32, 561–93.

Strahan, Randall, and Daniel J. Palazzolo. 2004. "The Gingrich Effect." *Political Science Quarterly* 119, 89–114.

Strout, Richard L. 1955. "Tariff Program a Bipartisan Victory." *Christian Science Monitor,* 18 February.

Sundquist, James L. 1981. *The Decline and Resurgence of Congress.* Washington, DC: Brookings Institution.

Swift, Elaine K., Robert G. Brookshire, David T. Canon, Evelyn C. Fink, John R. Hibbing, Brian D. Humes, Michael J. Malbin, and Kenneth C. Martis. 2000. *Database of Congressional Historical Statistics* (computer file). Ann Arbor, MI: Inter-university Consortium for Political and Social Research.

Taft, Philip. 1964. *Organized Labor in American History.* New York: Harper and Row.

Taylor, Andrew. 1995a. "Amendment Foes Hold Out Hope as Measure Heads to Floor." *Congressional Quarterly Weekly Report,* 21 January.

———. 1995b. "In Historic Turn, House Passes Balanced-Budget Amendment." *Congressional Quarterly Weekly Report,* 28 January.

Theriault, Sean. 2006. "Party Polarization in the U.S. Congress: Member Replacement and Member Adaptation." *Party Politics* 12, 467 81.

Thomas P. O'Neill Papers. John J. Burns Library, Boston College. Boston, MA.

Thurber, Timothy N. 2004. "The Second Reconstruction." Chapter 30 in Julian E. Zelizer, ed., *The American Congress: The Building of Democracy.* Boston: Houghton Mifflin.

"Thwarting Patients' Rights." 1999. *New York Times,* 5 November.

Tolchin, Martin. 1981. "House Foes See Reagan Victory on Budget Plan." *New York Times,* 5 May.

———. 1982a. "House Democrats Agree on Budget with Higher Taxes." *New York Times,* 11 May.

———. 1982b. "House Panel Adopts Democratic Budget on Party-Line Vote." *New York Times,* 14 May.

———. 1982c. "Leaders Say Veto Will Be Sustained." *New York Times,* 2 September.

Toner, Robin. 1989a. "This Was No Day for a House Party." *New York Times,* 8 February.

———. 1989b. "Foley, as Speaker, Begins to Take Fighting Stance." *New York Times,* 31 July.

Towell, Pat. 2000. "Hill Balks at Aid to Colombia in Supplemental Spending Bill." *Congressional Quarterly Weekly Report,* 4 March.

Trott, Harlan. 1950. "Kerr Bill Poses Nice Decision for President." *Christian Science Monitor,* 1 April.

Truman, David B. 1959. *The Congressional Party: A Case Study.* New York: John Wiley and Sons.

Turner, Ralph H. 1990. "Role Change." *Annual Review of Sociology* 16, 87–110.

Tyson, Ann Scott. 1999. "Congress Lets Congress Lead on Kosovo, for Now." *Christian Science Monitor,* 16 April.

"Uprising on a Minor Bill Hurts McCormack." 1962. *Business Week,* 17 March, 42.

U.S. Congress. House. 2005. *Constitution, Jefferson's Manual, and Rules of the House of Representatives, 109th Congress.* Washington, DC: Government Printing Office.

Valelly, Richard M. 2004. *The Two Reconstructions: The Struggle for Black Enfranchisement.* Chicago: University of Chicago Press.

VandeHei, Jim. 1999. "GOP Leaders Plan to Derail Campbell Bill." *Roll Call,* 19 April.

Vega, Arturo, and Ronald M. Peters, Jr. 1996. "Principal-Agent Theories of Party Leadership under Preference Heterogeneity: The Case of Simpson-Mazzoli." *Congress and the Presidency* 23, 15–32.

Vobejda, Barbara. 1996. "Welfare Bill Altered." *Washington Post,* 18 July.

Waggoner, Walter H. 1950. "President Vetoes Natural Gas Bill to Protect Public." *New York Times,* 16 April.

Wahlke, John C., Heinz Eulau, William Buchanan, and LeRoy C. Ferguson. 1962. *The Legislative System: Explorations in Legislative Behavior.* New York: John Wiley and Sons.

Walsh, Edward. 1986. "Intense Lobbying Efforts Focus on Swing Votes." *Washington Post,* 18 March.

"Washington in Brief." 2000. *Washington Post,* 28 March.

Weaver, Warren. 1971. "The Voters vs. House Leaders." *New York Times,* 23 August.

Weisberg, Herbert F., Eric S. Heberlig, and Lisa M. Campoli, eds. 1999. *Classics in Congressional Politics.* New York: Longman.

Welch, William M. 1999a. "House Passes Measure to Fund Airstrike Campaign." 7 May, 1999.

———. 1999b. "House Votes to Continue Funding for Troops in Balkans." *USA Today,* 11 June.

White, William S. 1955a. "Congress' Approval Likely; Resolution Wins First Test." *New York Times,* 25 January.

———. 1955b. "House Votes 409–3 to Back Eisenhower on Formosa; Senate Hears Joint Chiefs." *New York Times,* 26 January.

———. 1955c. "House Unit Votes Democratic Plan for $20 Tax Cuts." *New York Times,* 22 February.

———. 1957. *Citadel: The Story of the U.S. Senate.* New York: Harper and Brothers.

Whitfield, Stephen J. 1988. *A Death in the Delta: The Story of Emmett Till.* New York: Free Press.

Whitney, Robert F. 1949. "First Test Looms for Truman Today as Congress Opens." *New York Times,* 3 January.

Williamson, Elizabeth. 2007. "Support Wanes for Armenian Genocide Bill." *Washington Post,* 17 October.

Wines, Michael. 1993. "At the Congressional Brink: A Freshman Saves the Day." *New York Times,* 6 August.

———. 1995a. "GOP Tax Plan May Lack Support." *New York Times,* 13 January.

———. 1995b. "Budget Measure Likely but Which One?" *New York Times,* 17 January.

———. 1995c. "House Republicans Seek Edge for Their Version of Balanced-Budget Measure." *New York Times,* 24 January.

———. 1995d. "House Approves Bill to Mandate Balanced Budget." *New York Times,* 27 January.

————. 1995e. "Gingrich Acknowledges That Tax-Cut Plan Is in Trouble." *New York Times,* 29 March.

Wright, Jim. 1994. "Challenges That Speakers Face." Chapter 11 in Ronald M. Peters, Jr., ed., *The Speaker: Leadership in the House of Representatives.* Washington DC: Congressional Quarterly Inc.

————. 1996. *Balance of Power: Presidents and Congress from the Era of McCarthy to the Age of Gingrich.* Atlanta, GA: Turner Publishing.

Yang, John E. 1987. "Wright Backs Boosting Funds in FSLIC Bill." *Wall Street Journal,* 29 April.

Young, Garry, and Joseph Cooper. 1993. "Multiple Referral and the Transformation of House Decision Making." Chapter 9 in Lawrence C. Dodd and Bruce I. Oppenheimer, eds., *Congress Reconsidered,* 5th ed. Washington, DC: Congressional Quarterly Press.

Zelizer, Julian E., ed. 2004. *The American Congress: The Building of Democracy.* Boston: Houghton Mifflin.

Index

Foley, Thomas, 8, 29, 127, 215; congressional pay raise and, 121–23; district interests, 129, 173; floor advocacy by, 28, 31, 41–42, 214; floor voting by, 58, 232; going public, 180–82; leadership style of, 121; legislative leadership by, 113–14; 163, 167, 172, 174; MFN for China and, 173–75, 217; NAFTA and, 2–3, 51, 127–29; *1990* budget summit and, 51; *1993* budget reconciliation and, 133–36; view of speakership, 14–15

Ford, Gerald, 130, 164–65, 168, 180

Foreign Affairs Committee, House, 77, 85–86, 127, 241n34, 253n7

foreign policy: deference to president on, 13, 36, 44–48, 64, 206, 213, 240n30

Formosa resolution, 78–79, 240n30

Foster, Charles, 27

Freeman, Orville, 99

Frist, Bill, 2, 218

Fulbright, J. William, 85

Galloway, George, 4, 34

Ganske, Greg, 153

gas deregulation. *See* natural gas

Gephardt, Richard, 191–92, 242n43

Gingrich, Newt, 50, 184, 211, 226; balanced budget constitutional amendment and, 150–52; campaign finance reform and, 199; endangered species funding and, 123–24, 156, 249n10; expanded powers given to, 116; floor advocacy by, 24, 28, 33, 42–43; going public, 180–82; income tax reduction and, 152–54, 198, 252n39; legislative leadership of, 114–15, 163, 167, 172, 174, 253n2; in minority party, 150, 212; miscalculations by, 156, 202, 234n7, 252n39; negatives of, 185; personal policy goals of, 252n36; welfare reform and, 136–38, 250n24, 251n25

goal-driven leadership: alternatives to and counter-examples of, 48–51, 213–

15; applied to the Senate, 216–20; defined, 8–15; floor advocacy and, 35–37, 45–50, 208; going public and, 181–83; legislative leadership of Speakers and, 109–110, 154–56; predictions of, 17–21; recent versus older Speakers, 117–18, 210–12, 220–22. *See also* theories of congressional leadership

goals of Speakers. *See* goal-driven leadership

going public, 179–83, 198, 254n13

Gore, Al, 135, 193

Gramm, Phil. *See* Gramm-Latta budget bill

Gramm-Latta budget bill: 140–43, 212, 251n28–29, 254n11. *See also* O'Neill, Tip

Green, Edith, 82

Griffin, Robert, 107

Haines, Harry, 244n19

Halleck, Charles, 69, 71, 95, 99

Hansen, Julia Butler, 168

Hansen Committee, 168, 253n6

Hardy, Porter, 94

Harris, Oren, 94, 246n41

Hastert, Dennis, 50, 184–86, 201–3, 252n32, 254n1; anti-drug money to Colombia and, 186–88; campaign finance reform and, 199–201; floor advocacy by, 28, 36, 240n23; floor voting by, 56; Hastert doctrine, 185, 221; health care and, 3, 37, 239n17; intelligence bill and, 202, 255n6; Kosovo and, 189–92, 211; leadership style of, 184–85; miscalculations by, 191; patients' rights legislation and, 194–97; prescription drug bill and, 2–3, 193–94, 233n1; tax cut bill, 197–99

Hawaii, 70

Hays, Lawrence, 94

Herlong, Albert, 94

Holbrock, Greg, 244n19

Holifield, Chet, 81, 87, 245n27

Houghton, Amo, 252n37

House of Representatives: changes from
pre-reform to post-reform era, 111, 116;
expansion of, 70–71; required to initiate
tax measures, 240n31, 253n9; Speakers
serving interests of, 14–15, 19. *See also*
goal-driven leadership; Speaker's goals

Huddleston, George, 82

Hull, William, 105, 246n41

Hunter, John, 244n19

Hymel, Gary, 13, 141

Ichord, Richard, 246n41

Ikard, Frank, 247n47, 248n54

Imhoff, Lawrence, 244n19

income tax. *See* tax cut proposals; tax increase proposals; tax reform

Indochina. *See* Vietnam War

institutional presidency. *See* goal-driven
leadership; president; Speaker's goals

intelligence legislation, 144–45, 202, 221,
255n6

Interstate and Foreign Commerce Committee, House, 243n9

Jackson, Henry, 244n22

James, Scott, 236n26

Jefferson, Bill, 254n1

Jeffords, Jim, 193, 196

job creation bill, 138–39, 248n3

Johnson, Lyndon Baines, 48, 83, 177, 218,
220, 246n39, 247n45

Johnson, Nancy, 252n37

Johnson, Thomas, 248n54

Jones, Charles O., 5, 248n49

Jones, Hamilton, 94

Jones, Jim, 177

Jones, Robert, 81, 249n27

Josephy, Alvin, 83, 245n29

Judiciary Committee, House, 70

Kennedy, John F., 95–99

Kennedy-Ives. *See* labor legislation, in
1958–59

Kernell, Samuel, 179, 254n13

Kilday, Paul, 248n54

Kilgore, Joe, 247n48

King, Peter, 190

Kirwan, Michael, 244n22

Kosovo, 189–92, 202

Krehbiel, Keith, 234n5

labor legislation: in *1949*, 90–94; in *1958–
59*, 105–8, 248n49

labor unions: illegal or improper activity
by, 91, 105. *See also* AFL-CIO; Democratic Party in Congress; labor legislation; North American Free Trade
Agreement

Landrum, Phil, 107

Landrum-Griffin bill. *See* labor legislation, in *1958–59*

Lankford, Richard, 248n54

Latham, Henry, 243n11

Latin America. *See* Colombia; Mexico;
Nicaragua

Latta, Delbert, 141. *See also* Gramm-Latta
budget bill

leadership in Congress, theories of. *See*
theories of congressional leadership

leadership in Congress, tools of. *See*
Speaker of the House, powers of

Lebanon: U.S. troop deployment to, 23,
31, 49, 248n2

legislative leadership: categories of, 6,
157–58, 234n6; definition of, 5; predicting, 204–10; using sweeps to find,
226–28. *See also individual Speakers;*
floor advocacy; goal-driven leadership;
voting by Speakers

Lend-Lease program, 73, 168–69, 173

Lesinksi, John, 75, 91–93

liberal Democrats, 50, 73, 95, 110–11;
budget legislation and, 134, 148–49;
civil rights and, 102; economic legislation and, 139, 222; energy policy and,
68, 132, 243n8; foreign policy and, 85–
86, 125, 144, 146; labor and, 106–7;